ALEXANDER HAMILTON AND

THE DEVELOPMENT OF

AMERICAN LAW

ALEXANDER HAMILTON *and* *the* DEVELOPMENT *of* AMERICAN LAW

Kate Elizabeth Brown

University Press of Kansas

Published by the University Press of Kansas (Lawrence, Kansas
66045), which was organized by the Kansas Board of Regents and
is operated and funded by Emporia State University, Fort Hays State
University, Kansas State University, Pittsburg State University, the
University of Kansas, and Wichita State University

Portions of Chapter 6 were originally published as "Rethinking
People v. Croswell: Alexander Hamilton and the Nature and Scope
of 'Common Law' in the Early Republic" in the journal *Law and
History Review* 32:3 (August 2014), and are reprinted with the
permission of Cambridge University Press.

Library of Congress Cataloging-in-Publication Data

Names: Brown, Kate Elizabeth (Katherine Elizabeth)
Title: Alexander Hamilton and the development of American law /
Kate Elizabeth Brown.
Description: Lawrence, Kansas : University Press of Kansas, 2017. |
Includes bibliographical references and index.
Identifiers: LCCN 2017020132
ISBN 9780700624805 (hardback)
ISBN 9780700624812 (ebook)
Subjects: LCSH: Hamilton, Alexander, 1757–1804. | Constitutional
law—United States—History. | BISAC: HISTORY / United States /
Revolutionary Period (1775–1800). | LAW / Constitutional. | LAW /
Corporate.
Classification: LCC KF363.H3 B76 2017 | DDC 342.7302/9—dc23
LC record available at https://lccn.loc.gov/2017020132.

British Library Cataloguing-in-Publication Data is available.

Printed in the United States of America

10 9 8 7 6 5 4 3 2 1

For the Chief

Contents

Acknowledgments

There are so many whom I would like to gratefully acknowledge and thank for their help and support, including the following people, institutions, and four-legged creatures:

The University of Virginia has an excellent history department and law school, with professors who are tremendous advocates, teachers, and mentors for their graduate students. Thank you to Charles McCurdy, Paul Halliday, Max Edelson, and Risa Goluboff for giving me invaluable feedback on earlier versions of my manuscript. Mr. McCurdy (Chuck), the Chief, you are a truly outstanding mentor and teacher, and I am so honored to have been your (final!) PhD student. Thank you for being patient with me over my five years in graduate school, and for developing me into a scholar. I appreciate all of your guidance and advice as you helped me turn my high-school fascination for Alexander Hamilton into this, my first book, about Hamilton's impact on American law. Thank you also for writing all of those letters of recommendation for me, for sharing your extensive library with me, for continuing to be a friend and mentor to me in your retirement, and for twice letting me bring my Hamilton to your home when we graded all those final exams on the last night of the semester.

A very special thanks to Doug Bradburn, the founding director of the Fred W. Smith National Library for the Study of George Washington at

Mount Vernon. Doug, thank you for being a champion of me and my work, as well as a mentor to me as I transitioned from graduate student to early-career scholar. Also, many thanks to Mary Jongema, Neal Millikan (co-champion, with me, in Boy Band Trivia), Anna Millikan, Lucy Smith, Sarah Myers, Lindsay Chervinsky, Dana Stefanelli, Bruce Ragsdale, Brendan Gillis (my office mate), Holly Mayer, Tim Walker, Michael Blaakman, Stephen McLeod, Michael Kane, the Mount Vernon Ladies' Association, and the library staff at the Fred W. Smith National Library for the Study of George Washington at Mount Vernon. It was such an honor to be a fellow at the library, and to be immersed not only in George Washington's world but also in the intellectual world of the Revolutionary War and early republic scholarship fostered by Doug and the library.

I would also like to thank the New-York Historical Society, the Gilder Lehrman Institute of American History, the David Library of the American Revolution, and the Institute for Humane Studies. I am grateful to Elizabeth Dale and the *Law and History Review* for publishing parts of Chapter 6 as "Rethinking *People v. Croswell*: Alexander Hamilton on the Nature and Scope of 'Common Law' in the Early Republic" (vol. 32, summer 2014). Material from Chapter 3 has appeared in the Gotham Center for New York City History blog, and an excerpt from Chapter 1 previously appeared on the "Washington's Quill" blog published by the Papers of George Washington Project.

I owe a very special thank you to the history department at Huntington University as well. Jeff Webb, Tim Smith, and Dwight Brautigam—you are truly excellent colleagues, and I am grateful to know you and to work with you. Thank you for all of your support in my first few semesters at HU.

Also, thank you to Max Edling, Peter Kastor, Maeva Marcus, Patti Minter, John Moore, Cynthia Nicoletti, Peter Onuf, Gautham Rao, Sophie Rosenfeld, Vicky Woeste, and Olivier Zunz, as well as to the editors at the Papers of George Washington Project. I am grateful to Bill Ferraro, Tom Dulan, Ben Huggins, David Hoth, and Ed Lengel for all of the advice and experience I gained while working in the RevWar office. I miss being a part of your team and working on RevWar volumes 24 and 26.

I am grateful to Erik Seeman, Fred Konefsky, and to the late Richard E. Ellis who advised me at the University of Buffalo. Also, thank you to my former history teacher, David Ulrich, who inspired me to learn more about Alexander Hamilton during his truly awesome AP American history class. I am very grateful to Chuck Myers, Joyce Harrison, Larisa Martin, Mike Kehoe, Karen Hellekson, Stephen Knott, and Michael Federici, and to the staff at the University Press of Kansas for their wisdom and excellent guidance as I turned my manuscript into a monograph. I also thank Jim Westwood, a superb appellate lawyer from Oregon who graciously offered to be my consultant on modern law. This book is better and clearer because of you, and I truly appreciate your help.

To my amazing friends and family, thank you so very much! To my parents, Mike and Sue Brown, thank you for your love, selfless help, and support over the years. Thank you for visiting me all over the East Coast, and for always babysitting Hamilton (and for watching him closely so that he didn't fall into the pool). Mom, I hope this book makes it off of your unfinished bookshelf!

I am also very grateful to Mike Miranda (who, among many other things, took loving and special care of all of the feline members of the Buffalo and Charlottesville chapters of the IBPC), Lee B. Wilson (the other half of the Dynamic Duo), Kristen Lashua (my very excellent friend, confidante, and fellow scholar), Andrew Lashua, Mike and RaeAnne Caires, Ben Brady, Emily Senefeld, Ben Davidson, Jim Ambuske and Jim Hrdlicka (aka The Jimz), Asaf Almog, Erik Erlandson, and David Grant Smith.

To Jen Reeve and Chris Sutton: thank you for being such awesome friends to me! You are incredible teachers and scholars, and through your example, you have helped me to become a better educator. Jen, I am eternally grateful for your infinite patience (and no judgment!) as I vent to you and ask for your advice; thank you also for exposing me to the wonders of Facebook and, most importantly, to England and Scotland.

To my extended family—I hope you all enjoy receiving this book at Christmas! Thank you to Ed and Peg Brown, Alex and Steve Bernardi, Rev. Jim Krauser (to whom I am eternally grateful for the gift of tickets to see *Hamilton* on Broadway), the late Matt and Theresa Mytnik, Joanne and Leonard Milioto, Patty Mytnik, Jill and Pat Snyder, and Alison and Ben Szydlowski.

And last but never least, thank you to my other extended family of past and current four-legged creatures. These lovable critters include: L. G. Boogie (aka Little Guy Iredell), Stereo Boogs, Botetourt, So Smoke, Smellie Nellie, MoneyPenny, and Keela. But none of these cats and dogs are as special to me as my constant companion for these past twelve years, my sweet Hamilton. Thank you, Hamilton, for loyally accompanying me from Atlanta, to Buffalo, to Charlottesville, and now to Fort Wayne. You are a good doggie.

ᐁᐧ

Alexander Hamilton, Lawyer and Lawmaker

Alexander Hamilton never handed down decisions from a Supreme Court bench, nor did he write influential treatises on law. Yet he became the central figure in the development of American law during the early republic era. Hamilton's authority over the formation of a republican jurisprudence both fit for a newly independent nation and compliant with the recently ratified Constitution was extensive; he transformed inherited imperial law into legal and constitutional principles befitting the American experiment in government, one that aimed to divide sovereignty among a central national government, individual states, and the American people.

Hamilton's formative influence on American law was a direct result of his unique role in the American founding. During the two decades of his career after the army, Hamilton served as a powerful and effective statesman in President George Washington's Cabinet and as a preeminent attorney, representing the US government and private clients alike. His influence on the development of federal and state jurisprudence would persist decades after his death, well into the nineteenth century. Hamilton's impact was so foundational, in fact, that even Hamilton's political and ideological adversaries—Thomas Jefferson, James Madison, Andrew Jackson, and their partisans—adopted Hamiltonian constitutionalism to govern. We do not think of Hamilton as the father of his country, like we do Washington, nor is he considered the father of the Constitution, like Madison; but Alexander Hamilton deserves to be remembered as a father of American law.

Born in either 1755 or 1757 on the isle of Nevis, British West Indies, Alexander Hamilton grew up sensitive to the social stigma attached to his illegitimate birth. His mother died in 1768, and an impoverished but ambitious young Hamilton worked to support himself, joining the mercantile house of Beekman and Cruger in St. Croix as a clerk. When Hamilton demonstrated his perspicacity and managerial abilities on the job, Nicholas Cruger and another benevolent patron, the Reverend Hugh Knox, sponsored the young clerk's escape from West Indian obscurity by underwriting Hamilton's formal education in America. Hamilton arrived in New Jersey in 1772.

Soon after Hamilton moved to New York and enrolled in King's College (now Columbia University), revolutionary fervor swept through New York City, and he seized this opportunity to taste glory and to rise to prominence. Hamilton organized a company of provincial artillery, and soon after, in March 1777, General George Washington appointed the young artillery captain to join his family of aides-de-camp. Although he served Washington as a most trusted wartime subordinate, Lieutenant Colonel Hamilton eventually resigned as the general's aide to lead his own battalions at the battle of Yorktown. He left the Continental Army in 1781.

After the war, and with a new wife and son in tow, Hamilton began to read law in preparation for what would be an illustrious and lucrative practice in his adopted home. An astonishingly quick study, Hamilton was admitted to practice before the New York Supreme Court bar by July 1782; the state then admitted him as common law counsel in October 1782, and he qualified as both a solicitor and counsel in the Court of Chancery in 1783.[1] Hamilton practiced law in New York until he became the young republic's first secretary of the treasury in September 1789. Before taking the post in Washington's Cabinet, he also served in the Confederation Congress, in the New York assembly, and as a delegate to the Annapolis and Philadelphia constitutional conventions as well as the New York ratifying convention, during the 1780s. Hamilton then quickly resumed his private caseload after resigning his Cabinet post in January 1795. Ever the industrious attorney, Hamilton had pressing business awaiting him in the New York courts up until his untimely death at the hand of Aaron Burr, a fellow member of the New York bar, on July 12, 1804.

Like other members of America's founding generation, Hamilton trained and practiced in the tradition of the common law, a centuries-old amalgamation of homegrown English, and later American, colonial law that also incorporated elements borrowed from the civil, canon, and natural law traditions. English lawyers exported the common law, as well as European Enlightenment traditions grounded in reason, natural law, and scientific inquiry, to the British colonies and around the world. Enlightenment thought infused into legal communities on both sides of the Atlantic, such that even an obscure, provincial lawyer could be well versed in this cosmopolitan worldview. Before embarking on his legal training, Hamilton read Locke, Coke, Blackstone, Montesquieu, Postlethwayt, Grotius, Pufendorf, Burlamaqui, and "books and subjects on Ancient and Medieval history and philosophy." By the time Washington appointed him secretary of the treasury, he had studied Hume, Smith, Vattel, Lord Chief Justice Mansfield, and various volumes issued by English court reporters.[2] Hamilton was thus steeped in the day-to-day practice of English and colonial law, but he was also reading widely in enlightened English, Scottish, Dutch, and Swiss traditions.[3]

Up until the end of the Seven Years' War, when the British Parliament began actively legislating for its North American colonies, Englishmen and colonists alike celebrated the largely unwritten, customary British constitution for the rights, liberty, and balance of powers it ensured. Hamilton was no exception, and though he joined the American movement for independence, he never abandoned his admiration for the British constitutional system. It should therefore have come as no surprise that, when brainstorming during the debates of the 1787 Philadelphia Convention, Hamilton declared the British constitution to be "the best form of government—not as a thing attainable by us, but as a model which we ought to approach as near as possible."[4] In making this claim, Hamilton suggested a restorative approach to the American constitutional system; rather than make the radical plea to reinstate monarchy in the United States, he instead called on his fellow delegates to remember their past veneration of the British constitution and to use it to guide the American one they were in the process of drafting.

Hamilton thus did not become a pioneer of American law simply by looking backward to the British constitution or to English precedents—all eighteenth-century common lawyers referred to English case law. Instead, he did so by using English legal traditions instrumentally to accomplish his republican statecraft goals. When writing his authoritative commentary on the nature of federal constitutional power in *The Federalist,* he juxtaposed the British constitution with the new American one he helped to create; when proposing commercial, monetary, banking, administrative, or foreign policy in Washington's Cabinet, he used legal arguments to justify his desired course of action. In short, lawyering, legal innovation, and common law permeated Alexander Hamilton's professional career, Why, then, have scholars and biographers routinely ignored his influence on the development of American law?

Nineteenth-century Festschrift contributor Daniel W. E. Burke reflected on, and presciently anticipated, a formidable problem facing historians and biographers alike: though Hamilton was "retained in every important case and recognized as the ablest advocate in New York. Yet so chaotic was the system of reporting in those early days, that few of his great cases have come down to us in the books."[5] To be sure, scholars have caught glimpses of Hamilton's seminal influence on American law through a particular set of famous, well-documented cases—including *Rutgers v. Waddington, Hylton v. US*, and *People v. Croswell*—but largely gave up on piecing together the larger scope and importance of Hamilton's legal career.[6] Julius Goebel Jr. and Joseph H. Smith, the primary editors of Hamilton's law papers, are the two noteworthy exceptions to this general neglect.

During the course of his sixteen-year practice, Hamilton argued hundreds of cases and advised an even greater number of clients. Although case reporting was haphazard in the early republic, Hamilton's reputation as a superb lawyer persisted despite the incomplete legal record. Chancellor James Kent, for example, celebrated Hamilton's achievements in the New York courts. He described his posthumous reputation among jurists: "But among all his brethren Colonel Hamilton was indisputably preeminent. This was universally conceded." A century and a half later, historian Forrest McDonald described Hamilton's particular legal expertise: "For Hamilton did not like arguing the facts or merits of a cause nearly so much as he enjoyed doing battle on grounds of the law, and he became a master of the kind of special pleas that made argument on the latter grounds possible."[7] Still, generations of scholars and biographers have only superficially recognized Hamilton's influence on American law, acknowledging his brilliance but confining their exploration of his legal career to only a handful of high-profile cases.

Cursory studies of Hamilton's legal practice will not suffice, however, as Hamilton lived during a transformative era in American public and private law, and he contributed significantly to its development. Moreover, Hamilton used inherited English legal principles to help conceptualize, define, defend, and explain the distinctly American policies that biographers and scholars associate with Hamilton. Understanding the centrality of law to Hamilton's career is essential, therefore, because Alexander Hamilton consistently and purposefully used the law as an instrument to accomplish his national, economic, and republican policy goals.

The following chapters aim to recast our understanding of Hamilton's political career, his policy achievements, and his significant role in the American founding by considering him, first and foremost, as a preeminent lawyer who instrumentally applied law and legal arguments to accomplish his statecraft. By reexamining Hamilton's postwar accomplishments through the lens of the law, I argue that Hamilton's thoroughly studied political career, as well as his contributions to republican political science, cannot be fully understood without recognizing and investigating how Hamilton used Anglo-American legal principles to achieve these ends.[8]

Rethinking Hamilton's legacy as well as his place in the founding era proves perennially important because he engaged with, and is identified with, early national debates about domestic and foreign policy, constitutional law, governing practices, federal–state authority, and the ways in which the nascent American republic would interact with the rest of the world. In the conventional wisdom, Hamilton is the standard-bearer of an ideology turned political party, the Federalists, who engaged in nothing less than a struggle for the soul of the young United States against their rivals, the Anti-Federalists, and later the Jeffersonian Republicans. Except for the fact that both Federalists and Republicans wanted the young republic to survive and to thrive, on almost every relevant issue of their day, the two ideological factions disagreed on the proper course of action to take. As a consequence, the factions were seen as rivals, then as now, and their debates live on, in modified forms, into the present day.

Because we still identify these factions and their ideologies as "Hamiltonian" versus "Jeffersonian," a rethinking of Hamilton's objectives, arguments, and lasting influence consequently revises our notions of the development of political discourse and governmental power, and as I demonstrate below, the course of the development of American law. Hamilton waded into ideological debates made all the more imperative because he, like Washington, Jefferson, and Madison, was charting a completely novel course for the American nation. It turns out, however, that Hamilton and Jefferson's objectives were not as one-dimensional or as diametrically opposed as we so often think.

By presenting a legal analysis of Alexander Hamilton's career, this study juxtaposes a narrative of Hamilton's lasting legal legacy against the more familiar failures of his political career. After Secretary Hamilton's early legislative successes in the first Federalist-dominated Congresses, he faced increasing political opposition from Thomas Jefferson, James Madison, and their Anti-Federalist faction during the remainder of his term in office.[9]

Then, once out of office, Hamilton endured a series of political embarrassments and failures.[10] Some noteworthy indiscretions and political losses include an exposé written by Hamilton revealing his extramarital affair that aimed to clear him of alleged (and false) corruption charges; a miscalculated pamphlet published, again by Hamilton, to impugn President John Adams's suitability for office; the violent public outcry over John Jay's treaty with Great Britain; isolated rebellions over treasury-sponsored taxes; Jefferson's presidential election and the waning influence of the Federalists in state and national government; the Jeffersonians' repeal of the 1801 Judiciary Act, which Federalist lame ducks passed to restructure the federal courts; and Hamilton's ultimate demise in a duel with his political foe (and the sitting vice president), Aaron Burr.[11] Perhaps mercifully for Hamilton, he did not live long enough to witness the final death throes of the Federalist Party during the War of 1812.

The standard narrative of Hamilton's post-Cabinet career portrays the precocious lieutenant colonel turned brilliant minister's star as burning out quickly (perhaps even self-imploding) after reaching his apotheosis as policy maker in the early 1790s. This is true enough, as Hamilton's political losses outweighed his political victories after 1795. But even though Hamilton's political career had a losing trajectory, his legal legacy had a winning one.

If Jeffersonian Republicans and Jacksonian Democrats ultimately prevailed throughout the political battles of the early republic, then Hamiltonian jurisprudence proved victorious throughout the era's legal contests. Both in and out of public office, Alexander Hamilton developed the substantive foundations of American jurisprudence. This in turn allowed him to achieve some of his most important policy goals posthumously, through transformations in law, which he could not achieve through elections and party politics. To this end, Hamilton's most significant and enduring achievement was to translate and transform English legal traditions into explanations for and defenses of a robust federal judicial power. In addition, he also used the law as a flexible legal toolbox to enhance federal executive power, to increase the republic's commercial strength, to protect the federal government's fiscal powers, and to preserve the common law due process, jury trial, and press freedoms that secured the liberties enjoyed by ordinary Americans.

Hamilton's influence on the development of American law proved to be enduring and authoritative; the US Supreme Court upheld and cited Hamiltonian legal arguments well into the nineteenth century, and occasionally in the twentieth century.[12] Even Jeffersonian and Jacksonian jurists deployed

Hamilton's principles to support their legal claims. Hamilton's legacy thus extended beyond the usual summary of his contributions to the early republic—a national debt, a central bank, *The Federalist* essays, his party politics—to include an accomplishment befitting an American common lawyer in the founding era: a formative influence on the substance of federal and state jurisprudence.

The successes of Hamilton's legal legacy produced some unintended consequences, however. As I argue throughout, the main thrust of Hamiltonian constitutionalism focused on finding a balance between robust federal and state government authority. This is a more moderate and nuanced objective than scholars usually ascribe to Hamilton. Hamilton was undoubtedly a proponent of a strong central government, but he was also a practical realist, which meant that once the US Constitution delegated specific powers to the national government and reserved so much authority to the states, Hamilton set out to accomplish his statecraft goals within this legal framework, which allowed states to be powerful too. When Hamilton argued for robust federal powers, his aim was to exercise an untried, delegated authority that was new, untested, and vulnerable to encroachments by the states. Rather than seek opportunities to diminish the states' retained powers, Hamilton instead used his career as a statesman and attorney to offer his extended argument as to how to strike this delicate balance between state and national authority.

Yet one unintended consequence of Hamilton's prescription for balancing federal and state authority is that, when removed from the context of the initial, precedent-setting years of the early republic, Hamilton's arguments seem to be unequivocal calls for unfettered central government power. The problem is one of context. In Hamilton's day, he attempted to strike what he thought was the proper balance of power between the new central government and the preexisting states; subsequent politicians, rivals, jurists, and scholars instead interpreted and revived Hamilton's arguments as if increasing national government power were his only objective in an antagonistic, zero-sum struggle between the states and the central government. Because Hamiltonian sound bites make good fodder for pronationalist arguments, we think of Hamilton as a die-hard nationalist and nothing else; in the meantime, his more moderate perspective and nuanced legal arguments are lost.

Another unintended consequence of Hamilton's statecraft is that it generated political controversies that forever tempt subsequent generations to pit Hamilton as Thomas Jefferson's diametric opposite. The men were indeed political opponents, but on closer inspection, Hamilton, like Jefferson, respected the jurisdictional sovereignty and policy-making opportunities offered by the states. And Jefferson, like Hamilton, became, in practice, an advocate of robust executive power at the national level. When figures like Hamilton and Jefferson are flattened and fitted into easy, one-dimensional dichotomies, we lose sight of the complex and multivalent ways they influenced American history.

Although Hamilton was by all accounts an outstanding litigator and orator, he was only one of many excellent attorneys in the young republic. New York produced especially competent common lawyers, as New York modeled its court system on English institutions and thus relied heavily on English precedent. Hamilton worked intimately with this circle of top-tier New York attorneys, consulting with them on pending trials or appeals, serving alongside them as co-counsel, and even requesting their advice on national constitutional matters. Hamilton was not the only practicing attorney to realize the breadth and scope of the common law. Republican judges and lawyers like Jefferson, Madison, Edmund Randolph, St. George Tucker, and Spencer Roane also recognized—but feared—the enormous potential of the common law: if the common law were adopted too extensively, particularly at the federal level, it might swallow up America's nascent republican constitution. While Hamilton endeavored to aggressively incorporate English legal principles into American governance, Jeffersonians worked to minimize the adoption of common law into federal law.[13]

Because of his unique position as both lawyer and precedent-setting administrator and policy maker, Hamilton rigged the legal deck, so to speak. He had the opportunity to set practical and substantive precedents while in office, which he then defended with characteristically well-researched and well-reasoned legal arguments. These Hamiltonian precedents proved to be efficient, effective, reasonable, and even customary by the time his successors took office—and so they adopted them too. Another reason that Hamilton's influence over the development of American law has been lost to scholars of the early republic is that they tend to assume that Hamilton's political losses overshadowed his posthumous influence. This, however, was not the case, as we will see; Hamilton's authoritative constitutionalism pervaded the jurisprudence of Thomas Jefferson, Andrew Jackson, John Marshall, Joseph Story, Roger Taney, James Kent, Albert Gallatin, state and federal attorneys general, and federal administrators at all levels. Still, throughout the pages that follow, Hamilton's political failures will be noted alongside his concurrent legal successes.

Alexander Hamilton's legal legacy was closely related to the growth of federal judicial power during the early republic. Usually this increase in federal court power is attributed to Chief Justice John Marshall; yet the US Supreme Court was not the primary driver of federal judicial power in this formative era in American law. Instead, federal judicial power was enhanced at every turn by collaborations between executive administrators (from the treasury secretary down to the customs collectors stationed at faraway ports), by litigation strategies drawn up by common lawyers in lower state and federal courts, and by federal district judges who simultaneously acted in both executive and judicial capacities. Federal judicial power was thus inextricably tied to the energy and actions of the executive branch, as well as to the work of district judges and local attorneys.[14] These often forgotten jurists, administrators, and strategists expanded the scope of federal judicial power day by day, transaction by transaction, such that by the time a constitutional question about the scope of federal judicial power made it before the US Supreme Court's bench, the federal courts already had practice exerting a wider scope of power. This made it all the more feasible for the Court to adopt extensive federal judicial power as a principle of American constitutional law.

As a high-ranking administrator, as a frequent district judge collaborator, and as a public and private litigator, Alexander Hamilton considered the common law to be a flexible, adaptable tradition to be applied instrumentally in order to accomplish his statecraft as well as to shape the contours of American constitutionalism. When Hamilton applied common law principles to his statecraft goals, the common law provided the tools that did the work of governing. By focusing on the ways in which Hamilton translated and transformed inherited English legal principles into a distinctly American jurisprudence, this examination of early republican law demonstrates how, even after the United States ratified its new constitutional order, the new nation had no pressing desire to cut itself off from its English legal roots. America's continued embrace and reception of English law after the Revolution was enthusiastic and committed still—thus underscoring the founding era as a mixed bag of conservative and revolutionary events.[15]

Throughout his career, Hamilton consciously and purposefully looked backward to soak up the principles of English law while he simultaneously applied them forward to shape a distinct and novel American republic. That he continually referred to English legal concepts reflected how, in the day-to-day business of governing under a newly minted constitution, America's break from England was every bit as conservative as it was radical and innovative.[16] Like Hamilton, early republican common lawyers, judges, administrators, and statesmen all thought in English. These founding officials continued to scrutinize English constitutionalism in order to make sense of their own radical innovations, such as how to separate governmental power in practice, how to preserve federal and state sovereignty, and how to maintain popular sovereignty. That Hamilton too considered the English constitution to provide an authoritative reference for American jurisprudence did not make him unique; Hamilton's singular influence over the development of American law instead arose from a professional career that combined a lucrative law practice with his distinctive role as drafter, ratifier, expositor, and then, from the moment of its inception, administrator of the new constitutional order.

Hamilton's most profound influence on American law—and his greatest debt to British constitutionalism—is his adaptation of concurrence. In the American federal system, where sovereignty is divided and delegated between national and state levels of government, concurrence provides harmonizing rules so that the federal and state governments can simultaneously exercise the same powers, like taxing, borrowing, or adjudicating contract disputes. Hamilton provided preliminary guidelines for both the extent and limits of legislative and judicial concurrence in *Federalist* Nos. 32 and 82.

In addition to this federal form of concurrence (between the national and state levels), Hamilton advocated for functional concurrence. In practice, functional concurrence described how executive and judicial functions were often mixed and unified, with executive officers properly exercising judge-like discretion and judges acting as administrators themselves. Hamilton never used the term "concurrent" to describe these combined executive–judicial functions, yet he advocated for an executive–judicial relationship—what I refer to as the federal magistracy—that was concurrent in practice. The president, his ranks of administrators, and the judges of the federal Supreme Court as well as the judges of circuit and district courts each had concurrent authority to exercise discretion and to administer the law. Like federal concurrence, functional concurrence also included limits to the extent of each executive officer or judge's concurrent authority.

As suggested by the term "magistracy"—a term Hamilton and his contemporaries used to collectively describe executive and judicial officers—the practical model for concurrence in government derived from the British constitution. Constitutional theory in medieval, early modern, and eighteenth-century England organized around the idea that at the center of all law and justice sat the sovereign king. From this theoretical unity of power in the sovereign—the fount of law—sprang the inseparably interwoven executive, judicial, and lawmaking functions in the realm. The king's counselors acted on behalf of the king and for the benefit of his dominions by dispensing judgment in law courts and advice in Parliament. When the king sat in his Parliament, convened with the lords temporal, the lords spiritual, and the commons of his realm, he sat at the very pinnacle of his power. The ultimate sovereignty of England, and later Great Britain, vested in this unified body of the king in Parliament.

The British constitution was thus predicated on unity among its various jurisdictions. All courts, counsels, magistrates, and assembled lawmakers traced their authority to the sovereign, and through his two bodies—his political body (the body politic) and his natural body—unity among them was maintained.[17] The constitution emphasized harmony, sought to minimize conflict, and offered a variety of concurrent arrangements: the king, his counselors (including Parliament and the Privy Council, and his justices of the peace (magistrates) each exercised some degree of executive, judicial, and lawmaking authority. English litigants could choose their preferred venue when going to law among competing jurisdictions like common law, chancery, church, manorial, and prerogative courts. Before Americans challenged the notion, colonial governors and provincial "parliaments" made law for the American colonies concurrently with the king, his Privy Council, and the British Parliament in London.[18]

Great Britain offered examples for both federal (colonial and London) and functional concurrence that modeled concurrence for Hamilton. The theoretical and practical thrust of Hamiltonian concurrence was to unify the American federal system uniquely predicated on the delegated sovereignty assigned through a written constitution. To Hamilton, this harmonizing did not mean simply consolidating power in the federal government; however, concurrence did require lawmakers to understand the precise boundaries of federal and state authority. Hamilton advocated more aggressively for federal power because, compared to the states, federal power was untried and underdeveloped in the late eighteenth century. The US Constitution articulated the powers of the national government, but what that authority meant in practice remained undetermined. Instead, Hamilton wanted robust federal powers to be exercised concurrently with those plentiful existing state powers—that is, he aimed to unify the workings of the nation's various jurisdictions through the sovereign people's federal constitution. In doing so, Hamilton demonstrated that the states, when not encroaching on the national government's proper but inchoate powers, could also help him to accomplish his nationally oriented statecraft.

Hamiltonian concurrence sought to harmonize the combined executive and judicial functions of the federal magistracy, as well as the legislative and judicial authority concurrently exercised by the national and state governments. It was Hamilton's broadest, most far-reaching influence over American law—and it is evidenced by the judges and lawyers who continually cited Hamilton as the authority on the matter. By enacting functional and federal concurrence, Hamilton quite literally wrote the rules and set the precedents that configured the American federal system. Concurrence also rendered Hamilton, whom historians often consider to be the archnationalist of the early republic, a true, small-f federalist. Because concurrence and the contouring of American federalism form the center of Hamilton's legal work, they are the pervasive and unifying themes in this book.

That Hamilton borrowed models of concurrent governance from the British example suggests the extent to which early republic constitutionalism relied on English law, but this was by no means the only principle that he inherited and adapted from the British constitution. In each of the following chapters, I describe the many strands of this inherited law on which Hamilton relied in order to accomplish his statecraft.

In order for me to accurately present Hamilton as a masterful attorney deserving of his contemporary reputation, and as the innovative statesman who used law to instrumentally apply his statecraft, I must occasionally delve into the nitty-gritty of case law and legalese that either Hamilton used to make his legal claims or that demonstrate how later jurists adopted Hamiltonian legal principles. In many cases, exploring the legalistic details of a string of judicial decisions and lawyers' arguments offers the clearest paths to recovering Hamilton's legal legacy. Still, this book is intended for anyone interested in the founding era, not simply for legal historians or lawyers. Therefore, if you are willing to endure the occasional technical parts of the narrative, I will make clear the significance to be gleaned from those legal details and complexities. Technical arguments are never meant to be the destination but comprise some of the particulars of the journey in the chapters below; most important are the overarching themes of concurrence, increased federal judicial and executive power, retained state sovereignty, and the lasting significance of English law as the ultimate triumphs of Hamilton's legal career.

In addition, this reconsideration of Hamilton's influence on law offers three significant revisions to the conventional narrative about the founding of the early republic. First, as mentioned above, though Hamilton's political prospects withered, his influence persisted in American jurisprudence throughout the nineteenth century. Hamilton thus triumphed over his political adversaries by setting the rules for constitutional governance that subsequently regulated later administrations.

Next, by shifting focus away from the US Supreme Court and centering it instead on an executive official and his interactions with lower federal courts, administrators, and lawyers, the development of American law becomes less dependent on the decisions made by a single superior court exercising judicial review and more about augmenting federal judicial power incrementally, in various ways, across departments, and from the bottom up. For years, historians have described the growth of federal judicial power by celebrating the instrumental decisions of John Marshall, Joseph Story, and their brethren on the early national US Supreme Court.[19] Legal scholar Grant Gilmore even described the era overlapping with Marshall's thirty-four-year tenure on the Supreme Court bench as one defined by "great judges deciding great cases greatly"—and Chief Justice John Marshall was perhaps the greatest of them all.[20] But here an administrator takes center stage, demonstrating that much of the Supreme Court's reasoning filtered up from the processes established in the Treasury, as well as the substantive legal principles articled by Hamilton and his lawyer colleagues.

Perhaps most revealing, Hamilton's influence on the development of American law demonstrates how the inanimate, theoretical provisions of the US Constitution, as well as the abstractions of federalism and the separation of powers, assumed real, concrete meaning. Consensus on the original "true" meaning of the US Constitution's clauses eluded the Framers, just as it continues to elude judges in the twenty-first century. Therefore, statesmen and jurists who first imbued meaning into the Constitution—setting precedents about executive authority, for example, or determining the actual boundaries of state authority and federal power—had significant, lasting influence over the substance of American jurisprudence. Hamilton accomplished this feat not as a judge and not simply because he was the primary author of *The Federalist* but because he was one of the first statesmen to put constitutional provisions into practice. If the Framers of the US Constitution created a new constitution to address the numerous problems of the Confederation era, then Hamilton used the many varieties of law in his common law toolbox to ensure that the federal constitutional framework would work as he thought fit.

Finally, I intend to remind historians, in particular, that we study the Founding Fathers for a reason. Alexander Hamilton and his close circle of professional or elite, white, and male colleagues mattered indispensably to the development of the American nation, and crucially, they were key figures in the development of American law.[21] These men were privileged, learned, and influential, but they still matter greatly to our understanding of the early republic because it was they who turned abstract or aspirational concepts into concrete reality during the founding era.

Rather than reexamine the founding generation's contributions to American political science (through their political essays, pamphlets, or participation in constitutional conventions), I aim to highlight their less heralded, but no less important, accomplishments in solving the practical, day-to-day problems of running the new republic.[22] Alexander Hamilton and his supporting cast of lawyers, judges, administrators, insurers, merchants, Loyalists, and libelous printers faced the same problem: now that they had a new constitutional framework for government, how did it work in practice? Hamilton did much to figure it out, as well as to set legal and institutional precedents to guide the course of republican governance for the future. That is why he is at the center of the transformations in American law described here.

Each of the following chapters begins by outlining Hamilton's particular, desired statecraft objective and the English legal principles he instrumentally applied to achieve his policy goals. After describing how Hamilton used a particular legal tool to prevail in private litigation or to administer the Treasury Department, the chapter then explains how judges and jurists adopted, deployed, or modified Hamilton's legal arguments in early republican and antebellum jurisprudence.

The first two chapters explore functional concurrence. They describe how Alexander Hamilton articulated a lasting doctrine of necessary, inherent executive discretionary authority and put it to use in order to create an energetic executive branch. Hamilton's arguments about the executive's prerogative power were also related to the federal judiciary: both departments had discretionary authority, as well as administrative responsibilities, inherited from the practices of English and colonial magistracies. Therefore, judicial and executive magistrates constantly negotiated the balance between executive prerogative and judicial oversight, and in the process developed an enduring federal jurisprudence that delimited the contours of executive and judicial power. The federal courts set some limits on executive authority, but mostly the courts accommodated executive actions and even engaged with treasury officials to administer the law. Over time, the federal courts upheld the executive's robust prerogatives, while in turn the federal judiciary's coordinate and federal review powers expanded as a result of their close collaboration with the executive department.

Chapter 3 begins an exploration of federal concurrence that continues in Chapters 4 and 5. "Creating the 'Commercial Republic': Neutrality and Law in the American Courts" examines how Hamilton accomplished his statecraft goal of building a commercial republic through the federal courts' expanding admiralty jurisdiction. As long as the United States remained neutral during the French Revolutionary and Napoleonic wars, federal district and circuit courts administered neutrality law with the help of Hamilton's Treasury Department and port-side district attorneys. As a result, the federal judiciary's prestige and jurisdictional reach expanded to encompass more commercial jurisdictions, including lucrative marine insurance contract disputes. In Chapter 4, "Developing the Jurisprudence of Federalism: Hamilton's Defense of the Federal Fiscal Powers," I demonstrate how Hamilton's extended defense of the federal government's robust taxing and borrowing powers became legalized—that is, the legal arguments that Hamilton articulated as treasury secretary became incorporated into federal jurisprudence through two decades of Marshall Court decisions.

From fiscal constitutionalism, I proceed to the intricacies of land law in "'A Most Valuable Auxiliary': Securing Foreign Capital with the Law of the Land." As a sought-after attorney favored by land speculators and foreign investors, Hamilton relied on New York's chancery court and its variety of equitable trusts to attract foreign investment in state lands, as well as to transform the substance of land law in New York state. By working at both the state and federal levels to attract foreign capital, Hamilton proved that the states were critically important jurisdictions through which he could accomplish nationally oriented policy goals.

The final thematic chapter, "Litigation, Liberty, and the Law: Hamilton's Common Law Rights Strategy," focuses on Hamilton's career-long rights consciousness. This approach constitutes a major departure from the popular and scholarly misconceptions about Hamilton, which insist that he was a monarchical elitist who privileged creditor and mercantile interests above all else. What scholars and biographers have missed, however, is that Hamilton was always a common lawyer at heart; therefore, he held a deep reverence for the rights and liberties provided and protected by the Anglo-American common law. So, throughout his career, Hamilton fiercely and consistently fought to preserve common law rights for all Americans.

By surveying the span of Hamilton's law practice in New York state courts—from his defense of minority (Loyalist) rights in *Rutgers v. Waddington* (1784) to his defense of the freedom of the press in *People v. Croswell* (1804)—I demonstrate that Hamilton was dedicated to preserving the people's rights to due process, jury trials, and press freedom under common law. To Hamilton, the common law provided a common shield to benefit all Americans from their government's overreaching and abuse of power.

Hamilton defended common law rights in New York state courts. In doing so, he demonstrated, yet again, that he considered the states to be important jurisdictions for achieving republican policy goals. Federalism, and not the consolidation of power in a national government, mattered to Hamilton and figured prominently in his statecraft. I thus conclude the book by arguing that Alexander Hamilton's legal legacy presents us with a new portrait of him, not as a die-hard nationalist, but rather as a true federalist, dedicated to balancing robust federal and state sovereignty.

By focusing on these particular episodes and themes that span the entirety of his legal career, I offer an intensive—but not comprehensive—examination of Alexander Hamilton as both a lawyer and a lawmaker. I do not engage with Hamilton's proposed constitution, offered and rejected during the constitutional convention in Philadelphia, for example. While Hamilton was initially disappointed by the compromises ultimately codified in the final version of the US Constitution, he ended up making the most of the powers articulated in its articles. I do not examine Hamilton's ideal constitution; instead, I am interested in the way that Hamilton instrumentally used the constitutional provisions that actually became the law of the land.

Also, I do not focus on every type of law invoked by Hamilton, or on each instance of Hamiltonian lawmaking. Instead, I examine representative examples of Hamilton's lawmaking efforts that affected his policy agenda. I do not discuss all of the contexts in which Hamilton invoked international law, for example; nor do I explore the majority of Hamilton's extensive land dealings, where he helped to sort out and to quiet titles between feuding patroon families in upstate New York. Similarly, I do not detail the complex contractual litigation and arbitration proceedings in which Hamilton participated when representing French merchant Louis Le Guen or members of New York's mercantile class. These protracted disputes were important in Hamilton's day, as they sometimes yielded large settlements for his clients and they won acclaim for Hamilton as one of New York's premier lawyers. Yet while Hamilton clarified or innovated upon the procedural law involved in this litigation, his efforts had little impact on his greater statecraft goals, and therefore I omit them below. Similarly, I also exclude discussions of the routine or insignificant cases, mediations, or advisory opinions that occupied Hamilton's time but had a negligible influence on the development of the law.

In the pages that follow, I examine only those episodes in Hamilton's career in which his extensive legal practice intersected with his ambitious, republican statecraft goals. In doing so, I provide a selective but intensive way to understand, and thus to appreciate fully, the numerous and profound ways in which Alexander Hamilton developed the substance of American law.

ONE

❧

Creating the Federal Magistracy: Discretionary Power and the Energetic Executive

In the annals of American political science, Alexander Hamilton is often remembered for his prescription for a strong federal executive power: an administration replete with the necessary "ingredients" of "energy," including unity, duration, adequate support, and competent powers.[1] Although his general philosophy on executive power is well known, scholars have been much less interested in how the first treasury secretary converted his political theory into an enduring practical reality.[2] Hamilton spoke of the need for energy in executive action, but in practice and under the law, how did an energetic, republican executive act without overstepping his authority? Hamilton's answer to this delicate and momentous question relied on an implicit assumption of a limited, legally bound prerogative power—what customs collector Otho H. Williams referred to as Hamilton's "doctrine of discretionary Executive power."[3] In order to translate the theoretical executive power described in *The Federalist* essays into a smoothly running, capable, and efficient administration, Hamilton argued that an energetic executive was also a magisterial executive—that is, an administrator empowered to act with discretionary license. He spent his public career articulating enduring legal arguments to define and defend the executive's practical prerogative power, and in doing so, Hamilton transformed early republican political science into the foundations of American administrative law.[4]

This Hamiltonian doctrine of executive discretion has gone mostly unnoticed because Hamilton, the early republic's premier administrative genius, expressed it only through occasional yet careful and conscientious legal arguments dispersed throughout his voluminous correspondence.[5] Hamilton advocated for executive discretion through open letters to the public, as well as through arguments made in behind-the-scenes memos and in day-to-day correspondence with Congress, district attorneys, and other federal officials.

Hamilton's approach to defending executive discretion was produced largely on demand and as needed because during the first years after American independence, the idea of discretionary executive power proved to be complicated, if not outright controversial, in a constitutional republic. Executive power carried with it the unsavory taint of monarchism, and thus the potential for despotic abuse. During and after the Revolutionary War, newly ratified state constitutions either stripped state governors of their Crown-bestowed prerogatives or diluted their power in favor of legislative authority.[6] Nationally minded delegates to the 1787 Philadelphia Convention also expressed concerns about excessive executive power, and even President George Washington approached executive action cautiously so as to avoid the charge of being "monarchical."[7]

Despite this sentiment, the desire for a robust federal executive persisted among nationally minded Americans during the Confederation era and grew stronger under the Federalist-dominated Congresses of the 1790s.[8] During these years, Congress conceded that executive discretion was a necessary and convenient way to administer federal law; the House and Senate saw fit to grant the president certain discretionary powers in matters of calling out the militia, raising additional regiments in the regular army, fortifying ports, closing public debt-related transactions, administering embargos, and overseeing administrative districts and their staffs. Early Congresses also vested discretion in subordinate executive officials, especially in the valuation of goods and property for assessment, determining compliance with federal rules and policy, and initiating litigation to prosecute violators of federal law.[9]

These grants of executive prerogative were limited and based in statutory authority, however, and as such, they could be permitted and revoked at Congress's will. But to Hamilton, the business of administering good government required more nuanced discretion and administrative maneuvering than statutory language could articulate or anticipate. Moreover, exercises of administrative discretion often amounted to implementing executive policy that Hamilton and Washington did not want Congress or the courts to overturn. For Hamilton, prerogative powers were necessary but limited tools for the efficient administration of government. Restraining executive discretionary power not only prevented abuses of power, but Hamilton also intended for it to deter opposition to the administration's actions and therefore to discourage interference with his policy agenda.

In order to make the case that executive power required discretionary license, Hamilton made three moves. First, he wrote legal briefs, scattered across a variety of sources, about the discretionary nature of executive power: in his *Federalist* and Pacificus essays, in customs circulars, and in reports and letters addressed to Congress. Next, Hamilton translated his legal arguments about executive prerogatives into practical administrative precedent. Finally, he cultivated a close relationship between his energetic executive department that he led at the Treasury Department and the federal judiciary in order to demonstrate that executive prerogative in a constitutional republic was subjugated to law. By instructing his employees to combine both execution and judgment in the administration of the laws, while at the same time inviting federal judges to advise and oversee administrative action, Hamilton developed a new, informal institution in the new national government: the federal magistracy.

I use the term "federal magistracy" to refer to the administrative model that Hamilton envisioned and put into practice, which transplanted English administrative methods into America's new republican institutions. The federal magistracy collectively signifies the discretionary authority inherent in the administrator's power to execute law, the legal boundaries that limit this executive prerogative, and the oversight provided by judicial courts to ensure that administrative authority remained within its lawful bounds. In short, the federal magistracy denotes the constitutional relationship between the executive department and the judiciary, as well as the discretion and judgment inherent in both types of governmental power.

Through written briefs, through administrative practice, and through his interactions with the federal courts, Hamilton argued that executive power possessed significant discretionary authority, albeit a discretion bound by constitutional, statutory, and common law. As such, Hamilton understood the federal courts to have a duty to oversee administrative actions to ensure that the executive exercised his prerogative according to the law. Although Hamilton did not use the term "federal magistracy" to describe the relationship between the Washington administration and the federal courts, he frequently referred to executive officials, and occasionally to the courts, as "magistrates" or as part of the "magistracy."[10]

English and colonial magistracies served as models for Hamilton's energetic executive department and for a federal judiciary fully engaged in the day-to-day business of governing. Under Hamilton's federal magistracy, the executive and judiciary simulated the close relationship shared between English magistrates and common law judges in the administration and review of law. Executive officials at all levels—but particularly department heads and the president, or the "Chief Magistrate," as Hamilton referred to him—interpreted and administered the law with discretion and good judgment, and federal judges reviewed administrative actions to ensure compliance with federal law.[11] Federal judges administered law and policy as well.

The treasury secretary also sought out federal judges to review or to advise executive decisions, and he understood judicial oversight to occur in different ways: as tort litigation brought against a federal official by a wronged party, as a mandamus action asking the court to compel an administrator to act while executing the law, as part of the judiciary's inherent responsibility to protect individuals' rights, and through the federal judges' involvement in advising the Treasury about the administration of law. Although Hamilton thought it inexpedient to turn to the federal courts to approve all questions concerning executive discretion, he sought out judicial advice and oversight where it was necessary and practicable, when he thought it prudent to settle a political or statutory controversy, or whenever he could involve the federal courts in administrative matters. Hamilton did not seem to think that federal judges should sit idle, simply waiting for cases or controversies to come before their benches.[12] Hamilton is known for his crucial insight that in a republic, judicial power must be coextensive over legislative power, but he also intended judicial coextensivity to encompass executive actions. By creating the federal magistracy, Hamilton built judicial coextensivity into administrative practice and court precedent through formal courtroom proceedings as well as through informal advisory relationships between departments.[13]

Constructing a legal foundation for executive discretion also provided Secretary Hamilton with the opportunity to accomplish multiple statecraft goals: empowering executive officials with the energy required for good government, defending or deflecting the implementation of (usually Hamiltonian) administration policy, and encouraging the judiciary to enhance its authority by getting involved in the business of governing. Yet creating the federal magistracy was a multifaceted endeavor: Hamilton defined and defended executive discretion at the same time he encouraged the federal courts to actively participate in and oversee administrative action. This chapter examines the first of these endeavors, Hamilton's articulation of the discretionary authority inherent in executive power and its close connection to judicial power. No matter how much discretion Hamilton conceded to the executive, he always assumed that the executive prerogative was guided and constrained by the law, a principle intended to explain executive action when under review either by the federal courts or by the court of public opinion.

While Hamilton went to great lengths to describe presidential and administrative prerogatives, he only indirectly suggested to what extent the federal courts could limit executive discretion. When in office, the secretary did not test the constitutional limits of executive and judicial discretion, but subsequent administrations did—particularly after the Jeffersonian "Revolution of 1800" divided the federal courts and executive along opposing party lines. After 1800, Republican administrators began to challenge the Federalist judiciary's authority to limit or command executive action. In response, the federal courts elaborated on the federal magisterial relationship by establishing legal rules to balance executive discretion with the judiciary's duty to protect individual rights and to interpret federal law. These guiding principles included an affirmation of the courts' mandamus review authority, the ministerial versus political act distinction, and the strict construction of statutory executive discretion.

When expounding the federal magistracy, the courts built on Hamiltonian ideas about executive discretion and judicial authority in order to preserve—and under certain circumstances to carefully circumscribe—the executive's prerogatives. In doing so, federal judges both accepted and rejected those Hamiltonian administrative practices and legal arguments that Jeffersonian and Jacksonian administrations used to justify executive discretion. As the first head of the Treasury Department, Hamilton "had to trace out his own path" in the formulation and implementation of administrative practice; therefore, his arguments about the nature of executive discretion and judicial power had a particularly formative and lasting influence on the development of American law.[14] By orchestrating the federal magistracy, Hamilton created practical precedents for both the lawful exercise of executive discretion and the judicial review of executive action. In so doing, Hamilton set the terms of future legal debates about the proper constitutional relationship between the executive and the courts. Because Hamilton laid the conceptual and legal foundation for executive and judicial power in the new republic, the federal magistracy persevered in administrative practice and in federal jurisprudence long after Hamilton finished defending it.

Presidential Power and the Anglo-American Magistracy

When Alexander Hamilton described the constitutional nature of executive power in *The Federalist,* he focused on the limited and necessary prerogatives delegated to the president of the United States. Rather than classifying them as prerogatives outright, Hamilton prudently referred to the US Constitution's specific grants of executive power as those "competent powers" necessary for executive energy, and thus the crucial components for waging good government. Hamilton did not elaborate on the scope of the executive's discretionary authority, however, as New Yorkers were skeptical enough of a strong federal executive in 1788.[15]

Yet when practical administrative questions and political controversies arose during Washington's terms in office, Hamilton responded by publicly clarifying the contours of executive discretion. In those first, precedent-setting years of the federal republic, most administrative uncertainties resulted from either a lack of explicit direction from Congress or the use of ambiguous language in federal revenue laws. Indeed, the most important discretionary power exercised by the Washington administration was the ability to construe federal statutes—a routine task that could have major consequences. If the administration reasonably interpreted federal law, it could simultaneously minimize judicial challenges, avoid congressional meddling in administrative action, and prevent public dissatisfaction with the administration itself or with its policy agenda. Interpreting federal law required finesse, foresight, and most of all knowledge of the law.

While interpreting statutory law was the most frequently used—and thus the most frequently claimed and defended—discretionary power, Hamilton defined and explained other executive prerogatives, including the presidential pardon and the administration's statutory discretion to resolve Revolutionary War claims. Sometimes Hamilton made his case in order to address a question arising from internal, administrative circumstances, but just as often, public outcries and opposition politics challenged treasury policy and demanded redress from the administration. In response, Hamilton countered abuse-of-power charges by crafting legal arguments to defend the executive prerogative. In this way, the politics surrounding executive action influenced Hamilton's articulation and practice of executive power before and after the US Constitution was ratified. Therefore, both politics and practical administrative concerns shaped the legal contours of executive discretion.

Even before ratification, Hamilton had a federal magistracy in mind. Dispersed throughout his *Federalist* essays on executive and judicial power,

Hamilton described the basic contours of the magisterial relationship: administrators operated with some discretionary authority when executing the law, while judges ensured that governmental action (in this case executive action, rather than legislative output) conformed to the law of the land.[16] While the exercise of administrative and judicial power in a republic would necessarily depart from analogous practices in England's constitutional monarchy, the English magistracy had already informed American administrative and legal practices for over a century and would continue to influence the federal government under the US Constitution.

The English magistrate, or justice of the peace, served at the pleasure of the king and represented royal authority in England's localities. Justices of the peace presided as both judge and local governor of the county for which they were commissioned, and from the fourteenth century (when justices began exercising true judicial powers at quarter sessions) until the late seventeenth century, local magistrates had significant autonomy and little oversight.[17] The justices' administrative authority pertained only to local matters, but their particular powers and duties numbered in the hundreds. Local magistrates' most significant power was the discretion to levy taxes among the local community in order to accomplish local upkeep and other administrative tasks.[18] Because of these formidable taxing powers, justices of the peace could easily reign over their locality as either "a petty tyrant or a benevolent ruler."[19]

English magistrates also possessed judicial authority to hear and determine misdemeanors and some felonies, as well as the power of summary conviction. By the late seventeenth century, however, magistrates' judicial autonomy came increasingly under certiorari review (certifying the record produced in a lower court by a superior court) by the King's Bench. Over time, the King's Bench developed extensive judicial oversight of local magistrates and "had a flourishing jurisdiction as a court of review for both summary convictions and orders of quarter sessions relating to such matters as public works, licensing, and the settlement of the poor."[20]

Despite the robust administrative and judicial authority exercised by English magistrates, their discretion was, at least in theory, highly circumscribed. Michael Dalton's *Countrey Justice*, a popular handbook for English and American magistrates, warned, "The commission of the peace (in it selfe) doth leave little (or nothing) to the discretion of the Justices of the P[eace] but doth limit them to proceed *secundu Leges, Consuetudines, Ordinationes, & Statuta*."[21] In other words, the king's commission limited the magistrates' discretion, forcing them to proceed according to the law, customs, ordinances, and statutes of the realm.

CHAPTER ONE

Colonial British America relied on the English magistrate model to administer law and justice at the local level. American justices of the peace presided over county criminal courts (quarter sessions, or general sessions), but they enjoyed a broader civil jurisdiction than their English counterparts. In some southern and mid-Atlantic colonies, magistrates heard criminal trials for slaves as well. Even George Washington, who became America's first chief magistrate, served as a local justice of the peace in Fairfax County, Virginia, before the Revolutionary War. In America, justices of the peace also retained administrative duties—responsibility for maintaining local infrastructure, administering poor relief, and levying taxes, for example—but the extent and scope of these duties varied across the colonies.[22] As in England, the American magistrate's authority and autonomy decreased throughout the eighteenth century as the specialized, learned, and more centralized authority of common law judges, lawyers, and juries "challenged the hegemony" of local justices of the peace.[23]

Although neither the Framers of the US Constitution nor Congress organized the federal court system to include quarter sessions, courts of common pleas, or justices of the peace, Congress recruited federal judges to serve in administrative capacities. Similarly, Congress also expected federal administrators to exercise some discretionary authority, as spelled out in federal statutes, and authorized the federal courts to inherit the Crown's prerogative writs (like mandamus, meaning "we command,"and habeas corpus) to review governmental action.[24] Thus national lawmakers, as well as Alexander Hamilton, retained the English magistracy mind-set, if not its particular institutional arrangements, in the early years of the federal republic. Hamilton would further articulate the details and nurture the relationship between the republican executive and judiciary to encourage and support a federal magistracy.

Hamilton's first steps in devising and implementing a federal magistracy included defining both the chief magistrate's prerogative powers under Article II and the nature of republican judicial power under Article III. It was no accident that Hamilton organized his *Federalist* essays with a thorough account of judicial power directly following his eleven articles on executive power. Under Hamilton's exposition, executive and judicial power complemented each other with similar, overlapping authorities and responsibilities: the executive could properly exercise judgment, while the judiciary's effort helped to ensure lawful administrative practices and good government.

Borrowing from the inherited English conception of judicial duty, Hamilton defined the federal judiciary's particular, necessary purpose under the limited federal Constitution as "to declare all acts contrary to the manifest tenor of the Constitution void," since the "interpretation of the laws is the proper and peculiar province of the courts."[25] The judge's duty to review the constitutionality of congressional or executive acts ensured that the federal government did not overstep its delegated authority. Furthermore, Hamilton noted that "the judicial magistracy is of vast importance in mitigating the severity" of law, and that the courts served as "the best expedient which can be devised in any government *to secure a steady, upright, and impartial administration of the laws.*"[26]

In *Federalist* No. 78, Hamilton also emphasized the judiciary's responsibility to protect and uphold the rights of individuals. He argued that an independent judiciary (that is, one shielded from legislative or executive meddling by a fixed salary and good-behavior tenure) provided "that inflexible and uniform adherence to the rights of the constitution and of individuals," which he considered to be "indispensable in the courts of justice." Judges were "an essential safeguard against the effects of occasional ill humours in the society . . . [that] sometimes extend[ed] no farther than to the injury of the private rights of particular classes of citizens, by unjust and partial laws."[27] Under Article III, the federal courts would protect individual rights not only through the nature of their judicial office but also through their general appellate power to review the proceedings of other tribunals. US attorney Charles Lee would later refer to Hamilton's explanation of the federal courts' appellate and supervisory powers as justification for the US Supreme Court's mandamus authority in *Marbury v. Madison.*[28]

Although he never explicitly described judicial review of executive action in his *Federalist* essays, Hamilton endorsed judicial coextensivity over the executive department in practice. Judicial review of executive action derived from preexisting Anglo-American legal traditions, where the authority to review executive actions existed inherently in the common law judge's duty and office.[29] Moreover, Hamilton went out of his way to ensure that any administrative discretion exercised under his watch comported with statutory language or common law principles, indicating that Hamilton assumed that the official expounders of the law, the courts, could review executive actions to ensure conformity with the law. To this end, Hamilton initiated a mandamus suit in 1794, *US v. Hopkins,* to test the Treasury's construction of a federal revenue statute. By denying the writ of mandamus requested by the United States, the US Supreme Court reviewed and affirmed not only the executive's actions but also Hamilton's construction of a state-to-federal debt subscription statute.[30]

CHAPTER ONE

Hamilton's depiction of judicial power simultaneously evoked and complemented his description of executive power. Just as the federal judiciary reviewed federal acts to protect individual liberty, to ensure good government, and to oversee the "steady, upright" administration of the law, a sufficiently energetic and well-supported executive magistracy possessed a responsibility to ensure the same. He even used similar language to describe the judicial and executive powers: energy was to Hamilton the most vital, indispensable feature of executive power. Executive energy was "essential . . . *to the steady administration of the laws*" and "to the security of liberty against the enterprises and assaults of ambition, of faction, and of anarchy."[31] Discretion was essential to the exercise of judicial power, but it was no less so in Hamilton's formulation of executive power, which drew heavily from the British king's royal prerogative.

Englishmen debated the nature and extent of the royal prerogative throughout the seventeenth century, beginning with the Stuart kings' aggressive assertions of prerogative power, the mid-seventeenth century's civil wars, and the general constitutional upheaval that resulted in the Glorious Revolution of 1688–1689. By the middle of the eighteenth century, however, Parliament had somewhat tamed the British king, and Sir William Blackstone, a leading jurist and an advocate for parliamentary supremacy, described the royal prerogatives as they existed by the 1760s in his *Commentaries on the Laws of England*. The substantive royal prerogative, Blackstone reported, could be divided into three types: "first, the king's royal *character*; secondly, his royal *authority*; and, lastly, his royal *income*."[32] By nature, the American president lacked a royal character or royal income, but his office shared much in common with the British king's "royal authority."

Blackstone described the eighteenth-century royal prerogative with two maxims that came to influence and define Hamilton's conception of the executive's discretionary authority. First, quoting Bracton, Blackstone described a limitation on the royal prerogative, "Nihil enim aliud potest rex, nisi id solum quod de jure potest," or that the king has no other power than what is allowed by right.[33] But when acting within the bounds of a "lawful prerogative, the king is and ought to be absolute; that is, so far absolute, that there is no legal authority that can either delay or resist him." Blackstone followed this particular rule about royal authority with a list—"He may reject what bills, may make what treaties . . . may pardon what offences he pleases"—that overlapped significantly with the presidential prerogatives outlined in Article II.[34]

Of the king's prerogatives categorized as part of the "royal authority," most had to do with taking some form of action. Barring statutory prohibitions or desuetude, if the king wished to pardon a convict, he could pardon without parliamentary interference; or if he wished to veto a statute in Parliament he could, at least in theory, still exercise that prerogative right. The president shared some of the British king's actionable prerogatives, and within the bounds of the law, he enjoyed an exclusive sphere of action to be taken (or not) at his discretion.

As we will see, Hamilton also argued that the executive and his administrators had another type of crucial discretionary power: to interpret the law in order to execute it. This authority was one of interpretation rather than of action, but it too derived from the royal prerogative. Blackstone described the king's prerogative to issue binding proclamations as predicated on the discretionary license needed to enforce the law in practice—that is, "the manner, time, and circumstances of putting [the] laws in execution must frequently be left to the discretion of the executive magistrate."[35] In other words, inherent in the king's prerogative authority were the powers to decide when or when not to act, and to decide how to interpret statutes in order to enforce them.

In *The Federalist*, Hamilton devoted his most careful exposition of Article II to the executive magistrate's "competent powers," each an exercise of inherited royal prerogatives, and each comprising some degree of discretionary license. The Constitution's Framers modeled the president's veto power—or as Hamilton called it, the "qualified negative"—after one of the British king's most significant prerogatives.[36] When exercising his veto, the president not only partook in the business of lawmaking but also had the opportunity to adjudge the propriety and constitutionality of bills before they became law. The president also exercised discretion when appointing federal officers, when presenting Congress with information on the state of the Union, when receiving ambassadors, and when faithfully executing the laws.[37] Undoubtedly a strategic move, Hamilton did not explain in *The Federalist* what the executive prerogative required to faithfully execute the laws. But this discretionary authority—the ability to interpret the meaning or instructions embodied in federal statutes—cut to the heart of practical administrative discretion, and Hamilton would define it frequently during his tenure in the Treasury.

In these essays, Hamilton elaborated on the president's explicit, constitutionally ordained powers. Yet his arguments implicitly affirmed both that discretionary authority was inherent in the nature of executive power and that the president could not operate above the law (in this, Hamilton mir-

CHAPTER ONE

rored Blackstone's maxims about the royal prerogative). Indeed, the executive was "subordinate to the laws," including the US Constitution, and Hamilton evidenced this by confining his discussion of presidential power to its relevant constitutional provisions.[38]

Hamilton gave considerable discussion to two actionable prerogative powers, pardoning and treaty making, that would in time be associated with political controversies arising during Washington's tenure in office. Hamilton referred to the president's pardoning power as a "benign prerogative" required by "humanity and good policy," instituted primarily "for the mitigation of the rigor of the law," especially "in seasons of insurrection."[39] Hamilton was particularly prescient here, as George Washington made shrewd political use of his pardoning power in the aftermath of the 1794 Whiskey Insurrection. After Pennsylvania's circuit court tried, convicted, and sentenced insurgents Philip Vigol and John Mitchell to hang, Washington issued stays of execution and then pardons to spare the convicts' lives.[40] Washington strategically used his pardoning prerogative to demonstrate the fair-mindedness and mercy of the national government after he enforced the legitimacy of federal law.[41] In doing so, Washington substantiated Hamilton's observation that "in seasons of insurrection or rebellion, there are often critical moments when a well-timed offer of pardon to the insurgents or rebels may restore the tranquility of the commonwealth."[42] Because this critical period could pass quickly, only the chief magistrate, as opposed to the deliberative Congress, had sufficient energy and maneuverability to make a quick decision to pardon.

Hamilton and Washington also confronted a more uncertain, but less politically sensitive, occasion to use the pardoning prerogative in 1791, but this time the constitutional limits of the presidential pardon came into question. By the terms of the August 1790 Collection Act, customs officials could not land cargo after sunset. On October 7, 1790, Samuel Dodge, a customs inspector in New York, landed seven or eight hogsheads of molasses at port in New York harbor, in violation of the federal customs statute. Dodge was subsequently indicted in federal court in February 1791 for the infraction, but he maintained that he had been ignorant of the after-sunset unlanding provision of the statute because it had gone into effect only a few days before Dodge unloaded the molasses. After a grand jury handed down an indictment acknowledging that Dodge acted without fraudulent intent, Dodge pleaded guilty, but asked the court to suspend judgment against him so that he could plead his case to President Washington.[43]

Dodge's petition to Washington raised two legal issues.[44] The first was whether the fines and other penalties for Dodge's customs violation could be excused under a 1790 act to remit and mitigate penalties and forfeitures for customs violations (the Remitting Act), as Dodge claimed.[45] Under the act, Congress bestowed the treasury secretary—in this case Hamilton, who was also Dodge's supervisor—with a limited pardoning power; because Congress authorized the secretary to remit certain revenue-related penalties, Dodge hoped that his boss could relieve him. Secretary Hamilton was skeptical, however, but as he always did when faced with important legal questions, he consulted his close friend and colleague Richard Harison, the district attorney for New York. Harison did not think that the 1790 Remitting Act could relieve Dodge because Congress intended the act to mitigate penalties incurred by merchants and ship captains, not treasury employees. Also, as Hamilton noted, the presidential pardon was a more appropriate tool for redress.[46] Yet even the pardoning prerogative raised its own constitutional questions.

No one doubted that Washington could pardon Dodge and relieve him of the fines and penalties incurred under the federal statute and owed to the federal government. There was a catch, however; the Collection Act stipulated that half of Dodge's fine was to be paid to the informer who had reported Dodge's violation to John Lamb, the federal customs collector in New York. Therefore, Washington could pardon Dodge and forgive him the fine owed to the federal government, as well as reinstate Dodge as inspector, but could the presidential pardon divest the informer of his statutory right to half of Dodge's fine?

Hamilton raised the constitutional question to Harison "concerning the extent of the power to pardon," while Washington consulted the US attorney general, Edmund Randolph, as well.[47] Randolph's response has not been found, but Harison agreed with Hamilton that "the power to pardon which the Constitution has vested in the President of the United States cannot extend to affect the rights of Individuals."[48] Could the pardon be issued at all, then? Yes, but Harison suggested that the pardon be conditional on Dodge's payment of the informant fee, and possibly the expense of prosecution. He noted that "a Practice somewhat analogous to this, has prevailed in England."[49] In 1792, Washington issued the pardon to Dodge.[50]

The Washington administration's handling of Dodge's petition demonstrates how mindful Hamilton and Washington were to ensure that executive discretion conformed to existing law. The president's power to pardon derived from Article II of the US Constitution, but the prerogative's particulars had to be carefully delineated from English common law principles and case law. Also, Hamilton, Washington, and Harison were especially concerned about the monetary right vested by law in Dodge's informant, and thus were careful to preserve it. Hamilton and Harison's assumption that executive discretion could not infringe individual rights not only echoed Publius' claims in *Federalist* No. 78 but also presaged Chief Justice John Marshall's similar conclusion in *Marbury v. Madison*.

In his *Federalist* treatment of the presidential prerogative, Hamilton also detailed the executive's treaty-making powers, a discretionary authority unto itself, as the president made the decision to enter into a contract with another sovereign. After the parties involved drew up their agreement, only then would the Senate give its advice and consent. Like any other federal law, however, the president would also have to interpret existing treaties and act on his conclusions. This discretionary authority to interpret law and to act accordingly has become an integral part of executive power, yet it sparked fierce public outcry during the 1793 neutrality crisis. In defense of Washington's Neutrality Proclamation, Alexander Hamilton became the first and foremost expounder of the executive's discretion to interpret the law.

In the first of his four Pacificus essays, Hamilton defended Washington's constitutional authority to issue the Neutrality Proclamation by demonstrating that inherent in the power to execute the law is the necessary authority to interpret it. Hamilton described the executive "as the *organ* of intercourse between the Nation and foreign Nations—as the interpreter of the National Treaties in those cases in which the Judiciary is not competent."[51] Washington sought to faithfully execute his peacetime obligation to the nation (as Congress had not declared war on either the French or the British), and so "in fulfilling that duty, [the executive] *must necessarily possess a right of judging* what is the nature of the obligations which the treaties of the Country impose on the Government."[52] In this case, Washington and his Cabinet adjudged that American neutrality did not violate the provisions of the 1778 Franco-American Treaty of Amity and Commerce.

Hamilton's final summation in Pacificus No. 1 endures as a strong, definitive statement about the nature of executive power under the US Constitution. But it also had a particular public purpose: the Pacificus essays helped to soothe the political frenzy incited by the Washington administration's neutrality-based approach to Atlantic-world politics. Hamilton concluded his first Pacificus essay by forcefully articulating the discretionary authority inherent in executive power:

The President is the constitutional EXECUTOR of the laws. Our Treaties and the laws of Nations form a part of the law of the land. *He who is to execute the laws must first judge for himself of their meaning.* In order to the observance [*sic*] of that conduct . . . it was necessary for the President to judge for himself whether there was any thing in our treaties incompatible with an adherence to neutrality. Having judged that there was not . . . it was [the President's] duty, as Executor of the laws, to proclaim the neutrality of the Nation."[53]

When reflecting on Hamilton's contributions to constitutional law, legal scholar William R. Casto carefully combed through Pacificus' "careful and lucid argument . . . grounded in the structure and actual words of the Constitution," and concluded, "Simply put, Pacificus No. 1 is one of the best essays ever written on a specific issue of constitutional law."[54] Hamilton successfully argued that the US Constitution authorized the executive's necessary, inherent discretionary authority. While Pacificus developed his masterful exposition of executive power in the face of political opposition, Secretary Hamilton would continue to articulate these arguments under the pressures of maintaining his own administrative policy agenda.

The Prerogative in Practice

Alexander Hamilton was known to have run a "notoriously tight ship" in the Treasury Department.[55] He directed his own remarkable reserves of energy toward overseeing his far-flung employees by circulating departmental memos that kept them uniformly up-to-date and apprised of his directives.[56] Hamilton's close management style was a natural result of his personality— he loved to be at the center of the action—yet he also had policy and governance goals at stake: restoring and maintaining the public credit, successfully collecting federal taxes, and demonstrating how a strong, centralized national government would help, rather than harm, the constitutional republic. Hamilton realized early on that successful administration could help to accomplish these goals as readily as his various policy reports to Congress did.

Just as the chief magistrate relied on discretionary authority to act with sufficient vigor, so would the administrative department under Hamilton's direction. Hamilton's employees and colleagues in the Treasury exercised routine, discretionary authority as part of their day-to-day tasks. For instance, the comptroller's responsibilities were considered by Congress to be quasi-judicial in nature, and customs collectors had to make valuations and statutory construction decisions daily.[57] But whenever possible, Hamilton tried to insert himself into the collectors' decision-making processes to limit their interpretive latitude. The secretary did this to ensure administrative uniformity across the department, but also to be sure that collectively, the Treasury Department made smart, well-supported decisions that reflected well on the administration's policy goals.

Hamilton's defense of administrative action can be found throughout his work-related correspondence, including his Revolutionary War claims adjudication reports and his various memos and testimonies dealing with administrative interpretation of federal law. Sometimes Hamilton defended administrative prerogative proactively—that is, Hamilton claimed the authority to make quasi-judicial decisions or statutory interpretations so that he could direct the outcomes of the decisions. At other times, however, Hamilton articulated a defense of administrative prerogative in order to retroactively defend his or his department's actions in the face of political, and sometimes public, controversy. Whether proactively or not, Hamilton always grounded his defense of administrative discretion in law by demonstrating how the administrative decision-making process conformed to well-reasoned rules or common law principles by consulting legal counsel to inform and guide treasury action, or by defending discretionary authority inherent in the nature of executive power.

Hamilton took a proactive approach to adjudicating the Revolutionary War claims pouring into Congress during the first years of the federal republic. Scores of soldiers, merchant suppliers, and widows applied to the first federal Congress—the first solvent Congress that they had encountered, thanks to Hamilton's assumption and funding plan—requesting pensions, restitution for damages, back pay, reissued government securities, and compensation for contracted goods and services.[58] To dispose of each claimant's petition, research would have to be conducted to verify the veracity of the claim (if at all possible) before Congress could ultimately decide whether the claimant deserved payment, and if so, how much. This process of adjudicating claims seemed to fit better in a court of law: as a relatively large, deliberative body, Congress was bogged down by the time-consuming research, debate, and decision-making responsibilities that accompanied each individual's petitions for compensation. Yet rather than establishing a court of claims, Congress simply referred most of the petitions to the department heads for consideration. If Congress agreed with the advised dispositions provided by Secretary Hamilton or by Secretary of War Henry Knox, then Congress would appropriate money for the petitioner.[59]

Adjudicating claims provided Hamilton with an opportunity to further his goal of establishing and maintaining the public credit. Adjudicating compensatory petitions often amounted to weighing the interests of the public against the interests of the petitioners, which typically meant that the public good was better served by rejecting a questionable claim for money. Hamilton viewed some of the more dubious claims as potential threats to the public credit, and in these cases, he reinforced his own statecraft by denying the claim. Since Hamilton's public policy goals could be served by each of his decisions, the secretary would not want Congress to second-guess and overrule his hundreds of recommendations. Therefore, to validate his recommended outcomes, Hamilton ensured that his decisions conformed with reasonable, nonarbitrary rules and preexisting statutes of limitations. By adopting legal limitations in his adjudications, Hamilton effectively accomplished two things: first, he gave Congress less of a reason to overrule his decisions, and second, he helped to set a precedent for the exercise of administrative discretion.

On August 7, 1790, Congress read and approved a "Report on the Petition of Jacob Rash" as submitted by the treasury secretary.[60] Rash had originally petitioned Congress on June 29, requesting duplicates of Continental Loan Office certificates that were destroyed by fire in 1785.[61] Congress submitted the petition to Hamilton, and he responded favorably to Rash. In his report, Hamilton reasoned that many petitioners found themselves in the same predicament as Rash, and justice should be done for them by granting new certificates. However, Hamilton would not reissue certificates without assurances that the former certificates were actually destroyed and that the petitioner could be confirmed as the legal holder. These two concerns directly engaged Hamilton's larger administrative concerns over restoring and maintaining the public credit. If Hamilton authorized loan certificates to be reissued without confirming that the originals had been destroyed, then the value of public securities, as well as the public's confidence in the marketplace, would be undermined. Hamilton proposed a solution to help identify the creditors who lost their certificates through a verifiable accident, then applied these guidelines to Rash's petition.[62] On April 21, 1792, Congress received from Hamilton a batched submission of claims also requesting renewals of loan certificates.[63] Hamilton considered each petition on its own merits, but he applied the same rubric to help standardize his decision-making process. He also annexed a copy of his Rash report to remind Congress of his applied principles.

Because Hamilton's judgments had real consequences for the public credit, he set the claimant's burden of proof relatively high to ensure their

CHAPTER ONE

credibility. For example, Hamilton threw out the petition of Laurana Richardson, who, as the legal representative for her dead husband, claimed that the earth destroyed the certificates when they were buried with her husband.[64] Hamilton did not find Richardson's conjecture to be enough proof for a certificate reissue. But William Baker had a more credible claim: he gave his certificates to his mother for safekeeping, and while Mother Baker had the certificates in her cupboard, vermin destroyed them. Accompanying Baker's claim was testimony from his mother, a confirmation of the facts by a friend, and an advertisement run in the newspapers for the lost certificates. Baker had met Hamilton's general standard of proof, and so the treasury secretary recommended a reissue.[65]

In addition, Hamilton strictly construed and upheld statutes of limitations, and as a result, many petitioners with good, provable claims were barred from relief because the secretary declined to mitigate the effects of the various acts.[66] Hamilton also refused to give preferential treatment or to consider compensating petitioners for depreciation. In 1779, Joseph Bennett received payment in Continental money that he knew to be worth less than the amount of goods he provided to the government. Years later, Bennett sought compensation for the difference between the real value of his goods and the depreciated value of the Continental money, which he had accepted at its face value. Yet when considering his 1792 petition, Secretary Hamilton seemed unsympathetic to Bennett's loss, reasoning, "There is nothing in the Case of the Memorialist to distinguish it from the general Case of the Creditors who made similar Loans to the United States, and of course the Claim does not in the Opinion of the Secretary admit of a distinct treatment."[67] Hamilton did not think it good policy to compensate for depreciation on government accounts and securities, or to distinguish between creditors by favoring some over others.[68]

Claims adjudication gave Hamilton an opportunity to simultaneously exercise rule-bound discretion and to uphold his policy agenda. Of course, Congress could always overrule the secretary's decision and reconsider the petitioner's claim or refuse to appropriate money for its redress. This rarely happened, however, in part because Congress did not want to look into and resolve individual claims (that's why it punted them to Hamilton and Knox in the first place), but also because Hamilton wrote convincing, well-researched, and well-reasoned reports on each petition. While immersing himself in the administrative drudgery of claims adjudication, Hamilton set a precedent for how the executive's rule-bound, expedient discretion worked in practice.

When Hamilton was not busy reporting to Congress, he was in constant communication with his employees, and in particular his customs collectors. The collectors were both the front line and the face of the federal executive authority to Americans engaged in maritime commerce, and as such, they inherently executed the most important administrative prerogative: interpreting the law before executing it. Hamilton knew this, but he sought to limit his collectors' desire to interpret and execute federal statues independently of him. The Treasury's customs collectors were headstrong, smart, and personally liable in civil court for their actions, however, and so some collectors resisted Hamilton's authoritative interpretations of federal law.[69] Yet because Hamilton demonstrated the legal justification behind his statutory constructions and because he generally gave good advice, most of the time the customs collectors deferred to Hamilton.

But not always. When in the summer of 1792 Secretary Hamilton sensed that some of his customs collectors had been deviating from his instructions regarding the duty on spikes (fasteners) and fees collected under the Coasting Act, he issued a statement describing the executive department head's superintending power to interpret the law.[70] Concerned that "deliberate deviations from instructions . . . would be subversive of uniformity in the execution of the laws,"[71] Hamilton insisted that because Congress gave the secretary of the treasury the responsibility "to superintend the Collection of the Revenue," he had the definitive administrative authority to interpret the laws for the collectors.[72]

Hamilton argued that the "power to superintend must imply a right to judge and direct. . . . It is not possible to conceive how an Officer can *superintend* the execution of a law, for the collection of a tax or duty . . . unless he is competent to the interpretation of the law, or in other words, has a right to judge of its meaning."[73] But if superintending meant that Hamilton possessed a prerogative to interpret the laws, then he also had the necessary authority to fix statutory meaning for his inferiors: "The power of *superintending* the Collection of the Revenue . . . comprises . . . the right of *settling*, for the Government of the Officers employed in the Collection of the several branches of the Revenue, the *construction* of the laws relating to revenue, in all cases of doubt. This right is fairly implied in the force of the terms, 'to superintend,' and is essential to uniformity and system in the execution of the laws."[74]

This discourse was in line with Hamilton's other articulations of executive discretion, as judgment and discretionary authority were inherent in the nature of executive power, particularly for the crucial business of executing the laws. But the supervisory authority that Hamilton derived from the power "to superintend" merely allowed him to request that his inferiors abide by his constructions—at least, that is what the federal courts determined during Jefferson's administration. Hamilton understood, just as his collectors did, that because the collectors were personally liable in court for their actions, individual collectors might follow their own interpretations of their responsibilities and duties under the law. Despite the fact that Hamilton articulated an executive superintending power, neither Hamilton nor his collectors attempted to use the secretary's superintending authority as a shield against collector liability or as an excuse for the president to exercise his discretion in place of his employees' discretion in court. (The Jefferson and Jackson administrations made these arguments, however, but the courts largely rejected them.) By circulating memos declaring his authority to interpret the law, Hamilton could only reassert the executive's prerogative and guide his employees, with the hope that, for the sake of administrative uniformity, he convinced each collector to abide by his construction and his legal arguments.

Statutory interpretation caused another internal controversy, this time over the collectors' fee schedule provided under the 27th and 30th sections of the 1789 Coasting Act.[75] Through his multiple customs circulars addressing the Coasting Act, Hamilton clarified the construction of various components of the act, but he ultimately could not get his collectors to comply with his interpretation of its problematic fee provisions. The issue turned on how many times the collector could legally collect his 60-cent fee. Did the collector earn 60 cents after he received the entry of inward cargo and qualified each manifest on board (all considered to be one service, as Hamilton claimed), or did the collector earn 60 cents for receiving the entry of inward cargo, followed by 60 cents earned for each manifest qualified (multiple actions and thus multiple earnings, as the collectors claimed)?

Hamilton clearly wanted his employees to collect their fee only once per inward cargo, after the collector had properly received the cargo and qualified all of the related manifests. He admonished them, "Uniformity in practice as to the article of fees is particularly desireable. The want of it has already been a source of complaint, and is of a nature to produce both discontent and censure."[76] Moreover, he thought it "an important principle of public policy that allowances to officers should not be extended by implication or inference; as discretion on that head, must from the nature of the thing be liable to great abuses."[77] Hamilton devoted three customs circulars to explaining his construction of the law, the legal principles guiding his reasoning, and the public policy concerns he had. He also relied on his most frequently used statutory construction strategy: consult other lawyers for their input. The secretary asked Samuel Jones, New York City's recorder, and the Treasury's informal outside legal advisor, Richard Harison, for their thoughts on the matter, and they agreed with Hamilton's interpretation. When Hamilton consulted two Virginians, William Heth and US attorney general Edmund Randolph, however, they agreed with the collectors' interpretation of the law.[78]

After all the research, consultations, and informal legal briefs, Hamilton finally conceded that his collectors would not follow his interpretation of the fee schedule. He rescinded his instructions, but he still maintained that his construction of the Coasting Act's fee provisions was correct. A final brief demonstrated that he genuinely thought that his construction was correct, based in sound legal principles—and perhaps most importantly, the interpretation of the law that would protect his collectors in court. When constructing the fee provisions, along with other problematic sections of the Coasting Act, Hamilton had already reminded his collectors that if contested, their constructions could be "overruled by the Courts."[79] By soliciting legal advice from the nation's top commercial attorneys (including himself), the secretary attempted to limit his collectors' liability.

When trying to dissuade his collectors from charging 60-cent fees per manifest entered, Hamilton noted that already the practice garnered complaints from the public. Public or political outcry was a typical response to the administration's efforts to faithfully execute the law by faithfully interpreting the law (as the neutrality controversy demonstrated). Even though Secretary Hamilton tried to be proactive about minimizing controversy surrounding executive construction, he found himself retrospectively defending executive action.

Preliminary controversies that would eventually erupt into the Whiskey Insurrection plagued Hamilton even before Pennsylvanian distillers refused to pay the excise tax. When the offending excise on domestic and foreign distilled spirits first passed Congress in 1791, Hamilton anticipated uncertainties, and he attempted to resolve its statutory ambiguities from the start.[80] To this end, he circulated a memo to his customs collectors with an extensive enclosure detailing how the collectors were to construe particular provisions of the law.[81] Despite his best efforts, public protests induced Congress to ask Hamilton to report on the difficulties of executing the law.

In his "Report on the Difficulties in the Execution of the Act Laying Duties on Distilled Spirits," the secretary described various problems with the law and suggested solutions. One of the first issues addressed, however, was the public's outrage over the collectors' perceived arbitrary discretion including a "summary and discretionary jurisdiction" in the collectors that ran counter to common law and abridged the people's right to jury trials, and a general discretion to search and to seize indiscriminately.[82] Hamilton dismissed the first charge regarding the collectors' summary jurisdiction outright, as "there is nothing in the act even to give colour to a charge of the kind against it." But the collectors' discretion to search and seize did exist, and Hamilton inferred that the real issue was not that "general discretionary power of inspection and search" existed, but that the discretionary authority extended in this case to domiciles and dwellings. Nevertheless, Hamilton defended his collectors' prerogative to search: if the distiller would not separate his place of business from his home, then his home would necessarily be subject to inspection when the collector assessed the undistinguished distillery. He also recommended the practice of marking the distilleries as separate buildings or entrances from the home, so as to avoid as much confusion as possible for the collector.[83]

As noted above, the Whiskey Insurrection would also provide President Washington with the opportunity to exercise his pardoning prerogative. Together, there were three instances of executive discretion associated with the tax rebellion: Hamilton's proactive construction of the law, his report defending the collector's exercise of discretionary authority, and Washington's final pardon of the convicted rebels. These three exercises of executive power demonstrate how Hamilton relied on administrative discretion to implement his policy agenda (the tax on distilled spirits was Hamilton's idea in the first place) and how frequently the executive used judgment to interpret and execute the laws.[84] The prerogative exercised here ranged from behind the scenes and mundane to politically charged and extraordinary. Hamilton considered each to be inherent in the nature of executive power.

Hamilton devoted hours to defending his department's exercise of executive discretion while serving in the Washington administration, yet even when he left his Cabinet post, he found it necessary to continue explaining and justifying the administration's prerogative powers. In the fall of 1795, months after he left the Treasury, Hamilton published a signed open letter defending the Treasury's past and current practice of paying officials' salaries in anticipation of services rendered. President Washington, former treasury secretary Hamilton, and current secretary Oliver Wolcott Jr. had been accused in the press of corruption for paying extra compensation to the president.[85] To Hamilton, this was an attack on the Treasury's necessary discretion to decide when to disburse money that had been legally appropriated.

In his letter, Hamilton argued that appropriations had to be balanced against the availability of treasury reserves in order to avoid a serious cash flow problem. The department's head thus needed discretionary authority to disperse appropriated salary payments when treasury reserves could support them—even if the salary paid out was in advance of work done for that pay period. "The business of administration requires accommodation," Hamilton reminded his audience, and this accommodation was the secretary's discretionary authority to release salary payments when he thought the Treasury could best support and manage inflows and outflows of cash.

Hamilton denied that the Treasury violated the terms of the president's compensation statute with this construction, and to prove his point, he went on for pages with a record of warrants attached.[86] But he also had more to say on the exercise of executive discretion. Noting that a "discretion of this sort in the head of the department can at least involve no embarrassment to the Treasury," he claimed that it was nonarbitrary, partly because the secretary had been careful to act with an "eye to the public interest and safety," but also because he could be dismissed and punished for true misconduct. Moreover, he explained that this was "an example of a discretion to do what there is not a right to demand [by the president, or other officials]. The existence of this discretion can do no harm, because the head of the Treasury will judge whether the state of it permits the required advances."[87]

So exasperated was Hamilton to have to defend reasonable, nonarbitrary, necessary treasury practices that he took a moment to indulge in self-pity: "Preeminently Hard in such circumstances, was the lot of the man who[,] called to the head of the most arduous department in the public administration, in a new Government, without the guides of antecedent practice & precedent, had to trace out his own path and to adjust for himself the import and bearings of delicate and important provisions in the constitution & in the laws!"[88] Yet behind his dramatic tone, Hamilton neatly summarized what made his five years as treasury secretary so extraordinary. Without precedent to guide him, Hamilton was forced to "trace out his own path" in order to figure out how to interpret and execute statutory law within the untried bounds of the new Constitution. As a department head, Hamilton learned to improvise daily, and he relied heavily on the executive's inherent discretionary authority to allow him the freedom to maneuver, reason, and adapt accordingly.

The necessity of executive discretion prompted Hamilton's repeated defense of it: without prerogative license, and without the ability to accommodate vague statutory language or practical, administrative problems, the federal executive would be ineffective and inadequate. Hamilton would not tolerate an inept executive—not when he labored for so long to create the energetic executive magistrate. But neither, it turned out, would the federal courts. In the years after Hamilton left office, the Marshall and Taney courts would consider, accept, reject, and expand on Hamiltonian administrative practices. In doing so, the federal courts sustained and elaborated on the federal magistracy amid a changing political climate marked by interdepartmental clashes.

The Federal Magistracy in the Federal Courts

Hamilton lived just long enough to witness his ideological opponents challenge the federal courts' authority to review executive action. After a decade of mounting political opposition to Federalist policies and Federalist administrations, Jeffersonian Republicans now took control of the national government. With sweeping majorities gained in Congress, and with Thomas Jefferson peacefully acceding to the chief magistracy in March 1801, Jeffersonian Republicans triumphed over Hamilton's weakened and discordant Federalists. But with this peaceful electoral "Revolution of 1800" came the Jeffersonians' extended attack on the federal judiciary.

Federal judges became a target for Republicans in part because they represented a last bastion of Federalists in government, but also because judges seemingly had the will and the power to act against the will of the people. Before leaving office, lame duck Federalists passed the Judiciary Act of 1801, and with it attempted to secure sitting judges' tenure on the federal bench though political wrangling and statutory law. Incoming Republicans would have none of this, however, and quickly repealed the 1801 legislation; in subsequent years, Republicans also impeached federal judges, including District Judge John Pickering (who was successfully moved from the bench) and Supreme Court Justice Samuel Chase (who was acquitted by the Senate).[89]

President Jefferson also attempted to abridge the power of the federal courts in one final way: by seeking limits on federal judges' authority to review executive action. By confronting a federal bench filled with Federalist judges, however, Jeffersonians found themselves in the rather curious position of advancing Hamiltonian arguments about the extent of executive prerogatives against a Federalist Supreme Court sympathetic to Hamiltonian views on judicial power. Even though Alexander Hamilton was now permanently out of office and on the losing side of national politics, Hamiltonian constitutionalism had come to define the terms of the executive–judicial debate waged throughout the early national period.

Once in office, Jefferson, Treasury Secretary Albert Gallatin, and other Jeffersonian–Republican jurists advocated for robust executive prerogatives, but they did so by denying that the federal courts had any authority to limit executive discretion. To justify these claims, the Jefferson and Jackson administrations relied implicitly and explicitly on Hamiltonian arguments. Just by adopting the language and practice of a strong, discretionary executive, Jeffersonian and Jacksonian jurists ensured that Alexander Hamilton's model of the energetic executive became the norm for presidential and administrative practice. Yet at the same time, this political repurposing of Hamiltonian arguments forced the judiciary and the executive to clarify and further refine their constitutional relationship.

The introduction of ideological opposition dividing the national government into discrete departments raised questions about the federal magistracy that Hamilton had neither answered nor anticipated. While he expected judicial review of executive action (including mandamus review), he never had to clarify where, exactly, to delimit executive prerogatives and judicial review if the president or his administrators contested court oversight. Opposition politics soon made these distinctions imperative, however, and it was thus left to the courts to continue defining the limits of executive and judicial discretion.

Beginning with *Marbury v. Madison*, John Marshall incorporated the components of Hamilton's magistracy into the federal government's nascent administrative jurisprudence, but further elaborated on executive discretion by classifying it as either ministerial or political (discretionary) in nature. If the executive action under review was ministerial, then the courts had complete authority to limit or command the executive to act in a judicially prescribed way. Marshall's ministerial distinction provided a sturdy legal rule to balance Hamilton's energetic executive against the court's review powers should they collide. While in *Marbury* the Court carved out and preserved a political act category—a prerogative sphere—for executive discretion to thrive untouched by the Court, a year later it rejected a revived version of Hamilton's superintending power in *Little v. Barreme*.[90]

The federal circuit courts soon followed Marshall's lead. In *Gilchrist v. The Collector of Charleston*, the Circuit Court for the District of South Carolina affirmed its mandamus review authority over the class of discretionary powers delegated to the executive department by Congress while it simultaneously denied the president's and treasury secretary's asserted superintending powers. Rather than rely on Marshall's ministerial distinction, the court strictly construed the statutory language that granted the inferior administrator his discretion. The US attorney general protested the decision, however, arguing that only the president, and not the federal courts, had the authority to limit or command the executive official's decisions. Eventually, in *Kendall v. US ex. rel. Stokes*, the Taney Court reaffirmed and adopted the four legal rules articulated by these earlier decisions, including mandamus review, the ministerial distinction, the rejection of an intra-administration superintending power, and the strict construction of the executive's statutory discretion. In doing so, the Taney Court emphasized the Hamiltonian claim that discretion was necessary and inherent in the exercise of executive power, but that it must also conform to law and judicial review.[91]

When incoming secretary of state James Madison refused to deliver justice of the peace commissions signed by outgoing president Adams, William Marbury (along with four other would-be magistrates) asked the Court to issue a writ of mandamus commanding Madison to deliver the signed commissions. The Court ultimately determined that while Marbury had legal title to the office and thus had a legal remedy available to him, the Court could not grant the mandamus because in this particular case it lacked jurisdiction. Marbury was out of luck.[92]

Despite the Court's jurisdictional limitations, Chief Justice Marshall still wrote an opinion for a unanimous Court, offering dicta that would become the judicial touchstone for presidential and administrative litigation in the early national period.[93] Although the chief justice did not explicitly refer to Hamilton in his opinion (Attorney General Charles Lee cited the former secretary), it was the Hamiltonian magistracy that Marshall described, upheld, and adapted for a federal government divided along party lines.

When Marshall commented on the nature of executive and judicial power, which had collided in *Marbury*, he deferred to the executive's unquestioned prerogative powers to nominate and appoint officials to federal offices. When the executive had discretionary authority, "whatever opinion may be entertained of the manner in which the executive discretion may be used, still there exists, and can exist, no power to control that discretion . . . being entrusted to the executive, the decision of the executive is conclusive."[94] Marshall wholly acknowledged the legitimacy and finality of executive discretionary authority. But echoing Hamilton's careful consideration of the presidential pardon and Samuel Dodge's informant fee, Marshall also affirmed that the executive "cannot at his discretion sport away the vested rights of others."[95] Therefore, the Court determined that the president's appointment prerogative had ended, and Marbury's right to the office had vested, once the commission had been signed, sealed, and ordered to be recorded. The plaintiffs thus possessed legal title to their offices.

Marshall articulated two important dimensions of executive discretion that conformed to Hamilton's conception of executive power. First, where discretion was explicitly granted to the executive (like the pardoning or appointment powers), the executive had complete authority to judge when and how to wield these prerogatives. Second, because executive prerogatives were either explicitly or implicitly conferred by law, the judiciary was naturally authorized to ensure that executive discretion remain within its proper bounds. Marshall's distinction is slight but important: the Court may not "enquire how the executive, or executive officers, perform duties in which they have a discretion," but where that discretion ends, or where he is "directed by law to do a certain act affecting the absolute rights of individuals," then the Court can step in to review the executive's action and to command him to act.[96]

In this case, former president Adams exercised his proper presidential prerogative to nominate and appoint justices of the peace, and so the Court could not review his decisions. However, Secretary Madison had no discretionary authority to deny Marbury his commission because the executive's legal window for exercising his appointment prerogative had closed; the legal boundary was, according to the Court, after the commission was sealed and ordered to be recorded. Where the executive's prerogative ended, the individual's vested right began.

Chief Justice Marshall thus adopted both components of Hamilton's federal magistracy model. He acknowledged that executive magistrates necessarily exercise discretion, but that discretion had finite legal contours. In addition, Marshall upheld the idea, as articulated by Hamilton in *Federalist* No. 78, that the judiciary's particular constitutional duty was to protect individual rights. To this end, Marshall distinguished between the magistrate's ministerial and discretionary duties to use as a handy rule to guide the Court and future administrations: "It is a ministerial act which the law enjoins on a particular officer for a particular purpose."[97] If executing a ministerial duty, then the executive possessed no prerogative authority and thus the courts could command him to act. Yet if the executive performed a legitimately discretionary duty, then so long as he did so within the limits of his prerogative (for example, acting without violating an individual's right), the court could not review his decision or circumscribe his prerogative. The ministerial distinction provided a legal guideline to allow the Court to compartmentalize and navigate the overlapping exercise of judicial responsibility and executive prerogatives.[98]

Note, however, that though Marshall endorsed Hamilton's conception of magisterial authority, it was the chief justice, and not the former treasury secretary, who articulated this ministerial/discretionary distinction and assigned it the status of a legal rule. Marshall established the distinction partly through the influence of Hamiltonian constitutionalism and partly from what he divined to be the executive's natural obligation to administer specific duties assigned by sovereign law on which individuals' rights depend.

But Marshall was not the only jurist involved in *Marbury* to endorse Hamilton's conception of magisterial authority. During oral argument, former US attorney general Charles Lee, attorney for the plaintiffs, quoted from three of Hamilton's *Federalist* essays on judicial power in order to argue for the judiciary's right to give legal remedy to his slighted clients.[99] Lee broadly construed Hamilton's arguments about the Supreme Court's appellate authority to implicitly justify its exercise of mandamus review. Also, Lee cited Publius in order to persuade the court that Madison's denial of the commissions compromised the independence of the federal judiciary, as well as Marbury's rights. Lee referred to *Federalist* Nos. 78, 79, and 81 to convince the Court that it had a duty "to maintain the rights of [his clients'] office" as well as to maintain the integrity of an independent judiciary.[100] Moreover, since Hamilton initiated a mandamus suit in the US Supreme Court during his treasury tenure, Lee cited the unreported 1794 case, *US v. Hopkins*, as precedent for the Court's jurisdiction in William Marbury's mandamus action.[101]

Although Marshall's adoption of the federal magistracy model in *Marbury* occurred only through dicta, his opinion formalized the fundamental components of the Hamiltonian magistracy into a reported judicial opinion. *Marbury* also initiated a new phase in the development of American administrative law: the case marked the moment when the federal courts began refining the details of the executive–judicial relationship and sorting out where exactly the executive's discretion ended and the judiciary's oversight began. By establishing legal rules for limiting executive discretion, *Marbury* became the pivotal precedent for Federalist, Jeffersonian, and Jacksonian lawyers to use when arguing about the proper contours of the federal magistracy.

A year after *Marbury*, the Marshall Court adjudged *Little v. Barreme*, a civil lawsuit that raised questions about discretionary authority exercised within the administration's hierarchy. In a 1799 nonintercourse statute, Congress authorized the seizure on the high seas of US vessels bound for any port or place in the French Republic. The act did not authorize the seizure of vessels sailing from the French Republic, nor did it allow the capture of non-American vessels.[102] In December 1799, the US frigate *Boston*, led by Captain Little, seized a neutral Danish vessel leaving Jeremie, a French port, to Danish St. Thomas. Little then libeled, or brought the vessel, the *Flying Fish*, into federal admiralty court for violating the 1799 act.

As measured by the statute's provisions, Little blatantly violated his mandate, first by capturing a Danish vessel instead of an American vessel, and second by seizing a vessel headed from, rather than to, a French port. On the basis of these acts, Little seemed clearly liable for damages against Barreme, presumably the owner of the vessel. But there was one complication that could release Little from liability: President Adams had instructed the captain to act as he did. In 1799, Adams issued instructions to his merchant marine that badly misconstrued the provisions of the 1799 act.[103] He told his captains to capture vessels headed both to and from French ports, which directly violated the terms of the statute. Moreover, the president implied that seemingly "Danish" vessels were particular targets for seizure because they were often American vessels sailing under false papers. Captain Little therefore deliberately defied the terms of the 1799 act because he acted under orders from his administrative superior. The key question for the Court became: did Adams's instructions absolve Little from liability?

The Marshall Court thought not and held Little liable for the damages incurred by Barreme after the mistaken seizure. Writing the opinion for the Court, Marshall pointed out that the statute did not authorize seizures heading from a French port, nor did it give the president any power to authorize them. Therefore, Adams had badly misconstrued the law. While Marshall sympathized with the obedient Little for acting on his superior's instructions, it ultimately did not release the captain from liability for superseding his statutory authority. The chief justice decreed that the "instructions cannot change the nature of the transaction or legalize an act which without those instructions would have been a plain trespass."[104] Therefore, the Court would hold those administrators vested with statutory authority responsible for construing the law for themselves.

Although the Marshall Court never mentioned Hamilton or treasury practice in its opinion, by refusing to allow an administrative superior's instructions to substitute for an inferior's statutorily conferred judgment,

Marshall implicitly rejected Hamilton's notion of an executive superintending power. Moreover, the Court also demonstrated that it would strictly construe executive discretion conferred by Congress. These principles became reoccurring themes in administrative law, and only a few years later, the federal courts would reiterate them during another politically contentious mandamus action.

Gilchrist et al. v. The Collector of Charleston, or the *Case of the Resource,* reprised the themes of *Little v. Barreme* and sparked a politically charged debate between Federalist courts and the Jefferson administration about the limits of executive discretion and judicial oversight. The case arose when Robert Gilchrist, owner of the *Resource,* brought a mandamus action against Simon Theus, collector at Charleston, asking the South Carolina Circuit Court to command Theus to release his vessel detained under the 1807 Embargo Act.[105]

In his opinion for the court, Associate Justice William Johnson stated that under the act, the "granting of clearances is left absolutely to the discretion of the collector," and this right remained "in him unimpaired and unrestricted" as long as the collector suspected that the vessel had violated or was attempting to evade the embargo.[106] In other words, the collector's discretion was proper and binding, but only within the limited parameters spelled out by Congress; the collector did not have the authority to detain vessels for reasons unrelated to those specified in federal customs law. Furthermore, contrary to Theus's claims, Johnson determined that only the collector wielded a prerogative power; the statute did not grant discretionary authority for detaining vessels to Treasury Secretary Gallatin or to President Jefferson. (Nevertheless, Jefferson, acting through Gallatin, had advised Theus to detain the *Resource.*) In consequence of these findings, the court granted the mandamus and ordered the collector to issue clearance for the *Resource* to depart Charleston.

Whether or not Theus intentionally targeted the Federalist merchant Gilchrist for detention, the case took on an overtly political dimension when US attorney general Caesar A. Rodney published an open letter critiquing the court's decision. In it, Rodney relied on *Marbury's* jurisdictional demurrer to deny that the circuit court had authority to issue the mandamus.[107] Moreover, Rodney defended those Hamiltonian administrative practices that Jefferson and Gallatin had continued since taking office. Both the president and treasury secretary attempted to preserve Hamilton's suggested superintending hierarchy, whereby upper-level administrators directed the decisions of lower officials to ensure best practices as well as conformity to policy. The attorney general thus argued that the court violated the discretionary authority of both the collector and the president by granting the mandamus. Rodney insisted that the Embargo Act allowed the collector to detain vessels until he could consult the president, and therefore the chief magistrate had a supervisory authority (a "controlling power," derived from his authority to faithfully execute the laws) over the collector's decision to detain the *Resource*.[108]

Like *Little v. Barreme, Gilchrist* revolved around how much discretionary authority attached when Congress conferred administrative discretion through statute. But unlike *Little,* the court in *Gilchrist* was not reviewing the administrator's liability on the back end, after he had finished executing the law; rather, the *Gilchrist* court purported to command the administrator to act while he was still engaged in executing the law. In order to refute the federal court's authority to oversee the collector's actions, the Jefferson administration claimed that it possessed a Hamiltonian superintending power that excluded judicial oversight. To this end, Rodney argued that since Congress gave discretion to the collector, the court did not have any authority to review the collector's act in midexecution. Instead, Collector Theus was only responsible to his bosses, Jefferson and Gallatin, and they, rather than the courts, would decide whether Theus's actions faithfully executed the law.

In his open letter, Rodney articulated a modified, compartmentalized relationship between the executive and the judiciary. He observed that there did not "appear in the constitution of the United States any thing which favours an indefinite extension of the jurisdiction of courts, over the ministerial officer within the executive department," and he suggested that there were two ways to proceed, one acceptable under the Constitution and one not. Rodney thought that judicial intervention to retrospectively redress a wrong committed by an executive officer was proper (that is, nonmandamus litigation to determine executive civil liability), but "an interposition by a mandatory writ, taking the executive authority out of the hands of the president, and prescribing the course, which he and the agents of any department must pursue" was not. The difference was that "in one case the executive is left free to act in his proper sphere, but is held to strict responsibility; in the other all responsibility is taken away, and he acts agreeably to judicial mandate."[109] Whereas Hamilton and Marshall considered mandamus review to be appropriate, Rodney thought that such an intervention would violate the "proper sphere" of executive and judicial power. In making these claims, Rodney faithfully articulated the theory of coequal department first pronounced by Jefferson.[110]

In response, Justice Johnson published remarks of his own. He denied Rodney's claims to an intra-administration superintending power and affirmed the court's mandamus review. In addition, Johnson forcefully contested Rodney's "proper sphere" approach to delimiting executive and judicial power.[111] To him, the matter was simple: congressionally delegated executive discretion went only so far as the law explicitly allowed, and the court, as the constitutional organ responsible for declaring the law, could strictly police it. In *Gilchrist,* the Embargo Act gave discretionary authority to the collector only, according to Justice Johnson, and so only the collector could wield this discretion when he was suspicious of the vessel's intentions to evade the embargo. Since collector Theus admitted that he was not suspicious of Gilchrist's intentions but detained the *Resource* anyway, Theus violated the boundaries of his statutorily conferred prerogative powers. Therefore, because the collector transcended the bounds of his statutory discretion, the judiciary did not infringe on the executive's authority when it commanded the collector to give clearance to the *Resource* to leave Charleston.

The legal debate incited by *Gilchrist* simultaneously confirmed, rejected, and expanded upon Hamilton's formulation of the federal magistracy. By using *Marbury* as the key precedent informing *Gilchrist,* both the circuit court and Attorney General Rodney accepted Hamiltonian premises about discretionary authority as a necessary component of executive power. Disagreement arose over the scope of judicial review of executive action, however. Hamilton, Marshall, and Johnson endorsed mandamus review of executive action, against the arguments offered (again) by the Jefferson administration. Also, Hamilton understood executive and judicial power to be overlapping and complementary; he would have found it to be both difficult and undesirable to separate them into Rodney's distinct spheres.

Rodney, in contrast, sought to limit the court's mandamus review powers and instead sought to take advantage of Marshall's ministerial/political distinction in order to free the executive's prerogatives from judicial limitation. The Jefferson administration assumed an administrative hierarchy whereby the president and his department heads exercised a superintending power over their employees, whether or not statutory language specifically granted them that power. The courts, however, rejected this superintending claim and asserted their own authority instead: when administrative discretion derived from statute, the courts would strictly construe the law's provisions and police executive action. *Gilchrist* did not settle the matter for the administration, however, and in its aftermath, the debate over the contours of the magisterial relationship continued under Andrew Jackson.

Jackson's administration made the grandest claims yet about executive discretion and the federal courts' limited ability to review it. The resulting US Supreme Court contest, *Kendall v. The United States, on the Relation of William B. Stokes et al.*, gave the Taney Court the opportunity to reaffirm its mandamus review authority and the Marshall Court's ministerial rule, as well as to revisit judicial review of statutory executive discretion.[112] The *Kendall* litigation originated in executive noncompliance: Jackson's postmaster general, Amos Kendall, refused to comply with an 1836 special act passed by Congress directing him to pay disputed monies owed to four contractors who had transported US mail. Kendall's predecessor had approved payment to the creditors, but Kendall subsequently reexamined and denied the allowances and credits granted. When Stokes and three other contractors complained, Congress passed an act, which Jackson signed, for their relief. Under the terms of the act, the solicitor of the Treasury would calculate the balance due to the petitioners, then submit the bill to the postmaster for payment. However, after the solicitor calculated and submitted to Kendall the amount due (the creditors' award totaled approximately $162,000 owed), the postmaster general authorized payment for only $122,101.46. Kendall thus intentionally denied payment of $39,462.43 to the contractors (and President Jackson apparently approved). As a result, the deprived creditors brought a mandamus action to the Circuit Court for the District of Columbia, and the judges ordered Kendall to fully comply with the terms of the 1836 act; Kendall then asked the US Supreme Court to reverse the circuit court's decision on a writ of error.

The special act did not delegate any discretionary authority to Kendall (only the solicitor had judgment to determine the amount owed to Stokes), but the lawyers for Kendall nevertheless argued that the executive's discretionary authority inherently existed whenever he read, interpreted, and executed the laws. Kendall's lawyers, Francis Scott Key and US attorney general Benjamin F. Butler, resurrected Pacificus' arguments to make these claims, though they applied Hamilton's reasoning in a way that the former treasury secretary would have disputed. Key and Butler claimed that President Jackson's inherent discretionary authority—which he conferred on Kendall through his approval of the postmaster's noncompliance—was beyond the Court's authority to review. Key declared, "Not only is it the President's duty to see how the laws are executed: he is invested with discretion as to when they are to be executed." On what authority did the executive have such discretionary license? "One of the political powers or duties of the

President, as given by the constitution, is to see that the laws are faithfully executed; and both the late Chief Justice [Marshall] . . . and Mr. Hamilton . . . in the letters of Pacificus[,] say, that he must ascertain what the law means; 'must judge of it for himself.'" Because the executive possessed a discretionary authority inherent in his duty to execute the laws, Butler claimed that the judiciary had no power "to interfere in advance, and to instruct the executive officer how to act for the benefit of an individual."[113]

Butler's arguments echoed those of former attorney general Caesar Rodney. He cited an assortment of Hamilton's *Federalist* essays on executive power in order to make the point that since the Constitution vested the entire executive power in the president (an arrangement that both Hamilton and Madison vindicated), then only the president could be constitutionally responsible for reviewing the acts of his administrators "in advance." Faced with these formidable authorities, Richard S. Coxe, for the defendants in error, could only reply that the proposition "for the first time distinctly advanced by General Hamilton, in his Letters of Pacificus," made the executive authority into an unchecked power, commensurate with that of a "king or czar, emperor, or dictator." Therefore, according to Coxe, the Court should regard Hamilton as "a great and revered authority, but subject to occasional error."[114]

Kendall's attorneys made bold claims about executive power. They also used Hamiltonian arguments to make Jeffersonian claims about the coequal and cosovereign executive and judicial departments. Butler and Key pushed the logic of Hamilton's Pacificus arguments to the extreme, claiming that so important was the executive's inherent discretionary authority to faithfully execute the laws that the courts could neither review nor interfere with his ability to exercise discretion. They adopted a Hamilton-like superintending argument as well, and claimed that only the heads of the administration, and not the courts, could determine whether or not subordinate officials were faithfully executing the law. (Hamilton would have denied this.) The Jacksonian jurists thus denied Hamilton's magisterial relationship but still embraced the first treasury secretary's robust conception of executive power.

The Taney Court rejected their claims, however, and reaffirmed the components of the federal magistracy, beginning with the Court's authority to review Kendall's actions. Writing for the majority, Associate Justice Smith Thompson confirmed that "under this law the postmaster general is vested with no discretion or control over the decisions of the solicitor," rendering his duty a ministerial one.[115] Therefore, as Marshall had determined before him, the federal courts could review the executive's noncompliance and command him to act.

Thompson also denied that "the postmaster general was alone subject to the discretion and control of the President, with respect to the execution of the duty imposed upon him by law," because to allow the president to claim this sort of unchecked, superintending discretionary authority "would be vesting in the President a dispensing power, which has no countenance for its support in any part of the constitution."[116] To this end, he repudiated Kendall's claim that simply executing a statutory duty put the executive's actions into *Marbury*'s discretionary category and thus out of the reach of the courts: "There are certain political duties imposed upon many officers in the executive department, the discharge of which is under the direction of the President. But it would be an alarming doctrine, that congress cannot impose upon any executive officer any duty they may think proper . . . and in such cases, the duty and responsibility grow out of and are subject to the control of the law, and not to the direction of the President."[117] Furthermore, since executive discretion was "subject to the control of the law," the executive's political/discretionary duties were not wholly free from review; if Congress granted discretionary authority specifically to the executive, then Congress, and by extension the courts, had the authority to review and limit them. Taney concurred in this constitutional sentiment (though he dissented to the Court's holding), adding, "The office of postmaster general is not created by the constitution. . . . The office was created by act of congress; and wherever congress creates such an office as that of postmaster general, by law, it may unquestionably, by law, limit its powers, and regulate is proceedings; and *may subject it to any supervision or control, executive or judicial,* which the wisdom of the legislature may deem right."[118]

The Court's decision in *Kendall* sustained the various legal principles that previous federal courts had devised to balance the federal magistracy's competing forms of discretionary authority. *Kendall* upheld Marshall's ministerial/political distinction, which it then used to affirm its own mandamus review of the postmaster's nondiscretionary duty to Stokes. The Taney Court also rejected the administration's claims for an inherent, intra-administrative superintending authority and reaffirmed that the federal courts would strictly construe any executive discretion granted by statute. Stokes's special act did not grant discretionary authority to the postmaster general, and so the Court was not about to find it emanating from the executive's general authority to faithfully execute the laws.

At *Kendall's* conclusion, the federal courts had staked a limited claim to reviewing executive action, and they did so without smothering or dominating the executive branch. On the contrary, a theme underlying each decision was the courts' careful regard for the propriety and necessity of administrative discretion. The guiding principles developed by the judges to define their review reflect this cautious approach to preserving executive prerogatives. The courts acknowledged a wide berth for executive prerogatives, and the ministerial/political distinction carved out a prerogative sphere whereby executive actions could not be reviewed. The limits created by the courts included the ministerial distinction, where no executive discretion existed, and the vested rights boundary whereby even constitutionally guaranteed prerogatives, like the pardoning power, stopped where an individual's vested right began. (Hamilton assumed this to be true before Marshall declared it to be a rule.) Moreover, discretionary powers conferred by Congress were merely revocable prerogatives; that the federal courts construed them strictly did not impair the executive's inherent or constitutional powers.

The federal courts thus preserved the federal magistracy by acknowledging and maintaining the executive's prerogatives. At the same time, they developed a limited oversight of administrative action. *Marbury*, *Little*, *Gilchrist*, and *Kendall* constitute a line of cases that enhanced the executive's authority, as the administration's discretionary authority had been acknowledged and preserved in federal case law, in addition to the courts' powers. As Robert McCloskey has noted, in *Marbury* John Marshall asserted the mighty power to review congressional law by denying the Court's jurisdictional authority to do so.[119] Similarly, the federal judiciary assumed the power to review executive acts by acknowledging that the executive's inherent, constitutional prerogatives were off-limits to the courts. During the first fifty years of the early republic, judicial power expanded coordinately with executive power, and the Hamiltonian federal magistracy endured.[120]

The Hamiltonian Magistracy and American Administrative Law

By recovering the federal magistracy, a set of constitutional arguments that structured the executive–judicial relationship in the early republic, we can better understand how novel republican legal principles developed as a continuation of and innovation on inherited past practices. Administrative law developed not as a niche offshoot of the regulatory state in the twentieth century, not as an inevitable triumph of executive prerogative over judicial power, and not as a centuries-old power struggle between the coordinate branches of the federal government.[121] Instead, administrative law originated in the customs of an inherited English colonial magistracy, but it became an applicable jurisprudence for a republic through the various efforts of American jurists, Congresses, and administrators throughout the early national period. English and colonial magisterial practice exemplified and legitimated law-bound administrative discretion and a limited judicial oversight of it; the founding generation put these customs into practice by refracting them through the lens of republican principles and through the structural framework provided by federal Constitution. Despite this collaborative effort, no individual influenced the founding of administrative law more than Alexander Hamilton.

Hamilton's important contributions to administrative law can be found in his potent, foundational ideas about the extent of judicial and executive authority. Hamilton considered the federal courts to be the national government's ultimate constitutional expositor, while he also argued that the executive properly exercised prerogative powers. During his time in office, Secretary Hamilton did not have to reconcile these two conceptions of departmental power, but during his lifetime, John Marshall did. The Marshall Court compromised with the executive department, however, splitting the difference between the departments and their respective prerogatives. In *Marbury*, the ministerial versus political distinction carved a prerogative sphere for judicially untouchable executive action while reserving to the courts their authority to judicially protect individual rights—a limit on executive discretion recognized by Hamilton. The federal courts continued to place some limits on the executive's superintending powers but only to preserve administrators' civil liability (*Little*) or to strictly construe statutory grants of discretionary powers (*Gilchrist* and *Kendall*). The executive's prerogative sphere was consistently maintained by the federal courts, even if the judges simultaneously set limits on the boundaries of executive power.

As a result, the federal courts claimed a wider scope of authority as constitutional arbiters and as limited overseers of executive action. At the same time, however, executive power expanded in the early republic; presidents, department heads, and their far-flung employees exercised an increasing amount of inherent, constitutional, and statutory prerogative powers. The federal courts also strengthened executive discretionary authority by repeatedly acknowledging that it existed and that it was, in certain cases, not subject to review by the courts. In this way, both the executive department and the judiciary enhanced their authority while developing an American administrative jurisprudence distinct from, although originating in, the English magistracy.

Perhaps the most striking part of this extended negotiation between the two departments of the federal magistracy is that both the courts and the executive branch relied on Hamilton's arguments to make their claims. Hamiltonian administrative practice and constitutional theory sit squarely at the center of both Marshall and Jefferson's opposing visions of the executive and judicial relationship. Alexander Hamilton influenced Marshall's vision of the federal judiciary as final constitutional arbiter, and he also provided practical and legal foundations for Jefferson's (and later Andrew Jackson's) coequal department theory.

That Hamiltonian theory inspired John Marshall is familiar and unsurprising; both were staunch Federalists who deeply valued the judiciary's role in preserving popular sovereignty by reviewing exercises of governmental power.[122] *Marbury v. Madison* restated Hamilton's description of judicial power in *Federalist* No. 78, and William Marbury's attorney, Charles Lee, cited from *Federalist* No. 80 to argue that the Supreme Court's appellate power implicitly covered executive acts. Moreover, Hamilton participated in a precedent-setting mandamus suit before *Marbury*, never questioning the federal court's authority to oversee the executive action under review.

But Alexander Hamilton's model for the energetic executive, as well as his arguments for executive discretion, influenced Jefferson's coequal department theory as well. Of course, Hamilton would not have agreed that executive action was immune from judicial review—the ultimate takeaway of coequal department theory—but Jefferson and his political sympathizers adopted Hamiltonian arguments to advocate for an executive superintending power and discretion in the execution of law. Not only were both of these Hamiltonian claims incorporated into Jefferson, Gallatin, Jackson, and Kendall's administrative practices, but also lawyers for the Jeffersonian and Jacksonian administrations relied on these same Hamiltonian arguments, sometimes explicitly, to make the case for coequal department theory in court.

By recovering the federal magistracy, we see how American administrative law evolved from its monarchical roots into a republican jurisprudence, as well as how the federal courts and the executive enhanced their prerogatives through negotiating their constitutional relationship. Yet the federal magistracy also reveals how central Alexander Hamilton's constitutional theory and practice were to not only the development of administrative law but also to the republican constitutionalism of John Marshall and Thomas Jefferson. In the early republic, then, the federal magistracy was a Hamiltonian magistracy.

TWO

❧

Administrative
Accommodation in the Federal
Magistracy

Hamilton had a singular influence on the articulation and subsequent development of the executive's prerogative powers, the first component of the federal magistracy. But the second part—a close, symbiotic relationship between the executive and the judiciary—was established by a more collaborative effort among the treasury secretary, the federal courts, and Congress. Recall that the federal magistracy that Hamilton envisioned combined the judgment and discretion of vigorous executive officials with the judicial oversight and even administrative actions of federal judges. Both the executive and judicial departments shared inherited authorities from the English magistrate, or justice of the peace. In practice, this relationship between the magisterial departments of government grew out of separate but similar efforts by Congress and Hamilton to get federal judges actively involved in the administration of federal law and policy. Rather than exclude the federal courts from the day-to-day business of administering law, both Hamilton and Congress actively sought federal judges' input in the executive's decision-making process and in the supervision of national policy. For the most part, the federal judges eagerly complied.

Exploring the close-knit, collaborative relationship between executive officials and judges as administrators exposes a bustling, but usually forgotten, jurisdiction of the federal courts, as well as the day-to-day intricacies of the federal magistracy. As we have already seen, John Marshall and his brethren took the opportunity presented by those legal questions surrounding executive discretion to position the federal courts as the final expositors of constitutionality for the national government. The Marshall and Taney courts often made these sorts of constitutional claims in the early republic and antebellum eras.[1] The still-dominant narrative of federal court development tracks the Supreme Court's adjudications of great constitutional questions, and as a result, the judiciary appears to be aloof and distant from the day-to-day business of governing.[2]

This familiar and important narrative presents only one side to the development of federal courts' jurisdiction and authority in the early republic. The constitutional arbiter story ignores the early courts' active engagement in the business of administering law; it also almost always neglects the involvement of busy federal district courts in administrative matters. In fact, federal district judges most directly resembled their English and colonial magistrate forebears, as judges clothed with judicial power who also ensured that laws enacted by the sovereign would be executed within their districts. These judges also worked and corresponded with Secretary Hamilton and his customs collectors as part of a combined judicial–executive effort to execute federal law. In this way, the federal courts became, right from the start, a vibrant, busy federal venue for administering law and policy—a lucrative function set apart from, though contributing to, their tentative but developing role as constitutional umpires.

The federal courts did not get involved in administrative matters by pronouncing themselves to be administrators. On the contrary, Congress usually created administrative responsibilities for a particular federal court or its justices through statutes. The best-known example is Congress's failed efforts to include the federal courts in the administration of the 1792 Invalid Pensions Act.[3] In this instance, the federal courts protested their assigned roles in administering the act, citing the statute's purported violation of the separation of powers principle. Ultimately, federal circuit judges refused to fulfill their statutory mandate in *Hayburn's Case*.[4] Under the Invalid Pensions Act, the particular problem was that Congress gave the federal circuit courts administrative responsibilities, then allowed the secretary of war to revise their judicial decisions. When instead Congress assigned tasks to the judges as individuals, rather than to the judicial court on which they sat, the federal judges were willing to participate as administrators.[5]

Congress, for example, recruited district judges to administer the provisions of its 1790 statute concerning the seaworthiness of sailing vessels. In order to go to sea, Congress required the master of the vessel to petition a district judge (or local justice of the peace) to first appoint three mariners to appraise the vessels for statutory required food, water, and medicine chests as well as its general fitness for ocean voyaging. After the mariners reported back, the judge had the ultimate discretion to decide on the vessel's seaworthiness, or the steps that must be taken before the vessel could sail.[6] Similarly, under the Remitting Act, Congress also involved district judges in the administrative process by which the treasury secretary adjudged and mitigated statutory penalties relating to coasting law violations.[7]

In addition, Congress actively involved the federal district and circuit courts in the administration of federal policy by assigning them criminal and civil jurisdiction over neutrality, embargo, and nonintercourse act violations. When, for example, the Washington administration declared that the United States would remain neutral until Congress declared war, Congress responded by passing a criminal statute to prosecute violators of US neutrality.[8] Although Congress specified which actions constituted a breach of the law, it fell to the federal courts to translate and apply explicit statutory language to the many vagaries of wartime Atlantic-world commerce.[9] The success of federal neutrality policy thus hinged on how the courts would construe, apply, and prosecute Congress's statutory provisions. Also, the judiciary played a similar role in overseeing the Jefferson administration's embargo and nonintercourse acts, as well as the Adams administration's highly unpopular Sedition Act.[10] Because Alexander Hamilton was actively involved in prosecuting neutrality violations in federal court, the federal judiciary's responsibility for administering neutrality will be discussed in the next chapter; the importance of the courts' involvement in embargo litigation will be discussed in this chapter.

While Congress defined the courts' magisterial functions in national governance, Hamilton also recruited the federal courts to help him administer the law. In particular, the secretary looked to federal judges for their input and oversight over those treasury matters that affected his favored policies. For example, Hamilton took seriously the opportunity presented by the Remitting Act to delicately balance the collection of federal coasting and customs revenues against the growth of domestic and international shipping in American ports. Therefore, Hamilton actively engaged district judges in conversation so that both executive and judicial magistrates conferred on whether to remit or mitigate coasting law penalties. Secretary Hamilton also initiated and involved himself in federal court litigation in order to receive a legally binding interpretation (and most often, validation) of his construction and execution of federal statutes. By turning to the courts, Hamilton intended for the federal bench to authorize and validate treasury policy to answer political opponents who contested Hamilton's execution of the law.

The result of these combined legislative and executive efforts to involve the courts in the business of administering law was threefold. First, as noted above, the courts gained prestige, jurisdiction, and a busy docket by taking part in various administrative matters. Second, the courts and their justices developed their place within the federal magistracy, functioning as both judicial overseers of administrative action and administrators themselves. Finally, and most importantly for Hamilton, a functioning federal magistracy fostered a symbiotic relationship between the executive and judicial departments. The administration relied on judicial input to validate executive policy, while the courts gained jurisdiction and authority as part-time administrators and full-time overseers of national and state governance. Each time the courts reviewed an executive act, they exercised their constitutional function as expositors of national law and coordinate-department review. Sometimes this oversight allowed the federal courts to make constitutional claims about the limits of executive power or their role as umpire of the federal system, as demonstrated in *Marbury*, as well as in *US v. Hopkins* and in *Olney v. Arnold*.[11] Other times, however, federal court review simply authorized and executed federal policy, thus engaging and uniting federal judges and executive officials in a common purpose.

The ultimate result of this close cooperation was administrative accommodation—that is, judicial deference given to administrators' actions in the execution of federal law and policy.[12] Administrative accommodation prevailed despite the Jeffersonian attacks on the federal courts, and despite the fact that the Federalists who pioneered administrative accommodation never regained political dominance (but instead continued to lose their political prominence). Especially during the early years of the nineteenth century, Federalist judges found themselves working alongside (and therefore accommodating) Republican administrators. Although the federal courts policed the executive prerogative and occasionally placed limits on it, more often federal judges deferred to executive decisions and administrative proceedings when these actions were exercised within their proper (usually statutory) limits. Administrative accommodation meant that while both the executive and judicial departments cooperated in the administration of federal policy, federal judges tended to respect and to uphold the administrative decisions made by executive officials, their frequent collaborators. So not only did the federal magistracy enable executive administrators to act with discretionary authority, but it also encouraged justices on the federal bench to be both administrators and common law judges. For Hamilton, the constitutional theorist and practitioner behind the federal magistracy, accomplishing executive policy goals was an interdepartmental, collaborative affair.

The Remitting Act in Action

One of the first petitions that Congress handed over to Hamilton for review had nothing to do with Revolutionary War debt or missing loan certificates. Instead, it came from a foreign merchant who had been caught unaware by the federal government's newly enacted customs laws. Christopher Saddler, a shipper from Nova Scotia, petitioned Congress for relief "from the forfeiture of his vessel and cargo, which "ha[d] been seized in the port of Boston, for a violation of the impost law of the United States; of which law the petitioner was wholly ignorant."[13]

On January 19, 1790, the treasury secretary returned a "Report on the Petition of Christopher Saddler" to Congress, responding only ten days after Saddler submitted his initial plea for relief. Hamilton had not yet received all of the pertinent facts of the incident from Benjamin Lincoln, the customs collector at Boston, so he could decide whether or not Saddler's inadvertent violation should be forgiven.[14] But the details of the Saddler decision seemed less pressing to the secretary than the fact that the newly enacted impost laws were taking merchants involved in the seafaring and coastal trades—the federal government's primary revenue source—by surprise.[15] In response, Hamilton's report recommended to Congress a remedial course of action: the secretary proposed, undoubtedly with himself in mind, that circumstances like Saddler's required "vesting somewhere a discretionary power of granting relief." Furthermore, "the Secretary begs leave to submit to the consideration of the House, whether a temporary Arrangement might not be made with expedition and safety, which would avoid the inconvenience of a Legislative Decision on particular Applications."[16] After considering Hamilton's report in committee, the House took Hamilton up on his suggestion.

Congress subsequently passed "An Act to provide for mitigating or remitting the forfeitures and penalties accruing under the revenue laws, in certain cases therein mentioned"[17] (the Remitting Act) on May 26, 1790.[18] The act gave the secretary of the treasury the authority to decide whether or not shippers and merchants should receive reduced or outright remitted penalties when they inadvertently violated federal customs law. Congress also recruited federal district court judges to report to and to advise the treasury secretary before he made his decision. Rather than creating a federal court of claims to handle these equitable petitions, Congress conferred the power to adjudicate revenue penalties to an executive official acting on the advice of the federal district courts. Under the Remitting Act, Congress inverted and entwined the typical functions of executive and judiciary: the treasury secretary became a judge within a highly specified jurisdiction, while the district judge provided the relevant facts and circumstances to report to the secretary.

The Remitting Act helped to establish, right from the start of the early republic, the overlapping and collaborative functions of the federal magistracy. Hamilton suggested that Congress confer on the executive the discretionary authority to remit or mitigate revenue-related penalties, and Congress not only granted his request but also saw fit to recruit the federal district judges as investigators, reporters, and advisers to the treasury secretary. Therefore, the successful execution of federal customs law involved a cooperative effort among treasury officials (as collectors and compliance officers stationed at port), federal district courts (as sites for prosecuting statutory violations and as fact-finding venues), district judges (as reporters to the treasury secretary), and the secretary of the treasury (as head of both the administrative efforts and the remission adjudications involved).

Aside from mitigating the cumbersome and time-consuming process of initiating collections suits in court, the Treasury and Congress also had a vested interest in ensuring that they struck a balance between collecting a sizable revenue and maintaining a bustling merchant trade. The logic behind the act made sense in the particular context of the early republic. As the national government opened for business and thus sought to collect duties from trade, Congress frequently passed new laws, with different penalties attached, to generate this key source of government revenue. But foreign merchants, or even domestic merchants who had yet to hear about the new revenue or coasting trade laws, could easily arrive at port, inadvertently fail to comply with the various requirements, and then face penalties that they unintentionally incurred. Neither Hamilton nor Congress wanted to discourage maritime trade by imposing surprise penalties on otherwise well-meaning merchants, so the Remitting Act offered a way to get around the penalties—as long as the merchants had no intent to defraud the government from collecting duty revenue.

The treasury secretary had the best vantage for ensuring that consistent remissions comported with these policy considerations. Ideally, remissions of revenue penalties would be applied consistently across all ports, and therefore, it made sense to vest a single department head with the task of ensuring consistency rather than relying on the separate district courts. Furthermore, penalties computed by juries might be too sympathetic and lenient to the unsuspecting merchants (thus jeopardizing the national revenue), or they might be too harsh (which might discourage trade). If noncompliant merchants had only judicial remedies available to mitigate duty and tonnage penalties, then the extra cost and hassle incurred though litigation might also stifle trade.

Another advantage of the Remitting Act was to give merchants the option to petition for a remission or mitigation of penalties before or after going to court. Merchants thus benefited from the opportunity to forum shop, as they could opt for a trial in federal court or they could petition the American "Chancellor of the Exchequer"—as Hamilton referred to himself as the secretary of the treasury—for his equitable relief.[19] Overall, then, the design of the Remitting Act was to benefit all parties involved: coastal trade would be less hampered by lawsuits, remissions could be more consistently applied, federal revenue income would be protected, and from the merchants' point of view, the cost of doing business with the United States would be lessened.

In practice, the Remitting Act operated to engage both executive and judicial magistrates in the process of balancing law enforcement against the benefits of equitable relief. The procedural provisions of the 1790 Remitting Act specified that if a person could be liable, or had already been found liable by a court, for any fine, forfeiture, or penalty under the laws for collecting impost and tonnage duties, then he could petition a district judge for a remission or mitigation of the fine, penalty, or forfeiture. The judge would then give notice to the petitioner, as well as to the US district attorney, to show cause for or against the remission or mitigation of the penalty. After this summary hearing, the judge transmitted the facts of the summary hearing to the secretary of the treasury, "who shall thereupon have power to mitigate or remit such fine, penalty or forfeiture, or any part thereof, if in his opinion the same was incurred without wilful [sic] negligence or any intention of fraud, and to direct the prosecution, if any shall have been instituted for the recovery thereof, to cease and be discontinued, upon such terms or conditions as he may deem reasonable and just."[20] As provided by the act, Hamilton had the power to remit or mitigate the penalty if the petitioner could incur a fine but had not yet been convicted by a district court. The secretary also had the statutory authority to direct all prosecutions to cease once he decided to remit or mitigate the fine, forfeiture, or penalty.

As the foremost advocate for executive discretionary authority, Hamilton embraced his role as the final arbiter of remissions decisions. In contrast to his adjudication of Revolutionary War claims, he tended to be more forgiving toward the mishaps and extenuating circumstances that caused seafaring merchants to violate federal law. Though Hamilton had complete authority over the final decisions to remit or mitigate revenue-related penalties, he cultivated a cooperative partnership with the district judges who advised him on each petition. Because of this collaborative relationship, the district judges provided informal oversight as well as advice for Hamilton's Remitting Act adjudications.

The *Rising Sun* forfeiture demonstrates how the remitting process worked in practice. Jeremiah Olney, the customs collector at Providence, Rhode Island, initiated a suit against the British schooner *Rising Sun* because the schooner's tonnage was less than the thirty tons requisite, by law, to import foreign merchandise.[21] The owner of the vessel, Thomas Hazard Jr., did not realize that his schooner violated American tonnage requirements, and he petitioned the Rhode Island district court under the Remitting Act to avoid Olney's lawsuit. Henry Marchant, district judge of Rhode Island, sent Hamilton the necessary facts: even though Hazard's vessel had been to US ports in the past, Hazard did not realize that the American measurement for tonnage differed from the tonnage listed on the ship's British paperwork. Hazard had not captained the *Rising Sun*, or any other vessel, before this incident, and he did not anticipate the difficulty he encountered with new American tonnage requirements.[22]

Judge Marchant presented the "Truth of the Facts" to Hamilton, and in this written brief, the judge clearly thought that Hazard had been unaware of the penalties awaiting him at the port of Providence. Marchant also indicated that he found no fraudulent intent. A few weeks later, Hamilton sent Jeremiah Olney a note conveying his decision: Hamilton remitted the penalty, though Hazard still owed $50 to other parties (not the US government) "together with costs and charges."[23] Through the Remitting Act's summary process, Hamilton authorized Hazard's remission in advance of the lawsuit that Olney had set into motion, rendering it unnecessary.

The remitting process did not always go so smoothly, however. Hamilton relied heavily on accounts collected, written up, and sent to him, and when the evidence seemed suspicious or incomplete, Hamilton requested clarifications from the district judges. In regard to the petition of George

Tyler, Hamilton sent a letter to David Sewall, judge of the District Court for Maine, to clarify certain omissions and inconsistencies regarding the facts surrounding Tyler's possible fraudulent intentions.[24] John Lee, the Penobscot collector involved in prosecuting Tyler, suspected fraud in Tyler's request for a remission; yet Judge Sewall found the case, which went to trial, difficult to decide, indicating that he did not suspect ill intent. Sewall did not sufficiently explain why the decision was so difficult in his opinion, however, and on this point, Hamilton pressed for an explanation. In contrast to Sewall's uncertainty, Lee maintained that "the Petitioner had not the least claim to a mitigation," and should a remission or mitigation be authorized, it "would have a very bad effect upon the minds of people" of Penobscot, where they all suspected that Tyler had no claim to a mitigated fine. With this public relations opportunity, Hamilton wanted to be very sure that Tyler did not deserve a remission, for he had to decide between Tyler's pleas and the public's judgment. In order to do so, he needed Sewall's opinion on whether or not Tyler had intended to defraud the government.[25]

Hamilton's ultimate opinion on Tyler's case has not survived, but from his letter to Judge Sewall, Hamilton made it clear that his decision would not be arbitrary: Hamilton depended on the judge to provide the best account of the truth, and he upheld a quasi-legal standard for "admitting" evidence—it had to be consistent and verified by the judge or the collector—which lent a degree of legal accountability to Hamilton's decisions. With the additional supervision of fact-finding district court judges added to Hamilton's relatively rigorous decision-making process, Hamilton's adjudications self-consciously conveyed a sense of impartiality and fairness.[26]

As mentioned above, the Remitting Act served a policy-oriented purpose. Both Secretary Hamilton and Congress wanted to vigorously collect revenue without impeding trade, and the Remitting Act allowed for a more efficient administrative means of accomplishing this balance. The Remitting Act streamlined the remitting process by placing the treasury secretary in charge of the final decision, but Hamilton further unified the remitting process by issuing directives to the district judges as if the judges were treasury officials. In Hamilton's "Treasury Department Circular to the District Judges," a memo sent out to the judges to ensure uniform participation under the Remitting Act, Hamilton addressed the question of whether a petitioner awaiting resolution of his request could provide "some proper surety" in exchange for his confiscated vessel or goods. Hamilton informed them that he thought "it expedient to say that if such a proceeding should appear to the Judge, before whom the matter is brought, legal, I shall have no objection to its being adopted, due care being observed as well with regard to the competency of the sum, in which the security may be taken as of the sureties themselves."[27]

By advising the district judges to release the confiscated property on proper security, Hamilton directed his judicial administrators to ensure uniformity in the remitting process. Behind this request, Hamilton also had a commercial consideration in mind: since in all likelihood the confiscation penalty would be remitted, then the merchant's ability to trade should not be further hampered while awaiting Hamilton's decision. As long as a sufficient surety was in place, petitioner merchants had access to their confiscated goods and vessels, and commerce could continue. Always with his policy goals in mind, Hamilton used his limited quasi-judicial authority to meet executive ends.

Establishing the US Supreme Court as Umpire

The Remitting Act demonstrates how both Hamilton and Congress recruited the federal courts to participate in the execution of federal law and policy. As executive and judicial magistrates, Hamilton and the district judges had interwoven responsibilities for administering the provisions of the customs laws and the Remitting Act at the same time that both exercised various degrees of discretion over the prosecution and remission of statutory penalties. The Remitting Act relied extensively on interbranch cooperation, and because Hamilton took it upon himself to foster ongoing conversations between him and his judicial administrators, the Treasury and the federal courts began to develop a close, cooperative, and accommodating relationship.

As part of their magisterial relationship, Hamilton occasionally sought out the federal courts to give judicial sanction to his construction of revenue laws. Because the judiciary heard civil litigation arising between customs officials and merchants, Hamilton would get involved, advising his defendant employee about law and strategy. Federal judges would not allow the secretary's advice or direction to absolve the collector of his civil liability (as we have seen, the courts rejected this form of executive superintending power); still, Hamilton became involved not only to help his employee but also to influence, or at least be appraised of, the court's ruling on the customs statute involved. This was the case in the protracted litigation between merchant Welcome Arnold and Jeremiah Olney, the collector at Providence.

Hamilton liked to stage cases—that is, he often used the common eighteenth-century legal fiction of generating a legal dispute and enlisting opposing parties to the litigation so that the question or issue in dispute could be put before a court. Staged cases were useful mechanisms for recruiting the courts to rule on particularly pressing legal questions at that time rather than waiting for the issue to come before the bench organically. Hamilton helped to stage *Hylton v. US* in 1796, for example, in order to test the meaning of the Constitution's direct-tax clauses.[28] When in 1794 Hamilton could not convince the Virginia governor, Henry Lee Jr., to adopt the Treasury's construction of Hamilton's own enacted assumption plan, the secretary staged a mandamus case, *US v. Hopkins*, to test his construction in federal court.[29]

For Hamilton, the importance of *US v. Hopkins* was rooted in policy. A crucial part of Hamilton's public finance proposals pivoted on the assumption of the states' Revolutionary War debt into the national and foreign debt, which would then be funded by nationally levied taxes. As the coordinators of the assumption scheme and as the collectors of taxes, customs collectors and loan officers in the Treasury Department administered Hamilton's public finance policy through their routine activities enforcing revenue laws at port and exchanging old securities for newly issued certificates. The loan officers executed Hamilton's assumption policy by receiving the states' unpaid war debts and exchanging those state certificates of debt for federal certificates. This process was known as subscription (that is, subscribing the state debt to the national debt). This exchange could be accomplished at the Treasury itself or through the federal loan offices set up in each state. The federal loan officers, including Virginia's officer, John Hopkins, exchanged the state certificates only if the debt was eligible to be subscribed to the national debt under federal law (what I refer to as the Funding Act).[30]

Complicating this exchange of one debt for another was the fact that some state debt had already been redeemed. Redemption occurred when the state debt was either returned to the state treasury (for example, as payment of state taxes, for purchase of state lands, or through retirement) or by outright purchase by a state's "sinking fund."[31] The Funding Act made no provision for this redeemed debt, but Secretary Hamilton had; in communications with his loan officers stationed in the several states, Hamilton construed the Funding Act as not encompassing redeemed debt. He told the loan officers to refuse redeemed state certificates as ineligible for assumption into the national debt.[32]

Some states did not interpret the Funding Act in the same way, however, and Virginia, South Carolina, North Carolina, Georgia, and Rhode Island attempted to subscribe already redeemed certificates, and even to reissue the redeemed certificates for subscription into the assumption program.[33] Of course, Hamilton would have none of this; according to the treasury secretary, and corroborated by Attorney General Edmund Randolph, once a certificate had been redeemed by the state, the debt it represented ceased to exist, and it did not qualify to be assumed under Hamiltonian policy.[34] Both men based their interpretation of what qualified as subscribable certificates on a common law understanding of debt instruments.[35]

Hamilton thought that the Funding Act barred already redeemed state certificates, and his decision had been uniformly executed by his loan officers. But in 1792, the Virginia legislature indirectly challenged Hamilton's interpretation of the Funding Act by passing a statute that allowed holders of Virginia debt certificates issued after January 1, 1790 (the Funding Act's cutoff date, after which certificates could not be subscribed), to exchange those certificates for already redeemed certificates with earlier issue dates.[36] In essence, the Virginia legislature tried to pass off its post–Revolutionary War debt as debt eligible under Hamilton's assumption plan by reissuing redeemed state certificates.

This did not comport with Hamilton's interpretation of the Funding Act, and he wrote to Governor Lee, a close friend of President Washington's and a wartime colleague of Hamilton's, to clarify the law. Hamilton told Lee that "after full deliberation at The Treasury in conformity with the opinion of the Attorney General of the United States," the question had been settled: "The Certificates or evidences of debt of any state which had been once paid off or redeemed could not legally be received on Loan; upon the plain principle that they thereby ceased to constitute any part of the existing debt of a State."[37] Hamilton continued, relying on the common law definition of debt to explicate his understanding of what was eligible for subscription: "And though a state may[,] by a subsequent act[,] restore to such certificates the quality of *debt* which they had lost—this would plainly amount to the creation of a new debt, not in existence when the Act of Congress passed, not contemplated by it, and manifestly intended to be excluded by its provisions."[38]

Plainly, Virginia's statute violated Hamilton's interpretation of the Funding Act, and so, under his superior's direction, loan officer Hopkins could not accept Virginia state certificates unless he could verify that the certificates had not been redeemed. Still, Hamilton knew that even though his construction of the Funding Act had been in force for some time and that it had been uniformly applied to all the states, his interpretation of the law would be more readily accepted if it had the authority of a judicial adjudication behind it. Moving toward a resolution, Hamilton suggested that he and the attorney general stage a case in order to get the question before the federal courts: "If the Executive of Virginia should eventually disagree with the construction of the law . . . I shall with pleasure concur in any proper arrangement for revising, and, if found wrong upon further examination for rectifying it."[39]

New attorney general William Bradford and former attorney general Randolph recruited Richmond securities broker Richard Smyth to serve as plaintiff, and together they worked out the details and presented the action for *US v. Hopkins* to the Supreme Court.[40] Bradford arranged for Edward Tilghman to be Smyth's counsel, and Tilghman formally initiated the proceedings by requesting a writ of mandamus from the Court to compel Hopkins to accept Smyth's redeemed certificates. Bradford argued that the writ of mandamus should not be issued for redeemed certificates, thus directly testing the Treasury's construction of the Funding Act.[41]

After the case went before the US Supreme Court, Hamilton earned a somewhat ambiguous victory. The Court ultimately denied the writ, thus confirming that Hopkins's refusal to accept the Virginia certificates and Hamilton's construction of the Funding Act would stand. However, the Court seemed to have questioned the plaintiff's right to request the writ in the first place, and so it rejected Tilghman's arguments rather than outright endorsing the Treasury's construction.[42] Nevertheless, Hamilton's interpretation of the Funding Act endured without any new challenges to the Treasury's process of subscribing state debt.[43]

By the time the Court denied the writ, however, the subscription period for state certificates had expired (March 1, 1793), and the states had received final settlements for their revolutionary expenses from the federal government (states received credit for expenses not assumed through the subscription program). Legal historian Maeva Marcus suggests that the end of the subscription period and the finality of settlement could have "worked to bring about acquiescence to the Treasury Department's policy regarding redeemed state certificates" because no new subscriptions would be rejected since the subscription window had closed. Also, any uncertainties over outstanding state revolutionary debt had been resolved by the finality and credit provided by a final settlement of state accounts.[44] Despite these mitigating factors, states or individuals who had already attempted to subscribe redeemed debt during the subscription period could still have brought lawsuits or questioned the Treasury's actions; that no new challenges arose suggests a general acceptance of the Court's decision, and the ultimate triumph of Hamilton's statutory construction.

Hamilton's assumption plan was a hard-won, crucial component in his larger scheme to restore the nation's credit, and he was not about to allow a few crafty states to create and then benefit from a legal loophole in the Funding Act. Subscription was the actual mechanism for assuming state debt—it was the very process that enabled the assumption plan to work. Hamilton thus did not simply assert that he had the constitutional prerogative to declare, with finality, what this momentous law meant. By staging the mandamus suit, the secretary demonstrated that Hamiltonian constitutionalism depended on the courts to provide the ultimate interpretation of statutory law. The executive had the prerogative to exercise discretion when interpreting a law, but when a proper legal controversy arose (or was generated, as it may be), only the courts had the binding authority to review the executive's construction and declare the meaning of the provision in question.

US v. Hopkins demonstrates the cooperative federal magistracy in action. Hamilton exercised and defended his executive discretion, but he then recruited the federal courts to review and definitively declare the law. By simply denying the writ, however, the pre-Marshall Supreme Court provided the judicial oversight sought by Hamilton but declined to offer any extra commentary on the limits or extent of executive discretion. The court simply cooperated in addressing the mandamus question at hand and allowed both Virginia and the Treasury to quickly resolve their dispute. Staged cases like *Hopkins* as well as the direct-tax case, *Hylton v. US*, demonstrated the level of collaboration exercised among the various departments of the federal government as well as the states. In *Hopkins*, executive officers Hamilton, Randolph, and Bradford gathered documentation, selected the plaintiff and counsel, and initiated the legal action; Lee, Smyth, and Tilghman then willingly complied. The Supreme Court played along, hearing opposing arguments and providing a resolution to the contrived action before it.

Most interestingly, state legislatures cooperated with the ruling as well. *Hopkins* was a staged action, conjured up by federal executive officials and Virginia's governor, and yet every state government complied with the Supreme Court's ruling on the matter rather than bringing their own separate challenges to court. Importantly, Virginia's legislature accepted the fact that its remaining redeemed certificates would not be assumed or credited by the Treasury: in 1795, the state legislature resolved that the governor should destroy those redeemed certificates languishing in the state's sinking fund.[45] By accepting the Court's ruling in *US v. Hopkins*, the state legislatures tacitly acknowledged both the constitutional authority of the federal courts to interpret the Funding Act and to adjudge controversies arising over such federal statutes, as well as the implicit cooperation between executive, judicial, federal, and state authorities to interpret, execute, and adjudge the law.

Hamilton's success in *Hopkins* was repeated in the federal courts when the US Supreme Court construed select provisions in the 1790 Collection Act according to the secretary's interpretation. The protracted litigation, culminating in *Olney v. Arnold*, called into question the actions of customs collector Jeremiah Olney, as well as the Treasury's construction of its duty to extend credit to merchants arriving at port under sections 41 and 45 of the Collection Act. These provisions allowed importing merchants to obtain credit on their customs duties by submitting a bond to the collector promising payment on or before a future date. If a merchant did not pay on time, the act required the collector at port to bring suit against the merchant and to extend no further credit until the delinquent bond had been paid.[46]

In 1792, prominent Rhode Island merchant Welcome Arnold attempted to circumvent Olney's suspension of his credit after Arnold had become delinquent on a bond due to the collector. In order to do this, Arnold transferred his cargoes to other merchants, who then submitted duties for the goods under their names. While Arnold maintained that this transfer was a bona fide sale, the collectors and Hamilton thought it a collusive maneuver to avoid the terms of the act. Hamilton agreed with Olney that "the appearances stated by you afforded the presumption of a design to evade the law sufficiently strong to *justify* an Officer in refusing the credit." Moreover, Hamilton assured Olney that if Arnold sued him for damages for denying him credit, the Treasury would indemnify the collector.[47]

In November 1792, after Olney had already initiated a district court suit against Arnold for another delinquency, Arnold again had unpaid bonds outstanding. This time, however, Arnold transferred his latest cargo to Edward Dexter, who then offered a bond for the goods. Olney, in turn, declined to accept it, acting on Hamilton's advice. Arnold then demanded that Olney receive the bond, but the collector still refused and continued to detain the cargo. Only after the conclusion of the first lawsuit, *US v. Arnold*, restored Arnold's credit did Olney finally take Dexter's bond.[48] Although the bond had been accepted and his credit restored, Arnold and Dexter brought two separate trespass-on-the-case actions for damages against Olney in the Court of Common Pleas for Providence County.

Hamilton had anticipated Arnold's spiteful litigation and offered not only to pay Olney's legal costs but also gave the collector crucial advice for conducting his defense. The secretary wrote, "Should Mr. Arnold (as you say he threatens) commence a prosecution in the State Court, care must be taken so to conduct your defence as to admit of an appeal to the proper federal one."[49] Hamilton's proposed strategy, therefore, was to use section 25 of the 1789 Judiciary Act to bring the suit before the US Supreme Court on writ of error review from the Rhode Island courts.[50] In order to do this, however, Olney's state court defense had to raise a claim arising under the US Constitution, federal treaty, or federal law. Olney pleaded the 1790 Collection Act, citing the section 41 stipulation that collectors should deny credit to delinquent merchants. He also argued that the fraudulent collusion between Arnold and Dexter warranted the refusal of credit as well.[51]

After more than a year in state court, Rhode Island's highest judicial court, the Superior Court of Judicature, ruled that Olney's plea did not bar his actions toward Arnold and Dexter.[52] Again, Hamilton helped Olney to strategize, encouraging him to bring his case before the federal courts. The treasury secretary was acutely interested in the outcome, telling Olney, "I approve of your intention to take measures for an appeal to the proper Court of the United States. I could wish that you would request the District Attorney to forward to me the pleadings in the cause, and the reasons upon which the Court founded its decision."[53] Hamilton sensed the larger importance of Olney's suit, which tested the US Supreme Court's section 25 review of state court judgments on federal questions. Without section 25 review, state courts could impede or harass federal government operations simply by rejecting federal administrators' legitimate claims that they acted under federal law. Federal officials, who were already held liable to wronged third parties in court, would be hesitant or unwilling to enforce federal law if unaccommodating state courts willfully ignored the administrators' statutory duties and found them liable for damages.

Although Arnold's counsel introduced procedural questions about whether a bona fide federal question had been raised in the course of the state court proceedings, the US Supreme Court upheld Olney's plea and reversed the judgment of the Rhode Island Superior Court of Judicature.[54] By turning to the federal courts to view Olney's actions, Hamilton and the Treasury Department earned another federal court victory in their interpretation and execution of federal law. Congress even translated administrative policy into federal statute law by passing a 1799 Collection Act with provisions to prevent "frauds arising from collusive transfers."[55]

More was at stake, however, than simply Olney's reputation as an honest and meticulous, if somewhat uncompromising, collector. For Hamilton, the *Olney* suits became test cases to help establish the US Supreme Court's authority as arbiter of the federal system. If in *US v. Hopkins* the US Supreme Court exercised coordinate review over executive actions, then in *Olney v. Arnold* the US Supreme Court exercised federal review of state court decisions involving executive actions. Establishing the Supreme Court's federal question review powers was crucial for Hamilton for both practical and theoretical reasons. Hamilton and his collectors invested much time and energy into their faithful interpretations and executions of federal statutes; therefore, it was gratifying for the federal courts to uphold the executive's construction of the law. Also, by validating the Treasury's construction of the 1790 Collection Act, the federal courts prevented others from suing Treasury officials for similar acts. Hamilton sought out federal review of executive actions, and because of the executive's good-faith effort to faithfully construe the law, the Supreme Court approved treasury practice.

Hamiltonian constitutional theory also relied on the federal courts as the ultimate interpreters of federal law, particularly because states had concurrent authority to review questions arising from federal law. In *Federalist* No. 82, Hamilton anticipated and directly addressed the constitutional theory undergirding section 25 review, as well as the US Supreme Court's unique role as umpire of national and state governance. In that essay, Publius forthrightly asked: "What relation would subsist between the national and State courts in these instances of concurrent jurisdiction?" The answer: "The Constitution in direct terms [Article III] gives an appellate jurisdiction to the Supreme Court in all the enumerated cases of federal cognizance." This meant that while states acted as "natural auxiliaries to the execution of the laws of the Union," the US Supreme Court ensured that state decisions comported with federal law: "An appeal from [the states] will as naturally lie to that tribunal which is destined to unite and assimilate the principles of national justice and the rules of national decisions." Hamilton concluded, "To confine, therefore, the general expressions giving appellate jurisdiction to the Supreme Court to appeals from the subordinate federal courts, instead of allowing their extension to the State courts, would be to abridge the latitude of the terms, in subversion of the intent, contrary to every sound rule of interpretation."[56]

Since section 25 of the 1789 Judiciary Act inscribed Publius' constitutional vision into law, it was fitting that Alexander Hamilton helped to formulate the legal strategy that first made use of the provision's federal oversight machinery. When Hamilton turned to the federal courts for review in both *US v. Hopkins* and in the *Olney* lawsuits, his closely reasoned interpretation of federal statutes paid off; federal judges accommodated the

Treasury Department's efforts to faithfully read, interpret, and apply the first federal revenue code. And by intentionally recruiting the US Supreme Court in the review of executive action, Hamilton involved the courts in those administrative matters most important to the Treasury.

Administrative Accommodation and the Executive Prerogative Revisited

When surveying the existing scholarship on executive–judicial relations in the early republic, interbranch conflict persists as the dominant theme.[57] This narrative focuses on a line of cases, many of which involved judicial oversight of executive discretion, where the predominantly Federalist courts squared off against the Jefferson, Madison, and Jackson administrations. The case law includes *Marbury v. Madison*, *Stuart v. Laird*, *Gilchrist v. The Collector at Charleston*, and *Kendall v. US ex. rel. Stokes*, as well as Aaron Burr's 1807 trial for treason.[58] Andrew Jackson also contributed to this executive–judicial contest with his 1832 Bank Veto, a powerful retort to *McCulloch v. Maryland*. While these occasional conflicts were real and important—as we have seen, they generated a constitutional conversation about the limits and prerogatives of the national executive power—they are a select, splashy bunch of controversies that raised both political and constitutional questions. These occasional contests did not wholly define the relationship between the executive and judicial branches, however, and by focusing exclusively on these notorious clashes, historians have ignored and obscured the more frequent judicial accommodations made to uphold executive action.

During the first decades of the early republic, the executive and federal judiciary were not on a constant collision course; in fact, their relationship is better characterized by the many day-to-day interactions that brought executive magistrates in contact with judicial ones. During these frequent exchanges, the intense pressure of negotiating party-line constitutional politics lifted, and the federal courts and the executive's administrators worked closely and collaboratively to administer federal law. While the federal courts always heeded the limits of the executive's prerogatives, they simultaneously displayed deference to administrative action and a willingness to uphold the executive's interpretation and execution of the law.

Alexander Hamilton experienced administrative accommodation throughout his tenure in Washington's Cabinet. Simply enforcing federal customs laws sent Hamilton's collectors into federal district court weekly, if not daily, to participate in lawsuits arising from their statutory duties. The treasury secretary did not sit back, aloof from the courtroom action; instead, Hamilton involved himself in devising legal strategies, consulting lawyers for advice, and closely monitoring the outcomes of the port-side libel suits initiated by his employees. Yet Hamilton also engaged with the federal courts through congressional mandate and the remitting process, as well as through his own initiative in the *Hopkins* and *Olney* cases. The business of administering federal customs law inevitably required the executive and the courts to work closely together. Because the early national Congress enforced the most important federal policies in district court—including US neutrality policy, Sedition Act prosecutions, and the 1807 embargo—federal judges and executive officials shared the responsibility of administering the law.

District judges were the key judicial administrative personnel in the early republic. Under the various iterations of the Remitting Act, district judges reported to and investigated for the treasury secretary, but under the customs, coasting, embargo, and neutrality laws, they enforced federal policy within their courtrooms.[59] Take, for example, *US v. The Hawke*. The collector at Charleston initiated this 1794 suit in the South Carolina District Court, alleging that the claimant, Mr. Bolchos, had purchased the vessel in violation of the 1793 Enrollment Act.[60] Congress had passed this statute to enforce US neutrality during the early years of the maritime wars between France and Britain, as well as to enforce a short-lived trade embargo to any foreign port.[61] The libel alleged that the *Hawke* traveled on a foreign voyage without forfeiting its American coasting license, and that the captain of the schooner sold the vessel to Bolchos, a foreigner. Both of these actions constituted violations of the act.[62]

District Judge Thomas Bee determined that the *Hawke*'s convoluted voyage was nothing but a "fraudulent contrivance" meant to evade Congress's embargo.[63] The vessel violated the licensing provision of the Enrollment Act but not the foreign-sale clause; Bee ruled that because of the intentionally fraudulent nature of its voyage, the *Hawke*'s sale to Bolchos was illegal, and thus the ship retained its American character. Acting in concert with the collector and district attorney, Bee upheld national foreign policy.

Interestingly, the district attorney prosecuting the libel made the argument that since the United States had proof of the vessel's Enrollment Act violations, the court could not inquire into the motives or causes of the violation. The court should instead simply approve the libel. Also, the district attorney claimed that under the terms of the Remitting Act, only the secretary of the treasury—Alexander Hamilton at the time—had the power to investigate whether or not fraud was intended; if he thought not, then the secretary could mitigate or remit the penalty. Judge Bee resisted these claims, however, and construed the claimant's violations of the Enrollment Act through the lens of his fraudulent motives.

The *Hawke* libel demonstrates the multivalent role of the district judge in the early republic. On the one hand, the judge, collector, and district attorney represented the magisterial might of the federal government, each taking part in the investigation and prosecution of Congress and the Washington administration's foreign policy. On the other hand, although he took part in the administration of federal law, the judicial magistrate was still, first and foremost, a judge. To this end, Judge Bee upheld the integrity of the district court's jurisdiction by maintaining its judicial prerogatives. Bee resisted the district attorney's argument that because the Remitting Act was also in force, the district court should suppress its judicial operations and confine itself to fact-finding, or to simply rubber-stamping statutory violations.

US v. The Hawke also demonstrates how, in addition to collaborating on administrative matters, the federal magistracy operated as two separate jurisdictions, both adjudicating federal customs law. Coasting trade and revenue law violations could be brought to either the district court or to the treasury secretary for adjudication, and while the secretary could not overturn a conviction in court, he could direct court proceedings to stop once he determined to mitigate or remit a statutory penalty. Judge Bee would not follow the district attorney's suggestion to approve the seizure and forfeiture of the *Hawke* because, even though the claimant could have petitioned the secretary for a mitigated penalty, he had not done it. Because the *Hawke* found itself in a judicial venue, rather than in the executive's jurisdiction, the district admiralty court would properly and judicially adjudicate the libel.

Though the Remitting Act created a nonjudicial forum to which merchants could petition, federal judges still upheld and deferred to the treasury secretary's limited alternative jurisdiction. In the case of the *Cotton Planter*, for example, a libel originating in the District Court for New York but appealed to the New York Circuit Court, the claimant ship owner violated the December 1807 embargo by sailing to the West Indies in January 1808.[64] The claimant originally petitioned the treasury secretary, Albert Gallatin, for a remitted penalty, claiming ignorance of the law. Gallatin refused to remit the penalty, and subsequently the collector and district attorney for New York successfully libeled the *Cotton Planter* in federal district court.

On appeal, Circuit Judge Henry Brockholst Livingston reversed the forfeiture, determining that, while ignorance of the law was not a valid legal excuse, the embargo did not specify a commencement date; moreover, the ship owner's home port had not received timely news of the embargo. Therefore, the court granted relief to the ship owner for these mitigating circumstances. In his opinion for the court, however, Livingston noted "that there is power in the secretary of the treasury to relieve in case of an unintentional violation of laws relative to trade, and therefore the less occasion for the interposition of the judiciary; that the secretary has refused relief here, because he considered the alleged ignorance of the claimant a mere pretence." Did the secretary's decision preclude the federal court's jurisdiction? No, said Livingston, because the original libel and its appeal "is a question purely of judicial cognizance, and may be decided without interfering with any other department of government."[65] In other words, two separate adjudicatory processes existed under Congress's remitting acts; since the treasury secretary did not halt the district court's proceedings, the libel could continue.

Livingston continued by acknowledging the integrity of the executive's jurisdiction to remit revenue penalties: "Nor is there any doubt that the secretary of the treasury would have remitted the forfeitures, if any had accrued, if he had been satisfied of the bona fides of the transaction." But because Gallatin's decision occurred before the libel began in federal district court, did the subsequent judicial adjudication interfere with the executive's remitting powers? Livingston thought not: "As the decision of that gentleman has been incorporated with the proceedings in this cause . . . it may be thought by some that this court thinks itself competent to reverse what he has done. The court disclaims any such right."[66]

The federal courts continued to uphold the executive's jurisdiction under the remitting acts, even considering it to be a compulsory procedure for investigating suspect cargos. In 1825, Supreme Court associate justice Smith Thompson considered the remitting provision of an 1818 act (which incorporated the 1797 Remitting Act) in *US v. One Case of Hair Pencils*, and he interpreted the treasury secretary's remitting powers to be a procedural necessity for determining whether or not fraud was involved.[67] Thompson determined that "under the authority given to the secretary of [the] treasury, he may remit in whole or in part, so as to meet the equity of the various cases that may occur. He is entrusted with equitable powers to grant relief. . . . It is not an unlimited discretion, however."[68] To Thompson, the secretary's power was not unlimited, but it was required; he construed the 1797 Remitting Act and the 1818 Duty and Tonnage Act as requiring that the treasury secretary be involved if an invoice did not match its received cargo. Thompson reversed the lower court's decision, ruling that under the 1818 act, the question of fraud could not be submitted to a jury (that is, to any judicial proceedings), but only to the treasury secretary.

Chief Justice John Marshall, the chief combatant for the federal courts in the traditional narrative of executive–judicial relations, also deferred to the treasury secretary's remitting powers. When Marshall considered the provisions of the 1813 Remitting Act while riding circuit in Virginia, he explained how the district court and treasury jurisdictions continued to work with each other in the same ways Hamilton interacted with district judges like Marchant and Sewall. Marshall described the collaborative remitting process as it stood under an 1813 customs law:

> The legislature seems to have intended, that the act of the treasury department, should be final and conclusive, and that all the facts should be placed before him, before he performs that act. Those articles, the forfeiture of which is remitted, are of course restored to the proprietor. The prosecutions, if instituted, are to cease. It would seem to be a part, and an essential part, of the duty of the secretary, to define the articles on which this remission operates; or if it be only on a certain interest on those articles, to define that interest.

He noted the particularly Hamiltonian part of the process: "If the statement of facts made by the court, did not enable the secretary to ascertain this interest, it would seem to be his duty, to require a more full statement; and the case should go back to him for a final decision."[69] If district judges failed to provide a satisfactory account of the facts, then the treasury secretary would demand a better report from them—a precedent set by Hamilton decades before. Also, Marshall clarified another collaborative part of the remitting process: if the secretary chose to remit only a portion of the petitioners' seized property, then the secretary handed off the rest of the forfeiture to be adjudicated in federal court. Therefore, both departments could administer and adjudicate violations of the law for the same petitioner.

Marshall also noted, echoing his ministerial distinction in *Marbury v. Madison*, that the treasury secretary's properly employed statutory remitting powers fell within the executive's untouchable prerogative sphere: "Could the court in which the prosecutions were depending, have proceeded to an investigation of the extent of the interest of the petitioners, after receiving this instrument of dismission from the treasury department? I believe

CHAPTER TWO

it could not." Marshall concluded his opinion by declaring, "The secretary acts . . . and his acts cannot be revised by the court."[70]

The treasury secretary's statutory remitting powers also resembled the president's constitutional pardoning prerogative, a similarity not lost on early national judges and lawyers. In two separate but related cases, the federal courts considered the limits of the executive's remitting and pardoning powers on individuals' vested rights. In the 1821 federal circuit court case of *US v. Lancaster*, Associate Justice Bushrod Washington considered whether the presidential pardon used to remit the federal government's interest in a forfeited bond also negated the moiety of the penalty claimed by the customs collectors. This question recalled Alexander Hamilton's consideration of Samuel Dodge's pardon, and with a common law–based reasoning that echoed Hamilton's decision, the court determined that the presidential remission could not impair the right of customs officer to his lawful moiety.[71]

Only four years later, however, the US Supreme Court construed the collectors' moiety rights under a federal nonintercourse act to be conditional on the treasury secretary's remission decision. Determining that "the law was made for the benefit of those who had innocently incurred the penalty, and not for the benefit of the custom-house officers," the Court inferred from the statutory language that, at least under this particular statute, Congress specifically meant for the collectors' monetary reward to vest only if a forfeiture actually occurred. Therefore, the Court did not uphold the collector's asserted right to the seized property.[72]

These cases demonstrate how the federal courts cooperated with the executive department, balancing the treasury secretary's remission adjudications with their judicial libels. The federal courts also helped to enforce the executive's administration of federal law and policy by deferring to the treasury secretary's reasonable constructions of federal statutes. Encouraging this judicial deference is exactly what Hamilton had in mind when he explained and defended his construction of federal statutes by way of common law principles and accepted rules of statutory construction. If the treasury secretary construed federal statutes within the reasonable bounds of the text, then the courts tended to defer to the executive's interpretation and execution of federal policy.

In *US v. The William*, for example, the Massachusetts District Court upheld the constitutionality of 1807 and 1808 embargo statutes, and in doing so, it supported President Jefferson's bold foreign and commercial policy.[73] Under the embargo, the Jefferson administration's executive authority exploded—so much so that administrative law scholar Jerry L. Mashaw remarked, "Limited government was clearly out the window, as was congressional control of administrative authority."[74] Although the *William* decision signaled to the administration that the federal courts would support its embargo policy, the Massachusetts District Court also claimed for the federal courts the status of final arbiters of constitutional questions. It did so by citing a long line of Supreme Court case law, as well as extensive quotations from Hamilton's *Federalist* essays on judicial power, including Nos. 78, 80, 81, and 83.[75]

The federal courts continued to support the Jeffersonian embargo by deferring to the administration's construction and interpretation of customs laws during this period. In 1809, the US Supreme Court considered the Treasury's interpretation of federal duties on salt, and John Marshall affirmed, "If the question [regarding the proper duties on salt] had been doubtful, the court would have respected the uniform construction which it is understood has been given by the treasury department of the United States upon similar questions."[76]

In two other embargo-related cases—both reaching the US Supreme Court on writs of error from superior state courts—the Court gave an expansive reading to the customs officials' statutorily conferred discretion. In *Crowell et al. v. M'Fadon*, inspector of revenue Joseph Crowell detained the *Union*, a vessel waylaid in Barnstable, Massachusetts. Crowell suspected that the *Union* had attempted to evade or violate the embargo laws, so he detained it under his authority provided by an April 1808 act.[77] Although Crowell had an "honest" suspicion, he turned out to be incorrect; the *Union* did not act unlawfully. M'Fadon then sued Crowell, claiming that collectors had to have a "reasonable" suspicion—that is, a more rigorous standard than just a hunch—to detain vessels under the embargo laws. The Court disagreed, however, and upheld Crowell's discretionary judgment. Writing for the Court, Justice Gabriel Duvall noted, "The law places a confidence in the opinion of the officer, and he is bound to act according to his opinion; and when he honestly exercises it, as he must do in the execution of his duty, he cannot be punished for it."[78]

In a similar case, *Otis v. Watkins*, Chief Justice Marshall reaffirmed the *Crowell* principle: "In construing this [embargo] law it has already been decided in this Court that the collector is not liable for the detention of a vessel . . . whenever, in his opinion, the intention is to violate or evade any of the provisions of the acts laying an embargo." Furthermore, he added, "The correctness of this opinion [is that] he is not responsible. If, in truth, he has formed it, his duty obliges him to act upon it; and when the law affords him no other guide than his own judgment, and declares that judgment to be conclusive in the case it must constitute his protection, although it be erroneous."[79] Although the Court refused to hold the collector accountable for acting on what turned out to be an incorrect opinion, it did find Otis liable for acting outside his statutory authority; Otis had removed the vessel from port, when Congress had only authorized him to detain the vessel at port.[80]

What this demonstrates is that, through *Marbury*'s ministerial versus political distinction combined with the administration's reasonable attempts to interpret and execute federal law, federal judges gave the executive department leeway and deference when they reviewed administrative actions. When confronting the routine, day-to-day legal questions arising from commerce at port, the federal courts and the Treasury's administrators did not have a contentious relationship; rather, they worked collaboratively, both taking part in the process of administering and adjudicating federal law.[81] Their accommodating relationship benefited both parties as well. Treasury policy benefited from the secretary's discretion to remit or mitigate revenue penalties, judges aided port officials by providing a consistent, strict, but reasonable standard for the interpretation of revenue laws, and the federal courts continued to enhance their own authority and profile by constantly reviewing executive actions and state court decisions. Importantly, the US Supreme Court began exercising its powerful writ of error review of state decisions through the private liability lawsuits generated by administrative actions. In this way, the growth of federal court jurisdiction developed from its administrative interactions with and oversight of execution action.

Magisterial Constitutionalism

Administrative accommodation in the federal magistracy reveals the close, symbiotic relationship between executive and judicial power in the early republic, and the connection between administrative action (which scholars tend to ignore) and constitutional jurisprudence (which scholars tend to follow closely). The executive and the courts collaborated to administer the law on a day-to-day basis, and this relationship proved to be mutually beneficial. For the federal courts especially, their involvement in administrative matters meant enhancing their prestige and authority, as well as exerting their authority to review executive and state actions. Nationally oriented judges like John Marshall and Joseph Story, therefore, built celebrated constitutional jurisprudence like *Marbury v. Madison*, *Martin v. Hunter's Lessee*, and *Cohens v. Virginia* on the foundations laid by federal judges as administrators, and the magisterial relationship developed between the executive and judicial departments.

As the first treasury secretary, Alexander Hamilton's influence on the federal magistracy's tradition of administrative accommodation is significant. Hamilton proposed the executive's remitting power to Congress, then set a practical precedent for the executive/district judge relationship to result from the remitting process and from normal customs collection activities. He also used litigation as a means to find out whether the federal courts would accommodate his department's interpretation and execution of federal law. In *US v. Hopkins*, Hamilton's staged mandamus action set a precedent for federal court review of executive action; in the *Olney* case, Hamilton instigated the federal court's first writ of error review of a superior state court's decision. Both of these actions constituted opening moves in establishing the federal courts as umpires of the federal system (state–national government relations) as well as umpires of the coordinate system (among the branches of the national government). Administrative action and the development of federal court jurisdiction were thus inextricably entwined in the early republic.

Hamilton, as we have seen, was a precedent-setting practitioner of energetic executive discretion, of collaboration between the nation's executive and judicial magistrates, and of judicial oversight of executive action. He was also the foundational constitutional theorist for the federal magistracy. As such, Hamilton influenced both Federalist and Jeffersonian Republican legal thought, particularly about the nature of executive power under the US Constitution. It should be no surprise, then, that the Hamiltonian constitutionalism cultivated in the federal magistracy provided key foundations for Jacksonian constitutionalism as well.

Jacksonian federalism (dual federalism) did not comport exactly with Hamiltonian constitutionalism. Hamilton and Andrew Jackson would not have agreed on the proper construction of Congress's Article I, section 8, powers, for example, but Jacksonian constitutionalism developed from Hamilton's vision of the federal magistracy. Jackson embodied an energetic Hamiltonian executive who defended his prerogatives but abided by the ministerial duty/discretionary act distinction that somewhat limited his authority to act. This distinction was John Marshall's legal rule, but the chief justice articulated it in order to reconcile two Hamiltonian ideas: robust executive discretion and the judiciary's duty to protect individual rights.

Like Hamilton, President Jackson and the Taney Court also believed that the US Supreme Court provided the final word on constitutionality within the federal system.[82] Congress conferred the writ of error review to the US Supreme Court in section 25 of the 1789 Judiciary Act, but the intellectual origins and practical development of this power can be traced to Hamilton. He not only strategized about how to use this review machinery in Olney's litigation but he also anticipated and explained the need for it in *Federalist* No. 82. So when Joseph Story declared the Supreme Court's review of state court decisions to be constitutional in *Martin v. Hunter's Lessee*, he adopted Hamilton's reasoning and transformed it into formal constitutional law. In *Martin*, Story recognized the need for some ultimate tribunal to harmonize discordant state interpretations of federal laws, thus closely paraphrasing Hamilton's contemplation of the power in *Federalist* No. 82.[83] Andrew Jackson would subsequently agree with both Story and Hamilton that the US Supreme Court was the final arbiter of constitutionality across the federal system (if not among the coordinate branches of the federal government). Jackson asserted in his 1832 Nullification Proclamation that if a state could nullify federal law, thus assuming the authority to determine the constitutionality of federal law, then "the Union would have been dissolved in its infancy."[84]

Under Roger Taney's leadership, the Jacksonian-era Supreme Court continued to negotiate limits on executive prerogatives as well as accommodate them. Although President Jackson advocated for Jefferson's coequal department theory, the Taney Court subscribed to a limited and somewhat ambivalent vision of federal courts' coordinate review of executive action. In *Kendall v. US ex. rel. Stokes*, the Taney Court emphatically rejected the administration's arguments that only the president could review his administrators' actions. It upheld the federal courts' previous rules about executive power, including the ministerial versus political distinction and a strict construction of statutory discretion. Yet at the same time, Roger Taney and his brethren could also be accommodating toward executive action; for example, the Court allowed the navy secretary, James Paulding, to exercise a questionable prerogative to deny a widow's pension, and it also attempted to protect administrative officers who were sued at common law.[85]

The authority and activity enjoyed by the early republic's federal courts developed from its close interaction with the executive department, and in particular with its close working relationship with the Treasury. Beginning with Hamilton, executive and judicial magistrates shared an overlapping constitutional function, since both exercised discretion and both participated in the administration of law. But only the judiciary had the authority, according to Hamilton and Marshall, to oversee executive action. Therefore, executive action and executive legal arguments were crucial to the development of the federal courts' coordinate and federal jurisdictional oversight. During the early republic, the growth of federal judicial authority was rooted in, and inextricably bound with, its interactions with the executive. And so the federal magistracy and the Hamiltonian ideas animating it lived on, beyond Hamilton's tenure in office, to become foundational principles in early republican constitutional thought and jurisprudence. By overseeing the federal magistracy, the US Supreme Court established its authority as the constitutional umpire for the American republic.

THREE

⟡

Creating the "Commercial Republic": Neutrality and Law in the American Courts

The Washington administration's 1793 decision to remain neutral during the French Revolutionary wars, followed by the federal government's maintenance of this neutrality policy for almost two decades afterward, was the most important event to influence the development of American commercial law in the early republic. Neutrality amid a world at war—a policy endorsed and extensively defended by Alexander Hamilton—had tremendous implications for the American economy, resulting in a flourishing carrying trade into lucrative overseas markets, the growth of an American marine insurance market, and general prosperity at home.[1] But within state and federal courtrooms, neutrality had the effect of expanding the federal courts' jurisdiction over commercial transactions such that, by 1815, the US Supreme Court could preside over the vast majority of maritime commercial disputes. By contrast, in 1789 the federal courts' most direct claim over maritime commerce arose from its limited, but exclusive, admiralty jurisdiction over commercial litigation involving seamen's wages, bottomry bonds (maritime liens), and civil salvage suits. The federal admiralty courts did not even have exclusive jurisdiction over cases involving maritime matters.[2] Yet over the course of the early national period, federal admiralty jurisdiction expanded to encompass virtually all types of legal disputes arising from maritime commerce. By exploring this extension of federal power, we uncover the story

85

of how Alexander Hamilton used the law to create a unified commercial republic.

From the outset of America's experiment in self-government, Hamilton envisioned that the United States would thrive as a "commercial republic," a polity that united Americans through their commercial interests. Hamilton also hoped that under the US Constitution, a national government would emerge strong enough to protect and foster those commercial pursuits.[3] Hamilton considered it to be the particular and obvious goal for the new national government to facilitate this commercial republic by establishing some degree of unity and uniformity in commercial interests, policies, and law across the states. Writing as Publius, he warned his fellow New Yorkers, "A unity of commercial, as well as political, interests can only result from a unity of government."[4] For Hamilton, then, achieving commercial unity across the states meant aligning mercantile and state interests with the preservation of the national government (the same objective of his most noteworthy legislative achievements, his funding and assumption schemes) and enforcing a uniform, national commercial policy through the administration of government.

Hamilton's most famous efforts to achieve a unity of commercial interests, his planned assumption of states' war debts to be funded by a host of federal taxes, created the first political schisms at the national level that eventually produced two separate political factions. While serving as treasury secretary, Hamilton managed to increase the ideological gulf separating the Federalists and Republicans through his treasury-sponsored diplomacy with British envoy George Hammond, his marked preference for an American alliance with England rather than with France, and his sponsorship and support for the unpopular Jay Treaty in 1794. Ever the realist, Hamilton endorsed John Jay's diplomatic efforts as necessary to maintain American neutrality and to prevent a possibly disastrous war with Great Britain during the republic's infancy. The treaty was also an opportunity to win a few strategic and commercial concessions from England (the British agreed to finally evacuate western forts, for example, and they opened up Caribbean trade to select American carrying vessels).

Secretary Hamilton's political efforts at maintaining a cordial, preferential, and above all neutral relationship with Great Britain helped to fuel an opposition party to the Federalist policy agenda; it also exposed Federalist leaders to excoriation in Republican-friendly presses as well as to popular condemnation. When publically endorsing the Jay Treaty in New York City, for example, angry citizens pelted Alexander Hamilton with stones; other critics burned John Jay in effigy. Despite these political setbacks, the young republic managed to reach some of Hamilton's commercial and diplomatic goals during his lifetime—America stayed out of open Anglo-French hostilities—yet, over time, the state and federal courts became the guardians of Hamilton's vision for a commercial republic.

The political economy of the Hamiltonian commercial republic has been well studied; scores of economic, political, and even legal historians have noted the successes, political fallout, and significance of Hamilton's economic policies, including his various reports on the nation's credit, the benefits of a sound national bank, the wisdom of levying certain federal taxes, and the encouragement of manufacturing in America.[5] Hamiltonian fiscal policies relied on the enumerated powers of the national government to create economic stability, including unifying US creditor interests, levying uniform imposts, stabilizing the value of circulating currency, and in general stabilizing markets.[6] Hamilton considered the state and federal courts to be crucial actors in the creation of this unified, uniform commercial republic, yet neither his foresight in this regard nor his practical use of American courts to affect commercial unity has been acknowledged.

Moreover, historians overlook the ways in which the system of federal courts—not just John Marshall's Supreme Court—consistently increased its authority throughout the early national period, with assistance from the state courts. By focusing on a cannon of landmark decisions handed down by the Marshall Court, including *Marbury v. Madison, Martin v. Hunter's Lessee, McCulloch v. Maryland,* and *Gibbons v. Ogden,* scholars presume that the US Supreme Court developed the bulk of federal judicial power haltingly, one decision at a time.[7] The federal courts' authority accumulated either through occasional decisions otherwise intended to limit state power or through deliberate, aggressive power grabs inspired by the nationalistic jurisprudence of Marshall or Joseph Story.[8] Also, because Article I, section 8's commerce clause remained "dormant" in this period, historians assume that the federal courts took only an occasional interest in overseeing economic and commercial matters.[9] Beginning in 1793, however, neutrality gave the states reason to create, alongside the federal courts, an increasingly uniform set of commercial legal principles. Neutrality also prompted the federal courts to be consistently and actively involved in adjudicating matters related to the carrying trade, the most important sector of the early republic economy.[10]

Hamilton recognized the federal admiralty courts' potential to enact his vision of a commercial republic, and as we will see, his strategic engagement with the early federal courts helped them to develop an active oversight of national commercial matters. During each phase of Hamilton's legal career—including his first years practicing law in the 1780s, as chief administrator-lawyer of the Treasury Department, and finally his return to private practice in 1795—he considered the federal admiralty courts to be the key jurisdiction for adjudicating the nation's commercial questions. As treasury secretary, Hamilton provided attentive oversight and direction to his customs collectors when they initiated libels in federal court. By actively engaging the federal admiralty courts to adjudicate violations of US customs laws, Hamilton not only filled the admiralty docket but also protected the federal government's most lucrative revenue stream and upheld the nation's credit. As a private attorney, Hamilton took part in neutrality-related libels that contemplated and sometimes expanded the jurisdictional reach of the admiralty courts.

In addition, Hamilton also articulated the constitutional theory that anticipated and gave support to the federal courts' broad claims to commercial jurisdiction. In *Federalist* No. 82, Hamilton described the "rule" by which overlapping federal and state jurisdictions could coexist under the constitutional republic, sharing and dividing their jurisdictional authority in a concurrent system.[11] He premised his description of judicial concurrence on the notion that "states will retain all *pre-existing* authorities," except in three overlapping cases: "[1] where an exclusive authority is, in express terms, granted to the Union; [2] or where a particular authority is granted to the Union and the exercise of a like authority is prohibited to the States; [3] or where an authority is granted to the Union with which a similar authority in the States would be utterly incompatible."[12] Moreover, Hamilton envisioned that the state and national courts would work together "as parts of ONE WHOLE"—as a system collectively adjudicating matters of national concern (whether or not a question of federal law was actually involved).[13] Concurrence, therefore, described how the state and federal courts could work together toward creating his commercial republic.

Admiralty jurisdiction qualified under Hamilton's enumerated exceptions because Article III expressly delegated "all Cases of admiralty and maritime Jurisdiction" to the federal courts. As a result, whereas states presided over admiralty courts during the Revolutionary and Confederation eras, they could no longer do so under the Constitution. However, state courts could still consider cases that touched on matters of a national concern. The states adjudicated thousands of marine insurance disputes during the early republic period, and these cases quite literally influenced how the carrying trade was underwritten. Yet Hamilton's articulation of concurrence described the parameters of a reserved jurisdictional space to which only the federal courts had access; if state litigation overlapped with matters national in scope or kind, then the federal courts might also claim cognizance over those types of cases within this exclusive jurisdictional sphere.

Admiralty lent itself well to this sort of gradual accumulation of federal power: because admiralty was an exclusive jurisdiction delegated only to the federal courts, anything cognizable in admiralty was properly within the purview of the federal courts. In this way, if federal judges claimed that certain types of maritime commerce qualified as a subject for admiralty's consideration, then the federal courts could take cognizance of those matters that were historically adjudicated only by the state common law courts. The state courts would still maintain their "pre-existing authority" to hear those cases, but now the federal courts could hear them too. This was exactly the move Joseph Story made in his precedent-setting opinion in *De Lovio v. Boit*.[14]

American neutrality, a combination of both statutory law and general policy, created concurrence between the federal and state courts where there was little overlap before. During America's neutral years, the increasingly vibrant federal admiralty courts adjudicated neutrality violations, revenue libels, and prize cases, while state courts interpreted the effects of neutrality on the overseas carrying trade—the heart of American commerce. Thus, both the state and federal courts considered legal questions arising from national policy. While adjudicating these neutrality-related questions, state judges also demonstrated a willingness to look to other states and to the federal judiciary for guidance when considering neutrality's effects on maritime litigation. Over time, state action helped to unify American commercial law during an extended period of wartime uncertainty; this in turn forged the legal bonds of a commercial republic.

At the same time, the federal admiralty courts gradually expanded their jurisdictional reach and prestige, until in 1815 Story announced in *De Lovio* that all maritime contracts and torts previously considered cognizable only in the state courts were also within admiralty's jurisdiction. Because *De Lovio* made it official, the federal courts now had concurrent jurisdiction over the bulk of maritime commercial litigation and could, in theory at least, enforce uniformity over maritime commercial law. Story seized upon the opportunity to further unify maritime commerce that the federal and state courts had been working toward since the 1790s.

Neutrality was thus the crucial event in the development of commercial law in the early republic because it forced both the federal and state courts to contemplate neutrality's effects on the law. Neutrality was the consistent, common denominator between the federal and state courts: once the states routinely decided questions that not only arose from federal policy, but also affected interstate and international commerce, it became reasonable and even natural for the federal courts to lay claim to this jurisdictional territory. The federal courts' expanded admiralty jurisdiction over maritime commerce put them in a better position to oversee and unify America's commercial republic. And because Alexander Hamilton was actively involved in all types of neutrality- and revenue-related litigation, his legal practice offers unique insight into the federal courts' ascent over commercial law.

The Rise of the Federal Admiralty Jurisdiction

The American colonies-turned-states inhabited a transatlantic world connected through maritime commerce. Yet at the outset of the early republic period, litigation arising from these overseas transactions could only occasionally be resolved in an admiralty court; most often, state common law courts heard such disputes. More than a decade before Justice Story made his sweeping claim in *De Lovio*, the federal courts' admiralty jurisdiction first began to expand to revenue seizures brought under section 9 of the 1789 Judiciary Act; it then continued to grow, albeit gradually, under the prize- and neutrality-related litigation arising from congressional statute.

Alexander Hamilton's commercial litigation practice maps onto the gradual expansion of the federal admiralty jurisdiction, as he participated in section 9 revenue suits and neutrality prosecutions during and after his term in public office. As treasury secretary, Hamilton directed his customs collectors to initiate libels (the form of action used to initiate a suit in admiralty) in order to reinforce his larger commercial and economic policy goals, which included effectively collecting revenue (to service the assumed war debt) and fostering an equitable business environment for both foreign and domestic mariner merchants. Hamilton also prosecuted neutrality-related libels on behalf of the US government, and he represented libellants and claimants in prize cases as a private attorney.

Federal admiralty jurisdiction was limited in 1789 because state common law courts still enjoyed, to use Hamilton's words, their "pre-existing authorities" over maritime contracts and torts, and the prize side of the federal court was inactive during peacetime. However, under section 9, Congress gave the federal admiralty courts cognizance over federal revenue laws, a departure from the English High Court of Admiralty's traditional, limited jurisdiction.[15] Apart from this break from English convention, it seemed, at least before 1793, that the federal courts' cognizance over admiralty and maritime matters would remain quiet and unassuming. Indeed, Americans' experience suggested that the authority exercised by the state common law courts usually kept earlier federal admiralty courts in check.

The federal admiralty courts' initial, limited jurisdiction can be traced to the history of English admiralty and common law courts. During the fifteenth and sixteenth centuries, the High Court of Admiralty thrived, adjudicating the bulk of litigation arising from England's growing overseas commerce. But as so often was the case in English legal history, the landlocked common law courts at Westminster wrested judicial authority away from competing jurisdictions until, by the latter half of the seventeenth century, the English admiralty court's civil and commercial jurisdiction (its instance, or peacetime, jurisdiction) had been restricted to only a short list of cognizable actions. These included contracts made on the high seas (that is, not on land or in coastal waters) and executed on the high seas; torts committed on the high seas; suits for mariner's wages and civil salvage; in rem proceedings on bottomry bonds that merchants entered into abroad; and the enforcement of judgments of a foreign admiralty court.[16] The High Court of Admiralty's prize, or wartime, jurisdiction remained intact but was only active when England was at war.

Across the Atlantic, the American colonies received conflicting messages about what constituted the jurisdictional boundaries of admiralty courts. While the High Court of Admiralty endured its much-truncated jurisdiction throughout the eighteenth century, the vice admiralty courts created from Parliament's 1696 Navigation Act enjoyed an enlarged instance (civil/commercial) jurisdiction over the colonies in addition to authority over prize cases and cognizance over suits brought for violations of British acts of trade. By 1700, eleven vice admiralty courts functioned across Britain's American and West Indian colonies. Throughout the seventeenth century, however, some colonies found it expedient to adjudicate local admiralty matters in their own common law courts; therefore, the vice admiralty courts enjoyed an effective, concurrent jurisdiction with these colonial courts.[17] Appeals from the vice admiralty courts would lie before either the Lords Commissioners for Prize Appeals or, if arising from the instance side of the court, the Privy Council. Appeals arising from the Navigation Acts could be heard in either the High Court of Admiralty or the Privy Council.

After the Seven Years' War, the appellate structure of the vice admiralty system changed, as did the political implications surrounding admiralty jurisdiction.[18] As a response to the colonial sentiment that juryless customs suits in admiralty violated American civil liberties, the American states innovated on British practice by introducing the jury into state prize proceedings during the Revolutionary War.[19] Also during the war, Congress established, first, a committee to hear prize cases (the Commissioners of Appeals in Cases of Capture); they then created the first federal appellate court, the Court of Appeals in Cases of Capture, in 1780. The Court of Appeals, a limited jurisdiction that often encountered resistance from the states, would determine more than sixty appeals until it ceased operating in 1787.[20]

By the time the delegates to the Philadelphia Convention drafted the US Constitution, American admiralty law had become familiar with the notions of appellate review and concurrence, yet it remained fraught with jurisdictional tension among competing courts. States had administered their own bustling admiralty courts throughout the Confederation period, and many of the lawyers and judges practicing in state courts or in the Court of Appeals also participated in the Philadelphia Convention. Alexander Hamilton was one of those delegates.[21]

As a lawyer only newly admitted to the New York bar, Hamilton engaged with both the Confederation and New York's admiralty courts. For example, he served as proctor for the claimant John Riolz in a 1785 customs libel in the New York Court of Admiralty.[22] The libellant, a collector of customs for the port of New York named John Lamb, had seized two trunks of Riolz's merchandise, claiming that the trunks were landed without Lamb's permission and without the necessary inventory and bills of lading, making the landing contrary to state law.[23] Collector Lamb prayed for condemnation of the goods. Hamilton answered that Riolz was a Frenchman and was not well acquainted with New York's customs laws. In fact, Hamilton argued that Riolz had left his trunks unattended at the dock so that he could find a friend in town and inquire about the steps required to lawfully land the goods.[24] After much litigation, Riolz eventually lost his claim, but Hamilton later recorded that, in sympathy for this "bad business" experienced by the "poor fellow," Hamilton would not charge Riolz a fee for his services.[25]

During these early years of Hamilton's career, he also represented libellants and claimants in suits involving bottomry bonds and civil salvage in New York's admiralty court.[26] His practice extended to the Confederation's highest court as well, as Hamilton was involved in at least three Court of Appeals cases.[27] From these experiences, he learned not only the particulars of American admiralty process (a mixture of English admiralty procedure combined with elements of common law) but also the practice of enforcing customs laws within admiralty jurisdictions.

Once Article III divested the state courts of their formal admiralty jurisdiction, Hamilton spent a good deal of time as head of the Treasury Department directing and advising his customs collectors when they became involved in revenue-related libels. Section 9 of the 1789 Judiciary Act gave the federal district courts an "exclusive original cognizance of all civil causes of admiralty and maritime jurisdiction, including all seizures under laws of impost, navigation or trade of the United States," but specifically "where the seizures are *made, on waters which are navigable from the sea.*"[28] The US Supreme Court would, in time, broadly construe the waters "navigable from the sea" clause in order to ensure that the federal admiralty jurisdiction became robust. Further, the district courts had to share their jurisdiction over certain maritime matters with the state common law courts. With the Judiciary Act's "saving to suitors" clause, the first federal Congress created a concurrent jurisdiction for litigants with in personam claims so that the suitors chose whether to litigate by filing a libel in federal admiralty court or by initiating an ordinary common law action state court.[29] Still, the exclusive federal jurisdiction over revenue libels enabled Hamilton to look to the federal courts as an instrument for his statecraft: the admiralty courts could provide equity, unity, and uniformity over the revenue laws that put his commercial policies into effect.[30]

Secretary Hamilton's day-to-day responsibilities included overseeing the libels initiated across the various federal district courts by his customs collectors. Usually Hamilton acted as a gatekeeper of sorts, giving advice and direction to his staff right before or soon after a collector reported a revenue law violation to the local district attorney. Although the customs collectors had strict instructions to follow the letter of the revenue statues, discretion and negotiation crept into all steps of customs collection, usually to ensure goodwill with the merchants paying the duties.[31] Therefore, Hamilton kept a watchful eye on his collectors to be sure that they initiated prosecutions that were fair and consistent with the course of the law.

Hamilton had a self-serving interest in ensuring that customs collection be (and be perceived as) fair, lawful, and equitable: the federal government depended on customs revenue to finance its operations and to service its debt, and Americans were notoriously suspicious of taxes and tax enforcement. Also, because the specter of Stamp Act prosecutions in the colonial vice admiralty courts remained fresh in the revolutionary generation's minds, the district court judges were most likely aware that customs prosecutions should be adjudicated with care.[32]

Hamilton often confirmed for his collectors that certain libels were worth pursuing, and he also wrote to his staff to instruct them as to which vessels to seize and bring into court.[33] For instance, the secretary directed Jeremiah Olney, the collector at Providence, Rhode Island, to seize the *Sloop Polly of Sandwich* for fraudulently landing rum, molasses, and sugar at port.[34] When collector William Ellery responded on Olney's behalf, he conveyed a tale of deception and intrigue whereby the master of the sloop evaded detection by blacking over the name *Sloop Polly* on the sloop's stern. The master also reported fake specifications when obtaining his license at port to further hide the vessel's true identity. When Ellery heard of a suspicious sloop tucked away in a small harbor, he guessed the mode of the master's deception and then confirmed his hunch by washing off the blackened *Sloop Polly* and measuring the vessel's dimensions. Ellery ended his account by assuring Hamilton that he would convey all information to Edward Pope, the New Bedford collector, who would then "cause her to be libelled and prosecuted as the law directs."[35]

Just as the customs collectors looked to Hamilton to interpret the nuances of federal revenue laws, they also posed legal questions to the secretary relating to seizures and revenue suits.[36] William Ellery, ever the diligent official, wrote to Hamilton with a list of concerns. First, Ellery asked, "To have your opinion on this question whether an officer making seizure of a vessel without his District may not remove her from the Place where she is seized, to an adjoining District provided it can be done with convenience and safety[?]"[37] Next, he wished "to be directed to what Collector to apply to commence a prosecution," and to know how to interpret the moiety provision of the Collection Act to be sure that all parties involved were paid lawfully.[38]

Finally, Ellery posed a more complex legal question regarding a buyer's right to access cargo that Ellery held until the seller made payment on a bond due to the Treasury Department. Ellery remarked, "I find a case will probably occur in this Custom house altogether new, and in which unless I am early favoured with your direction I may incurr censure embarrassment and expense," indicating how crucial Hamilton's legal expertise was to the everyday operations of his department.[39] Ellery was sensitive to any "embarrassment" caused by his actions as an executive official, and as evidenced by the volume and length of the customs circulars issued by the treasury secretary, Hamilton shared the same concern. Customs collection in the young republic was new and tremendously important, and part of Hamilton's responsibility was to ensure that the national revenue was collected seamlessly and lawfully. Although Hamilton's answers to these questions do not survive, Ellery acknowledged the receipt of Hamilton's responses with a gentle reminder to his boss that he also had queries pending on "the credit on salt &c," "drawbacks on Spirits distilled in the United States," "the Act [concerning] certain fisheries &c," and even more questions relating to the case of the *Sloop Polly*.[40]

The various sorts of legal guidance that Hamilton provided to his employees extended beyond the interpretation of revenue laws and pretrial libel preparations to the enforcement of the Washington administration's neutrality policy. To address the enforcement of American neutrality, Hamilton released, in characteristic fashion, a detailed circular letter to the customs collectors in August 1793 intended "to assist the judgment of the officers" while they kept a watchful eye out for "repeated contraventions of our neutrality . . . taken place in the ports of the United States." The circular relayed a "schedule of rules, concerning sundry particulars, which have been adopted by the President, as deductions from the laws of neutrality, established and received among nations." The secretary warned, "Whatever shall be contrary to these rules will, of course, be to be notified" to the governor and district attorney overseeing the state and district where any such contravention occurred. Hamilton was preparing his staff to intercept those vessels that would be subject to prize proceedings in federal admiralty courts.[41]

As the French Revolutionary wars persisted, Hamilton's collectors—like Meletiah Jordan, collector at Frenchman's Bay in the district of Maine—continued to update the secretary and to seek confirmation from him regarding the seizures and libels initiated in the wake of neutrality and the thirty-day embargo passed in March 1794.[42] Again, Hamilton exercised his option to confirm, correct, or countermand the revenue and neutrality-related lawsuits that the Treasury Department initiated in federal admiralty court. This discretion, combined with Hamilton's license to remit or mitigate revenue penalties, and his consequent close correspondence with federal district judges, meant that not only did Hamilton have a great deal of influence over the types of cases reaching the admiralty court but he also worked with the judiciary to meet shared national goals. As an executive agent, Hamilton influenced the way commercial laws were enforced, interpreted, and adjudicated in the young republic. He set a precedent for how an energetic, highly involved treasury secretary could successfully monitor and intervene in the legal matters facing customs collectors, a tradition followed by successors Oliver Wolcott Jr. and Albert Gallatin. [43]

In peacetime, the admiralty "side" of the federal courts was relatively quiet, but for the libels initiated by Hamilton's staff (which went unreported in early court records). With the beginning of the French Revolutionary wars and the declaration of American neutrality, however, the volume of federal admiralty business boomed, increasing from just three reported admiralty cases in 1793 to ten cases only a year later. Between 1793 and 1815, court reporters included 193 admiralty cases in their volumes of federal cases, from both the instance and prize sides of the courts, in addition to adjudicating other maritime suits involving the decisions of foreign admiralty courts.[44]

By closely mediating the relationship between the district courts and the Treasury's collectors, in addition to vetting customs libels, Hamilton helped to ensure that the federal admiralty courts successfully opened for business. But when America found itself a lonely neutral in an Atlantic world at war, neutrality-related lawsuits gave the federal judges their first opportunities to expand the boundaries of the admiralty jurisdiction.

In 1793, it was not clear that the federal courts would adjudicate neutrality-related cases, but the Supreme Court soon declared, in *Glass v. The Sloop Betsey* (1794), that the federal courts could hear privateering cases that involved neutral powers.[45] When district and circuit court judges declined to hear Swedish and American claims against a French privateer, the Supreme Court affirmed the federal courts' jurisdiction. In their decision, the Court determined, without citing any precedent, that the district courts had plenary admiralty jurisdiction—that is, they possessed all the instance and prize powers of admiralty courts. This sweeping declaration of the admiralty courts' powers quickly came to mean that the federal admiralty courts would hear many (though not all) privateer cases brought by British litigants. Privateering cases took up about half of the Supreme Court's docket from 1794 until the US entered into its Quasi-War with France.[46]

When Hamilton participated in federal neutrality prosecutions, he partnered with his close friend and colleague Richard Harison, the US district attorney for New York. Together, Hamilton and Harison libeled violators of the Registry Act of 1792 and the Enrollment and Licensing Act of 1793.[47] The duo handled prosecutions in the following way: Hamilton or both Hamilton and Harison would compose court documents or agreements made with the opposing counsel, and Harison would file any necessary paperwork with the court. Hamilton often appeared for the government in court, and both he and Harison shared the responsibility of arguing before the judge and jury.[48]

Often the federal courts made decisions about their jurisdictional limits, like whether or not the dispute under question qualified as an admiralty or common law action. In one such case, *US v. The Ship Young Ralph*, Hamilton appeared for the claimant, Robert Cummings, and made a winning argument against the cause being heard in admiralty.[49] The case arose under the Slave Trade Act of 1794, which forbade the fitting out or equipping of vessels in the United States for the purposes of trading or trafficking slaves in any foreign country. Unlike other navigation acts that expressly provided that seizures should be within the federal admiralty jurisdiction, the Slave Trade Act was silent on the matter.[50]

Hamilton represented the party requesting a dismissal of the libel, and the district court granted his petition in March 1802. After the courts' decision, however, Hamilton and Harison, the opposing counsel in this case, each issued written opinions on the ruling. As measured by his opinion, Hamilton thought the most decisive component of his argument had to do with the fact that the statute involved was penal and thus required "full consummation"—that is, a complete fitting out as a slave-trading vessel, in order for Cummings to be found guilty. His client's vessel did not meet the criteria of "complete preparation for the [slave-trading] voyage."

Yet accompanying this well-developed exposition was a brief and uncharacteristically short-sighted argument—but a winning one—claiming that "the proceeding was irregular[,] the case being plainly of common law not of Admiralty Jurisdiction." Presumably, Hamilton considered the case "irregular" and "plainly of common law" because the seizure of the *Young Ralph* occurred not on the high seas but in waters considered to be part of the county, which, according to English admiralty practice, would have triggered a common law action.[51] Also, as noted above, the statute did not specify admiralty jurisdiction, and Hamilton exploited this technicality on behalf of his client.[52]

Harison argued that the *Young Ralph* should have been libeled in the federal admiralty courts because other federal statutes had provided for seizures taking place in local tidewaters (that is, not on the high seas) to be prosecuted in admiralty. Moreover, Harison thought that regardless of a specific provision in the Slave Trade Act, any seizure would automatically come under section 9 of the 1789 Judiciary Act.[53]

The fact that Hamilton argued against admiralty's cognizance over *US v. Young Ralph* underscores the real constraints of the muddled English admiralty tradition that American jurists inherited and still abided by in the early republic.[54] In *Young Ralph*, Harison may have made the better legal argument about the propriety of admiralty jurisdiction (especially in hindsight), but Hamilton, ever the clever advocate, made the winning argument for his client. The *Young Ralph*'s strict adherence to English admiralty principles also gives us a sense of how great a legal transformation had to take place before the Taney Court could plausibly claim, decades later in *The Propeller Genesee Chief v. Fitzhugh*, that Article III's grant of admiralty jurisdiction extended to all navigable waterways—including "county" waters, rivers, and the freshwater Great Lakes, in addition to the high seas—where vessels carried on interstate or foreign commerce.[55] The common law argument was put forth by Hamilton on behalf of his client because even in 1802, it was still somewhat persuasive to some federal judges, even after the US Supreme Court upheld the contrary in *US v. La Vengeance*.[56] The expansion of federal admiralty jurisdiction progressed gradually but was far from complete.

In *US v. La Vengeance*, the Supreme Court rejected the notion that its admiralty jurisdiction was confined only to the high seas, and it thus broadened the federal courts' territorial jurisdiction over US coastal waters. Although Hamilton participated in *La Vengeance*, Harison prosecuted the case, and Hamilton represented Don Diego Pintado, the libellant in *La Vengeance*'s companion suit, *Don Diego Pintado v. The Ship San Joseph*.[57] Hamilton teamed up with Richard Harison, and they worked both cases simultaneously.

Pintado v. San Joseph arose after Pintado's ship, the *San Joseph*, was seized by the French privateer *La Vengeance* (Pintado was a Spanish subject and France was at war with Spain). *La Vengeance*'s master, Jean Antoine Berard (the claimant), brought the *San Joseph* into New York as a prize, and Hamilton filed a libel on Pintado's behalf for restoration, claiming that because Berard outfitted the vessel in the United States, the capture was in violation of the 1794 Neutrality Act.[58] At almost the same time, Harison filed a libel against *La Vengeance*, charging that the ship was outfitted in New York City, with the intent to be employed in the service of France, and in violation of the Arms Embargo Act of 1794.[59] The cases overlapped so much that the lawyers used the same testimony and exhibits in each.[60]

At the end of much litigation, the district and Supreme courts sided with Berard, affirming that *La Vengeance* had not been fitted out as a privateer on American waters.[61] Despite the ruling against the government and Pintado, the Supreme Court's decision claimed a more expansive admiralty jurisdiction in three ways. First, and most importantly, the Court surreptitiously extended its jurisdiction in admiralty to waters previously considered "local," and not solely confined to the high seas, which in this case were the waters off of Sandy Hook, New Jersey. Next, the Court held that an action of forfeiture for illegal arms exportation was a matter of civil admiralty jurisdiction as encompassed by section 9 of the 1789 Judiciary Act. (Recall, however, that the Court's holdings on these matters were still somewhat tentative, as the district judge in *Young Ralph* allowed a seizure to be prosecuted at common law.) Finally, by holding that embargo violations were matters of admiralty, seizures made under trade, navigation, or impost laws did not require a jury trial.[62]

In the years following Washington's 1793 Neutrality Proclamation, the US Supreme Court considered its admiralty jurisdiction to be expanding, and part of the larger effort to enforce US neutrality policy. *La Vengeance* was a landmark in this regard, and the US Supreme Court thought it settled the law with regard to the fact that federal admiralty jurisdiction was not confined only to the high seas, and that jury trials would not be necessary for seizures made under US revenue laws. Nevertheless, the Court still faced challenges to both holdings.

Despite the New York District Court's decision in *Young Ralph*, the US Supreme Court effectively overturned it in 1805 by citing *La Vengeance* and by maintaining that vessels seized under Congress's 1794 Slave Trade Act were matters of admiralty, not of common law.[63] In *US v. The Schooner Betsey*, Congress passed an act forbidding trade with St. Domingo, and the Supreme Court had to decide whether a vessel seized in violation of the act should be tried in the district courts as an admiralty or common law proceeding.[64] Citing *La Vengeance*, the Court determined that since the seizure was made on waters navigable from the sea, and not on waters considered to be within the body of the county, the proceedings would be in admiralty and without a jury.

In a preview of his sweeping pronouncement in *De Lovio*, Joseph Story described the admiralty's prize jurisdiction in 1813 as "not only tak[ing] cognizance of all captures made at sea, in creeks, havens and rivers, *but also of all captures made on land*, where the same have been made by a naval force, or by co-operation with a naval force. This exercise of jurisdiction," he affirmed, "is settled by the most solemn adjudications."[65] Therefore, once the Court broke away from the English precedent that confined admiralty's jurisdiction only to the high seas, the federal courts generally refused to retreat or to give up on any of the jurisdiction they had claimed for their admiralty side. James Kent considered the question of the admiralty's jurisdiction to be a mostly settled matter in American law.[66]

During the early republic period, the federal admiralty courts actively participated in commercial litigation through revenue suits and neutrality prosecutions. Along the way, they established and maintained an expanded prize and civil instance jurisdiction over all coastal waters, a departure from English precedent and a firm resolve against encroachment from either state or federal common law jurisdictions.[67] The federal admiralty court's activities in the years before 1815 are therefore significant because they demonstrate not only a gradual expansion of admiralty's jurisdiction, a trend upon which *De Lovio* would capitalize, but a constant participation in commerce and maritime commercial law. The admiralty docket transformed this initially quiet side of the federal courts into a feasible and vibrant jurisdiction to eventually oversee most of maritime commerce. Still, while admiralty grew in importance, the state common law courts would simultaneously take part in a national legal conversation about how to underwrite the carrying boom brought about by American neutrality.

Creating the Commercial Republic in the State Courts

The federal admiralty courts' oversight of national commerce began with section 9's assignment of revenue law seizures to the district courts, and it continued with the surge of prize and neutrality statute cases heard after 1793. Yet because the central common law courts at Westminster had gained cognizance over maritime contracts and torts in England, the federal judiciary did not claim that Article III's grant of admiralty and maritime jurisdiction included marine insurance contracts until *De Lovio* in 1815.

During the years after the Neutrality Proclamation, the American marine insurance business, which was in its stagnant infancy during the Revolutionary War, became suddenly active, growing tremendously after 1793.[68] Investment in insurance corporations exploded, as $600,000 of investment capital in 1792 ballooned to $10 million by 1804. The number of American insurance companies increased from one to forty across the same thirteen years.[69] The early national period was also a unique time in the American marine insurance market, as it marked an extended period where private individual underwriters coexisted with the growing number of incorporated insurers. The 1798 Quasi-War with France gave insurance corporations a distinct risk-pooling advantage in the insurance marketplace, but private underwriters persevered, both before and after the Quasi-War, using brokers to organize the hundreds of privately underwritten insurance contracts transacted each year.[70]

This boom in the insurance industry corresponded to the increased demand for American international shipping services and underscored the uncertainty inherent in the business of carrying goods during wartime. European warfare meant that as neutrals, American "free" ships could carry "free" goods (including enemy goods, but not articles deemed contraband by the belligerents) to any and all of the warring countries or their colonies without hassle. While neutral American carriers were always subject to the regulations imposed on them by various nations, including treaty provisions, blockades, or decrees made by foreign sovereigns, these restrictions did little in the aggregate to diminish the booming reexport trade carried out by American merchant mariners from 1793 to 1808.[71] During this fifteen-year period, writes one economic historian, "the economic development of the United States was tied to international trade and shipping."[72]

The growing marine insurance sector served the nation's larger commercial goals by providing crucial financial intermediation services to the young American economy. Insurers provided security against financial loss and prevented individual merchants from having to hold large caches of "precautionary savings" in order to remain solvent if their ship or cargo was lost at sea; therefore, insurance firms enabled risk-averse merchants to take advantage of the high-risk, high-return carrying trade opportunities enabled by American neutrality.[73] Marine insurance companies contributed to the development of American law as well, introducing the logic of actuarial statistics to common law judging.[74]

Questions arising from the new volume of marine insurance disputes were largely adjudicated in state common law courts in commercial cities like New York, Philadelphia, and Boston. Yet even though the federal courts' admiralty jurisdiction was formally closed off from considering most of the special assumpsit (contract) actions initiated against marine insurance policies, the common law side of the federal courts occasionally adjudicated marine insurance litigation before 1815. Because the federal judges already had experience adjudicating those insurance cases arising from the era of American neutrality, Story's claim in *De Lovio* was less of an overreach and more of a natural extension of federal power.

The common law side of the federal judiciary could always hear marine insurance disputes arising from their diversity jurisdiction—that is, if the insurer and insured were from different states, or if one were a noncitizen alien.[75] Also, when Congress created the Circuit Court for the District of Columbia in 1801, it gave the court jurisdiction over all cases in law or equity (including marine insurance disputes) where either or both parties were resident or found within the district.[76]

Admiralty courts also heard cases arising from maritime liens such as bottomry bonds.[77] Bottomry created an obligation whereby the master or owner of a ship borrowed money from a lender at a foreign port in order to continue the ship's voyage (to make repairs, or as a line of credit to continue the voyage). If the ship or cargo now underwritten by the loan was lost at sea, the borrower did not have to pay the lender (though the lender would have to be paid from anything salvaged from the voyage). The nature of these transactions prompted New York jurist James Kent to analogize bottomry with marine insurance, calling the lender "in effect, an insurer," where both lender and underwriter "contribute to the facility and security of maritime commerce."[78]

With the federal admiralty courts already adjudicating select maritime contracts like bottomry bonds, in addition to some marine insurance disputes, it was not such a great extension of logic or of jurisdiction to allow the federal admiralty courts cognizance over all maritime contracts. As marine insurance law developed among the various state courts, and to a degree in the federal courts, neutrality policy forced these disparate jurisdictions to grapple with the same pervasive problem: how should each jurisdiction's marine insurance law address novel questions about neutrality? As marine insurance law developed around the exigencies of American neutrality, the state and federal courts adjudicated the consequences of national policy.

While states could (and sometimes did) decide legal questions by looking only to their legal precedent, the nature of marine insurance litigation discouraged this sort of inward-looking judging. First, all of the jurisdictions considering marine insurance contracts faced the same questions arising from American neutrality. In this way, neutrality became the common denominator—that is, the basis of an effective federal–state concurrence that united, at least in substance, the decisions of all the commercial courts across the United States. Also, if another court had already reasoned through a particular problem—the status of a foreign court's judgment, for example—it made sense to borrow that court's logic in order to settle the dispute arising at home.

But most importantly, the creation of any sort of uniformity in commercial decisions benefited the merchants, shippers, and underwriters facilitating America's prosperous reexport trade; therefore, unity and uniformity in maritime commercial law added an element of certainty to an already highly uncertain wartime atmosphere. Just as nineteenth-century judges had an incentive to apply the law instrumentally in order to facilitate transactions and "release energy" in the domestic marketplace, the judges of the early republic had similar reason to create uniformity in the transnational marketplace.[79]

From 1795 until his death in 1804, Hamilton participated in at least 136 marine insurance actions and was generally regarded as one of the finest lawyers ever to litigate maritime questions in the early national period.[80] The New York legal scene was such that Hamilton and a group of six other colleagues litigated most of the marine insurance caseload, partnering on and off with each other, sometimes working together for one client, other times representing the plaintiff (usually the insurer) and defendant (usually the underwriter).[81] During the years 1796–1798, he also served on retainer as general counsel for the newly established United Insurance Company.

The jurisprudence that Hamilton litigated in New York state became part of a national judicial conversation about neutrality and marine insurance. As the French Revolutionary and Napoleonic wars dragged on, the marine insurance industry grew in the United States as well as in England, producing volumes of case law on insurance. With such a vast literature compiling, and with individual firms proliferating, marine insurance litigation in the early nineteenth century was quickly becoming complex and nuanced. Despite the intricacies of the developing law, the two most pervasive questions in marine insurance law coming before federal and state judges were: what were the obligations of the insured as a consequence of American neutrality, and what was the status of a foreign decree (a determination from a foreign admiralty court) in the American courts?

These neutrality-related concerns arose from the particulars of the insurance disputes adjudicated in New York, Massachusetts, and Pennsylvania, as well as in federal courtrooms. In order to address them with consistency, the courts consciously looked to each other in order to synthesize and unify the law. In this way, the state and federal courts acted as "one whole" of a concurrent system, as Hamilton predicted. While the judges' efforts did not create a unified code of maritime law, the state and federal courts created enough uniformity and consistency in marine insurance law that treatise writers like James Kent and Wendell Phillips could summarize the principles of neutrality warranties and foreign decrees in their respective commentaries on insurance law.[82]

Perhaps the most controversial question arising out of American neutrality was the status of foreign decrees, or whether the American courts would give comity to decisions made by foreign admiralty courts. Although jurists in America considered it to be settled in English law that foreign decrees would be adjudged conclusive, it was a momentous and difficult question for American courts to settle.[83] The question of the conclusiveness of foreign decrees arose frequently, usually as a result of the following fact pattern: the underwriter insured a voyage and stipulated that the ship or the cargo insured be warranted neutral. While undertaking the voyage, a belligerent intercepted, seized, and condemned the ship or cargo for any number of reasons, and consequently the insured made a claim to the insurer for compensation of the ship or cargo's loss. The insurer denied the claim, citing the condemnation as conclusive evidence of a breach of the neutrality warranty.

The difficulty of the question arose from the insurer's assumption that the foreign court correctly determined that the insured's actions were nonneutral. Foreign admiralty courts considered the neutrality violation midvoyage, and were thus spatially and temporally closer to the insurer's actions. The foreign courts' proximity to the neutrality violation suggested that they were better situated than an American court to determine evidence against the insurer. Yet what if, during the extended, tense years of wartime, the decisions of foreign courts were vindictive, faulty, or appeared, at least to Americans, to be inequitable?

Alexander Hamilton represented the defendant insurer in *Ludlow & Ludlow v. Dale*, and assisted the defense in *Goix v. Knox* (along with its companion case, *Goix v. Low*) and in *Vandenheuvel v. United Insurance Company*; together, these cases comprised New York's precedent-setting opportunity to grapple with the question of foreign decrees.[84] In *Ludlow v. Dale*, the Ludlows opened a policy of insurance for cargo, warranted as American property. The vessel transporting the cargo was owned by an American. When at sea, the vessel and cargo were captured by the British, libeled, and condemned in a vice admiralty court as lawful prize; the Ludlows then brought suit against the underwriter, Dale, when he refused to compensate them for the loss of the cargo. The defendant argued that the vice admiralty's decision was conclusive evidence of the nonneutral character of the property, and the New York Supreme Court agreed.

In *Goix v. Low* and *Goix v. Knox*, each defendant insurer had underwritten a ship and cargo, respectively; while no neutrality warranty existed in the policy, the ship was described as "the American ship," and the cargo was insured "against all risks." The vessel and cargo were condemned by a foreign admiralty court in Antigua, with no reason given, and Knox and Low refused to compensate Goix for his losses. Goix brought suit. The question before the New York Supreme Court was whether or not the Antiguan courts' decree amounted to a breach of the policies. Citing both *Ludlow* and English precedents, New York's justices upheld the conclusiveness of the foreign court's determination in *Low* but thought the expansive language "against all risks" covered the plaintiff's loss in *Knox*.[85]

The facts and holding in *Vandenheuvel* were similar to those in *Ludlow*, except that the case was taken, on writ of error, to New York's highest appellate court, the Court for the Correction of Errors. In 1802, the Court of Errors—a hybrid court made up of New York's chancellor, lieutenant governor, the justices of the supreme court, and the senate—reversed the lower court's holding. Because of the Court of Error's intervention, New York would ultimately reject the rule of the conclusiveness of foreign decrees upheld in the New York Supreme Court's rulings in *Ludlow*, *Low*, and *Vandenheuvel*. The rest of the state courts would largely ignore the Court of Error's decision, however.[86]

When determining the politically sensitive, and legally momentous, question of foreign decrees, both the state and federal courts looked to each other for cues and justifications for adopting the rule that foreign decrees were conclusive. As early adopters of the rule, however, New York and Pennsylvania referred back to the annals of English history, rather than to their sister states, in order to find the rule conclusive.

The Pennsylvania Supreme Court was generally more skeptical of foreign-decree comity than New York's court. Two years before the New York Supreme Court heard *Ludlow v. Dale*, the Supreme Court of Pennsylvania considered the validity of a foreign decree on a ship and cargo warranted American. In *Vasse v. Ball*, the court refused to find the French admiralty court's determination conclusive because there were manifest inconsistencies and errors in the libel.[87] Under less suspicious circumstances, however, the Pennsylvania courts determined that foreign decrees were conclusive in *Dempsey v. The Insurance Company of Pennsylvania*—that is, until savvy Philadelphian insureds began inserting clauses into their policies that read, "Warranted by assured to be American property, *to be proved, if required, in this city, and not elsewhere.*"[88] This clause effectively forced the courts to reconsider all available evidence concerning the foreign libel at home. Ultimately in Pennsylvania, like in New York, once the state's legislature became involved, the foreign decree was no longer considered conclusive in state law.[89]

By the time the US Supreme Court considered the matter during its 1806 term, the justices were aware of the jurisdictions that had adopted the foreign-decree rule. In *Croudson v. Leonard* and *Fitzsimmons v. The Newport Insurance Co.*, suits brought on writs of error from the circuit courts for the districts of Columbia and Rhode Island, the Court heard arguments about the conclusiveness of a foreign admiralty decree as evidence against insured plaintiffs.[90] In *Fitzsimmons*, counsel referred to *Vandenheuvel*, *Vasse*, and a previous federal case, *Maley v. Shattuck*.[91] In *Maley*, Chief Justice John Marshall set aside the question of the conclusiveness of foreign decrees and just assumed for the sake of argument that the decree was conclusive. After hearing arguments about the status of the rule in both English and state case law, the Court again dodged the question when delivering its opinion in *Fitzsimmons*, but it ruled in *Croudson* "that the sentence of the court of admiralty . . . is conclusive evidence in this case against the insured, to falsify his warranty of neutrality."[92]

Although the US Supreme Court made no move in any of these cases to assume jurisdiction over maritime contracts, the Court was aware of the fact that its admiralty jurisdiction frequently overlapped with state common law jurisdictions. In *Fitzsimmons*, counsel noted, "The common law courts have exclusive jurisdiction of questions of insurance, and wherever the question of neutrality is necessarily involved in a question of insurance, they have as complete jurisdiction to try the question of neutrality, as a court of prize has."[93] Resolving the legal issues raised by America's neutral status thus united both state and federal courts around their common national policy.

By 1810, when Massachusetts had finally gotten around to deciding the status of foreign admiralty decrees, federal and state case law on the matter had been largely settled. Massachusetts adopted the rule that foreign decrees were conclusive, and Justice Theodore Sedgwick went on at length surveying all of the other jurisdictions that had already adopted the rule. He began summarizing English cases, but he moved on "to consider how this question stands, in point of authority, in the United States."[94]

Connecticut had determined that the sentence of a foreign court was conclusive in *Stewart v. Warner*.[95] In *Vandenheuvel*, the New York Supreme Court had determined the same, and though the Court of Errors reversed the decision,

> When I [Sedgwick] consider the character of the judges of the two
> courts—the first composed of grave, respectable, and learned lawyers,
> and the second constituted by popular elections—I derive, at least, as
> much satisfaction from the unanimity of the former, the result of their
> laborious investigation, as from the opposing decision of the latter. It
> can hardly be supposed that the reversal of a judgment so rendered can
> be considered as finally deciding, in that state, this important question.[96]

CHAPTER THREE

To Sedgwick, as well as to the other state courts considering the rule, the fact that the New York Supreme Court had initially adopted the rule of conclusiveness mattered more than the fact that the Court of Errors had reversed the holding. Sedgwick continued, noting that the courts of "the great commercial state of Pennsylvania" had adopted the rule that foreign decrees were conclusive, citing *Dempsey* and *Calhoun*. Finally, he briefly discussed the Supreme Court's decision to adopt the rule in *Croudson*. According to Kent's *Commentaries*, South Carolina could have been added to this list as well.[97]

Sedgwick was an old Federalist, so it was fitting that one of his final comments in *Baxter v. The New England Insurance Co.* would conjure a Hamiltonian vision of commercial unity and uniformity, as enforced by the federal courts. After noting that the US Supreme Court adopted the conclusiveness rule in *Croudson*, Sedgwick concluded, "If this decision is to be considered as an authority in the national courts, (and I think it will), it would be with extreme reluctance that I should feel myself bound to dissent from it, by prescribing a different rule for the administration of justice in the courts of the state."[98] He then articulated the unspoken move that Story would make five years later in *De Lovio*. Sedgwick continued: "There seems to be a peculiar propriety in respecting the decisions of the Supreme Court of the United States upon this subject; because *there is delegated to the national government an authority to regulate commerce, and because it is highly interesting to commerce, that the same rule of decision, in this respect, should pervade the whole country.*"[99] In this concluding comment, Justice Sedgwick implicitly noted the way in which neutrality had created concurrence between the federal and state courts. He also paid tribute to Hamilton's commercial republic by recognizing the national government's responsibility to oversee interstate and foreign commerce.

By surveying the state and federal cases addressing foreign decrees, it becomes clear that in this one particular, but important and reoccurring, question of marine insurance litigation, neutrality created concurrence between the state and federal courts. Over time, American courts concurred with each other in order to achieve a roughly uniform commercial law consensus on the rule of conclusiveness. This concurrence and consensus occurred as well when courts considered other marine insurance law matters—like what, exactly, were the insured's obligations in order to uphold his neutrality warranty?

When composing his lectures on American law, James Kent discussed the particulars of the neutrality warranty, even though it had long been out of use, because of its importance to American jurisprudence during the early national period. Kent wrote that of all the legal questions arising out of the "long maritime wars that grew out of the French revolution," the neutrality warranty found in marine insurance policies "attracted great attention" as "a fruitful topic of discussion in the courts of justice."[100] The American courts strictly construed neutrality warranties, along with any other explicit warranty, and put the burden of appearing and acting neutral on the insured.[101] As a premier practitioner of commercial law, Alexander Hamilton helped to devise and settle the legal obligations of neutral insureds in New York's courts.

In *Blagge v. New York Insurance Co.*, the insurance contract at issue contained both a clause prohibiting illicit trade—an innovation on insurance policies ostensibly drafted by Alexander Hamilton—and a warranty that the cargo was American property.[102] Blagge (the insured) had entered into a joint venture with Lovett, the master of the *Flora*, to ship goods to La Guaira, Venezuela. After encountering legal troubles in Cartagena, Colombia, Lovett made an arrangement with a Spanish shipper named Thomas Thorres to ship some of the goods—ingots and doubloons—as Spanish property. In order to accomplish this, Lovett drew up a false invoice that omitted the cargo of ingots and doubloons from the vessel's documentation. When the *Flora* was subsequently seized by a British man-of-war, British officers discovered the omitted cargo and the paperwork listing the Spanish Thorres as owner of the goods. The cargo was then condemned and sold as lawful prize. The question before the New York court was whether the false invoice produced as a consequence of Lovett's side deal with Thorres voided the insurance contract.[103]

Hamilton, appearing on the underwriter's behalf, argued that the master's actions voided the contract because the creation of false papers subjected the cargo to an additional risk for which the insurers did not insure, and "if the assured has it in his power to give any aspect he may think fit to the property insured," then how can the underwriter know how to calculate his risk?[104] Richard Harison, appearing for the plaintiff insured, argued that the insurer was aware that the voyage was an attempt to evade Spanish import restrictions, and so Lovett's creation of the false documentation was in good faith and "a means of carrying on the trade." Although Harison indicated that the insurers understood that Blagge and his ship's master would try to circumvent Spanish trade restrictions, the court ultimately sided with the underwriters and Hamilton. In doing so, the bench clarified the obligations of neutrality warranties. The clause warrants not only the property as neutral but also implicitly requires that the neutral property be accompanied by documentation to insure it as such, as accustomed by the law of nations.[105]

The appellate courts of Pennsylvania, Maryland, and the US Circuit Court for Pennsylvania adopted similar principles. In *Calbreath v. Gracy*, the court found that because the underwriters insured cargo warranted as American property, the warranty and policy were voided when Spaniards were revealed to be one-third owners of the cargo.[106] In subsequent cases before the Pennsylvania and Massachusetts courts, opposing counsel would often refer back to the circuit court's holding in *Calbreath*.[107]

In *Phoenix v. Platt*, the Pennsylvania Supreme Court ruled that when the insured ship's captain attempted to "cover" or disguise cargo on board from his British captors, his actions voided the insured's neutrality warranty.[108] And while sitting on the Court of Appeals of Maryland, Justice Samuel Chase came to the same conclusion. In *Carrere v. Union Insurance Co.*, Chase declared that in his opinion, "The concealed papers, the artifice practised to prevent detection of them, the fictitious names used, and the mystery in which the whole are enveloped, contradict and discredit the legal documents . . . which cover the whole property insured as his property."[109] Needless to say, the insurer's actions had voided his neutrality warranty.

By the 1820s, marine insurance law had become so complex that Kent found it "difficult to bring the subject within manageable limits" for his lectures on the law. Also, by this time, those "very vexed discussions" arising from wartime—particularly over the status of foreign decrees—had faded in importance because of the long peace that followed the War of 1812.[110] Still, the lasting effects of American neutrality continued to be felt in insurance law: the decisions that arose from the United States' many years of neutral commerce created enough unity and uniformity in maritime law that Kent summarized the leading principles of marine insurance as part of an *American* law.

De Lovio v. Boit and Neutrality's Influence on Commercial Law

In the early republic, neutrality significantly impacted the development of American commercial law, allowing the federal courts to claim an expanded jurisdiction over commercial matters usually adjudicated by the states. Neutrality influenced the federal courts in two ways: first, neutrality vitalized the federal admiralty jurisdiction, increasing its volume of business and giving the admiralty side of the federal courts opportunity to gradually expand its authority over coastal waters. Second, neutrality created a point of convergence for federal and state courts, whereby both considered the effects of neutrality on maritime commerce. While the federal courts initially had limited access to the routine litigation arising from such commerce, questions arising from the thriving marine insurance industry were routine in the state courts.

Neutrality, however, revolutionized the business of marine insurance—the number of insurance policies underwritten, and thus the volume of insurance litigation initiated, exploded because of the neutral carrying trade—and it forced the nascent body of American marine insurance law to innovate in order to answer questions arising from the nation's neutral status. Because this innovation occurred at both the state and federal levels, the American courts began to create, for the first time, a roughly uniform, constantly unifying body of American commercial law.

Along with Alexander Hamilton's financial programs, neutrality—the common denominator converging state and federal maritime commerce decisions—helped to create Hamilton's commercial republic. When adjudicating cases arising from neutrality-related suits, the federal and state courts acted in concert, just as Hamilton predicted they would in *Federalist* No. 82. Both courts worked as part of a system united around the common purpose of creating a stable commercial environment, marked by certainty and uniformity in maritime commercial law. Hamilton's active participation in federal and state courtrooms—first as an administrator, then as a practicing attorney—demonstrates how the expansion of federal admiralty jurisdiction and the gradual unification of marine insurance law developed over the course of the early national period.

So when Justice Story officially announced, in *De Lovio v. Boit*, that the federal admiralty jurisdiction encompassed those maritime contract and tort disputes that had been adjudicated primarily, but not exclusively, by the state common law courts, he did so not as "an aggressive extension of the jurisdiction of the federal courts at the expense of the state courts."[111] Instead, *De Lovio* was the natural extension of the federal courts' gradual accumulation of power and the state courts' complicity in generating a national commercial law. Although Story grounded his decision in the annals of English legal history (a true enough claim; once upon a time, the High Court of Admiralty did have jurisdiction over maritime contracts and torts), his extension of federal power was politically and legally legitimated by the effects of nearly two decades of neutrality-related litigation in the federal and state courts.

Story also implicitly modeled his decision on Hamilton's notion of concurrence. The states retained their preexisting sovereignty to hear common law contract and tort suits, but the states could not erect admiralty courts. The federal courts had an exclusive authority to sit in admiralty, however, and because Story declared that admiralty encompassed maritime torts and contract disputes too, the federal and state courts truly exercised concurrence over the legal questions that had the greatest effect over the national commerce.

Once the United States chose war over neutrality, the common denominator uniting state and federal commercial decisions disappeared. *De Lovio* was an action brought by the libellant, De Lovio, specifically to test the viability of adjudicating a marine insurance suit in admiralty; had the case been brought a few years later, instead of right at the conclusion of Anglo-American hostilities, Story's claim might have been less feasible. After 1812, the courts were no longer grappling with the consequences of American neutrality. Story therefore took advantage of a propitious moment to further claim an expanded federal admiralty jurisdiction—a moment generated by the past two decades of federal and state courts working in tandem on neutrality-related legal questions. In the years after the 1814 Treaty of Ghent, however, the federal and state courts had reverted back to their separate spheres, adjudicating maritime contracts and torts independently, and without concern for neutrality or war, while transforming domestic commercial law in the face of a market revolution at home.[112] The only difference was that now the federal admiralty jurisdiction had officially expanded, in a postneutrality America, to encompass the bulk of maritime commercial litigation as well.

After *De Lovio*, a petitioner could initiate his marine insurance suit in either his state's common law court or in the admiralty side of the federal district courts without regard to diversity or alien jurisdiction stipulations. In the wake of Story's decision, however, James Kent expressed concern that perhaps the federal courts would now reduce the states' authority to adjudicate maritime contracts and torts—perhaps even to deny the states' jurisdiction over those matters at all. It was only a few years after *De Lovio* that Justice Story asserted the US Supreme Court's authority, in *Martin v. Hunter's Lessee*, and ruled that where the federal courts had jurisdiction, exclusive or concurrent, over a federal statute, treaty, or constitutional question, the US Supreme Court stood as the ultimate, final arbiter.[113] Kent worried that as an exclusive grant from Article III, the admiralty power might soon be construed by the Supreme Court to deny the states any cognizance over matters like maritime contracts and torts that were considered part of the federal courts' exclusive admiralty jurisdiction. He only grudgingly accepted the possibility that the federal admiralty courts could theoretically take exclusive cognizance of maritime contracts and torts, but he hoped that because their new jurisdiction was a recent innovation, the federal judges would not be so bold.[114] Perhaps as a precautionary gesture, Kent emphasized in his *Commentaries* the Hamiltonian premise that state courts retained their preexisting authority, even after *Martin*.[115]

As the nineteenth century progressed, however, Kent's fears went unfulfilled. Federal judges did not assume that they had an exclusive jurisdiction over maritime contracts and torts, but merely a concurrent one, shared with the state common law courts. Still, the federal admiralty courts continued to expand their jurisdiction over maritime commerce, sometimes even directly citing Hamilton's *Federalist* No. 82 to explain commercial concurrence between the state and federal courts.[116] Neutrality was no longer a concern for American maritime commerce, but by creating a concurrent, federal jurisdiction over such commerce, neutrality had a lasting effect on federal judicial power, American law, and the creation of Hamilton's commercial republic.

FOUR

~∽~

Developing the Jurisprudence of Federalism: Hamilton's Defense of Federal Fiscal Powers

During the particularly fraught summer of 1791—that season in which speculation in Bank of the United States scrip brought the young republic's first financial panic to Philadelphia—treasury secretary Alexander Hamilton received an alarming piece of news from Boston. William Lowder, the chairman of the town's board of assessors, wrote an open letter to the secretary asking to see the federal government's "public books of loans," the Treasury's record of US bondholders. Lowder requested the names and valuation of Boston-area federal securities holders because the town had levied a tax on its residents' personal property, which included the interest income earned on US bonds.[1] This news could hardly have been worse for the secretary, who had only managed to launch the major components of his fiscal program within the last year.[2] Now the town of Boston sought to tax the lucrative product of Hamilton's assumption scheme—the highly liquid, in-demand 6 percent, deferred 6 percent, and 3 percent securities issued to domestic holders of the newly nationalized war debt—and in response, the treasury secretary strenuously denied Lowder's request, citing the levy's harmful effects on the public credit. Despite the threat Boston's tax posed to his fiscal statecraft, Hamilton offered no legal or constitutional arguments to support his opinion, choosing instead to defend his position on policy, rather than legal, grounds.

Contrast Hamilton's reticence with Chief Justice John Marshall's bold assertions in *Weston v. Charleston*, an 1829 tax case adjudicated before the US Supreme Court.[3] The facts of *Weston* are nearly identical to the 1791 Boston incident: in February 1823, the city council of Charleston, South Carolina, passed an ordinance to raise revenue that taxed all sorts of personal property, including "all personal estate, consisting of bonds, notes, insurance stock, *six and seven percent stock [bonds] of the United States*, or other obligations upon which interest has been or will be received during the year."[4] (Note that when speaking of securities in the eighteenth and nineteenth centuries, Hamilton and his contemporaries often referred to bonds as "stock.")

Yet nearly four decades after Boston sought to levy a similar local tax on federal securities, Marshall pronounced that Charleston's attempt to do the same was unequivocally unconstitutional. The chief justice cited a number of legal arguments to bolster his argument: he pointed out that US bonds taxed by the ordinance were direct manifestations of the federal government's enumerated power to borrow, and that those securities represented an inviolable contract made between the federal government and its creditors. Therefore, the state had no authority to infringe on the national government's sovereign, and supreme, authority to borrow money, nor to interfere with the terms of its contracts. Furthermore, Marshall thought that Charleston's tax impaired the federal government's implicit responsibility to maintain the public credit.

Why did Hamilton and Marshall, both nationalists who opposed the city taxes levied on US bonds, offer such different responses to Boston's and Charleston's assessments? During the years separating the Boston tax from Plowden Weston's lawsuit against Charleston, American constitutional law developed the legal tools necessary to justify and to defend the federal government's power to tax and to borrow. Though he invoked no constitutional arguments to Lowder in 1791, Alexander Hamilton was the pivotal figure in the development of this fiscal jurisprudence, as he articulated, then put to use, the key constitutional principles that enabled jurists like Marshall to mount a legal defense of the federal government's fiscal powers.

Hamilton's fiscal jurisprudence—the legal strategy he employed to defend the federal government's taxing and borrowing powers—also became part of the early republic's jurisprudence of federalism. It had two main components. First, Hamilton sought to realize the potential of the expansive taxing and borrowing powers permitted to the federal government under the Constitution. Whereas the states exercised their considerable powers to tax and to borrow since declaring their independence in 1776, the national government had only enjoyed its theoretically concurrent, but not yet realized, fiscal authority with the states since ratification in 1788. To this end, Hamilton was the single most important figure in the early republic: when he joined the Washington administration, he quickly refinanced outstanding foreign loans and engineered the assumption and swap of domestic war debt for new US securities. In addition, his funding plan relied on a variety of newly proposed federal taxes that not only brought in revenue to service the national debt but also discouraged desuetude (the potential that dormant fiscal powers would enervate from disuse). By legislating the treasury secretary's proposals into law, Congress helped Hamilton to establish early on that the federal government had a vastly expanded power to tax.[5]

In addition to establishing the reality of federal fiscal concurrence, Hamilton also developed legal arguments to justify and to defend the federal government's taxing and borrowing powers when various state and national challenges threatened them. His articulation of legislative concurrence helped to quell the states' fears of plenary federal fiscal powers, and his successful defense of the carriage tax in *Hylton v. US* thwarted Virginia's attack on the national government's taxing power.[6] In addition, Hamilton developed arguments in favor of a broad construction of federal fiscal power, and he convinced Congress that US securities should be treated as inviolable, tax-immune contracts. Hamilton developed these legal maxims to assert and to defend the vigorous and concurrent federal fiscal powers that he had proposed and exercised as head of the Treasury Department.

While some of Hamilton's legal arguments are familiar to scholars of the early republic, historians have overlooked the coherence and long-term impact of his constitutional defense of the federal fiscal powers. This is surprising, particularly because Hamilton's defense of the federal government's taxing and borrowing powers made him a partisan lightning rod. Hamilton's funding scheme, an exercise of the central government's taxation might, garnered political opposition from Jeffersonians; further, one of Hamilton's proposed taxes, an excise on distilled spirits, catalyzed western Pennsylvania's 1794 Whiskey Insurrection. Yet another Pennsylvania tax revolt, Fries' Rebellion of 1799, galvanized in response to a Hamilton-supported and Oliver Wolcott Jr.–sponsored direct tax on houses. Moreover, Hamilton's proposed central bank, followed by his constitutional argument in support of Congress's authority to charter a national bank, also constituted part of Hamilton's ongoing defense of the federal fiscal powers. These measures, along with his funding and assumption schemes, enraged

Hamilton's ideological opponents and fueled vitriolic partisan politicking. Yet while Hamilton's fiscal-legal strategy helped him to accomplish desired policy goals during his term in Washington's Cabinet, it also became a lasting legal framework that persevered in constitutional jurisprudence long after Hamilton was out of office. Once again, Hamilton's legal legacy triumphed in spite of political setbacks.

The existing scholarship consistently underestimates the extent of Hamilton's efforts to restore and maintain the public credit through law. It also fails to acknowledge his seminal influence over the jurisprudence of federalism in the early republic. Political and economic scholars, for example, have meticulously examined Hamilton's financial programs and argued that Hamilton's combined funding, assumption, and central banking policies were effective at jump-starting the US economy and restoring the nation's credit.[7] Others have scrutinized the political consequences of Hamilton's financial programs or parsed his partisan motivations for recommending such a centralizing scheme for the young republic.[8] Economic historians interested in wealth distribution and taxes also take interest in Hamilton's policies and the new Constitution's fiscal powers, but they remain mostly unconcerned with the intersection of tax policy and the development of constitutional law.[9]

These accounts demonstrate the particulars of Hamilton's policy recommendations, along with their economic and political consequences, but historians assume that his efforts were complete—apart from a rhetorical defense continued through partisan squabbling—once Congress passed the requisite statutes to enact Hamilton's recommendations. This approach misses the fact that Hamilton did not rely solely on enacted policy to accomplish his statecraft. Instead, his work to restore the nation's credit continued through each and every treasury transaction and through a strategic, legal defense of the federal government's fiscal powers.[10]

Legal historians have missed Hamilton's fiscal defense strategy as well. Because legal scholarship so often clusters around particularly noteworthy cases, legal developments that arise across multiple, interconnected, or little-known cases can be obscured. For example, Hamilton frequently appears in the huge volume of commentary on the Marshall Court's "aggressive," nationalistic decision in *McCulloch v. Maryland* because his opinion on the constitutionality of the first Bank of the United States provided key legal arguments for Marshall's opinion.[11] Yet Hamilton's involvement in *McCulloch* is never compared with his related arguments before the Supreme Court in *Hylton v. US*, and *McCulloch* is not put into conversation with his other significant legal legacy, Hamiltonian concurrence. And though Hamilton figures prominently in scholarly treatments of *Hylton*, a case concerned with the meaning of the Constitution's "direct tax" clauses, the *Hylton* historiography is particularly disjointed and does not attempt to recognize a Hamiltonian legal strategy over and above the arguments he pursued in that case alone.[12]

The legal strategy that Hamilton used to maintain and sustain the public credit, as well as to defend the national government's fiscal powers, is thus in need of recognition and reconstruction. In order to do so, this chapter examines the intervening legal developments, and Hamilton's role in crafting them, that explain why Marshall's assertions in *Weston v. Charleston* are so different from Hamilton's reply to William Lowder in 1791. Hamilton's legal arguments, and particularly his articulation of concurrence, provided the legal tools that both he and subsequent jurists—nationalists and states' rights proponents alike—used to discuss the increasingly robust nature of the federal government's taxing and borrowing powers. Hamilton's legal strategy succeeded in defending those institutional and administrative measures enacted to restore and to maintain the nation's credit; his arguments also became a fundamental part of the early republic's language of sovereignty and federalism.

When, after Hamilton's death, antebellum jurists adjudicated questions involving collisions between the federal and state governments, Hamiltonian principles provided them with an articulated framework (legislative concurrence) and a set of legal tools for discussing and resolving these inevitable clashes of sovereignty. Hamilton's legal arguments originated a jurisprudence of "defensive" federalism in American constitutional law. That is, Hamiltonian concurrence, broad construction, and his securities as contracts arguments comprised a legal defense to be deployed specifically to protect the federal government's expansive taxing and borrowing powers. What Hamilton had yet to completely articulate in 1791, Marshall expressed fully in 1829. In this way, then, Alexander Hamilton's legal legacy sits squarely at the center of the jurisprudence of American federalism.

Establishing Legislative Concurrence

While Hamilton would eventually articulate a variety of legal arguments to counter challenges posed to the federal taxing and borrowing powers, his primary defense was in response to lessons learned from the American Revolution. Anglo-American constitutional law had taught Hamilton that hastily conceived taxes could threaten (or be perceived as a threat to) the security of individual rights, and that sovereign power could in fact weaken, or altogether disappear, if not regularly exercised. More importantly, Hamilton understood that even after the Confederation Congress's impotence was fully on display during the 1780s, Americans still remained skeptical of a strong, centralized authority and its power to tax them.

In response to these wartime lessons, Hamilton transformed the Constitution's abstract grant of federal fiscal powers into a reality. During the debate over ratification, and throughout his tenure as treasury secretary, Hamilton defined, then executed, the concept of legislative concurrence in American law. Rather than operate in wholly separate spheres, the federal and state governments often had the authority to simultaneously exercise the same types of power. The taxing power exemplifies this concurrent authority, as both the federal and state governments could and did tax the same articles of real and personal property, like dwelling houses, slaves, or carriages, at the same time.

Concurrence provided Hamilton with both a challenge and an opportunity. Because concurrence meant that the federal government had a vastly expanded arsenal of revenue-generating powers, the states would naturally be jealous of this power and concerned that it would impair their abilities to collect revenue. Hamilton met this challenge with a well-articulated argument made both in speech and in print that described how concurrence would work in practice. Hamilton assured the states that under the new Constitution, they retained most of their legislative sovereignty (and particularly their still-ample powers to tax), but he also enumerated the circumstances that would result in an alienation of these prerogatives. Concurrence formed the intellectual framework for Hamilton's overall legal strategy because it explained how the federal government could be just as fiscally assertive as the states, but without denying the states their legislative sovereignty or the majority of their traditional revenues.

But the federal government's potential for fiscal assertiveness provided the real opportunity for Hamilton. In 1782, Hamilton spent a frustrating few months as a continental tax receiver, working under the superintendent of finance, Robert Morris, and attempting to collect New York's share of continental taxes. Despite Hamilton's best efforts, he did not make headway collecting all of the arrearages owed by the state; nor did he succeed in reforming New York's tax system.[13] But as treasury secretary, Hamilton could achieve what the Confederation Congress could not. If he could execute the newly minted federal taxing and borrowing powers, he could accomplish the new nation's highest priority: to restore the public credit.[14] Hamilton took immediate advantage of this opportunity through his policy proposals as well as through his leadership and oversight of the Treasury Department. Therefore, the first component of Hamilton's legal defense of the federal fiscal powers was defining and exemplifying concurrence in action.

The federal government's power to tax proved to be contentious before it was even exercised. In a momentous departure from the Articles of Confederation, the Constitution gave the national government an extensive power to tax the American people directly. Whereas the Articles made the Confederation Congress dependent on the states to raise money for national exigencies (under the inefficient requisitions system), the Constitution authorized a taxing power completely independent of state action. In fact, the few limitations proscribed on the national taxing power seemed inconsequential to the vigorous potential of Congress's Article I, section 8, authority "to lay and collect Taxes, Duties, Imposts and Excises, to pay the Debts and provide for the common Defence and general Welfare of the United States . . . [and] to borrow Money on the credit of the United States." The limitations, in contrast, were comparatively minor to what they were under the Articles. They included rules for apportioning direct taxes (Article I, sections 2 and 9), the requirement that duties, imposts, and excises should be levied uniformly across the states (Article I, section 8), a cap on the amount of tax that Congress could levy on imported slaves (Article I, section 9), and a prohibition on taxing the states' exported goods (Article I, section 9). The Constitution made no mention of a limit on Congress's authority to borrow.

At the same time that the Constitution vested the national government with unprecedented fiscal authority, it deprived the states of their ability to tax imports and exports without Congress's consent (Article I, section 10). The states still retained the rest of their preexisting fiscal powers (which left them many options for raising taxes), but the federal government now shared with them a concurrent jurisdiction over most articles of revenue.[15] This yet-to-be-realized concurrent federal power became cause for much alarm during the debate over ratification. (In general, however, Anti-Federalists did not object to Congress's power to borrow.)[16]

Anti-Federalists strongly resisted the national government's newly augmented taxing power in part because a distant central authority now had the potential to pass onerous taxes that could in turn suppress individual rights.[17] Just as a far-off British Parliament once insisted on its right to tax and "to bind" its colonies "in all cases whatsoever," so too could an American Congress, the Anti-Federalists feared, if allowed such an extensive power to tax the people directly.[18] Federalists, in contrast, thought that the new republic needed exactly this sort of vigorous taxing power so that the national government could act appropriately in times of national crisis, but also so that it could accomplish fully the duties of a modern fiscal-military state.

Anti-Federalists had another concern as well: if the federal government could assess a person's land, slaves, luxuries, or home—among the many other articles of taxable personal property—would the states still be able to tax these things too? Or would federal taxes end up starving the states? Concurrence alarmed the states because it created a regime where state governments might have to compete with the federal government to collect their traditional revenues. In theory, then, the federal government's concurrent taxation powers had the potential to make the Anti-Federalists' consolidationist nightmares come true.

In order to address these fears, Alexander Hamilton presented his first arguments in defense of the federal fiscal powers. He offered this opening salvo in both the New York ratifying convention and in his *Federalist* essays, notably No. 32, and he intended for his claims to explain how legislative concurrence would work in practice in the new federal republic. Whenever possible, Hamilton exemplified his claims with tax examples.

When members of the New York ratifying convention raised concerns that concurrence could ultimately lead to the eradication of state governments, Hamilton answered them, first by associating the federal government's robust taxing powers with their proper objectives: the restoration of the nation's credit and the ability to meet exigent circumstances. He implored the convention: "Limiting the powers of government to certain resources, is rendering the fund precarious; and obliging the government to ask, instead of empowering them to command, is to destroy all confidence and credit." He then added the very Hamiltonian maxim: "A government, to act with energy, should have the possession of all its revenues to answer present purposes." He next directly addressed the perceived threat of concurrence: "With regard to the jurisdiction of the two governments," the Constitution did not "prevent the states from providing for their own existence."[19]

Concurrence did not invite a collision between the two independent sovereigns because "both might lay the tax; both might collect it without clashing or interference. . . . The states have an undoubted right to lay taxes in all cases in which they are not prohibited." Moreover, if a tax was laid on an article by both the federal and state governments, and if the individual assessed could not pay, both sovereigns would be treated as coequal creditors. According to Hamilton, this meant that the first government to sue for the collection of the tax debt would be the first creditor in line to receive payment.[20] He further denied that any other collisions between the federal and state sovereigns would result from their concurrent powers.

Richard Harison and James Kent in particular thought Hamilton's convention remarks persuasive, but it was his explanation of concurrence in *Federalist* No. 32 that would provide American jurists with a lasting, and much cited, framework for comprehending the federal and state governments' shared legislative powers. In this essay, one of seven discussing the federal government's power to tax, Hamilton made two main points. The first was yet another assurance to the states that they "should possess an independent and uncontrollable authority to raise their own revenues [. . . and] they would, under the plan of the convention, retain that authority in the most absolute and unqualified sense," with enumerated prohibitions excepted.[21] Note that when Hamilton discussed the states' retained, concurrent taxing powers, he spoke only of their preexisting authority to collect taxes; Hamilton's goal was to assuage the Anti-Federalist fears that New York's usual revenue streams would be overtaken by the federal government's new taxing powers.

Yet Hamilton's second point also spelled out the three instances where, under the Constitution's "partial union or consolidation," the "alienation" of state sovereignty occurred. These exceptions included: "[1] where the Constitution in express terms granted an exclusive authority to the Union; [2] where it granted in one instance an authority to the Union, and in another prohibited the States from exercising the like authority; [3] and where it granted an authority to the Union to which a similar authority in the States would be absolutely and totally *contradictory* and *repugnant.*"[22] He acknowledged the states' retained rights to their legislative sovereignty, and particularly their still-robust authority to tax, but he emphasized that when states exercised their taxing powers, any "direct contradiction or repugnancy in point of constitutional authority" would result in the alienation of state prerogative.[23] By carving out this "repugnancy" exception, Hamilton left an opening in his articulation of concurrence for a legal trump, whereby a true clash of federal–state sovereignty could be resolved in the national government's favor. During his career, Hamilton shied away from making this argument more explicit, or even from using this subtle suggestion of federal supremacy to defend the federal fiscal powers. Yet as we will see, this nationally oriented loophole empowered federal and state judges to consider the effect of federal supremacy on the states' concurrent powers.

Once enough state conventions ratified the US Constitution, concurrence was enacted but not yet put into practice. This unrealized potential of the federal government's concurrent fiscal authority was especially important at the beginning of Hamilton's tenure in office, when national powers were untried and potentially vulnerable. In order to transform concurrence from a theoretical to a practical legal doctrine, Hamilton operated strategically, suggesting those taxing and borrowing policies that asserted federal power while they simultaneously restored the public credit. In this way, making concurrence a reality became the cornerstone of Hamilton's legal strategy. Through his tax proposals, assumption scheme, foreign loan refinancing, and revenue collection efforts, Hamilton successfully executed the federal government's concurrent powers to tax and borrow.[24]

Although his policies proved to be politically controversial, Hamilton's programs were unquestionably successful. The treasury secretary succeeded at using the federal government's fiscal powers to restore the nation's credit. During his tenure in office, the federal government enacted a tariff-heavy tax policy, whereby Congress imposed relatively few internal taxes but many ad valorem customs duties, which fell mostly on merchants. As Max M. Edling and Mark D. Kaplanoff demonstrate, this program allowed the federal government to collect the maximum amount of revenue with the least amount of imposition on individual citizens. It worked. After Congress assumed approximately 70 percent of the states' debt under Hamilton's plan, the states were then able to reduce their direct-tax levies by 75 to 95 percent. Thus, the Constitution's grant of fiscal power, combined with the particulars of Hamilton's financial policy, created real tax relief for the majority of Americans.[25] Moreover, this federal fiscal policy also met Hamilton's primary goal of restoring the nation's credit. In addition to raising the value of federal securities, the combined components of Hamilton's financial program introduced "institutions of debt management"—including the initial program to pay down the principal of the domestic debt—that allowed the federal government to gradually reduce and ultimately to completely redeem both its domestic and foreign debt.[26]

Yet Hamilton had another reason to vigorously exercise the federal fiscal powers: to create what Fisher Ames called "habits of acquiescence" to the national government's authority among the American people.[27] In other words, new fiscal power should be put to use so that Americans would become accustomed to the federal government's authority and so that this authority did not weaken through disuse. This too was a lesson learned from the recent imperial crisis.

Desuetude was an old principle found in the annals of Scottish and English law that described how disuse of a law or custom could, over time, effectively repeal it.[28] Scotland adhered to the doctrine openly and considered desuetude to be a legitimate form of repeal for its statutes. English lawyers, on the other hand, rarely admitted to its legitimacy, though eighteenth-century jurist Richard Wooddesson noted that in practice, desuetude worked to quietly repeal customary and statutory law in England as well.[29] In America, Supreme Court justice James Wilson noted, "Disuse may be justly considered as the repeal of custom," an idea that the colonists had invoked during the Stamp Act crisis.[30] After Parliament levied the 1765 stamp tax, a revenue tax that funded the British treasury, rather than a duty on imports, American Whigs claimed that Parliament lacked the authority to tax the colonies in such a manner. The colonists argued that according to the Anglo-American constitution of customary rights, Parliament had never before exercised an authority to raise a revenue tax, and thus they lost their right to do so in 1765.[31] To the American Whigs, Parliament's disuse of their taxing power led to desuetude.

So if the imperial crisis preceding the American Revolution taught Anti-Federalists to be wary of a strong, centralized government and its prerogative to tax, it demonstrated to Federalists the importance of exercising taxing powers so as not to lose them. Hamilton learned this lesson: he proposed eight duties in his first 1790 report on public credit, and he offered various critiques and suggestions to Congress's tax policy during his five-year term in office.[32] By the time he left the Treasury, Congress had passed fourteen revenue acts, imposing taxes of different varieties: imposts, excise, and luxury good taxes before 1795, and a few years after Hamilton left office, the first federal direct tax on dwelling houses.[33] Defining and exercising concurrence thus comprised the first part of Hamilton's legal efforts to defend the federal taxing and borrowing powers. Hamilton's next step was to articulate specific legal arguments to preserve these fiscal powers when challenged by the states, by his colleagues in Washington's Cabinet, and by Congress.

Developing Hamilton's Legal Toolbox

When William Lowder, chairman of the board of assessors for the town of Boston, published his open letter to Secretary Hamilton in July 1791, Boston had already enacted the personal property assessment that taxed the interest earned from "monies in the public funds." Lowder contacted Hamilton because Nathaniel Appleton, the commissioner of loans for Massachusetts, refused to open the federal record books to the assessors, thereby denying the city tax collectors the names and holdings of the Boston-area residents who owned US securities. The board wanted to avoid the "disagreeable necessity of taxing the stock-holders according to their reputed property in the funds," so Lowder appealed to Hamilton to direct Appleton "to expose the public books of loan to the inspection of the assessors of the town of Boston."[34]

The secretary replied two weeks later with his own open letter in which he denied the request, respectfully submitting "that every thing, in the nature of a direct tax on property in the funds of the United States, is contrary to the true principles of public credit and tends to disparage the value of the public stock." Surely, Hamilton continued, neither Boston nor Massachusetts would pass a tax with the intent of impairing the public credit; thus, the treasury secretary felt confident that even in denying Lowder's request, he did not challenge the integrity of Boston's tax law. Nowhere in the letter did Hamilton mention the assessment as a threat to the sovereignty of the federal government's power to borrow; nor did he argue that securities were contracts and thus states were forbidden—on principle as well as by Article I, section 10—to impair their obligations. Perhaps it was because he was writing a public letter and not a legal brief that Hamilton chose to omit any legal grounds for denying Lowder's request; instead, he chose to defend the first direct challenge to the federal fiscal powers on public policy alone.[35]

It is not known for sure how successful the board of assessors was in collecting their tax, but their request inspired alarm, bitter feelings, and possibly breaking and entering. Writing to Hamilton in July and September from Boston, Fisher Ames reported that certain "country gentlemen have thought less favorably" of the secretary's letter and would applaud "acts of rapine in the shape of a tax" against all holders of federal securities. Also, in spite of Hamilton's refusal to open up federal records to them, "The Assessors are, in some places, disposed to pry into the entries at the Custom House, and the Loan Office Books."[36] In October, Tobias Lear alerted the president to the situation, commenting to Washington that if the assessors had the right to tax federal bonds, "it would appear that it is in the power of the state governments or corporations to ruin the public Credit; for if they have a right to tax them at all, there seems to be no limits set to the quantum—and it may be laid on so heavily as to make the securities hardly worth holding."[37]

CHAPTER FOUR

This direct collision between Boston's tax and the federal government's ability to borrow money (and therefore to restore the public credit) was a collision of sovereignty between the national and state governments. Boston's city council believed that the federal government had the constitutional authority to borrow money and to issue securities, but the council also thought that it had the prerogative to tax the interest earned from federal debt. During his lifetime, Hamilton would not have to contend with another direct collision of sovereignty like this; the next time a state would threaten federal sovereignty with its taxing prerogatives occurred in 1817, when Maryland sought to raise revenue by taxing the Baltimore branch of the second Bank of the United States. Instead, Hamilton devoted his efforts as both secretary and as a private lawyer to defending challenges made to the national government's ability to exercise its taxing and borrowing powers.

Take, for example, a question about concurrence that arose in New York in 1799. In 1794, Congress passed an act that taxed property sold at auction; it included provisions regulating the appointment of auctioneers, who, along with running the auction, would also collect federal duties on the goods sold.[38] While Congress took care to prevent any inconvenience to the states, the act made these auctioneers federal officials, appointed by Congress and overseen by federal, rather than state, authorities. Because a levy on goods sold at auction was typically an exercise of the states' taxing powers, the 1794 federal tax demonstrated concurrence in action, along with the questions that could arise from it.

New York's governor, John Jay, did not doubt the federal government's authority to exercise this concurrent tax power, but he questioned the constitutionality of Congress's ability to oversee the auctioneers. Jay consulted one of Hamilton's close colleagues, New York lawyer Josiah Ogden Hoffman, to inquire into the auctioneers' legal status, and Hoffman subsequently posed the question to Hamilton as well. As Hoffman described Jay's concern to Hamilton, the governor believed that under the US Constitution, any auctioneers would have to be considered "municipal Officers" and not federal appointees. Jay thought that the auctioneer would collect the federal tax, but "without any of the Checks contained in the Act of Congress."[39] Hoffman disagreed, however, telling Jay and recounting to Hamilton that the "Government of the United States and the State Government possess a concurrent Jurisdiction, in this Article of Taxation, as they do in ma[n]y other Instances," and if "Auctioneers were *exclusively* subject to the State Governments, it might be in *their* [the states'] power by a non-Appointment, wholly to defeat the Laws of the Union, or . . . the payment of the Tax might be liable to evasion."[40]

Hamilton's reply has not been found, but it seems likely that he would have agreed with Hoffman. Because the federal government's power to tax property sold at auctions was concurrent and constitutional (which no one doubted here), then, as Hamilton had previously argued in defense of the first Bank of the United States, the government had a "right to employ all the *means* requisite, and fairly *applicable* to the attainment of the *ends* of such power."[41] Appointing and overseeing federal auctioneers to collect a federal tax qualified as a fairly applicable and requisite means to accomplish the end goals provided in the act.[42]

This exchange among New York's elite jurists demonstrates that as the federal government exercised its concurrent authority, questions arose as to the nature and extent of its fiscal powers. It was unclear how, in practice, concurrence could be satisfactorily executed without compromising either state or federal sovereignty. The interstitial rules of federalism would only develop as questions were asked of, and challenges were mounted against, specific exercises of the federal fiscal powers. As the chief theoretician of legislative concurrence, Alexander Hamilton took part in these challenges, developing legal arguments aimed at defending the most expansive exercise of the federal government's taxing and borrowing powers against threats coming from both the national level and from the states.

The first principle that Hamilton articulated to uphold the federal government's concurrent fiscal powers is perhaps his most famous legal argument: that the federal powers enumerated in Article I, section 8, should be construed broadly. First pronounced in his 1791 opinion on the constitutionality of a national bank, Hamilton's principle of broad construction had two components, both of which helped to make his case not only for the first Bank of the United States but also for a broad construction of the means to implement the federal taxing and borrowing powers.

Because Secretary of State Thomas Jefferson and Attorney General Edmund Randolph had both looked through the Constitution's list of Congress's enumerated powers and failed to find a power to erect corporations, they both denied that the federal government could charter a bank.[43] Hamilton disagreed, however, arguing that the Constitution contained both express and implied powers, and that erecting corporations qualified as an acceptable, implicit exercise of national sovereignty. To test the propriety of such an implied power, Hamilton proposed the following rule: "If the end be clearly comprehended within any of the specified powers, & if the measure have an obvious relation to that end, and is not forbidden by any particular provision of the constitution—it may safely be deemed to come within the compass of the national authority."[44] Because a bank would assist the federal government to exercise its other enumerated powers—to tax, to borrow, to regulate commerce—then, Hamilton thought, the implied authority to incorporate a bank to be constitutional.

The next component of Hamiltonian broad construction addressed the problem of construing the Constitution's explicit text. Hamilton critiqued Jefferson's narrow interpretation of the "necessary and proper" clause, noting that Jefferson would give the text such a *"restrictive* operation" that only an *"extreme necessity"* could possibly justify any unenumerated exercise of federal authority, which Hamilton and other Federalists regarded as an impossible standard for a government tasked with responding to innumerable national exigencies.[45] Instead, Hamilton proposed that the words of the clause be construed by their "obvious & popular sense." He also advocated that any policy justified as "necessary and proper" be judged by how well its proposed means accorded with the proper ends of governing.[46] In other words, constitutional text should not be hamstrung by restrictive definitions; rather, "the powers contained in a constitution of government, especially those which concern the general administration of the affairs of a country, its finances, trade, defence &c ought to be construed liberally, in advancement of the public good."[47]

Generations of scholars have contemplated the treasury secretary's persuasive, and ultimately successful, arguments to justify his desired bank to President Washington, but Hamilton offered his principle of broad construction as more than just an argument to secure part of his financial program. Indeed, Hamiltonian broad construction offered a far-reaching defense of the federal government's authority to tax and to borrow.

The power to tax, for example, was never far from Hamilton's mind as he contemplated the constitutionality of the bank.[48] He noted that the federal government's authority to tax rum was an already accepted, implied exercise of its general, explicit power to lay and collect taxes, and he later made the case, "A Bank relates to the collection of taxes in two ways; *indirectly,* by increasing the quantity of circulating medium & quickening circulation, which facilitates the means of paying—*directly,* by creating a *convenient species of medium* in which they are to be paid."[49] Just in case Washington had not yet been persuaded, Hamilton directly affirmed that "the sovereign power of providing for the collection of taxes *necessarily includes* the right of granting a corporate capacity to such an institution, as a *requisite* to its greater security, utility and more convenient management."[50]

Broadly construing the federal government's constitutional powers also protected its ability to borrow, as the bank had "a direct relation to the power of borrowing money, because it is [a] usual and[,] in sudden emergencies[,] an essential instrument in the obtaining of loans to Government."[51] Furthermore, the implied power to incorporate a bank had an obvious relation to the enumerated power to borrow: "The legislative power of borrowing money, & of making all laws necessary & proper for carrying into execution that power, seems obviously competent to the appointment of the *organ* through which the abilities and wills of individuals may be most efficaciously exerted, for the accommodation of the government by loans."[52] Hamilton intended the principle of broad construction to incorporate policy considerations into constitutional adjudication: if the policy means accomplished constitutional ends, then the Constitution should be interpreted to accommodate those means. Constitutional interpretation should not stray too far from the text, but it should take into consideration national exigencies and public policy goals and empower the federal action whenever possible.

Hamilton's arguments for the constitutionality of the bank simultaneously accomplished multiple goals. Most directly, Hamilton persuaded Washington to sign the bank bill into law, thus enacting one of the components of Hamilton's financial program. At the same time, Hamilton used the principle of broad construction to justify the most useful institutional means with which the federal government could facilitate tax collection or borrow money in a pinch. By defending the means used to execute or assert the federal taxing and borrowing authority, broad construction in turn protected these fiscal powers. Hamiltonian broad construction also introduced a particularly potent, well-articulated legal principle into American constitutional law that empowered, rather than restricted, federal actions. Finally, Hamilton's explicit defense of the bank, as well as his implicit defense of the taxing and borrowing powers, directly served his overarching statecraft goal of restoring the nation's credit.

Hamilton relied on his principle of broad construction again, five years later, when he defended the United States against Virginia's attack on the federal taxing power. The resulting litigation, *Hylton v. US*, marked not only Hamilton's first and only oral argument before the US Supreme Court but also the first time the high court reviewed the constitutionality of a federal law.[53] Also, *Hylton* is noteworthy because federal actors—including Hamilton, before he left office, and US attorney general William Bradford—worked in conjunction with the plaintiff-in-error, Daniel Hylton, to put a test case before the US Supreme Court. The staged case turned on the meaning of "direct tax," found in Article I, sections 2 and 9.

The facts of the case were as follows: Congress passed "An Act laying duties upon Carriages for the Conveyance of Persons" on June 5, 1794, to set uniform duties on various types of carriages (that is, for example, across the states, all coach owners would have to pay a $10 duty, but chariot owners owed only $8).[54] When the bill was still in committee, however, Southern congressmen objected to the tax in part because they viewed it as a discriminatory levy on the South, and they raised the question of whether the carriage tax should be considered a direct or an indirect tax. The distinction was significant; if Congress categorized the carriage tax as an indirect duty or excise, then the Constitution required it to be levied uniformly across the states (as Hamilton intended when he proposed it, and as the act's framers designed the tax to be).[55] If, however, Congress determined that carriage taxes were actually direct taxes (like poll, land, or capitation taxes), then the Constitution stipulated that the tax be apportioned by population.[56] Arguing that the carriage tax was actually a direct tax because "all taxes are direct which are paid by the citizen without being recompensed by the consumer," the Virginia delegation in the House led the protest against the nonapportioned, and thus possibly unconstitutional, carriage tax.[57] Despite their efforts, a glum James Madison lamented to Jefferson in May 1794 that "the tax on carriages succeeded in spite of the Constitution."[58] Washington signed the bill into law a month later.

Yet Virginia's protests did not stop there. Secretary Hamilton got wind of Virginia's continued grumbling in the summer of 1794 and advised Tench Coxe, the US commissioner of revenue, to instruct Edward Carrington, the supervisor of the revenue for the district of Virginia, "to give facility to a legal decision in any case where it may be desired—taking care to secure an appeal in the last resort to the Supreme Court."[59] Hamilton assumed that Virginia's claims about the unconstitutionality of the carriage tax would have to be resolved in court, and in early 1795, Attorney General William Bradford devised a two-tiered strategy to bring the case into both state and federal court.[60] When a prominent cadre of Virginian gentlemen—including Daniel Hylton, Spencer Roane, Edmund Pendleton, and John Taylor of Caroline—refused to pay their carriage taxes in September 1794, Bradford and Hamilton brought an action of debt against Hylton, their willing defendant, for a total of $2,000 in taxes owed plus penalties.[61] This outrageously inflated sum, along with the collusion between the parties, demonstrates the extent to which all participants used legal fictions and extensive maneuvering to bring *Hylton* before the federal courts. For their part, Hamilton and Bradford calculated the inflated amount of back taxes and penalties in order to meet the jurisdictional thresholds stipulated by the 1789 Judiciary Act for the federal circuit courts.[62] After the Circuit Court for the District of Virginia issued a split decision, the case rose to the US Supreme Court on a writ of error. As the litigation proceeded, the federal government agreed to pay for all of Daniel Hylton's incident expenses, including his lawyers' fees.[63]

This complicity and maneuvering suggests the high stakes involved in *Hylton v. US*. If Virginia's direct-tax argument were adopted, it would have had dangerous consequences for the federal government's taxing powers. In their arguments before the federal courts, both Virginia and the federal government spent an inordinate amount of time discussing the proper definition of "direct tax"—a debate that has been discussed elsewhere and does not need to be repeated here.[64] The extant evidence strongly suggests that no precise, technical meaning existed for the term "direct tax," so both parties could only muster their most authoritative arguments to persuade the Supreme Court as it determined for the first time what exactly qualified as a direct tax (besides capitation, land, and poll taxes).[65] This debate over definitions masked the real threat that Virginia's direct-tax strategy posed to the federal fiscal powers: if a tax like the carriage tax qualified as a direct tax, then the federal government's concurrent authority to tax the American people would be severely limited in practice.

Because the Constitution required that taxes categorized as direct had to be apportioned, a direct tax on personal property would result in grossly unfair, skewed tax burdens across the states. The carriage tax offered a perfect example of this inequity in practice. Relatively few Americans owned carriages, and the 18,384 carriages that belonged to US taxpayers in 1796 were unevenly spread across the states. If Congress levied the carriage tax as a direct tax, then carriage owners would owe their tax on the basis of a complicated calculation that combined the number of carriages in their state plus the state's population.[66] Robin L. Einhorn has calculated what this hypothetical direct carriage tax would have looked like in practice: Delaware, with the most carriages per person, would end up paying 73 cents per carriage, while Georgia, the state with the fewest carriages per person, would have paid a relatively extravagant tax of $5.69 per carriage. Virginian carriage owners would have been taxed $2.93 per carriage.[67]

Direct taxes, therefore, were not only more difficult to calculate than uniform, indirect taxes, but they also easily produced unfair, unequal, and even "absurd" results.[68] Under a direct-tax computation, carriage owners in Pennsylvania ($4.11 per carriage) and Georgia would have been saddled with a disproportionately onerous tax bill—not because they chose to own so many carriages but because they lived in a state where so few carriages were owned relative to the population (calculated on the basis of the number of free persons, plus three-fifths of enslaved persons). Surely if Congress drafted the 1794 carriage tax as a direct tax, then every state but Delaware would have balked at their disparate, and increasingly disproportionate, tax burdens. Therefore, if most federal property taxes had to be categorized as direct taxes—the outcome that Virginia sought in *Hylton*—then most internal federal taxes would immediately become not only highly unpopular but also politically impracticable.[69] Virginia's direct-tax strategy would effectively strangle the federal taxing power and severely limit the extent of federal concurrence.

Thus, *Hylton* offered Virginia the opportunity to accomplish a number of its states' rights goals, including the limitation of the federal government's concurrent tax powers and the defeat of one unpopular federal tax in particular. Virginia perceived the carriage tax to be a discriminatory measure inflicted on the South, but this was based on an incorrect assumption that the South had more carriages than the North.[70] In addition, the state's counsel complained that any "local" tax (what attorney John Taylor defined as a federal tax on goods that did not circulate between the states) should be considered a direct tax, presumably because direct taxes were harder to levy, and this would protect the usual objects of state taxation from additional federal tax burdens.[71]

Virginians also feared that the carriage tax set a precedent for a future slave tax to be levied on the South. In his arguments before the circuit court, Taylor admitted as much, alluding to slaves as the next type of Southern property to be "peculiarly exposed" if the carriage tax remained on the books.[72] Typically, Southerners feared any threat to slavery, and according to Robin L. Einhorn, they successfully used early republic and antebellum tax policy as a shield to protect their peculiar institution. For Virginia, then, *Hylton* was an opportunity to prevent the potential of a uniform federal tax on slaves by defeating a tax precedent.

Taylor also relished the setback Virginia's strategy would cause for Hamilton's despised financial program: if Hylton prevailed, then the federal revenue streams on which Hamilton's funded debt depended would be severely limited in practice, perhaps leaving imposts as the only reliable federal revenues. To accomplish this end, Taylor invoked the boogeyman of national consolidation by openly questioning the wisdom and constitutionality of federal legislative concurrence: "For if . . . Congress can tax the drink, the food—the cloathing [sic]—and all necessaries, raised and kept by individuals for their own ease and subsistence, without limitation, is there any *real* restriction of their power of taxation?"[73] According to Hamiltonian concurrence, there was no real limit on the national government's power to tax but for the Constitution's few and explicit prohibitions. Taylor denounced this position, however, referring to it as a "web of pretended federalism." He also suggested that federal taxation was particularly vulnerable to corruption and manipulation "by the will of a minister."[74] Undoubtedly Hamilton was not amused at this oblique reference to him, nor to Taylor's other jabs aimed at his administration.[75]

In response, Alexander Hamilton met Virginia's attack on the federal taxing power with a variation on his own principle of broad construction. When arguing before the Supreme Court, Hamilton averred that direct taxes had no precise legal or technical meaning, and thus the case required the Court to determine the text's meaning for the first time: "Such a Construction must be made," Hamilton noted in a brief prepared for his oral arguments, that the "Power to tax may remain in its *plentitud[e]*."[76]

Just as he argued in his opinion on the bank, Hamilton stressed that the task at hand—the interpretation of the Constitution's text—required the Court to construe the relevant clauses in context with the federal government's responsibilities and appropriate policy goals. "In such a case," Hamilton argued, "no construction ought to prevail calculated to defeat the express and ne[ce]ssary authority of the Government."[77] The Court should consider the carriage tax to be either an excise or a duty because such a construction allowed the federal government to exercise the expansive taxing powers intended and granted by the Constitution's tax provisions. To determine otherwise—to force internal federal taxes to be inequitably apportioned as direct taxes—would be to deliberately limit federal authority in spite of Article I's broad granting of power. Hamilton noted, "It would be contrary to reason and every rule of sound construction to adopt a principle for regulating the exercise of a clear constitutional power, which would defeat the exercise of the power," and to adjudge the carriage tax as a direct tax would defeat the federal power to lay taxes on personal property.[78]

When faced with two alternatives—a broad interpretation of the Constitution's tax clauses that empowered the federal government to collect revenue, versus a confining construction that limited federal power—Hamilton aimed to persuade the Court to adopt a broad construction. If the end was constitutional (a robust federal taxing power), then any fairly applicable means to attain that end should "come within the compass of national authority" as well.[79] If Congress intended its uniformly assessed carriage tax as a means to exercise its constitutional power to tax, then the Court should not construe the relevant tax clauses so as to defeat or to restrict Congress's ability to do so.

In February 1796, the justices of the Supreme Court sided with the federal government in *Hylton*. They maintained in their seriatim opinions that the 1794 carriage tax was constitutional. Justice Samuel Chase adopted Hamilton's principle of broad construction when he declared, "The great object of the Constitution was, to give Congress a power to lay taxes, adequate to the exigencies of government."[80] Therefore, the Court disavowed a construction of "direct tax," "excise," or "duty" that implied otherwise and limited the federal concurrent power to tax. Furthermore, Justice William Paterson noted how "absurd" and "inequitable" a direct tax on carriages would be: "A tax on carriages, if apportioned, would be oppressive and pernicious. How would it work? In some states there are many carriages and in others but few. Shall the whole sum fall on one or two individuals in a state who may happen to own and possess carriages?"[81] Justice James Iredell added, "If any state had no carriages, there could be no apportionment at all. This mode is too manifestly absurd to be supported."[82]

But Virginia knew that a direct tax on carriages would be ridiculous and inequitable—it was the key component to their legal strategy. If direct taxes resulted in a reasonable, equitable distribution of the federal tax burden, then it would not really matter if the 1794 carriage tax was declared unconstitutional; Congress would just have to pass it again, this time with apportionment built into the bill, and the federal taxing power would remain robust. Yet because direct taxes did create inequality and absurdity, and were thus politically impracticable, it mattered that the Court declared the "indirect" carriage tax to be constitutional. Their decision in *Hylton v. US* not only upheld the constitutionality of congressional law but also maintained the federal government's ability to exercise a robust, concurrent tax power.

Hamilton's principle of broad construction helped him to defend the federal taxing powers from both national- and state-level challenges. Yet the treasury secretary also articulated a second principle in defense of the federal fiscal powers, though it is not nearly as well known: that federal securities should be considered as federal contracts, and that this contract status conferred tax immunity on the securities. Hamilton developed this second principle not because a state attempted to tax federal bonds but because Congress threatened to do so. In 1795, Hamilton offered this securities-as-contracts argument to convince federal lawmakers that preserving the sanctity and tax immunity of US bonds protected both the public credit and the national government's ability to borrow money.

Hamilton first made the argument that Congress should treat federal securities with the sanctity of a legal contract in 1790, when he opposed the suggestion that the federal government discriminate between original and current debt holders. In his first report on public credit, Hamilton denounced discrimination as "inconsistent with justice" and "a breach of contract; in violation of the rights of a fair purchaser."[83] Five years later, in his parting advice to Congress, the outgoing secretary reiterated this argument in his "Report on a Plan for the Further Support of Public Credit." This time, however, Hamilton was responding to four proposed House resolutions discussed during the previous spring. Two of the resolutions provided that any debts owed from American citizens to British subjects be sequestered and paid into the Treasury instead of to British creditors. The seized proceeds would be used to indemnify Americans who had suffered at the hands of privateers or who had their rights as neutrals violated by the British.[84] Although the proposed resolutions did not mention it specifically, Hamilton worried that Congress would also deny payment to British subjects holding federal securities, and he wanted to explicitly argue against such a policy before leaving office. The second set of resolutions called for a tax of 5 cents per every $100 to be levied on both transferred US bonds and Bank of the United States stock.[85]

In the third and final section of his 1795 report, Hamilton expressed his concerns over the 1794 resolutions. He bluntly asked, "Is there a right in the Government to tax its own funds?" before steadfastly denying that such a right existed. Premised on the implicit authority of a legislature to raise revenue from the property of the state, the supposed right of a government to tax its own funds would be, according to Hamilton, in violation of the contract made between the government debtor and citizen creditor, as well as in contradiction of the "maxims of credit."[86]

Federal securities were by nature federal contracts; a creditor loaned money to the federal government in exchange for interest paid on the money borrowed. The federal government in turn raised revenue through taxation in order to pay the creditor the principal and interest stipulated by the terms of the security. If, after the federal government issued these security contracts, it then decided to tax the debts held by foreign creditors or to claim a transactional fee every time a holder transferred their securities to another creditor, it would retrospectively violate the terms of the contract.[87] To charge a transfer tax or to otherwise tax the security itself would be tantamount to denying payment of the interest owed or principal borrowed. And "who," Hamilton exclaimed, "would not pronounce this to be a breach of contract, a fraud, which nothing could disguise?"[88]

Congress's proposals created an interesting tension between the power to tax and the power to borrow: if Congress had the constitutional authority to exercise both, then what was to stop Congress from taxing federal securities? When Hamilton balanced the federal government's authority to raise taxes against both its power to borrow and the moral and contractual obligations due to its creditors, he determined that the federal right to tax should be abridged:

> When a Government enters into contract with an individual, it deposes as to the matter of the contract its constitutional authority, and exchanges the Character of Legislator for that of a moral Agent, with the same rights and obligations as an individual. Its promises may be Justly considered as excepted out of its *power to legislate*, unless in aid of them. It is in Theory impossible to reconcile the two ideas of a *promise which obliges* with *a power to make Law which can vary the effect of it*. This is the great principle, that governs the question, and abridges the general right of the Government to lay taxes, by excepting out of it a species of property which subsists only in its promise. . . . If the Government had a right to tax its funds, the exercise of that right would cost much more than it was worth.[89]

Indeed, by proposing taxes on federal securities, Congress imperiled the restoration of the nation's credit and the federal government's practical ability to borrow in the future. What creditor would loan money to a government who could then reduce his return after the fact? Moreover, by infusing riskiness into the market for federal securities, Congress would drive up interest rates on the federal bonds and thus increase its own cost of borrowing. A federal tax on federal securities was thus bad on principle, and it was bad in practice.[90]

The Road to *Weston v. Charleston*

When appraising Alexander Hamilton's tenure in the Treasury Department, his combined efforts to make federal fiscal concurrence a lived reality stands out as the defining accomplishment of his career as a statesman. Hamilton's financial policies aimed to mobilize the federal government's fiscal powers, not only to restore the public credit but also to fight the possibility that a concurrent authority to tax and to borrow would eventually atrophy from disuse or underuse. While Hamilton acted as both lawmaker and energetic administrator, he also developed legal arguments to defend the federal government's concurrent powers to tax and to borrow. These principles, including broad construction and the tax immunity of federal securities, along with Hamilton's articulation of concurrence in *Federalist* No. 32, would reemerge long after Hamilton deployed them to become a lasting part of the jurisprudence of federalism.

The road to *Weston v. Charleston* demonstrates how, over time, Hamilton's "defensive" federalism became embedded in American constitutional law. In the early years of the nineteenth century, a change took place in the jurisprudence of fiscal concurrence. Congress and federal and state judges began to readily assert that the federal government's claims to tax, to borrow, and to exert its sovereign authority were supreme to those claims made by individual creditors or by the states. Although the supremacy clause had been in Article VI since 1787, jurists did not readily wield it because state legislation rarely clashed with exercises of federal sovereignty during the first years of the early republic. Yet in the first two decades of the nineteenth century, judges at both the state and federal levels began considering cases involving outright collisions of federal and state power. When lawyers brought these direct confrontations before state and federal courts, judges invoked federal supremacy, in addition to Hamilton's principles, to resolve the controversies before them, and ultimately to defend and uphold the federal government's fiscal powers.

Recall that when Hamilton championed federal concurrence in both the New York state ratifying convention and in his *Federalist* essays, he downplayed the likelihood that state and federal power would collide, suggesting that even if the two sovereigns did clash, the federal government had more to fear from state action than vice versa. Hamilton presented concurrence in language designed to ease the fears of New York's Anti-Federalists and to assure them that the states' preexisting authority to tax remained under the federal Constitution. Yet he still incorporated one rule into *Federalist*

No. 32 that suggested how state exercises of concurrent powers could regularly be subordinated to federal action. This rule—Hamilton's "repugnancy" caveat—posited that where the Constitution granted power to the federal government, if "a similar authority in the States would be absolutely and totally *contradictory* and *repugnant*," then the state's power would be alienated. As we will see, subsequent jurists would use this caveat to justify federal supremacy over the states' concurrent authority when state and federal power collided.[91]

As time passed, these collisions became more frequent, raising novel legal questions in their wake. In life, Hamilton did not take part in settling these conflicts, but in death, his past actions and writings set the terms for their resolution: Hamilton's articulation of concurrence lent the framework for the jurisprudential debate over how far, exactly, a state's sovereign, concurrent powers could extend when they challenged or overlapped with federal authority. *Federalist* No. 32 came to define the very nature of concurrence in American law, and according to Justice Joseph Story, the "correctness of these rules of interpretation has never been controverted; and they have been often recognized by the Supreme Court."[92]

Hamilton's *Federalist* No. 32 did not explicitly contemplate the kind of direct federal–state collisions that began to occur in the first few decades of the nineteenth century; in consequence, the lawyers and judges contemplating these controversies built on Hamiltonian concurrence—particularly his repugnancy caveat—by asserting federal supremacy over the states. Smith Thompson, an associate justice on the New York Supreme Court, described the principle of federal supremacy in an 1811 steamboat monopoly case, *Livingston v. Van Ingen*: "The only restriction upon the State government, in the exercise of all concurrent powers is, that the State must act in subordination to the general government."[93] Federal supremacy could be used as an absolute trump over state action (as John Marshall would do in *McCulloch v. Maryland*), but not necessarily. Thompson acknowledged the federal government's supreme authority to regulate patents and commerce, for example, but he still upheld the New York legislature's prerogative to grant exclusive navigation rights on state waterways. In this case, Thompson did not think that the state law interfered with the federal government's powers.

In *Livingston v. Van Ingen*, counsel for the respondents (the party lacking navigation privileges) argued that the New York act violated the federal government's Article I, section 8, authority to regulate commerce and to grant patents. But the state's highest appellate court disagreed. In his opinion for New York's Court for the Correction of Errors, Thompson explained, "It is not a sufficient reason for denying to the states the exercise of a power, that it may possibly interfere with the acts of the general government"—though, when a conflict did arise, states would "surrender the power" to the federal government. As for the act in question, the court determined that no "interference or collision of power" occurred.[94] In a concurring opinion, Chief Justice James Kent agreed with Thompson and affirmed that if New York's grant came "in collision with the actual exercise of some congressional power," then "state authority would so far be controlled, but it would still be good in all those respects in which it did not contravene the provision of the paramount law." To justify this, Kent cited Hamilton's repugnancy caveat, noting, "This construction of the powers of the federal compact has the authority of Mr. Hamilton."[95]

Livingston v. Van Ingen illustrates how Hamilton's articulation of concurrence set the framework for debating collisions of federal and state power in the early republic. Counsel for the respondents attempted to persuade the court that New York had no authority to grant exclusive access to commercial waterways. To do so, they contended that a concurrent legislative power in the states "must be either in conformity with that of Congress . . . and so nugatory, or else, in collision with, or contradictory to, the law of Congress, and so void." According to the respondents' counsel, including John Wells, John V. Henry, and Abraham Van Vechten, because Congress had exercised its power to regulate patents, the federal government's concurrent power became, in effect, an exclusive power. Van Ingen's attorneys did not explicitly cite *Federalist* No. 32 to make this argument, but they did credit their interpretation of the US Constitution to the former treasury secretary: "The true meaning of [concurrent legislative power] has been stated and explained by a very able commentator, an illustrious statesman and distinguished lawyer."[96]

Hamilton's description of concurrence in *Federalist* No. 32 could also align with the appellants' position. The counsel for Robert Livingston and Robert Fulton, the beneficiaries of New York's exclusive grant, argued that states always enjoyed a right to grant navigation privileges, and in absence of any constitutional language prohibiting or excluding this prerogative, the New York act was valid. Attorney Thomas Addis Emmet quoted Hamilton's rules of concurrence in order "to secure him on the side of the appellants, and avail myself of [Hamilton's] authority to show that some of the powers granted to Congress are concurrent." He dismissed Hamilton's repugnancy clause, however—the maxim most likely to undermine his argument—and deemed it "wholly unnecessary." Emmet focused instead on the fact that

Hamilton absolved any "occasional interferences in the policy of a branch of the administration" from qualifying as a constitutional repugnancy. Naturally, then, Emmet considered his clients' privileges to be nothing more than "an accidental or occasional interference" in federal policy.[97] Emmet would not convince the court to reject Hamilton's repugnancy caveat—Kent would cite it as authoritative—but he was ultimately persuasive; the court upheld the appellants' exclusive privileges as constitutional.

Judges and lawyers continued to rely on Hamiltonian concurrence when considering a spate of federal cases concerning sovereignty and concurrence after *Livingston*. In *Houston v. Moore*, for example, the US Supreme Court referred to *Federalist* No. 32 in order to uphold Pennsylvania's power to regulate its state militia, and in *Gibbons v. Ogden*, counsel from both parties relied on Hamiltonian concurrence to discuss competing state and federal claims to regulate steamboats on interstate waters.[98] When considering these cases, along with other commerce-related lawsuits, the Marshall Court often used federal supremacy as a trump to the state's concurrent power, voiding state law where the Court thought that the state's action directly collided with federal law. However, the Court would sometimes allow the states to exercise a concurrent power—to pass bankruptcy laws, for example—if Congress had not yet legislated on the matter.[99]

Though Congress did not pass much commercial legislation during the early national period, it did assert the federal government's fiscal supremacy as early as 1797. In that year, Congress passed an act making the United States the preferred creditor over any other creditor in bankruptcy proceedings, thus establishing that no matter how many creditors awaited payment from an insolvent debtor, the federal government would be paid back first.[100] By enacting this law, Congress quietly revised what Hamilton had promised his fellow delegates in convention: that the federal government would follow a "first-come, first-served" protocol, as one of many creditors waiting to receive payment.

The assignees of one insolvent debtor tested the constitutionality of this preferred-creditor status in litigation culminating in *US v. Fisher*.[101] In this case, Peter Blight was indebted to the United States before becoming insolvent, and after his death, the federal government brought suit to establish the priority of its claims to Blight's estate. Although the Pennsylvania Circuit Court denied the federal government's first-priority claims, the US Supreme Court upheld the plaintiff's preferred status and the act establishing it. To do so, the Court used federal supremacy to resolve the concurrent creditor conflict arising explicitly between the federal government and individual creditors, as well as implicitly between the federal and state governments. The Court also applied Hamiltonian broad construction to uphold the act and to defend the federal power to borrow.

Chief Justice Marshall wrote the opinion for the court. First, echoing Hamilton's arguments in defense of the bank, Marshall affirmed that "Congress must possess the choice of means, and must be empowered to use any means which are in fact conducive to the exercise of a power granted by the constitution." The Constitution grants a robust power to tax and to borrow, and thus it also permits the federal government to vigorously collect revenue to pay back its debts: "The government is to pay the debt of the union, and must be authorized to use the means which appear to itself most eligible to effect that object." In other words, Marshall relied on Hamilton's principle of broad construction to defend those means (tax collection and Congress's asserted preferred-creditor status) that the federal government used to exercise its constitutional taxing and borrowing powers.[102]

Marshall then went one step further. Taking note of the states' concurrent authority to collect on debts owed to them, Marshall added, "This claim of priority on the part of the United States will, it has been said, interfere with the right of the state sovereignties respecting the dignity of debts, and will defeat the measures they have a right to adopt to secure themselves against delinquencies on the part of their own revenue officers." Yet Marshall would not allow the states' sovereign authority to impair the federal government's ability to enact reasonable means to exercise its own constitutional authority. This was an "objection to the constitution itself," he wrote. "The mischief suggested, so far as it can really happen, is the necessary consequence of the supremacy of the laws of the United States on all subjects to which the legislative power of Congress extends."[103]

In *US v. Fisher*, the Marshall Court used Hamiltonian broad construction to defend the federal government's power to borrow money and to pay it back, and added a dash of federal supremacy to further justify the national government's preferred-creditor status. Of course, a direct collision between the federal and state governments could also have been resolved in the first-come, first-served manner that Hamilton proposed to the New York ratifying convention. But if Congress had already declared federal claims to be supreme, then Marshall could not resist the opportunity to uphold national law with Article VI's supremacy clause.

Years later, when reflecting back on the significance of Marshall's decision in *Fisher*, James Kent concluded, "It would seem, therefore, that the concurrent power of legislation in the states is, not an independent, but a subordinate and dependent power, liable, in many cases, to be extinguished, and in all cases to be postponed, to the paramount or supreme law of the union, whenever the federal and the state regulations interfere with each other."[104] With Marshall's decision in *Fisher*, federal supremacy, along with Hamilton's more subtle repugnancy caveat, had been successfully integrated into constitutional law, and subsequent litigation would only affirm this doctrine.

The fiscal controversy at the heart of *US v. Fisher* arose between the federal government and an individual, not between the federal government and a state. Thus, though *Fisher* had implications for federal and state creditor collisions, no state had actually challenged the federal government's preferred-creditor status in the litigation. *McCulloch v. Maryland* presented a wholly novel challenge to the courts, however, as the case involved an actual, direct collision between a state's sovereign, concurrent power to tax and the federal government's presumably sovereign power to erect a corporation (which in turn allowed the federal government to exercise its taxing and borrowing powers). *McCulloch* required the first true judicial defense of the federal government's concurrent fiscal powers.

In 1817, the state of Maryland needed to raise revenue and thus decided to tax the notes of all banks not chartered in Maryland, including the Baltimore branch of the second Bank of the United States.[105] The bank's branch manager, James McCulloch, refused to pay the tax, and as a result, Maryland sued to collect the taxes owed. When the case reached the US Supreme Court, Marshall combined a number of Hamiltonian principles, plus a full-throated assertion of federal supremacy doctrine, to declare the Maryland tax unconstitutional and void.

In oral argument, Hamilton's ghost pervaded the courtroom. Counsel for McCulloch, including Daniel Webster, US attorney general William Wirt, and William Pinkney, relied on Hamilton's opinion on the constitutionality of the first Bank of the United States to argue that the federal government had the constitutional authority to erect a corporation. But counsel for Maryland relied on Hamilton even more.

Maryland's attorneys, including Luther Martin (the state attorney general), Joseph Hopkinson of Pennsylvania, and Walter Jones of Washington, DC, countered the plaintiff-in-error's claims by exploring Hamiltonian concurrence and its implications for the controversy at hand. Hopkinson quoted the text of *Federalist* No. 32 directly, focusing on passages where Hamilton affirmed that the right of taxation in the states was inviolable—except for duties on imports and exports. To Hopkinson, then, Hamilton's interpretation of the US Constitution clearly intended for the states to retain this authority "in the most absolute and unqualified sense; and that an attempt on the part of the national government to abridge them in the exercise of it, would be a violent assumption of power, unwarranted by any article or clause of its constitution."[106] Furthermore, Hamilton clearly asserted, in *Federalist* No. 34, that the states "would have CO EQUAL authority with the Union, in the article of revenue, except as to duties on imports."[107] Hopkinson even cited a federal statute authorizing a federal tax on state banknotes as evidence of the constitutionality of Maryland's tax and the state's truly concurrent taxing powers. With on-point quotations like these coming from Alexander Hamilton, no less, Hopkinson, Jones, and Martin had no shortage of authoritative commentary to bring to the Court's attention.

After reading from *The Federalist*, as well as from the New York and Virginia ratifying debates, Maryland's attorney general, Luther Martin, also noted that the plaintiff-in-error's arguments—that the supremacy of federal law abridges the state's taxing authority—ran wholly contrary to the promises made by Federalists in these preratification debates. Hamilton, and others, denied that the Constitution "contained a vast variety of powers, lurking under the generality of its phraseology, which would prove highly dangerous to . . . the rights of the States"—yet was this not exactly what opposing counsel contended?[108] Martin implored the Court to resist the urge to depart from the Federalists' early interpretations of the US Constitution and to uphold Hamilton's own exposition of concurrence.

Of course, John Marshall would have none of this. Because Maryland relied so heavily on Hamiltonian concurrence, however, Marshall had to distinguish between Hamilton as the authority on broad construction, the power to erect a bank, and the meaning of the necessary and proper clause versus Hamilton as the authority on the state's absolute right to exercise concurrent taxing powers. To do this, Marshall noted that the times had changed, and in his day, Hamilton did not address the same sort of federal–state collisions that the federal and state courts now encountered with regularity (this was true for Hamilton's articulation of concurrence). Marshall thus dismissed Maryland's invocation of Hamiltonian concurrence as not quite relevant to the present collision of federal and state authority:

> The objections to the constitution [noted in Hamilton's *Federalist* essays on taxation] . . . were *to the undefined power of the government to tax*, not to the incidental privilege of exempting its own measures from State taxation. The consequences apprehended from this undefined

power were, that it would absorb all the objects of taxation, "to the exclusion and destruction of the State governments." The arguments of the *Federalist* are intended to prove the fallacy of these apprehensions; not to prove that the government was incapable of executing any of its powers, without exposing the means it employed to the embarrassments of State taxation.[109]

The chief justice acknowledged that the states retained their concurrent taxing powers under the US Constitution, just like Hamilton promised, but decided that because Hamilton's commentary on concurrence addressed a fundamentally different scenario than *McCulloch* did, Hamilton would object to the present conclusions drawn from his essays by the state of Maryland.[110] Undoubtedly Marshall was right; Hamilton would not have meant for his 1788 comments to justify such a direct threat to the federal government's fiscal sovereignty.

Thus, while it remained true for Marshall that the states retained their concurrent taxing powers, it was also true that the federal government had acted within its sovereign authority to charter a bank. Therefore, because federal law was the supreme law of the land, and because Maryland's tax was "on the operations of the bank, and is, consequently, a tax on the operation of an instrument employed by the government of the Union to carry its powers into execution," Maryland's tax on the second Bank of the United States could not stand.[111] While composing the Court's unanimous opinion, the chief justice borrowed from Alexander Hamilton's past legal arguments so directly that Marshall must have had Hamilton's "Opinion on the Constitutionality of an Act to Establish a Bank" open on his desk. Marshall concurred with Hamilton's defense of the bank and his arguments in *Hylton*, and restated, almost word for word, Hamilton's principle of broad construction to interpret Article I, section 8, clauses to justify the federal government's implied power to erect a corporation. Just as he did in *US v. Fisher*, Marshall virtually quoted Hamilton's legal maxim that as long as the ends are legitimate, any related, relevant, and nonprohibited means may be used by the federal government to exercise its constitutional powers.[112]

Livingston v. Van Ingen, US v. Fisher, and *McCulloch v. Maryland* demonstrate how, after his death, Hamilton's arguments in support of a "defensive" federalism had become loudly articulated in and fully integrated into the jurisprudence of American federalism. Hamiltonian concurrence provided the legal language and standard for discussing all manner of federal and state collisions; in fact, Hamilton's *Federalist* No. 32 had become such an authority that John Marshall had to specifically acknowledge Hamilton's state-centric arguments and distinguish them from the Court's decision in *McCulloch*. Also, the Marshall Court regularly used Hamilton's principle of broad construction to uphold federal laws, particularly those that maintained the federal fiscal authority, like erecting a bank and claiming a preferred-creditor status. Though Hamilton did not assert federal supremacy as strongly as the federal and state courts would in the nineteenth century, his repugnancy caveat created enough legal and intellectual space so that judges could assert federal supremacy without contradicting the rest of Hamiltonian concurrence.

With its direct collision between the fiscal powers of the state versus those of the federal government, *McCulloch* was one of two directly on-point legal precedents to influence the Court's decision in *Weston v. Charleston*. The other case, *Bulow and Potter v. The City Council of Charleston*, arose in South Carolina, but it never made it into the federal courts. During the second decade of the nineteenth century, Charleston's city council passed an ordinance that laid a tax on all bank stock held within the city, except those exempted from taxation by legislation. The exemptions did not exclude stock from the second Bank of the United States, and in *Bulow*, the question before South Carolina's Constitutional Court of Appeals was whether the city could tax Bank of the United States stock held by individuals. In a 3–1 decision, the South Carolina court said that it could. Reasoning that Charleston's tax applied to the individual property owner rather than to the bank itself, the majority opinion acknowledged that *McCulloch* immunized the bank from a state tax, but it correctly held that Chief Justice Marshall did not intend for his decision to extend to individuals who owned stock in the bank.[113] The court held that "the interest of the *United States* and the *individual stockholders* are distinct and independent," and thus the state—or, in this case, the city—retained its authority to assess any and all "legitimate subjects of taxation," including Bank of the United States stock.[114]

One South Carolinian justice dissented, however. Justice Abraham Nott suspected that the federal courts might interpret the majority's decision as an unconstitutional challenge to federal authority. Any tax levied on securities made those investments look less attractive. (Hamilton made this argument about the Boston tax and Congress's proposed bond resolutions.) Therefore, if a state or local government taxed securities related to or derived from sovereign federal law, then that tax directly—if not deliberately—defeated "the object intended to be effected by Congress." Nott most likely had Hamilton, Marshall, and Kent in mind when he noted that all commentators on the US

Constitution concurred that "where the *exercise of any power* by a State is *inconsistent* or *incompatible with* such delegation, it must be considered as *exclusively* granted to the general government."[115] In other words, the states were constitutionally prohibited from interfering with the federal government's sovereign powers, concurrence notwithstanding.

With *Bulow* on the books in 1818, only five years passed before the Charleston City Council was at it again. In 1823, the council passed another ordinance, this time assessing the "six and seven per cent stock of the United States" held by Charleston residents. Rather than tax privately owned stock issued by a federally incorporated bank, this time, Charleston taxed US bonds. This was a significant departure from past practice. In *Bulow*, the court could reasonably claim that enough separation existed between a local tax laid on individually held bank securities and the sovereignty of the Congress chartering the bank to prevent state interference with federal authority. No such claim could be made under the new ordinance, however, as Charleston now potentially threatened the federal government's ability "to borrow money on the credit of the United States." Plowden Weston, along with other holders of US securities, decided to challenge the city ordinance in court, but he lost in both Charleston's court of common pleas and South Carolina's highest court of appeals. Weston would eventually prevail in the Marshall Court.[116]

A divided US Supreme Court handed down its decision in *Weston v. Charleston*, and Marshall spoke for the majority. In his opinion, Marshall put together a Hamiltonian defense of the power to borrow, resting his arguments on the contractual nature of federal securities, federal supremacy, and the importance of an unrestricted federal borrowing power to the maintenance of the public credit. Echoing Hamilton's defense of the federal borrowing power in his "Report on a Plan for the Further Support of Public Credit," Marshall declared, "The tax in question is a tax upon the contract subsisting between the government and the individual," and this contract was intimately related to the government's power to borrow money. The power to tax was "one of the most essential to a state, and one of the most extensive in its operation." Yet for Marshall, it was "not the want of original power in an independent sovereign state" that restrains Charleston from taxing US securities, but rather the fact that the local tax interfered with the federal borrowing power. When federal and state actions collide, the supremacy of federal law trumps the state's authority. "The American people," Marshall explained, "have conferred the power of borrowing money on their government, and by making that government supreme, have shielded its action, in the exercise of this power, from the action of the local governments." Therefore, "the tax on government stock is thought by this Court to be a tax on the contract, a tax on the power to borrow money on the credit of the United States, and consequently to be repugnant to the constitution."[117]

Marshall avoided any explicit discussions of Hamiltonian concurrence by referring his reader to the Court's previous comments on *Federalist* No. 32 in *McCulloch*. Yet dissenting Associate Justice Smith Thompson, who, when presiding on the New York Supreme Court, had concurred in *Livingston v. Van Ingen*, would not let this omission slide. Thompson thought that Charleston did not tax the "means used by the government to carry on its operation" but only assessed *"property acquired through one of the means employed by the government to carry on its operations, viz.* the power of borrowing money upon the credit of the United States."[118] Also, *Weston* did not overturn *Bulow*, and Thompson failed to see any distinction between US securities and Bank of the United States securities, as both qualified to him as private property acquired through federal means, rather than as the means themselves.

To support his opinion, Thompson turned again to Hamilton's words in *Federalist* No. 32, noting that they were "often referred to as a work of high authority" on questions of federal power. Thompson observed that "the author has seldom been charged with surrendering any powers that can be brought fairly within the letter or spirit of the constitution," so surely Hamilton anticipated that the national government exercise its power to borrow money, and as a result create US securities. Yet "it never entered into the discriminating mind of the writer . . . that merely investing property, subject to taxation, in stock of the United States, would withdraw the property from taxation." Thompson was thus unconvinced that Hamiltonian concurrence addressed a fundamentally different type of federal–state conflict; to him, Hamilton was clever enough to foresee the dispute at issue in *Weston*, and thus if Hamilton thought a state tax on federal bonds unconstitutional, he would have said as much.[119]

Thompson was wrong on this last point, however. Hamilton encountered a *Weston*-like scenario in 1791, when Boston taxed federal securities, and he thought then that the tax was ill-advised and refused to comply. Furthermore, when Congress threatened to interfere with US securities during the French Revolutionary wars, Hamilton argued, just as Marshall would in *Weston*, that US bonds should be treated as contracts, thus inferring that the securities enjoy a tax-immune status. For Hamilton, these arguments not only sought to maintain the nation's creditworthiness but also protected the federal government's ability to exercise its borrowing powers in the future. Thus, Hamilton had experience, rather than simply foresight, regarding the legality of taxes imposed on federal securities. Still, he was never called on to articulate a legal response to the constitutionality of a state tax on federal securities, and that is why Thompson would not find Hamilton commenting on the matter.

Even though Hamilton would have agreed with Marshall rather than Thompson in *Weston v. Charleston*, Thompson's dissent demonstrates just how extensively Hamilton's legal principles had permeated American constitutional law. In the cases concerning federal–state concurrence, Hamilton often provided legal arguments for both parties involved—for the advocates of the state sovereignty and for those in favor of federal supremacy. Hamilton's legal defense of the federal fiscal powers had become a foundational part of the jurisprudence of federalism.

Alexander Hamilton's Defensive Federalism

While *Weston v. Charleston* is most often overlooked by modern scholars, the US Supreme Court never forgot the principles of federalism at issue in the case. When contemplating the nature of American federalism in the wake of the Civil War, for example, the Chase Court looked to both *McCulloch* and *Weston* in order to determine that a federal income tax could not be levied on state officials. In *Collector v. Day*, a ruling that echoed Hamilton's defense of the federal fiscal powers, the Court decided that the national government could not tax the "means or instrumentalities" used by the states for "carrying on the operations of their governments" or for "preserving their existence."[120]

Over twenty years later, the Supreme Court again looked to the fiscal defense principles adopted in *McCulloch*, *Weston*, and *Collector v. Day* to consider whether a federal income tax levied in part on state and local municipal bonds was constitutional. In *Pollock v. Farmers Loan & Trust Co.*, the Fuller Court cited *Weston* directly to explain why a federal tax on state bonds was unconstitutional: "We have unanimously held in [*Weston*] that, so far as this law operates on the receipts from municipal bonds, it cannot be sustained, because it is a tax on the power of the States, and on their instrumentalities to borrow money, and consequently repugnant to the Constitution."[121] The main question before the Court in *Pollock* was whether Congress's nonapportioned income tax violated the Constitution's direct-tax clauses; because the majority thought that it did, the *Pollock* decision overturned *Hylton v. US*'s narrower definition of a direct tax. Still, over a century after Alexander Hamilton recommended various federal taxes in his first report on public credit and endorsed the federal taxing power in *Hylton*, the US Supreme Court continued to look to his defense of the federal fiscal powers for guidance.

Hamilton's fiscal defense principles thus became inseparable from the jurisprudence of federalism that developed during the long nineteenth century. By recognizing and reconstructing the various components of Hamilton's fiscal defense, we see that his influence over the establishment of the public credit extended far beyond his various reports, which have become the focal point of many historical analyses of Hamilton's accomplishments. Yet the first treasury secretary achieved the restoration and maintenance of the public credit just as much by legal strategy as by policy proposal. Both his lawmaking and lawyering strategies had a lasting effect, but as *Collector* and *Pollock* demonstrate, Hamilton's legal principles outlasted his proposed taxes, his funded national debt, and his central bank.

Alexander Hamilton's defense of the federal fiscal powers also helps us understand how constitutional law developed during the early national period. Hamilton offered specific legal arguments that the Marshall Court adapted into its adjudication of federal–state questions, and Hamiltonian concurrence became the legal framework undergirding discussions of federalism in state and federal courts, for both national and states-oriented litigants. The ubiquity of Hamiltonian concurrence can seem to be a puzzling reality, however. If Hamilton was perceived, then and now, as "the most nationalist of all nationalists in his interpretation of the clauses of our federal Constitution," and if Marshall followed his lead, then why did Hamilton's articulation of concurrence become the standard authority on both sides of the aisle for resolving federal–state conflicts?[122]

Because Secretary Hamilton set key precedents, he became the natural expert on the matter. Hamilton was the first to articulate a widely disseminated explanation of concurrence, and he was the first administrator to give it meaning and scope through practice. Crucially, however, Hamilton's emphasis on preserving federal power persisted in law, even when the nature of the challenges arising from the American federal system changed over time. Hamilton's emphasis on the defense and preservation of federal power suggests why he had such a long-lasting influence on questions of federalism: Hamilton did not advocate for overly aggressive federal power but rather for the constitutionally authorized federal power contemplated by the Framers and ratified by the people in convention. Hamiltonian concurrence did not aim to trump the states but to balance a newly vigorous federal power with the preexisting vigor of the states.

Therefore, Hamilton's legal strategy was inherently defensive, rather than offensive, in its contemplation of national authority, and this had implications for the subsequent jurisprudence built from Hamiltonian foundations. When a seemingly aggressive decision like *McCulloch v. Maryland* is considered in a larger jurisprudential context relating to Hamiltonian concurrence, *Hylton*, *Fisher*, and *Weston*, the decision becomes less an assertion of "aggressive nationalism" and more a statement of Hamiltonian defensive federalism.[123]

Like any judge trained in the common law, Marshall built his opinions in *Fisher*, *McCulloch*, and *Weston* from the legal principles and decisions preceding them: the Court's adoption of broad construction in *Hylton*, the learned commentary of Publius, and Hamilton's brief on the constitutionality of a central bank. But because these cases directly involved or contemplated the collision between federal and state fiscal powers, Marshall applied precedent with the added element of federal supremacy to defend the federal government's taxing and borrowing powers and to resolve the impasse. The seeds of this defensive federalism came directly from Hamilton, and by applying the secretary's legal arguments, the Marshall Court embedded Hamilton's defense of the federal fiscal powers even deeper into American constitutional law. If Alexander Hamilton developed his defense of the federal fiscal powers to restore the nation's creditworthiness, then the Marshall Court ensured that the public credit could always be maintained.

❧

FIVE

"A Most Valuable Auxiliary": Securing Foreign Capital with the Law of the Land

Alexander Hamilton often emphasized trade, banking, and manufacturing interests when he spoke of his commercial vision for the young republic, but he, like Washington and Jefferson, was also interested in maximizing the productive uses of American land and natural resources. For example, Secretary Hamilton and Tench Coxe, the assistant secretary of the treasury, established the Society for Establishing Useful Manufactures, a private, government-sponsored corporation in order to leverage the mechanical power of the Passaic River's Great Falls for mill operations. Hamilton also identified the "Interests of Agriculture" along with those of "Commerce & Manufactures" as highly promising areas of growth for American economic development. Although commerce often took place overseas or across stock exchanges and money markets, agricultural production, manufacturing ventures, and commercial intercourse in everyday goods and services relied on the plentiful resources gleaned from the nation's vast terrain. Hamilton viewed land as an important resource that could be leveraged to create his thriving commercial republic; yet in order to realize the untapped agricultural, manufacturing, and commercial potential of both settled and sparsely populated lands, the United States required a large infusion of capital. To find this investment capital, Hamilton looked across the Atlantic Ocean.[1]

In his 1791 "Report on Manufactures," Secretary Hamilton made the case for attracting foreign capital to Congress by describing its "instrumentality." Foreign investment enhanced "not only our funds"—those critical European loans that first floated American independence and then funded and refinanced its lingering war debts—but also strengthened American commerce. Already, Hamilton affirmed, "our Agriculture and other internal improvements have been animated by it." Rather than fearing foreign investment as an external menace to rival American interests, the treasury secretary encouraged Congress to consider foreign funds as "a most valuable auxiliary" because "in a Country situated like the United States, with an infinite fund of resources yet to be unfolded, every farthing of foreign capital . . . is a precious acquisition." In time, Hamilton imagined, foreign investments would strengthen and improve American manufacturing as well as "the Public Communications, by cutting canals, opening the obstructions in Rivers and erecting bridges."[2] During his lifetime, Hamilton would, in fact, witness European capitalists investing in American public works projects such as canal building in New York, Virginia, and Pennsylvania. But he personally participated in and encouraged a different sort of foreign capital transaction: the buying, selling, and securing of title to American land.

Speculative land frenzies perpetuated by both foreign and domestic investors helped to define, inflate, and depress economic development in the early republic (in addition to other speculative ventures, like the scrip mania surrounding Bank of the United States stock).[3] This agitation to buy land, then quickly resell it at a profit, attracted the more preeminent statesmen and financiers of the era, and it caused no small number of ruined livelihoods and an even greater amount of stints in debtors' prison. Even Hamilton briefly joined the ranks of the statesmen as speculators like Washington, Jefferson, and Robert Morris when he purchased a small parcel of land in western New York (part of a large tract owned first by American speculator extraordinaire Alexander Macomb).[4] Land speculation produced surveyed and parceled-out plots, as well as some commercial profits (particularly for the politicians and lawyers like Hamilton who negotiated, advised, and transacted the complicated land sales). However, the frenzy for buying and then quickly reselling unimproved land was not an ideal use for foreign capital. Instead, Hamilton hoped that foreign funds would underwrite long-term settlement or would encourage agricultural, commercial, or manufacturing ventures that would in turn lead to American economic prosperity.

A crucial component to establishing Hamilton's vision of economic development was securing long-term foreign investment in the young republic. By the time Hamilton left the Treasury in 1795, Dutch, French, English, and even some Spanish investors had already poured millions of dollars into a diversified portfolio of American investments, including American independence (with principal and interest, a total of $11,710,378 financed by foreign loans), US treasury notes (the product of Hamilton's funding and assumption scheme), Bank of the United States stock (another Hamiltonian venture), private canal and navigation companies, and New England, Maine, and Ohio Valley land ventures.[5] Land speculators often focused solely on making quick profits, but if those proprietors invested their money for a longer term, then the foreign capital could become the "valuable auxiliary" Hamilton intended. Time was needed so that land titles and all conflicting claims could be quieted, and the land itself could be properly surveyed, parceled out with care, improved, and gradually sold to yeomen farmers, merchants, or manufacturers.

As a practicing attorney in the heyday of American land speculation, Hamilton facilitated some speculative ventures, but he also devoted much time and effort using the law as a tool to assist a group of Dutch proprietors as they secured long-term investments in New York state lands. As we have seen, Hamilton leveraged the concurrent judicial and legislative authority shared by the national and state governments to exercise robust fiscal powers and to build a thriving commercial republic; in order to attract productive foreign capital, Hamilton again relied on the concurrent federal and state jurisdictions to accomplish his statecraft. At the national level, Hamilton used the policy-making opportunities provided by his office, as well as through Congress's borrowing powers, through the federal courts, and through his efforts to cultivate a federal magistracy, to attract stable, long-term foreign investment in land. And though the federal government proved crucial to the task of selling western lands, Hamilton also counted on the states as sovereign jurisdictions to facilitate foreign investment within their dominions.

That Hamilton relied on sovereign state powers to accomplish his statecraft runs counter to the notion—born from his focus on strengthening the national government—that throughout his career, he utterly disdained and dismissed the authority of the states. Hamilton took every opportunity, so goes this notion, to clothe the national government with extraordinary (even supraconstitutional) authority, refusing sovereign power to the states, and thus diminishing them to mere provincial municipalities.[6] While Hamilton may have seriously considered a severe diminution of state authority—even the abolition of the states—to be a viable option in the 1787 constitutional convention, he dismissed it as soon as the US Constitution formally created a federal system of delegated national powers.[7] The diminution of the states had no significant place in his post-Constitution legal thought. Rather, Hamilton's professed and practiced constitutionalism consistently upheld the sovereignty of the states, in context with the newly enlarged sovereignty of the national government. Alexander Hamilton was, after all, the chief exponent and theoretician of judicial and legislative concurrence—and, as demonstrated by his practice and application of American law, he advocated for robust national power while preserving concurrent and sovereign state authority. After ratification, Hamilton recognized that the state and national governments were no longer locked in a zero-sum power struggle; state authority could be plentiful and strong at the same time that federal powers were robust because of the guiding blueprint provided by the US Constitution.

Therefore, when it came to advancing Hamilton's favored policy of attracting foreign investment, the states in general, and New York state in particular, provided equally instrumental, if not more effective, jurisdictions to accomplish his statecraft compared to the national level. While the federal government presided over western territories and lands ceded from the states, the states controlled the law of the land within their boundaries. This meant that state legislatures and state courts set the rules for selling, buying, using, and improving the land that was, in the early republic era, closest to commercial ports (New Orleans excluded), to Atlantic markets, and to a mobile population. The states controlled the land that would be first settled and first connected with existing commercial markets and infrastructure.

Inherited English law, as modified by American statutes, controlled the disposition of this agriculturally and commercially viable land within the states. And as a highly sought-after land lawyer, Alexander Hamilton understood that New York, the state in which he practiced, provided a particularly advantageous legal environment to secure foreign investments because it had a powerful tool to sort out and adjudicate complex land transactions: a vibrant law of equity and a powerful, stand-alone Court of Chancery.

Although the rules governing the use and disposition of land derived mainly from the common law, the colonies turned states also inherited equity, a body of law that complemented the common law and sought to right wrongs or to give remedies in circumstances where the common law was too rigid or too poorly equipped to do justice. In practice, equity developed in England as a competing jurisdiction to the common law courts, and to attract litigants, courts of equity acknowledged legal rights and interests unknown to the common law. One particularly significant branch of land law developed in the English High Court of Chancery to govern trusts, a wholly novel legal relationship structuring land use, which developed unknown to and therefore unacknowledged by common law.

In his *Commentaries on Equity Jurisprudence*, Justice Joseph Story described trusts, a highly useful Chancery invention, in their broadest sense: a trust was "an equitable right, title, or interest in property, real or personal, distinct from the legal ownership thereof." He then clarified, "In other words, the legal owner holds the direct and absolute dominion over the property in the view of the [common] law; but the income, profits, or benefits thereof in his hands, belong wholly, or in part, to others."[8] By developing the trust relationship, equity acknowledged and upheld property rights and interests of parties who did not actually own the property according to the rules of the common law.

In New York, the Court of Chancery provided equitable rights to land users to counteract the stringent limitations placed on land transactions at common law. At common law, for example, aliens could not legally own land outright; the state could always move against the alien and divest him of the property. Therefore, foreign investors interested in purchasing allodial land (that is, property held in freehold ownership, without any landlord or tenurial obligations attached to it) could not simply acquire lands in the state without first getting the state legislature to pass a statute exempting the aliens from the common law prohibition.[9] Then, as now, lobbying for such an exemption took time and money, and it was subject to an ever-shifting political climate, making private statutes an unreliable method to subvert the common law ban on alien land ownership. Therefore, Alexander Hamilton used a combination of trusts and other equitable interests as tools to strategically skirt around and supplement this legal limitation in order to secure long-term foreign investment in the state's available lands.

By examining in detail how Hamilton used equity principles to secure and quiet titles for one prominent foreign client, Dutch financiers organized as the Holland Land Company, we can also see Hamilton's broader influence over the development of equitable interests in American law. Hamilton's legal strategy on behalf of the Holland Land Company was affected by, and must be framed against, his separate efforts to develop and to innovate upon the legal and equitable principles governing mortgages (a legal device that was simultaneously a covenant or debt obligation enforceable at common law and a trust acknowledged in equity). By pursuing his policy goal at both the federal and state levels, Alexander Hamilton harnessed the powers of both jurisdictions to attract and secure foreign capital investment in the new nation. By developing the tools of American chancery courts, Hamilton created lasting changes in the law of the land.

The Federal Magistracy and the Law of the Land

In ways familiar to us, Hamilton helped to secure foreign investment in the United States using a set of preferred legal tools to accomplish his statecraft. When it came to disposing of land in economically productive ways, the federal government controlled western lands and territories, and the states presided over the sale of lands within their own borders. In the early republic, the state and federal governments had generally concurrent powers to dispose of lands and to secure foreign capital within their wholly separate jurisdictions. This general concurrence included adjudicating land disputes. In these types of cases, both the state courts and the federal courts (under diversity jurisdiction) had concurrent authority to hear claims made by citizens of different states or by aliens.[10] Hamilton appeared in federal court to defend New York's sovereignty in a series of land-related diversity cases, but he found the experience frustrating and detrimental to his client's interests.[11] He had more success in state court. Still, the federal government had substantial authority to adjudicate land claims as well as to attract foreign capital, and Hamilton exercised these powers when he served in the Treasury. As treasury secretary, Hamilton worked to secure foreign investment in the new nation at the federal level before representing the Holland Land Company's interests in New York.

Throughout his tenure as treasury secretary, Hamilton arranged for the nation's foreign debt to be serviced and refinanced, effectively paying down wartime debts contracted with Spain and France with new loans floated mainly from the Netherlands.[12] Prioritizing the complete and timely payment of foreign debts under the new constitutional republic became the crucial way for the United States to establish and maintain its creditworthiness abroad—a fact that both Hamilton and the first Congresses recognized. While managing the payment of these foreign monies owed abroad, Hamilton developed a relationship with the Dutch bankers who, when organized in partnership as the Holland Land Company, would later become his clients.[13]

Although Hamilton's posttreasury law practice focused on securing landed investments for his foreign clients, while in office, Hamilton's economic policies enticed European investors to invest heavily in US government securities.[14] British and Dutch bankers also invested in a portfolio of

American corporate stocks, which included the Bank of the United States, various state banks, and the growing number of insurance and turnpike/canal corporations. By 1803, the value of US corporate stocks held by foreigners totaled $48.4 million, or 33 percent of the outstanding corporate stocks floated in the US domestic market.[15]

Investors from both Holland and England speculated heavily in American lands, though the Dutch considered their land investments in Maine, Pennsylvania, and New York, as well as their corporate investments in mills and road and canal companies, to be long-term.[16] Given that foreign capital was hard at work underwriting American creditworthiness, commercial development, and land surveyance, Hamilton must have been pleased; these were the productive outcomes he imagined in his "Report on Manufactures." As an added bonus, if US government lands could be sold to foreign or domestic buyers, then the money raised from the land sales would also help to pay down the existing debt.

Although western land sales were sluggish during the 1790s, Hamilton considered vacant federal lands to be assets that, if managed properly, could add a valuable revenue stream into the US Treasury. After Congress directed the treasury secretary in January 1790 "to report to this House on a uniform system for the disposition of lands and property of the United States," Hamilton responded with a short, detailed list of how the national lands could be productively managed and sold. At the top of Hamilton's list was "that no land shall be sold, except such, in respect to which the titles of the Indian tribes shall have been previously extinguished"—that is, the federal government should deal only in secure and quiet titles. In the rest of his report, he advised and anticipated land sales on credit, land commissioners adjudicating "controversies concerning rights to patents or grants of land," and above all, vesting "a considerable latitude of discretion" in the executive commissioners staffing the federal land office. As befitting the chief proponent of the federal magistracy, Hamilton emphasized that ample executive discretion was needed to skillfully manage the complexities of land sales. He reminded Congress that land-office legislation must "leave room for accommodating to circumstances which cannot, beforehand, be accurately appreciated." This suggested foresight to accommodate executive discretion was made in an effort to "avoid the danger of those obstructions and embarrassments in the execution, which would be to be apprehended from an endeavor at greater precision and more exact detail."[17]

From his post in the Treasury, Hamilton thus helped to direct federal policy in order to attract foreign capital and to manage the sale of federal lands. The federal executive and judicial departments also contributed to these policy goals through their efforts to quiet and secure titles to lands caught up in the private land disputes and interstate boundary controversies that arose in the early national era.

Interstate boundary disputes plagued the states before and under the Articles of Confederation, and they proved crucial in shaping the federal system created by the US Constitution.[18] The land-dispute court authorized by Article IX of the Articles of Confederation gave way to the enhanced jurisdiction of the US Constitution's Article III federal courts, which Alexander Hamilton helped to define while sitting on the committee of style during the Philadelphia Convention.[19] Thus, land controversies had already led to increased national power by the end of the 1780s. Because the federal courts now had jurisdiction over most interstate land disputes, and because the national government controlled the sale of western lands, land controversies provided the Supreme Court and federal circuit courts with significant opportunities to weigh in on public land policy.

Once Congress passed its first post-Constitution land statute in 1796, the federal courts began adjudicating real property disputes arising from inaccurate surveys and contested land claims.[20] These intricate and lengthy proceedings often took years to resolve, and according to administrative law scholar Jerry L. Mashaw, they constituted "the largest single category of substantive nonconstitutional cases on the Supreme Court's docket between 1815 and 1835."[21] Still, like the revenue and admiralty cases brought by executive officials and adjudicated in the federal courts, land disputes enhanced the prestige and authority of the federal courts by making them an indispensable government service to Americans seeking to settle western lands. Settlers relied on the treasury officers staffing federal land offices to acquire land, and then, if a competing claim or unsolvable problem arose, land grantees turned to the federal courts to quiet their titles. Also, by injecting "a sense of regularity and evenhanded equity" into land disputes at the national level, federal judges, as well as executive land commissioners, helped enhance the prestige and authority of the federal government.[22]

Moreover, the federal magisterial relationship thrived between the executive branch's land grantors and the federal judges who oversaw land distribution. Regulating land sales required executive discretion, a fact anticipated by Alexander Hamilton and officially confirmed by Congress when in 1800 it authorized the treasury secretary to prescribe regulations "as to him may appear necessary and proper" to Congress's more general statutory rules.[23] Jeffersonian Albert Gallatin was the first treasury secretary to exercise this discretion, and he did so by continuing the Hamilton–Wolcott practice of issuing directives via circulars to the various land offices and surveyors.[24]

Congress also clothed magistrates appointed as land commissioners with traditional magisterial powers, such as the ability to examine witnesses, and to hear and determine private land claims "according to justice and equity," with Congress serving, if necessary, as the *dernier resort* for unsatisfied parties to the dispute.[25] In practice, this system worked much like Hamilton's war-claims adjudication process: the commissioners, like the treasury secretary, did their due diligence, made a determination, and then Congress would simply confirm, rather than question, their decisions.[26] For reasons relating to the complexity of land disputes, the fact that executive land officers did not hold title to the lands they sold (the US government owned the lands), and Congress's willingness to act on grantees' petitions for relief, the federal courts rarely reviewed or overturned executive or legislative decisions regarding land titles.[27] In fact, the federal courts were so accommodating toward the decisions made by land office personnel and land commissioners that one legal historian has argued that the federal courts considered the executive decisions to be those of a coordinate tribunal.[28]

Land commissioners could not adjudicate all types of land claims, however; they could only resolve those claims arising between the United States government and the grantee. Third-party claimants, as well as alien landholders, citizens of different states, and occasionally the states themselves, took their land-based controversies to judicial courts at either the state or federal level. When adjudicated in the federal courts, land cases often gave rise to important decisions relating to constitutional jurisprudence (for example, the Supreme Court's interpretation of Article I, section 10's contract clause in *Fletcher v. Peck*) and to statements of robust federal judicial power (as in *Martin v. Hunter's Lessee*).[29] The US Supreme Court even resolved a title dispute involving the Holland Land Company and the state of Pennsylvania (Hamilton was not involved). In *Huidekooper's Lessee v. Douglas*, the Court interpreted a troublesome Pennsylvania statute in favor of the Dutch proprietors and against the wishes of Governor Thomas McKean, his board of property, and the Supreme Court of Pennsylvania.[30] In doing so, the Marshall Court riled the state's Republicans, who then complained that "the Federal Courts prostrated the sovereignty of Pennsylvania at its feet by a sophistical construction of the Constitution."[31]

Yet the federal courts were not always equipped for successfully resolving land disputes, even in cases that seemingly involved a state as a party to the dispute. Alexander Hamilton represented New York's interests in a group of interrelated suits, including *Fowler v. Lindsley*, *Fowler v. Miller*, and *New York v. Connecticut*, that involved a contested eight-mile-wide strip of land (known as the Connecticut Gore) running along the border between New York and Pennsylvania. The Gore seemingly formed a part of New York state, but it was instead claimed by Connecticut under a "sea to sea" grant in its 1662 charter.[32] Connecticut sold its claim to the Gore in 1795 to proprietors who then established the Connecticut Gore Land Company and sold shares of stock in the company. Outraged at the sale, New York asserted that neither the company nor the state of Connecticut could hold (or had held) valid title to the disputed land.

At each stage in the protracted litigation initiated by the company, neither the Circuit Court for the District of Connecticut nor the US Supreme Court considered the merits of the cases—that is, neither ruled on the question of which state actually held a valid title to the Gore.[33] Instead, the circuit court, followed by the Supreme Court sitting first in law and then in equity, only considered matters relating to the procedural and jurisdictional particulars of how the cases should be adjudicated, and to whom. At bottom, these questions revolved around the fact that neither New York nor Connecticut was a formal party to the controversy, yet the states' interests were intimately tied to the outcome of the litigation. Although federal law intended for the federal courts to adjudicate interstate boundary disputes according to the rules of the common law, the legal particulars of the Gore controversy produced what was, to New York, inequitable and biased proceedings.

New York was involved in the litigation at every turn, even though the federal courts consistently ruled that it was not a party to the dispute. The state's interest in reclaiming the Gore was evident from the outset, as it recruited state attorney general Josiah Ogden Hoffman, as well as other prominent lawyers like Hamilton, to represent the defendants dragged into court by the Connecticut Gore Land Company. Hamilton made strenuous arguments that New York was in fact a party to the litigation, and as such, neither of the circuit courts for the districts of New York or Connecticut should hear the cases, as both had natural biases. In the April 1798 term of the Connecticut Circuit Court, Hoffman and Hamilton asserted that the US Supreme Court was the natural mediator in what was essentially an interstate boundary dispute, and thus the ejectment trials should be removed to that superior court.[34] The court, however, denied the defendants' challenge to their jurisdiction. When New York subsequently convinced the US Supreme Court to weigh in on the question, it also denied the defendants' argument that New York was a party to the case.[35]

In August 1799, New York attempted a different legal strategy and initiated a third suit, *New York v. Connecticut,* by a bill in equity. (Associate Justice Bushrod Washington had hinted that Hoffman and Hamilton's case might be helped if they brought the case to the Supreme Court on a bill of equity instead of at law.) By turning to equity, New York could potentially solve all of its procedural and jurisdictional problems. First, the bill brought the controversy, which now defined the states as the opposing parties, into the exclusive jurisdiction of the US Supreme Court for resolution. Even better, because the bill would be adjudicated in equity, no biased juries from either state would be involved, and the Court could issue an injunction to the company to immediately stop any land dealings in the Gore.

Although the Court denied issuing an injunction to the company (arguing, again, that the state of New York was not truly a party to the underlying dispute), New York's tactical move to initiate *New York v. Connecticut* demonstrated how equity offered a complementary, competing, and more just process by which land claims could be resolved. Yet the federal courts gave preference to common law proceedings over those in equity, as the 1789 Judiciary Act stipulated that the federal courts should not hear equity cases "where plain, adequate and complete remedy may be had at law."[36] Moreover, federal common law process seemed unable to cope with the particulars of the Connecticut Gore controversy. The federal courts continually denied New York's stake in the litigation even though New York had an obvious and compelling interest in the suit: no less than the territorial and jurisdictional boundaries of a sovereign state would have been decided by a jury of Connecticut citizens if the litigation proceeded in due course.

Hamilton's frustrating experience with the Connecticut Gore litigation suggests how equity could provide significant advantages over the common law process to resolve the complexities of title disputes. The case also demonstrates how political and legislative solutions could augment judicial resolutions of land controversies. After the Connecticut Gore Land Company unsuccessfully attempted to settle with New York state, it began to consider the bill proceedings as a quick way to finally resolve the dispute.[37] Yet the company sought the benefits of equity too late; in 1800, Congress and Connecticut brokered a deal to end the dispute, and by 1803, the federal courts had dismissed all three cases, leaving the company to settle compensatory claims with the Gore's 1795 vendor, the state of Connecticut. The congressional deal effectively ended the controversy with a legislative solution: Congress would confirm the property rights of Connecticut citizens who held lands in the Ohio territory (known as the Western Reserve) if Connecticut renounced all jurisdictional claims in Ohio and any other territories west of its border with New York (which included the Gore).[38] In his dealings with the Holland Land Company, Hamilton too would strategically seek combined equitable and legislative solutions to acquire, quiet, and sell titles to his Dutch clients' New York lands.

Adjudicating Trusts and Quieting Titles in the New York Courts

Hamilton's land-related law practice was extensive and varied. Throughout his career, he represented a vastly divergent set of clients, often with antithetical interests. These clients included common freeholders, heirs and heiresses, municipalities (Hamilton served as the attorney for Kingston, New York), foreign and domestic land speculators, and landed patroons. The fact that Hamilton represented such a diverse array of interests derived in part from the fact that New York was a divided state: the western and northern portions of the state encompassed allodial lands that could be bought and sold on the free market in "fee simple" (that is, land owned outright, free from any other claims or obligations attached to the real property). But a sizable eastern section of the state—the lands surrounding the Hudson River Valley—bore resemblance to feudal Europe. Because the eastern segment had first been settled by the Dutch before being conquered by England in the late seventeenth century, Dutch-descended manor lords (patroons) owned much of the Hudson Valley lands, and their nonallodial property holdings had tenurial obligations attached to them. A tenant living on Schuyler or Van Rensselaer land, for example, might owe "four fat fowl," rent payments, fines on alienation, or other incidents to their manor lord, thus rendering the eastern portion of republican New York state "more feudal than monarchical England."[39]

Hamilton married directly into the Schuyler family and therefore, through their extended relations, into the Van Rensselaer clan. Inevitably, then, he represented the interests of this elite landholding class in court, even introducing a procedural innovation, the writ of right, into New York law to help the manor lords enforce their tenurial rights against their tenants.[40] This system of feudal landholding turned out to be surprisingly sturdy; as legal historian Charles W. McCurdy has shown, neither American law nor its political system was up to the challenge of dismantling New York's inherited brand of feudalism.[41] Still, the law of the land supported the buying and selling of western New York's nonfeudal lands, and in particular, New

York law developed to enhance the rights and benefits conveyed by equitable trusts. Hamilton had a prominent role in this legal transformation, and so his dealings with western allodial lands, rather than with New York's patroons, will be discussed below.

Trusts developed in the English High Court of Chancery as a mechanism to work around the strictures of the common law (its rules of inheritance, for example) or to separate the beneficiaries of property (minors, women, "unthrifty" sons) from the legal owners of the land.[42] Recall that trusts are simply an equitable relationship whereby the beneficiary of the trust (also known as the "cestuy," "cestuy que use," or "cestuy que trust") did not own legal title to the property in question. The beneficiary might inhabit, farm, or otherwise have use of the real property, but the beneficiary did not own the real estate. The trustee held legal title to the property for the benefit of the cestuy. Chancellors and judges sitting in equity, therefore, had the task of determining where the trustee's rights or obligations ended and where the beneficiary's rights began.

Hamilton relied on the trust, as well as other equitable principles, as tools to secure the Holland Land Company's interests in New York real estate. By examining the legal maneuvering necessary to protect the company's investment, we see how Hamilton's strategy for this particular client depended on changes in the law of mortgages (a form of trust), as well as the political whims of the New York legislatures and occasionally the oversight of the state and federal courts sitting in equity.[43]

When acquiring land in the state of New York, the Holland Land Company faced a difficult, though not insurmountable, problem: their alien status. In its 1777 constitution, New York adopted the English common law, as modified by state statute, as the law of the land.[44] One component of this adopted common law was the feudal rule, which dated to time immemorial, stating that an alien could not own real property for his own use within the realm. Any foreigner caught defying this prohibition would forfeit his property to the king.[45] Furthermore, if a subject—or, in New York, a citizen—took title to real property that had been purchased by an alien, then the subject/citizen was deemed a trustee for the foreigner, and the state attorney general could bring a bill in equity to have the state declared the beneficiary of the trust.[46] Given these inherited limitations, not even equitable trusts could circumvent the common law prohibition against alien landholding in New York without a statutory modification to the common law.

As one of the company's dedicated attorneys, Hamilton sought to attain a statutory exemption for his clients—a legislative feat that was in no way guaranteed. The Holland Land Company was in a precarious position as it was: they had already purchased lands through intermediaries, and if taken to court, New York's chancellor could force the company to forfeit its property to the state. To remedy this, the company's agent in America, Théophile Cazenove, attempted to acquire a statutory exemption from the New York legislature in 1794, but his efforts were unsuccessful. Fortunately for the Dutch financiers, Hamilton had more luck. Hamilton's memorial to the New York legislature resulted in a temporary, statutorily sanctioned trust arrangement for his clients: the 1796 act allowed the Holland Land Company to be a statutorily valid cestuy, and the existing title holders to the company's land (the intermediaries who made the original purchases on behalf of the company) would become bona fide trustees, holding title in fee simple, in trust, for seven years.[47] During this seven-year period, however, the legislators expected the Dutch proprietors to either become citizens or to convey their real property to Americans. When the period expired, the legally sanctioned trust reverted to its former, illegal status and the company's real property would again become subject to forfeiture to the state.

Problems ensued, however, that convinced Hamilton that the company would have to seek a longer exemption period from another private act in order to protect the company's investment. First, the Holland Land Company eventually purchased around 3.3 million acres of land—much of western New York—from Robert Morris, but to its dismay, Native Americans still claimed title to some of the acreage.[48] Through a 1797 treaty with the Seneca nation, however, the company eventually secured title to those lands. Yet a second problem remained: this vast tract of purchased land was wild and unsurveyed. This proved harder to solve without more of a statutory grace period. Thus, the Holland Land Company followed Hamilton's suggestion to petition for an extension, and, with the assistance of assemblyman Aaron Burr, the company secured passage of an act that allowed all aliens not subjects of a power at war with the United States to hold real property in New York.[49]

Under the 1798 Alien Act, the Holland Land Company could hold the title to its purchased lands outright despite its foreign status. Yet Hamilton, along with his co-counsel, Richard Harison and David A. Ogden, still suggested that the company maintain the trust, and therefore its status as cestuy. The attorneys had two practical reasons in mind for maintaining the trust, even after the passage of the Alien Act. First, if the company held title to their lands outright, then at least one of the Dutch partners would have to sail to New York to either formally appoint and record a power of attorney for an agent (so that the agent could then sell lands on behalf of the company) or to acknowledge and record the company's deeds in person if the company wanted to convey lands to other alien buyers (like interested English purchasers).[50] If the company wanted to sell any part of its New York holdings, then there was no way around the fact that one of the Dutch partners would have to make an in-person appearance in New York. At that moment at least, none of the proprietors wanted to incur the inconvenience of a transatlantic voyage.

Counsel's second consideration had to do with geopolitical tensions. Hamilton, Harison, and Ogden advised their client, "In Case of War between [the United States] and France, Holland will most probably be implicated in it." Thus, "so far as it respects Sales contemplated" in England or in any other country with which the Dutch may be at war, "the Propriety of having the Title vested in Citizens of the United States, must be obvious."[51]

On their attorneys' advice, the Holland Land Company arranged for their existing trustees to convey the company's lands to American citizens to hold the property in trust for the company. Under this temporary trust arrangement (the company soon after recorded a power of attorney in New York and disbanded the trust), the proprietors held their New York lands as alien purchasers, but the company still benefited from its hard-won statutory exemptions.[52] The Dutch partners also avoided the hassle of making a transatlantic voyage to New York until it was convenient for them, and they temporarily protected their ability to convey lands to English buyers in case of the outbreak of war.

In order to combat the prohibitions and administrative hurdles accompanying alien landholding in New York, Alexander Hamilton relied on the trust, which in this case had to be sanctioned by statute, as a strategic way to secure the interests of the Holland Land Company. Here, trusts worked as legislatively granted mechanisms to avoid the common law's prohibitions against foreign landowners. They also served as practical tools that Hamilton used in order to give his clients the convenience of selling land in New York without incurring the immediate hassles arising from transatlantic wars and ocean voyaging.

Circumventing the problem of alien landholding was the first, most pressing problem that Hamilton encountered as one of the Holland Land Company's attorneys. He also provided long-term strategies and arbitration services for the company to resolve two other pressing issues: the first a tactical maneuver to protect the company's interests in light of the changing law of mortgages, and the other a major problem concerning conflicting title claims.

CHAPTER FIVE

Because the Holland Land Company intended to invest in New York state for the long term, Hamilton advised his clients as to what type of legal instrument they should use to convey land to settlers. The mortgage was simultaneously a contractual relationship used to convey real property as well as a form of trust whereby the mortgagee held title to the real property and the mortgagor inhabited or used the property as the beneficiary. Mortgages developed in medieval England, and by the Tudor period, the mortgage had come to denote any arrangement whereby a loan was secured by a conveyance of real property.[53]

Traditionally at common law, judges interpreted mortgages as strictly enforceable covenants between the mortgagee and the mortgagor. The mortgagee (the lender) held a conditional fee simple in the real property until the mortgagor paid the mortgagee a specified sum of money. If the mortgagor failed to make the specified payment, title to the property completely vested in the mortgagee.[54] While this arrangement could be a fair contractual bargain, the English Court of Chancery heard enough stories of individual hardships—"hard facts of particular cases, as where the penalty [for default] was grossly excessive, or where punctual payment was prevented through misfortune or sharp practice"—that an equitable doctrine of mortgages began to develop outside of the common law. When considered in equity, the mortgage resembled a trust more than it did a covenant or debt obligation at law. While the mortgagee was still entitled to payment on his loan, and he could, at some point, reclaim the mortgaged property, the Chancery gave the mortgagor more leeway, considering him to be a beneficiary with equitable rights attached. In particular, equity granted the mortgagor an "equity of redemption." This meant that "if the legal estate passed to the mortgagee for nonpayment, the mortgagor was nevertheless always entitled to a reconveyance" within a reasonable time period, until the Chancery foreclosed on the right.[55] The mortgagor's equity of redemption—this right born from and acknowledged only in equity—became so inseparable from the mortgage that the parties to the agreement could not even contract out of the right.[56]

Equities of redemption shifted the power balance between the creditor (the mortgagee) and the debtor (the mortgagor), giving debtors relief when they encountered hard times or misfortunes. Moreover, during the late eighteenth century, the law of mortgages transformed again, moving even further toward a robust notion of debtors' rights. As attorney for the Holland Land Company, Alexander Hamilton was aware of the transformations in the law of mortgages in England and America, and in 1804, he helped adapt and extend English precedent into New York law.

The change began in England, in the common law court of King's Bench. There, Lord Chief Justice Mansfield suggested that a mortgage had become only a security, a lien, in the law; if upheld, Mansfield's dicta meant that the mortgagee no longer possessed title to the real property mortgaged as security to the loan.[57] In America, South Carolina formally adopted Mansfield's suggestion as a statutory modification to its common law in 1791, passing an act stating that if the mortgagor was still in possession of the property, then he was "deemed owner of the land," and the mortgagee became only the "owner of the money lent or due."[58] New York adopted the same policy through incremental moves made in case law, originating from a suit decided by Chancellor John Lansing Jr. This dispute, *Waters v. Stewart*, culminated in the Court for the Correction of Errors (Court of Errors), the highest court of the state, in 1804.

In *Thomas Waters, and Richard Thorne and Sarah His Wife v. John Stewart*, Hamilton and his *Fowler* co-counsel, Josiah Ogden Hoffman, represented the respondent Stewart on appeal in order to resolve a complicated set of facts and interests involving the Waters family and a judgment issued at law to settle their debts.[59] The basic facts were these: Sarah Waters and her brother, Thomas, claimed to be the legal owners of a mortgaged farm in Goshen, New York, though Sarah's deceased husband had mortgaged the property after their marriage. Eventually the original mortgagee assigned the farm to Stewart, another creditor. After the husband's death, a common law court ordered the local sheriff to sell the widow Waters's equity of redemption in the property in order to pay off debts owed by her deceased husband. Stewart, who still held the mortgage to the farm, purchased the equity of redemption sold by the court.

In spite of legal sale, Sarah Waters and her brother wanted to pay off the mortgage held by Stewart in order to regain ownership of the farm. Stewart, however, claimed that he owned the property outright (as he had purchased the equity of redemption). Waters then brought a bill in the New York Court of Chancery claiming that that a common law court could not force the sale of an equity of redemption to a judgment creditor (Stewart), because that equitable right had remained in the Waters family and was a right foreign to the common law.[60] The chancellor dismissed the bill, and Waters appealed to the Court of Errors.

Complicating the situation (which included intermediary buyers and sellers of Sarah Waters's mortgaged property) was the fact that New York passed a statute in 1787, and reenacted it in 1801, governing the property eligible to be sold at common law in execution of outstanding debts.[61] These qualifying properties included "all and singular the lands, tenements, and real estate of every debtor." For the chancellor and the Court of Errors, the question at hand was whether or not the statute's operative phrase "real estate" included the mortgagor's right to an equity of redemption.[62]

The distinguished counsel for the appellant Waters built their case around the traditional distinction between law and equity, and the fact that equities of redemption were historically acknowledged only in Chancery. Therefore, they argued, the Goshen common law court could not have ordered the mortgaged property sold to cover Sarah Waters's deceased husband's debts because that move forfeited her right of redemption, a right unacknowledged at law. Hamilton and Hoffman, arguing on Stewart's behalf, framed the issue differently, asking, "Who is the owner of lands or real estate mortgaged?"[63] Because Chancery precedent, as well as Lord's Mansfield's recent dicta, strongly suggested that, for all intents and purposes, the mortgagor, and not the mortgagee, held title to mortgaged property (that is, the mortgagee's interest had been reduced to a mere security interest), then the Waters family's (the mortgagor's) title-holding interest in the property qualified as "real estate" under the statute.

Note the distinction and significance between the opposing counsel's arguments. Waters's counsel argued that the right of the equity of redemption was merely a right in equity. Therefore, the equitable right to redeem the property remained with Sarah Waters and her brother because no common law court could force them to forfeit it (at common law, the equity of redemption was not acknowledged, claimed the attorneys). Hamilton and Hoffman built their case from arguments made by Chancellor Lansing and urged the Court of Errors to recognize instead an innovation in New York law that underscored how powerful the mortgagor's property right had become. They argued that the mortgagor's right to an equity of redemption had become so absolute, and had produced such a strong title-holding status in the mortgagor, that the common law now acknowledged the equity of redemption and, implicitly, that the mortgagor actually held the title to the property. This was a major claim.

Recall that initially, at common law, the mortgagee (the creditor/lender) was considered to be the legal owner of mortgaged real estate, and as such, he possessed immediate, complete, and final ownership to the property as soon as the mortgagor missed a payment. Equity provided an alternative to this unforgiving common law reality by granting the mortgagor a right to an equitable redemption, and thus giving the mortgagor the right to the property up until the moment that a chancery court foreclosed on that right.

Hamilton and Hoffman's argument therefore extended equity's beneficence in the law of New York state. They proposed to the court, first, that the mortgagor in possession actually held title to the real estate, and second, that the common law in New York had adapted to acknowledge equities of redemption, as well as the mortgagor's status as holding title to the property.

The Court of Errors agreed with Hamilton and Hoffman, and affirmed the chancellor's decree.[64] Justices Ambrose Spencer and James Kent spoke for the court, acknowledging that yes, common law and equity tended to treat mortgages differently, but in certain ways, "the courts of law follow the notions of a court of equity."[65] More recently, common law began recognizing the absolute nature of the equity of redemption as well as the diminishment of the mortgagee's interest to a mere security.[66] Because New York's statute did not specifically exclude the equity of redemption as property eligible to be sold to judgment creditors, it seemed acceptable to Kent to interpret the statute in light of the changes in English precedent.[67]

Waters v. Stewart thus ushered in a new era in the law of mortgages in New York. After *Waters*, the mortgagor routinely benefited from a robust conception of his rights as title holder to the mortgaged property. Julius Goebel Jr. and Joseph Smith observed that the *Waters* decision led to the New York Supreme Court's 1806 holding that mortgagees must give mortgagors a certain amount of notice (called "notice to quit") before commencing an ejectment action to evict the mortgagor from the premises.[68] And the mortgagor's title-holding status became official eight years later in *Runyan v. Mersereau*, when the New York Supreme Court confirmed that in the mortgage transaction, the mortgagor held the ownership interest, and the mortgagee only a security interest on his loan.[69] After serving as chancellor of New York, James Kent cemented the influence and permanence of these decisions in the annals of both New York and American law in the fourth volume of his influential *Commentaries on American Law*.[70]

Hamilton seemed to have anticipated that eventually changes in the respective rights of mortgagors and mortgagees would likely affect his Holland Land Company clients, so he proactively advised his Dutch clients to sell their New York lands through installment sales contract rather than through mortgages. While Hamilton never articulated why he considered installment contracts to be preferable to mortgages for the company, given the changing legal rights of mortgagees in England and in the American states, it made sense that Hamilton selected the conveyance method that better protected his clients' interests. By the late 1790s, it was likely that as mortgagees, the Holland Land Company would lose their title-holding status in law; therefore, the "contract to convey" suggested by Hamilton safeguarded the company's interests by protecting their claims to title. In addition, Julius Goebel Jr. and Joseph Smith have concluded that in the pre-*Waters* world, Hamilton likely thought that, as alien sellers, the company would incur extra inconvenience like "double suits and double expense" if they had to go to both a court of law (as judgment creditors, to obtain an execution of debt) and to the Court of Chancery (to get permission to foreclose on the equity of redemption).[71] Furthermore, Goebel and Smith note that because mortgages had to be recorded in both a central New York office as well as in the counties where the land was situated, this "posed an extreme inconvenience" to a foreign seller with a land agent stationed at a remote location and far from many acres of land owned by the company.[72]

As equitable principles transformed the law of mortgages in the Anglo-American world, Hamilton anticipated and adapted his clients' legal maneuvering in order to better protect their interests, as well as to ensure that the company encountered as little hassle as possible when selling or improving their investments. As a prominent and distinguished attorney representing various classes of clients, Hamilton simultaneously worked to protect creditor interests (in this case, the Holland Land Company's holdings) as well as to enhance the rights of debtors (the many mortgagors who benefited from the *Waters* decision), which existed in tension.

Alexander Hamilton's service to the Holland Land Company had one final act. Hamilton, along with attorneys David A. Ogden and Thomas Cooper, arbitrated clashes between at least three competing groups of creditors and the company.[73] As a result their decision, the Holland Land Company finally acquired full title to the western lands they had inadvertently mortgaged so precariously. Yet the company's creditors in trust were not pleased with the arbitration settlement. One of the trustees, Thomas Fitzsimmons, subsequently brought suit in federal court to review the Hamilton–Ogden–Cooper decision. Eventually the US Supreme Court, sitting in equity, heard the creditors' claims, in *Fitsimmons v. Odgen*. The Court affirmed the Holland Land Company's title and the Hamilton–Ogden–Cooper award; the Court also implicitly praised the legal strategy pursued by the company's counsel in order to secure the company's title.[74]

Through these extraordinarily complex and prolonged land dealings, we have seen how Hamilton developed portions of New York's land law concerning debtors' rights, and in order to preserve and protect the foreign capital invested in the state, he also worked to enhance creditors' rights. During the years he practiced law, Hamilton helped to secure creditors' rights on many occasions, particularly as they related to commercial transactions.[75] But right before his death, Hamilton effected one final, important change to the land law of New York state, this time concerning creditor liens and their order of priority.

In English law, the "tacking" doctrine governed the priority given in the Chancery to multiple mortgagees' claims to property. To understand the doctrine, imagine that A holds the first mortgage (or judgment) on Z's property, B holds a second mortgage on the same property, and then C holds both a third mortgage on Z's property as well as a purchased interest in A's mortgage. By the tacking doctrine, C "tacked" his mortgage interest onto that of the first creditor, A. Therefore, when the chancellor subsequently divides up Z's assets among his existing creditors, A and C have first priority, because through tacking, C's interest tacked onto A's and trumped B's interest—even though B's loan to Z predated C's loan. As Chancellor Kent explained, tacking meant that "the junior mortgagee may purchase in the first mortgage, and tack it to his mortgage, and by that contrivance 'squeeze out' the middle mortgage, and gain a preference over it."[76]

A dispute over the tacking doctrine arose in the New York courts when Bissett (Z) mortgaged the same handful of New York City lots to three mortgagees, including Onderdonk (A), Taylor (B), and the Bank of the United States (C), and then went bankrupt. After Bissett had entered into his agreement with Taylor, Taylor then assigned his security in Bissett's mortgaged lots to McGregor, and then McGregor assigned the interest to James Grant (who then became the new B). The Bank of the United States also bought into—that is, it tacked onto—Onderdonk's mortgage. After Bissett went bankrupt, the bank (C) claimed that its interest had priority over Grant's loan (B), and initially, Chancellor Lansing applied New York's relevant statutory law, found it consistent with the doctrine of tacking, and decided in favor of the bank. Grant appealed to New York's Court of Errors, and Alexander Hamilton represented him against the bank.[77]

Hamilton and his co-counsel, Caleb Riggs, broke with English precedent and argued that New York statutes intended to establish absolute priorities among mortgages. Moreover, they noted, fraud would be encouraged if a newer creditor could trump the interests of an older creditor simply by buying into a preexisting mortgage.[78] The Court of Errors agreed. Speaking for the court, Justice Ambrose Spencer declared that under New York law, tacking had been abolished.[79] Many years later, after serving as chancellor,

James Kent noted that *James Grant et al. v. The Bank of the United States* marked not only the moment when New York state formally abolished tacking, but it was also "the earliest case that I am aware of in this country, destroying the system of tacking." Kent went on to praise Hamilton's efforts to more equitably secure creditor liens, remarking, "I had the satisfaction of hearing that profound civilian, as well as illustrious statesman, General Hamilton, make a masterly attack upon the doctrine, which he insisted was founded on a system of artificial reasoning, and encouraged fraud."[80] By helping to transform the law of mortgages in New York, Alexander Hamilton developed the rights of both debtors and creditors in American law.

Land Law, Hamiltonian Concurrence, and the Power of the States

Hamilton's efforts to change some of the key equitable principles surrounding debtor and creditor relations in New York led to permanent revisions to the doctrine of tacking and to the law of mortgages in state jurisprudence. These transformations also affected equitable trusts in general, for as the law of equity changed in New York, those financiers organized as trusts now held altered rights as landholders, secured creditors, and mortgagees under state law. What Hamilton's land law practice demonstrates is that in order for foreign investors to secure their capital in American lands, land law became a crucial tool (and an occasional impediment) that could make or break their investment.

In New York, the common law set a barrier to entry for foreign investors, but at the same time, equity provided foreign financiers with a legal mechanism, the trust, that offered investment flexibility as well as the ability to skirt the alien-landholding prohibition when approved by the state legislature. Equity also supplied the basic legal principles used by the Hamilton–Ogden–Cooper arbitration settlement, as well as the operative doctrines behind shifting debtor–creditor relations in New York. Changes to the doctrines of tacking and equities of redemption transformed the options available for landed investors as well. In order for foreign investors to protect their capital as the law evolved around them, they needed to find well-versed attorneys to navigate and strategize for them. These lawyers helped to secure foreign investment in the early republic.

From time immemorial, engaging with the law of the land at common law or in equity was a complex endeavor requiring clever lawyers to sort through the convoluted intricacies of property claims in order to be effective advocates for their clients. But after the ratification of the US Constitution, American attorneys worked with a new complexity: they could take their claims to either or both the federal and state levels to quiet titles for their clients, to suggest the best conveyance instruments, to arbitrate among conflicting claims, and in general to undertake whatever legal maneuvers were necessary to secure investment.

Hamilton engaged both jurisdictions to secure foreign investment. Because he was an influential statesman as well as a sought-after legal advocate in a state with a westward-moving population, he had a unique perspective for recognizing that under the American federal system, foreign and domestic capital could be secured in the two separate but concurrent jurisdictions. While the national government had its own sovereign sphere in which to sell western lands, to adjudicate conflicting claims, and to support manufacturing, commercial, or agricultural endeavors, so did the states. The states were concurrent spheres in which to attract foreign investment, to sell land and adjudicate title disputes, and to encourage commercial ventures within their boundaries. In the early republic, the states were powerful jurisdictions for attracting foreign capital, and Hamilton not only recognized this fact but also used his private law practice to help secure those investments that he first sought as treasury secretary.

According to Hamiltonian concurrence, the states, as well as the federal government, had robust authority to legislate and to adjudicate. Hamilton therefore relied on both to build his commercial republic, to ensure that both levels of government enjoyed ample taxing powers, and to secure foreign investment in American lands. Although we remember Alexander Hamilton as *the* consummate nationalist, in reality, he recognized and embraced the fact that the states also exercised formidable powers to accomplish nationally oriented statecraft. Hamilton helped New York state to realize this potential.

There is no doubt, of course, that Hamilton endeavored to create a strong national government, but as we have seen, Hamilton strategically maneuvered at the state and national levels. Particularly when engaged in his private practice, Alexander Hamilton embraced the states' abilities to contribute to the development of the nation's commercial, manufacturing, and agricultural pursuits. His evaluation of the states' importance in the Union thus changed over time: the Confederation-era Hamilton who scorned state power evolved into a (small-f) federalist statesman who recognized the states' potential to advance the nation's policy objectives in the early national era.

It was the structure of the US Constitution that made all the difference for Hamilton. The guaranteed powers delegated to Congress in Article I, section 8, the empowered, energetic magistrate created by Article II, and the independent judiciary created by Article III to preside over the supreme law of the land (Article VI) provided a way to keep the states in check. Although the federal system was still largely unproven—after the Federalist Party lost the battle over the repeal of the 1801 Judiciary Act, Hamilton feared that the US Constitution had been rendered a "frail and worthless fabric"—the former secretary still pursed his preferred policies through any means constitutionally available.[81] But by establishing a federal system that delegated specific powers to the national government while reserving for the states a large cache of both exclusive and concurrent powers, the US Constitution created two jurisdictions from which Hamilton could pursue his statecraft. That he used national laws and institutions to enact policy goals is not surprising. But that Alexander Hamilton also relied on state courts, statutes, and inherited law to accomplish national aims demonstrates that his accomplishments and legacy are more complex and far-reaching than historians and biographers have acknowledged.

The states figured prominently in the statecraft of Alexander Hamilton, not as impotent localities prostrated before a centralized nation-state but as concurrent jurisdictions that acquiesced only in the face of the national government's constitutionally delegated powers. To accomplish his policy goals, Hamilton consistently turned to the jurisdictional options made possible by federalism, proving in theory and in practice that concurrence was the most important legal tool in Hamilton's inherited legal toolbox.

SIX

◆

Litigation, Liberty, and the Law: Hamilton's Common Law Rights Strategy

Over the past five chapters, I have demonstrated how Alexander Hamilton created substantive American jurisprudence, influenced and guided by principles of English law. Hamilton used the law as an instrument to achieve his preferred statecraft, and by defining his policies through law, Hamilton legitimized his own programs. Still, one of Hamilton's career-long legal pursuits has been absent from this study thus far; in addition to the constitutional, fiscal, and commercial law influenced by the first treasury secretary, Hamilton also demonstrated a consistent, indefatigable rights consciousness. His critics have long ignored Hamilton's advocacy for liberty under the law by alleging that he was an antidemocratic closet monarchist. Yet Hamilton dedicated his legal practice to crafting strategies based in common law that preserved and sought to expand English liberties in the American courts. Throughout his career, Alexander Hamilton worked to ensure that crucial civil and political rights remained robust for the inhabitants of the new republic.

Hamilton's legacy has been tarnished by charges levied against him by his contemporary political opponents, as well as nearly two centuries of censure from historians. Critics accused him of making unholy alliances with money men and the propertied class, favoring the establishment of an American monarchy, and being contemptuously elitist, all the while harboring a deep suspicion of democracy.[1] These charges mischaracterize Hamilton's genuine concern for the fate of America's experiment in republican government and his formulation of American political science. Hamilton was not a villainous monarchist; nor did he have complete disdain for ordinary Americans. On the contrary, as we will see, Hamilton built his fledgling legal practice by defending a broad spectrum of common and powerful clients alike, including persecuted rich, poor, and widowed Loyalists in the aftermath of the Revolutionary War. Throughout his career, Hamilton also represented feuding New York landowners, argued on behalf of seafaring traders suing insurance firms for claims on damaged or lost property, and successfully defended New York City's notorious carpenter, Levi Weeks, in his 1800 murder trial.[2] Hamilton ended his career by championing a robust conception of the freedom of the press by representing a convicted partisan printer, Harry Croswell, who dared to criticize the Jefferson Republicans then in power. Despite these efforts, American iconography and historiography insist that other Founders like Thomas Jefferson—but never Hamilton—wear the mantle of liberty.[3] On closer inspection of his public rhetoric, and most importantly his legal practice, however, Alexander Hamilton rivals even Jefferson as a rights-conscious statesman.

We should not be surprised that Hamilton paid close attention to the preservation of American liberty. After all, like other radical American Whigs, a college-age Hamilton publicly spoke out against King George III and Parliament's tyranny before the outbreak of hostilities. During the war, the captain turned lieutenant colonel fought for American independence both in battle and at General Washington's side at headquarters. But most importantly, after the war, Hamilton trained as a common lawyer, just as Jefferson, John Adams, James Madison, James Wilson, John Marshall, and Andrew Jackson did. It is from this common law instruction that Alexander Hamilton developed a successful legal strategy to use to enforce his rights consciousness in court. Hamilton became a staunch advocate of due process and freedom of the press liberties that protected Americans from governmental overreach.

The key to Hamilton's rights strategy was the distinction he made between a "strict" versus an "extensive" conception of the common law. Under their new constitutions, the states received, in various forms, English common law, but these reception provisions created ambiguity and legal uncertainty.[4] Determining what parts of the common law applied in state jurisprudence proved to be a tricky endeavor, as seemingly basic questions uncovered uncertain and complicated answers. Under New York's reception clause, for example, what authorities provided definitive evidence of the common law?[5] Only the central English courts at Westminster? What about "ancient" English statutes, or Parliament, or—after the adoption of the federal Constitution—Congress?

While serving in the New York assembly in 1787, Hamilton identified the key ambiguity in New York's reception clause and asked aloud, "What is meant in the constitution, by this phrase 'the common law'?"[6] He then went on to describe the important common law distinction animating his legal and constitutional thought:

> These words have in a legal view two senses, one more *extensive*, the other more *strict*. In their most extensive sense, they comprehend the [British] constitution, of all those courts which were established by immemorial custom, such as the court of chancery, the ecclesiastical court, &c. though these courts proceed according to a peculiar law. In their more strict sense, they are confined to the course of proceedings in the courts of Westminster in England, or in the supreme court of this state.[7]

After suggesting that the state constitution's reference to "common law" encompassed more than just the case reports generated by the central courts in Westminster, Hamilton thus determined, "I view it as a delicate and difficult question; yet, I am inclined to think that the more *extensive sense* may be fairly adopted." Although Hamilton referred here only to a particular intestacy bill under consideration, this distinction between a strict and an extensive common law would pervade Hamilton's litigation strategies for the rest of his career.

For Hamilton, then, the extensive common law was an enormous corpus of law—understood by him as synonymous with the entire English constitution—that offered strategic flexibility as well as a vast body of legal precedents from which to draw in order to make arguments about the substance of law in the American republic. When Hamilton wanted to make a rights claim for his client, he drew from this expansive body of common law principles and precedent to make his argument. As we will see, the strategic flexibility allowed by his extensive common law approach meant that Hamilton looked to principles and practices beyond English case law in order to effectively represent his client. English common law—that is, the English constitution itself—became a tool for Hamilton to instrumentally apply to promote his client's interests while simultaneously furthering his own political goals. Note, however, that when I refer to these differing interpretations of the common law as strict versus extensive below, I borrow Hamilton's 1787 distinction as a helpful analytical label. Neither Hamilton nor his lawyer colleagues used the terms "strict" or "extensive" to describe their conceptions of the common law.

Hamilton's extensive common law strategy proved to be effective for two reasons. First, Hamilton was by all accounts a brilliant lawyer, with an encyclopedic mind, a disciplined work ethic, and an innate forensic talent that allowed him to piece together and recall winning arguments from the annals of English legal history. Yet Hamilton's litigation strategy also succeeded because it so perfectly fit the legal uncertainty characterizing his time at the bar: Hamilton and his lawyer colleagues practiced law when much of the substantive law of New York was unsettled and still up for grabs. When thinking back to these postwar decades, Chancellor James Kent explained the uncertainty at the New York bar: "We had no precedents of our own to guide us. . . . Nothing was settled in our courts. Every point of practice had to be investigated, and its application to our courts and institutions questioned and tested."[8] In these first early years of the American republic, the state of American law was thus highly contingent. For Hamilton, the best way to take advantage of this opportunity was to maximize the legal options available to the courts to consider, and his extensive conception of the common law provided those options. Hamilton devised and applied this strategy when arguing for expansive conceptions of due process and freedom of the press liberties, and in doing so, he permanently changed the substance of New York state law—and the course of American law.

Hamilton's Defense of the Loyalists

"Legislative folly has afforded so plentiful a harvest to us lawyers that we have scarcely a moment to spare from the substantial business of reaping."[9] In 1784, Hamilton could boast about the number of Loyalist defendants retaining his legal services but not about the ease of winning their cases. This "legislative folly"—that is, the Anti-Loyalist statutes passed by New York state during and after the Revolutionary War, including the Confiscation, Citation, and Trespass acts—deprived Hamilton's Tory clients of their rights and property, and challenged Hamilton to creatively circumvent statutory law in order to craft successful defenses. These discriminatory statutes remained in effect after the official end to hostilities, thus making it difficult for sympathetic attorneys to be effective advocates for their Loyalist and British clients.

The persecution and exile of Loyalists in New York has been well documented.[10] America's break with England, coupled with the British occupation of New York City, caused irrevocable divisions across New York communities and forced families to choose either to leave behind their homes and property or to be branded as traitors for remaining behind enemy lines. The war exposed the depth of Patriots' hatred and fear of the British and their sympathizers, but also the extent of Patriots' wrath against those whom they once considered fellow subjects and now reckoned foes. Yet while Loyalist scholarship describes in detail the hardships endured by American Tories, it gives little account of how Loyalists and their lawyers attempted to resist such persecution through the law. The efforts of Loyalist attorneys like Hamilton to shield their clients from legal persecution have been largely overlooked.[11]

Hamilton found the persecution of Loyalists and their subsequent flight from the state to be unjust and alarming, as their exodus was a serious detriment to commerce and an impediment to New York state's economic growth. But he did not simply advocate for judicial review as the remedy to the Loyalist problem. Indeed, historians have generally put too much analytic weight on the development of judicial review, and the Mayor's Court's opinion in *Rutgers v. Waddington,* as Hamilton's solution to the Loyalist problem in New York, as well as to explain the judiciary's ascendancy in the early republic. Judicial review was an extraordinary act, and it occurred too infrequently to explain why and how Americans now embraced their former colonial magistrates as republican judges. Alexander Hamilton's defense of Loyalists, however, offers an alternative insight into how an independent judiciary developed in the new nation. Hamilton attempted to revise the courts' image and function in the eyes of the New York public in order to win favorable results for his clients. As a part of this strategy, he suggested that it was the judiciary's essential purpose to safeguard the people's liberty by providing due process of law in ordinary, everyday legal matters. To Hamilton, judicial process, but not necessarily judicial review, was crucial for sustaining America's republican experiment.

By examining Alexander Hamilton's defense of both Loyalists and British subjects in court, in the press, and ultimately in the state assembly, it becomes clear that the guarantees of the due process of law were fundamental to both Hamilton's litigation strategy and to his simultaneous attempt to convince New Yorkers to repeal the Anti-Loyalist statutes. Rescinding Anti-Loyalist laws benefited even Patriots, according to Hamilton, because denying legal process to the Loyalist few also imperiled the rights and liberty of the Patriot many.

Hamilton equated the protection of the rights and liberties of the state constitution with the guarantee of due process that judicial courts provided. To defend his clients against litigation arising from Anti-Loyalist legislation, Hamilton used various legal strategies derived from his extensive conception of inherited English common law in order to circumvent the limitations on due process written into these statutes. Having to maneuver around statutorily imposed constraints on judicial process gave Hamilton a profound appreciation for the protections afforded by the due process of law and the courts' role in enforcing and guarding it. Thus, when Hamilton made his case to the public in his first and second *Letters from Phocion*, he argued that common law due process was a constitutionally guaranteed right, and that this process protected everyone from arbitrary confiscation, banishment, disfranchisement, and punishment. Anti-Loyalist statutes set a precedent for the persecution of anyone through legislative fiat, as statutes denied British sympathizers their rights to traditional judicial process, including presentment, review of errors, and a fair defense.

Considering the entirety of Hamilton's use of a broad conception of common law to defend Loyalists also provides a fresh insight into his early formulation of the nature of republican judicial power.[12] He emphasized the courts' responsibility to provide guarantees of due process, which derived from the common law, and thus, to Hamilton's mind, should temper, if not override, the procedural restrictions in New York's Anti-Loyalist statutes. Moreover, because the common law provided due process, ensuring that no person would be divested of life, liberty, property, or the franchise without a complete and fair judicial prosecution, Hamilton also argued that New Yorkers should look to the common law courts, and not to the legislature, to protect their liberty. As Hamilton learned through practice, even with statutory limitations on legal process in place, the common law proved flexible enough for him to win some degree of justice and relief for his clients. For Alexander Hamilton, then, the broadly conceived common law, and the courts that ensured its due process guarantees, protected the American people not simply through the extraordinary act of judicial review but through the everyday guarantee of the due process of law.

Statutory Limitations on Common Law Due Process

During the course of the American Revolution, New York passed over thirty statutes aimed at persecuting those who sympathized with the British or resided behind enemy lines, yet only three of these statutes figured prominently in postwar litigation.[13] While Trespass Act litigation would consume most of Hamilton's law practice in the 1780s, he also litigated cases involving the Confiscation Act and the Citation Act. Each act denied defendant Loyalists some of the traditional forms of judicial process.

The Trespass Act authorized transitory trespass litigation (that is, trespass actions prosecuted in courts beyond the vicinity where the offense occurred), which gave Patriot plaintiffs their pick of favorable local courts. Crucially, the act forbade Loyalists from justifying their trespass by military permission, and it stipulated that not only the defendant but also his representatives, executors, and heirs were subject to prosecution.[14] In addition, the act made the first court to hear a case also the final court of record, thus denying removal to a higher court or appellate review.

The New York legislature modeled the Confiscation Act after English law regarding high treason, but it added broader language and fewer procedural safeguards.[15] The Confiscation Act attainted some well-known British subjects by name, but it also provided that anyone found "adhered to the Enemies" of the state were subject to the forfeiture and confiscation of their real and personal property.[16] English treason prosecutions required trials in the vicinity of the offense, the testimony of two witnesses, and an overt action to constitute treason. Under the Confiscation Act, however, indictment could be brought in any county (not necessarily the county of the offense), with the testimony of only one witness, on general suspicion of adherence to the enemy. If the accused failed to appear to traverse, or deny, the indictment, the Supreme Court of New York would automatically adjudge them guilty, and their property would be forfeited and confiscated.[17]

The Citation Act stayed all suits initiated by Loyalists to collect on debts owed to them by Patriots. The act also coerced Loyalist creditors to settle with their Patriot debtors on more favorable terms than their original contracts stipulated. The act allowed Patriots to secure abatements on the amounts they owed and to pay back their remaining debt in paper currency instead of pounds sterling. After the British withdrew from New York, the act stipulated that any Patriot debtor could "cite" his Loyalist creditor to fulfill the debt on these terms, and if the Loyalist creditor refused to settle, he would be permanently barred from recovering the debt.[18]

These acts placed limits on the legal process available to Loyalist defendants by preventing removal to superior judicial courts, by prohibiting military command as a justifiable defense, by creating hardships and alternative procedures for collecting debts, and by making it difficult for Loyalist defendants to travel to or obtain notice of actions pending against them in transitory courts located in Patriot-friendly counties. Legislative restrictions impeded the normal course of judicial process and forced Hamilton to be creative when crafting a defense litigation strategy for his Loyalist clientele. The limits of New York Anti-Loyalist legislation made it almost impossible to successfully defend British subjects and Loyalists after the war, so Hamilton worked to mitigate as much as possible the unjust effects of the Trespass, Citation, and Confiscation acts.

Defense Strategies

The majority of Hamilton's Loyalist practice came from trespass lawsuits, brought under the Trespass Act or common law trespass actions, which allowed Hamilton to try alternative defense theories depending on the circumstances of the trespass.[19] When first preparing for lawsuits arising from the Trespass Act, Hamilton posited two defenses: a plea of the law of nations and a plea of the Treaty of Peace (1783).

The Trespass Act forbade defendants to plead any military justification for the use and occupation of Patriots' property located behind enemy lines during the war. This restriction severely hampered possible defenses because during the British occupation of New York, British military personnel granted permission to those residing in the city to use otherwise vacant buildings (usually owned by Patriots who had fled the city). In addition, defendants paid rent to the British for their use of these vacant dwelling houses, storerooms, and workhouses. Military justification was thus the actual reason for the defendants' use of the plaintiff's property. The law of nations, a constituent part of the broadly conceived English common law, accepted this justification for the use of vacant buildings (when permitted by an occupying force). To Hamilton, the universal law of nations was part of the "extensive common law" received under New York's 1777 constitution, and it thus trumped the Trespass Act's restriction on a military justification plea.[20]

For those defendants who considered themselves to be British subjects during and after the war, Hamilton added the "plea of the Treaty," along with the "plea of the law of nations," to a Trespass Act defense. Once the treaty was ratified by Congress on January 14, 1784, Hamilton argued that the language of the treaty granted a general amnesty to any further prosecutions of wartime offenses committed by British subjects. When pleading in court, Hamilton planned to submit both theories on behalf of British clients, like Joshua Waddington, or limited the plea to a law of nations justification for Loyalists, whom he considered members of New York state.[21]

During the Revolutionary War, Elizabeth Rutgers abandoned her brew house in British-occupied New York City. Eventually two merchants occupied her vacated property with permission from British officials. When the British ultimately evacuated the city, Rutgers sued Joshua Waddington, the agent for the two merchants, under New York's Trespass Act. The New York Mayor's Court heard the resulting litigation in 1784, at the height of the Anti-Loyalist fervor sweeping the city.[22]

Rutgers v. Waddington has long been considered a pivotal case in the development of the distinctly American concept of judicial review. Yet when placed in the context of Hamilton's other Trespass Act litigation, *Rutgers* represents Hamilton's splashy introduction of a novel defense, not an overt attempt to persuade the Mayor's Court to declare the Trespass Act unconstitutional and void.[23] Hamilton cited the law of nations—which he considered to be part of the law of the land via the New York constitution's common law reception clause—as well as the Treaty of Peace as the basis of Waddington's defense. Hamilton argued that both bodies of law were superior to New York's statutory law as they applied to Waddington, a British subject.[24]

As judges determined how to reconcile these claims about conflicting superior and inferior laws, they could equitably interpret the statute to conform to the superior law (as Judge James Duane, of the Mayor's Court, did in the *Rutgers* case), or they could apply the highest-ranking law to the case at hand.[25] Hamilton did not attempt to persuade the court to declare the Trespass Act void; instead, he argued that military justification derived from higher-ranking laws of the land and thus should be admitted as a plausible defense. In *Rutgers*, and subsequently in other Trespass Act litigation, Hamilton aimed to expand on and take advantage of any viable defenses for his clients. He intended to use the common law to challenge and to override the effects of statutory law for his client, but not to outright nullify the law with an exercise of judicial review.

Judge Duane accepted Hamilton's law of nations plea and agreed with the defense counsel that the *ius gentium* (law of nations) became part of the law of the land under the state constitution.[26] To this end, Duane equitably interpreted the Trespass Act so as to smooth over the edges of conflicting laws: the New York legislature did not explicitly say in the text of the Trespass Act that it wished to violate the laws of nations or to supplant the common law, so the court would assume that contravening this law was not the legislature's intent. Therefore, when construing the Trespass Act and applying it to *Rutgers*, the court applied the Trespass Act without breaching the law of nations.[27] From this, the Mayor's Court determined that a plea of the law of nations was admissible, but for only the time periods that Waddington had permission from the British commander in chief to dwell in and use Rutger's property (but not permission from other British officials, like the commissary general).[28]

Duane did not accept Hamilton's plea of the treaty. Rather, he ruled that the text of the treaty bestowed no express amnesty for the defendant, and thus gave no further benefit than what the law of nations already provided.[29] Hamilton planned to use the plea of the treaty in other lawsuits, including *Tucker v. Thompson*, but he subsequently dropped the plea after the *Rutgers* decision (see, for example, *Gomez v. Maule*, a Trespass Act case in which Hamilton relied solely on the plea of the law of nations).[30]

Hamilton's partial victory in *Rutgers* gave him a viable defense for his British and Loyalist clients, and he used this law of nations plea in subsequent Trespass Act actions such as *Quackenbos v. Underhill* and *Morton v. Seton*.[31] To Hamilton, this legal leeway came as a welcome reprieve from an otherwise dire situation where seemingly no Trespass Act defense could be made. Reflecting back on this scene of general despair among Loyalist attorneys, Hamilton recounted to George Washington in 1795 his search for an effective defense:

> The fact is that from the very express terms of the [Trespass] Act a
> general opinion was entertained embracing almost our whole bar
> as well as the public that it was useless to attempt a defence—and
> accordingly many suits were brought and many judgments given
> without the point being regularly raised and many compromises were
> made and large sums paid under the despair of a successful defence—I
> was for a long time the only practicer who pursued a different course
> and opposed the Treaty to the Act.[32]

Although Hamilton's comments refer only to his plea of the treaty, pleading the law of nations proved to be a more viable defense. In fact, extant in Hamilton's law papers is a law of nations plea drafted by Hamilton for use by another attorney in *Shaw v. Stevenson* (1784), indicating that Hamilton's strategy circulated among other defense attorneys as a potentially effective remedy to counter the "extensive operation" of the Trespass Act.[33]

Hamilton's Loyalist clients also faced common law trespass actions that encompassed the destruction of property, instead of or in addition to the mere use and occupation of property, and were not always prosecuted under the Trespass Act. To answer both common law trespass and Trespass Act lawsuits, Hamilton pleaded other defenses such as duress inflicted by military authority (as in *Lloyd v. Williams*, where the defendant was impressed by the British military to harvest the plaintiff's wheat to be used by British forces); military orders to destroy the plaintiff's property (the defendant in *Lloyd v. Hewlett* had been a member of the Loyalist militia); citing the "customs and usages of war" (similar to invoking the plea of the law of nations under Trespass Act actions and used in *Hendrickson v. Cornwell*); and pleading the general issue, or general denial, to the trespass (*Lloyd v. Sneathen*).[34]

Loyalists and British subjects found themselves facing statutory and common law trespass actions without clearly admissible or effective defense options available to them, so it became Hamilton's challenge to devise workable defenses to present in court. Although he was not always successful in winning these lawsuits, Hamilton found that certain pleas could be used to counteract the seemingly oppressive limitations of the Trespass Act. Justice could be served to his British and Loyalist clients in court, even when legislatures tried to make it impossible.

Settlement Strategies

Coupled with his novel defense strategies, Hamilton held out hope that settling a case out of court (or removing to a superior court) would ensure that his client would have to pay a smaller amount to Patriot plaintiffs than would be the case if lower court decisions were final. While the Trespass Act prohibited removal to superior courts, common law trespass cases could be removed to superior courts, as could Confiscation Act or Citation Act cases. Hamilton thus added the possibilities of removal and settlement to his overall strategy.

Hamilton's first tactic toward settlement was to delay proceedings for as long as possible in the hope that during the delay, statutory law would be amended or rescinded in his client's favor. In February 1784, for instance, Abraham Cuyler asked Hamilton for an opinion on whether the Treaty of Peace might be used to challenge the forfeiture and confiscation of Cuyler's property under the Confiscation Act (Cuyler was attainted by name in the act). Advocating patience and delay, Hamilton cautioned Cuyler against bringing any challenges in court at the time because "there has not hitherto been any judicial decision upon this point, and in the present temper of this Country it would be very unadvisable for Mr. Cuyler to hazard an experiment."[35] Similarly, when reflecting on past Trespass Act litigation, Hamilton wrote, "I effected many easy compromises to my clients . . . & produced delays till the exceptionable part of the Act was repealed."[36] Delay could either encourage settlement or prevent judgments from being issued during the height of Anti-Loyalist fervor in New York.

Removal to a superior court (or the threat of removal) also helped to broker settlements out of court.[37] To some degree, Hamilton was wary of removal to the New York Supreme Court out of a concern that his successful pleadings would be found inadmissible by the superior court. Yet at the same time, opposing counsel also feared removal because, in the wake of *Rutgers*, a superior court decision might work against the plaintiff's interests.[38] Because the Trespass Act provided that the inferior court to first take cognizance of a case would be the final court to adjudge it, removal was not an option under the act. This stipulation benefited Patriot plaintiffs because it denied Loyalist defendants the writ of error, a judicial safeguard that allowed superior courts to review lower court decisions for errors in law (not in fact). Also, the provision made it more likely that plaintiff-friendly judgments would be handed down from the more informal, inferior courts (lower courts were not as finicky about the technicalities of pleading, for example, as superior courts).[39]

With the Trespass Act's restriction of removal on the books, it would seem, then, that plaintiffs would lack incentive for settling a Trespass Act action. It turned out, however, that Hamilton's partial victory in *Rutgers* had the effect of making removal an option in Trespass Act cases despite the statute. After the decision, Rutgers's astonished and outraged counsel contemplated, then set into motion, the "people's writ of error" to force review of the Mayor's Court decision in the New York Supreme Court. In July 1785, their writ of error was still pending when Rutgers and Waddington reached a settlement out of court for an undisclosed amount. Given that Waddington ultimately settled after a jury of inquiry awarded Rutgers only £791 (instead of the £8,000 for which the suit was instituted), Julius Goebel Jr. believed that the settlement amount was much closer to the jury award than Rutgers's original request for damages.[40] The *Rutgers* decision and the admissibility of Hamilton's law of nations plea cast widespread doubt that plaintiffs would inevitably succeed in their Trespass Act lawsuits.

The Trespass Act's stipulation against removal also seems to have been generally disregarded by New Yorkers during the mid-1780s, especially after the *Rutgers* decision. *Rutgers* incited the New York assembly to declare the judgment to be "subversive of all law and good order, and leads directly to anarchy and confusion," and it provoked a committee of nine men to denounce the Mayor's Court for having "assumed and exercised a power to set aside an act of the state."[41] Yet commentators still assumed that unfavorable outcomes in Trespass Act lawsuits could have judicial remedies. After the immediate *Rutgers* controversy, for example, Hamilton participated in at least one other Trespass Act action that originated in the Queens County Justice's Court in 1785 and was removed on certiorari to the New York Supreme Court in 1786.[42]

Petitions and Procedural Technicalities

Hamilton used the judicial options available to him, including alternative defenses, removal, delay, and settlement, to mitigate the limited due process imposed by statute. In addition to these tactics, Hamilton sought remedies for his clients through extrajudicial petitions to the legislature and through the exploitation of procedural technicalities in court.

Occasionally Hamilton submitted petitions to the assembly when he thought that a private act—a quasi-judicial adjudication handed down by the legislature—could serve his clients' interests. The executors of John Aspinwall's estate, for example, encountered problems executing Aspinwall's will because of the Citation Act. Aspinwall died with personal debts owed and debts due him from Patriots, but the Citation Act impeded the estate's executors from collecting on the debts owed to Aspinwall to pay back the debts owed by the estate. Hamilton's petition requested that the legislature grant the executors the power to sell real property to meet the estate's debts (Aspinwall's will did not empower the executors to sell real property). In this case, the Citation Act proved an insurmountable impediment to the execution of the will, and legislative action could provide relief by allowing the executors to meet the obligations of the estate and to free up the remaining assets for Aspinwall's heirs.[43]

During the war, Phoebe Ward's husband was convicted under the Confiscation Act, and his real estate was sold. After the judgment, but before the sale, the state forcibly evicted Phoebe Ward and her children from the property. She then wrote a petition and gave it to Hamilton to submit to the legislature claiming that "notwithstandg. my inofensive [*sic*] Conduct [during the war] I am Dispossessed of all my Living & am brought almost to Desperation."[44] Although her petition did not specifically ask that her former property to be restored to her, Ward sought—most likely after seeking Hamilton's counsel—any relief the legislature could offer to her.

Nonetheless, because petitions relied on the mercy of Patriot-controlled legislatures, Hamilton preferred to seek justice for his clients through the courts. His final legal strategy was to use any procedural technicalities available to him to lessen the oppressive effects of Anti-Loyalist statutes, as he did in *People v. Nicholas Hoffman*. Nicholas Hoffman had been indicted and convicted under the Confiscation Act in 1782, but because of a clerical error, the name on the indictment and judgment misspelled Hoffman's name as Huffman. Consequently, in 1783, Hoffman was again indicted, as the court did not have a record of a Nicholas Hoffman's indictment in the past. Hamilton's defense attempted to capitalize on this error as the basis of a sort of "double jeopardy" defense.[45]

In his plea of *autrefois attaint* (previously attainted), most likely submitted by Hamilton to the court, Nicholas Hoffman "says that the judgment aforesaid [from 1782] still remains and exists in full force and effect in no wise [sic] revoked reversed annulled or pardoned," indicating that the real and personal property confiscated under the 1782 judgment would still be owed to the state.[46] But if Hamilton could convince the court that the 1782 judgment fulfilled Hoffman's prosecution under the Confiscation Act, and that because of the misspelling the 1783 indictment did not apply, then the real and personal property acquired by Hoffman since the first judgment issued against him would not be subject to any further confiscation. Hamilton would thus argue that Hoffman was once attainted and thus always attainted, and the state had no claim to any property acquired after the attainder.

To make his case, Hamilton contemplated a number of different tactics. He questioned, but rejected, whether the first judgment could be overturned (through abatement or reversal); he then considered whether the second indictment could be quashed.[47] To this end, Hamilton contemplated using the plea of the treaty so that Hoffman could claim an express amnesty from the second indictment. Yet because the treaty was provisional at the time, Hamilton instead pursued the plea of *autrefois attaint*, claiming that Hoffman's first judgment still stood, thus invalidating the second indictment.[48] While it is unknown how the *Hoffman* case resolved in court, Hamilton's argument that property acquired after a Confiscation Act judgment was not subject to further confiscation was upheld in *Leonard v. Post*.[49]

Defending Loyalists to the Public

New York's legislature passed the Trespass, Citation, and Confiscation acts before the Treaty of Peace ended official hostilities, but these statutes remained part of the law of the land after the formal end of the war. As we have seen, Alexander Hamilton worked to circumvent, as much as possible, the limitations on process that Loyalists faced in court after the war, but he considered it a gross violation of the New York constitution, the state's "received" body of common law, and the treaty that Loyalists and British subjects should even have to contend with such restrictions. Hamilton thought that since the treaty had been signed and ratified, it was time for New York to come to terms with the fact that the war was over, independence had been won, and the British threat was gone. More importantly, New Yorkers had to abide by the legal realities that accompanied the end of war: the treaty protected British subjects from further confiscations and prosecutions, and everyone else, no matter their sympathies before the war, became an inhabitant of New York state.

Given the prolonged British occupation of New York's southern district during the war—and the Patriots' lasting fears and hatred of the British after evacuation—it is not surprising that editorialists warned Tories that "we are not disposed to admit you as fellow citizens."[50] But in response to this widely shared, vindictive sentiment, Hamilton penned the first *Letter from Phocion* in January 1784, aiming to convince Patriots that the security of their rights and liberties depended on the restoration of these privileges to Loyalists. By arguing that former Loyalists who, after the war, identified themselves as Americans were bona fide New York citizens, Hamilton associated the intentionally spiteful due process violations endured by Loyalists with America's tenuous republican experiment.[51] The legislature's denial of legal process to an unpopular few posed a looming threat to the rights and liberties enjoyed by everyone—even Patriots. In making this claim, Hamilton also gave the judiciary, the overseers of due process, a necessary institutional role in the new republic: counterweight to legislative tyranny.

Implicit in Hamilton's first and second *Phocion* essays is the premise that by denying or limiting due process in civil suits prosecuted after the war (like trespass actions), the legislature punished a whole class of people for treasonous behavior without legally convicting them for their individually committed, overt acts of treason. By classifying all Loyalists as adhering to the enemies of the state without conducting individual treason prosecutions to demonstrate, by law, that each Loyalist was actually an enemy of the state, the New York legislature violated, postbellum, the constitutional rights and privileges accorded to all. Becoming a traitor required presentment, indictment, prosecution, and determination by a jury according to law. Thus any statutory penalties incurred from general legislative indictments of treason did not constitute the required judicial prosecution at law, and could not justify any revocation or diminution of rights or privileges enjoyed through citizenship.

To begin his case, Hamilton reminded his Patriot brethren of the "spirit of Whiggism" that "cherishes legal liberty, holds the rights of every individual sacred, condemns or punishes no man without regular trial and conviction of some crime declared by antecedent laws, [and] reprobates equally the punishment of the citizen by arbitrary acts of legislature."[52] Yet Phocion noted, despite this ardent Whiggism that animated the Revolution, arbitrary legislatures had "expell[ed] a large number of their fellow-citizens unheard [and] untried"—a frightening thought to liberty-loving citizens because "if [the legislature] may banish at discretion all those whom particular circumstances render obnoxious, without hearing or trial, no man can be safe."[53]

Yet under New York's 1777 constitution, all "member[s] of this state" should be safe because the legal process was guaranteed:

> The 13th article of the constitution declares, "that no member of this state shall be *disfranchised* or *defrauded of any of the rights or privileges* sacred to the subjects of this state by the constitution, unless *by the law of the land or the judgment of his peers.*" If we enquire what is meant by the law of the land, the best commentators will tell us, that it means *due process of law, that is, by indictment or presentment of good and lawful men,* and trial and conviction in consequence.[54]

After citing this constitutional guarantee of judicial due process, Hamilton focused on its implications. Regarding those "obnoxious" Tories, they were all safe from any further prosecutions: the treaty expressly protected those who considered themselves to be British subjects, and the rest, the Loyalists who chose to be Americans, were already genuine citizens of New York and enjoyed protections under the constitution (as well as residual benefits from the treaty's prohibitions of further wartime prosecutions).[55] Again, as Hamilton was keen to emphasize, imperiling any person's right to the due process of law imperiled everyone's rights and liberties protected by law.

After publication, the first *Letter* met with various criticism in the New York press, but the most notable responses came from "a Mechanic" and "Mentor" (Isaac Ledyard). The Mechanic flung knowing, nasty personal insults at Phocion—"Your pedigree is of the *bastard* and *degenerate* kind"—and condemned Hamilton's advocacy of "an impure nest of Vipers . . . the very blood-hounds and blood-suckers of our lives and liberties!" The Mechanic could not hide his outrage that to such "inveterate and intestine enemies—vipers" Phocion "would wish to introduce and restore to the rights of citizenship!"[56] Mentor's response, however, was more legalistic and level-headed because he based his denial of Loyalist citizenship on the language of the Treaty of Peace (though he too could not resist inserting some personal and professional digs at Hamilton). Mentor assessed all Loyalists as traitors, and by the treaty, they either remained British subjects or became British subjects—but either way, all British sympathizers were aliens in New York. Moreover, Mentor denied that any judicial prosecutions were necessary to legally determine treasonous acts because the treaty's language provided the necessary legal stipulations.[57]

Knowing that his claims concerning Loyalist citizenship had not fully resonated with New Yorkers, Hamilton wrote again in April 1784, and this time, his *Second Letter from Phocion* put forth a more legalistic argument that denied Mentor's interpretation of the treaty and more precisely established, rather than just asserted, the Loyalists' legal status as citizens.[58]

The *Second Letter* built on and enhanced Hamilton's previous arguments concerning the interdependence of Loyalist citizenship, due process, and the rights and liberties guaranteed to "member[s] of this state." Hamilton first defined five premises undergirding these larger arguments, each describing a fundamental aspect of due process according to the law of the land.[59] Next, he set the date for determining citizenship as July 9, 1776—the date New York acceded to the Declaration of Independence—thus firmly demarcating the moment in time when any person remaining on New York soil was a member of the state and owed allegiance to the state. British sympathies did not renounce this allegiance, nor did peacefully residing behind enemy lines during the occupation of New York City. Neither circumstance could legally revoke the privileges of citizenship, or a citizens' requisite allegiance to New York.[60]

Furthermore, if legitimate treason was suspected of a Loyalist, then such an accusation presumed two things. First, for a legally valid charge of treason to stand, the treasonous actor must be presumed a citizen, for aliens could not, by definition, commit treason against a government to which they are alien, and thus have no allegiance.[61] Also, as emphatically indicated in the first *Letter*, citizens were constitutionally entitled to the due process of law to indict, prosecute, and legally adjudge their treasonous acts before any punishments could forfeit their legal rights and privileges. Hamilton made it clear that Patriots could not have it both ways: either Loyalists were aliens, and thus protected by the treaty and not subject to further prosecutions under Anti-Loyalist statutes, or they were bona fide members of New York state, and thus legally entitled to the due process of law before any further punishments, forfeitures, banishments, confiscations, or discriminatory limitations to civil process could be inflicted upon them. Anything less would be a "barefaced tyranny" perpetrated by arbitrary legislatures acting against the true nature of republican governments.[62]

Hamilton addressed these *Letters* to the people of New York to persuade them that it was the legislature, not the British nor their sympathizers, that posed the most imminent threat to the people. The elected assembly threatened the rights of all, not just the rights of the "obnoxious" few. By addressing the public, Hamilton hoped that their subsequent outcry would demand that representatives change the existing law that limited the legal process available to Loyalists. Just as Hamilton did not attempt to persuade the Mayor's Court to void the Trespass Act, Hamilton did not suggest in his public commentary that courts could or should void the Anti-Loyalist statutes that threatened the rights of New York citizens. Instead, by insisting that the privileges of citizenship were protected through judicial process, Hamilton defined the particularly important role of the judiciary in republican government: as guardians of the people's rights and liberty through the due process of law. The courts had a constitutional mandate to provide the process that prevented a citizen from arbitrarily losing his civic and political rights.

By invoking Whig rhetoric and by demonstrating how postbellum treatment of Loyalists endangered the privileges of citizenship, Hamilton positioned the common law courts as serving a crucial role in republican government because they provided the legal safeguards necessary to protect "member[s] of this state" against the asserted supremacy of the legislature. Moreover, Hamilton made it clear that when any legislature imposed statutory indictments and forfeitures on its inhabitants without allowing proper prosecutions under the due process requirements, such a legislature effectively usurped judicial powers and rendered itself a tyrant.[63] To resist this unauthorized seizure of power, Phocion called on the people to demand change in the existing law, and ultimately to preserve the republic that they had just created.

Alexander Hamilton and the Freedom of the Press

Hamilton relied on his extensive conception of common law to combat Anti-Loyalist discrimination by arguing that New York had received the law of nations into the law of the land, by attempting to use writ of error review to circumvent statutory law, and by appealing to the due process rights provided by the common law as a privilege of English, and now American, citizenship. He also advocated for other procedural safeguards, like a motion for new trials in civil cases, throughout his career as a practicing attorney.[64] Although Hamilton devised this rights strategy in the 1780s, he returned to it throughout his legal career, including his final famous defense of Federalist printer Harry Croswell and the freedom of the press.

In *People v. Croswell*, a criminal libel prosecution initiated in 1803 and decided the following year, Hamilton argued Croswell's motion for a new trial based on his extensive interpretation of common law received under the New York constitution.[65] During posttrial arguments, the question at hand was a constitutional one: what exactly was the common law of criminal libel, as received by New York's 1777 constitution?[66]

Croswell is most often considered in the context of an emerging free press doctrine—that is, historians are usually interested in the case for how it fits within a developing narrative of a free and open press.[67] While Hamilton can seem a vanguard of sorts in these accounts for arguing in favor of truth as a viable defense to libel prosecutions, some legal scholars take the opposite approach, because Hamilton openly praised the Sedition Act in *Croswell*. He also instigated and participated in criminal libel suits of his own, notably against publisher David Frothingham, during the last years of Adams's term in office.[68] As the Federalists' political fortunes waned, Hamilton and his faction seemed to be in favor of suppressing political critiques from rivals. For these reasons, *Croswell* can be viewed as a missed opportunity or as a stagnation of free press doctrine. Hamilton has frequently been cast as a historical villain for his failure to move legal practice further along from politically motivated sedition prosecutions and the Blackstonian doctrine of "no prior restraint."[69]

Yet the lawyers arguing for and against Harry Croswell's motion for retrial were not asking the court to change the law of criminal libel. Instead, they were concerned with establishing what the law of criminal libel was in the first place. Hamilton and his colleagues asked the court to declare, but not to change, the law of criminal libel as received by the 1777 constitution.[70] *Croswell* thus marked a pivotal moment of constitutional uncertainty in New York law, and it sparked a high-profile debate over the meaning of common law in the early republic. New York's preeminent lawyers used arguments about the nature and scope of the common law received by New York's constitution as a way to answer a pressing question facing the state: what was the law of seditious libel in the American republic?

Hamilton led the defense's case for an extensive interpretation of the common law, as received by the New York constitution. He argued that common law encompassed much more than just the decisions of the justices in Westminster. The jurisprudential circumstances surrounding *People v. Croswell* provided the defense with a particularly ideal opportunity to invoke Hamilton's extensive common law. The prosecution first cited Lord Chief Justice Mansfield for articulating what they claimed was a clear, unassailable statement of the law of seditious libel. But in reality, the law in England was muddled, and the defense would leverage this imprecision and confusion by advancing a broad and historical approach to English precedent.[71]

Next, the defense merged this broad conception of common law with a strategy of sifting through the entire history of English constitutionalism in order to make their argument. This methodology had particular resonance under New York law. The state's 1777 constitution had modeled New York's highest court after the House of Lords, one of England's oldest and most distinctive institutions. By creating the Court for the Correction of Errors, the state constitution also retained a Parliament-like body: a combined upper legislative house and highest judicial court that predisposed its members, including the justices of the New York Supreme Court who presided over the *Croswell* case, to be responsive to past and current parliamentary precedent as part of or relevant to the law of seditious libel upheld by New York law.

Finally, both the defense and the prosecution recognized the opportunity to insist that the common law, as their side defined it, provided the ultimate bulwark for individual liberty in a republic.[72] The attorneys enhanced this argument by associating their version of common law libel doctrine with certain legal rights—for instance, a right to protect one's reputation or a right to equal treatment under the law—which in turn, they claimed, helped thwart partisanship, the unsavory unintended consequence of American republicanism. The lawyers positioned their opponents' version of common law, on the other hand, as undercutting common law rights, enabling partisanship, and producing legal outcomes that were repugnant to republican government and to the New York constitution.

Determining Seditious Libel Law in New York

Harry Croswell's counsel placed its motion for a new trial on two grounds, both of which disputed the common law doctrine declared by trial judge

Chief Justice Morgan Lewis. Lewis had presided over the trial, which proceeded at a circuit court convened at Claverack, New York, on July 7, 1803. First, the defense attorneys insisted that the jury had been misdirected by Lewis. The chief justice had stated that the common law of criminal libel restricted the jury to consider only the fact of publication and whether the publication's innuendos meant what the prosecution said they meant (that they referred to President Thomas Jefferson). The defense's second ground for retrial was that the common law allowed evidence of truth to be proffered, making it necessary that the original trial should have been put off until the next circuit so that the defense could round up those witnesses who would testify to the truth of the publication. At trial, Lewis had instructed the jury not to consider the truth or falsity of the publication, or Croswell's intent.[73]

After reassembling their respective legal teams for oral argument, the prosecution and the defense met in the New York Supreme Court at Albany on February 13–14, 1804.[74] Chief Justice Lewis presided, along with justices James Kent, Henry Brockholst Livingston, and Smith Thompson, to resolve the question: what was the law of criminal libel in New York? William W. Van Ness opened for the defense, and he was followed by both of the state's attorneys, George Caines and Attorney General Ambrose Spencer. Arguments concluded with Richard Harison and Alexander Hamilton for Croswell.

Caines and Spencer agreed with Chief Justice Lewis's understanding of common law doctrine, which comported with the law declared in Peter Zenger's case (New York, 1735) and most recently by Lord Mansfield in *Rex v. Shipley*, more commonly known as the *Dean of St. Asaph's Case* (King's Bench, 1784).[75] In the *Dean of St. Asaph's Case*, Mansfield made clear that the law of criminal libel differed from other types of criminal prosecutions; that is, the jury did not decide on the general issue—whether the defendant was guilty or innocent of criminal libel—but rather it deliberated only on the narrow factual question of whether or not the accused had published the libelous piece. Mansfield cited a string of King's Bench cases, including *Queen v. Tutchin* (1704), *Rex v. Franklin* (1731), and *Rex v. Owen* (1752), to support this position.[76] According to England's former chief justice, if the jury determined guilt on the basis of the publisher's intent, this would permit the jury to determine law, rather than fact, which would invite a dangerous instability into English law.[77] The *Croswell* prosecution echoed this warning against inviting "chaos" into the law, should the defense's version of common law libel be adopted by the court.[78] Mansfield's account of criminal libel law conformed to Chief Justice Lewis's jury instructions at trial.

Lord Mansfield's statement of the law of criminal libel constituted the core of the prosecution's position in *Croswell:* the common law adopted in New York reflected only what the judges in Westminster said it was. And with few exceptions—notably the *Seven Bishop's Case* (1688)—the King's Bench had ruled that juries did not decide on both law and fact in criminal libel actions. Also, for actions of criminal libel, truth was never a viable defense.[79]

Yet the English law of seditious libel had been changing over the course of the late eighteenth century—a development obscured by Mansfield's declaration of the law of seditious libel in the *Dean of St. Asaph's Case.* Beginning after 1770, prosecutions for politically motivated criminal libels emphasized the seditious effects of the publication in question (that is, the potentially deleterious effect of the words on society) rather than the text's unlawful nature. The lawyers involved in late eighteenth-century English libel trials began to frame their arguments around the question of whether the effect of the publication was seditious (an increasingly contextual, and thus factual, matter for the jury to decide) rather than the question of whether the words were libelous (a point of law for the judge to determine).[80] Mansfield's assertion that the jury could decide only the narrow question of publication thus proved unworkable. Consequently, before Parliament passed Fox's Libel Act to allow the jury to decide on the general issue, the English law of seditious libel had already begun blurring together the questions of libel and sedition (law and fact) such that both matters had to be left to the jury.[81]

This muddled, transitory state of English criminal libel law could work to Croswell's advantage, however: if Mansfield's pronouncement of criminal libel law did not even match the true state of the law in England, how could it be an authority for the law in New York? The defense's extensive conception of the common law allowed them to mine other sources of English law in order to present a more advantageous (and more accurate) description of the English law of seditious libel to the New York Supreme Court.

Because the *Croswell* court was familiar with Mansfield's ruling on criminal libel law, the prosecution moved on to deflecting critiques of its strict version of common law and to elaborating the benefits of King's Bench doctrine. For example, both sides suggested that the infamous Star Chamber, a prerogative court abolished in 1641, originated the doctrine of libel law embraced by eighteenth-century King's Bench justices. But to the defense, libel law coming from the Star Chamber was tainted. Van Ness called the Star Chamber "corrupt" and "a tool of despotism," while Hamilton rather dramatically described it as "one of the most oppressive institutions that ever existed" whose "horrid judgments cannot be read without freezing the blood in one's veins."[82] In response to and in anticipation of these sentiments, Caines reassured the *Croswell* court that the Star Chamber's reputation was tarnished only by the fact that it did not use juries in its often ex parte operations. Those legal principles handed down from the Star Chamber court were not only good law but also represented law that was in accordance with the true common law of criminal libel.[83] Furthermore, the prosecution added, the ancient statutes and supposedly common law proceedings presented by the defense did not even hint at true common law doctrine.[84]

The prosecution attempted to demonstrate to the court how their strict conception of common law comported with (and thus was not repugnant to) New York's constitution. To meet this end, the prosecution connected the particularities of the "course of settled law" to republican purposes.[85]

Caines anticipated possible criticism of the strict approach by pointing out that King's Bench doctrine was not just a set of rules. Behind those formalistic rules rested an important substantive concern: criminal libel law had developed to protect the public against breaches of the peace.[86] Moreover, if incendiary speech went unpunished, this would facilitate not only breaches of the peace but also political partisanship. With this in mind, Caines refuted the defense's contention that true but libelous publications were necessary for republican elections:

> In a republic, it is not a spirit of liberty which we have to keep
> alive,—it is a spirit of faction that we have to repress: and this right
> [the purported "power of libeling" for a better informed electorate],
> thus contended for, without benefiting the first, begets the second; the
> only enemy of our real liberty. It creates the calumniator; that civil
> incendiary, who uses as firebrands, scandal, slander, and invective . . .
> with these he kindles the flame of party spirit.[87]

In seeking to avoid the "inevitable consequences of a factious spirit," Caines reminded the court that Lord Mansfield had already provided New Yorkers with the appropriate solution. Thus, "to prevent these deleterious results," Caines proclaimed, "the strong corrective of common law principles . . . is the only remedy."[88] By this, of course, he meant King's Bench principles of common law.[89]

By introducing political partisanship as a substantive concern of criminal libel law, Caines opened up an opportunity to discuss certain rights protected by their strict version of common law in connection with the evils of political faction. He first suggested that criminal libel law provided for the legal protection of a person's reputation, and later in his speech, he openly declared that the common law protected the "rights of reputation," which were "as sacred as those of property."[90] As a corollary to this point, Caines skeptically questioned whether a right to vote in republican elections also conferred the right to abuse other Americans, be they magistrates or private citizens seeking elected office.[91] Through this comment, Caines attacked the defense's contention that true but libelous information about a candidate or public officer was crucial and relevant to preserving republican elections.[92]

Finally, Caines asserted that to allow truthful libels to be protected under New York law was to invite a double standard into the law, which would be repugnant to the constitution. To this end, Caines presumed a right to equal treatment under the law: if the court declared that truth was a viable defense in criminal libel law, then a double standard would be set for magistrates and private citizens. The law would protect the private citizen from any sort of published libels (under an action of private libel), but the magistrate would not receive the same treatment under the law, for true libels aimed at him would receive no legal protection. Moreover, the damage wrought by unpunished libels of a public official's reputation would affect not only his peace of mind and his character but also his property and the peace of mind of his family.[93]

Attorney General Spencer reinforced Caines's arguments about these rights protected by the King's Bench account of criminal libel law. Spencer reminded the court that because the law of New York state was concerned with the protection of an individual's rights and liberties, it followed that no judge could allow one person to infringe on the rights, property, and happiness of another when acting in accordance with his prescribed judicial duty.[94] But for the most part, Spencer left all talk of rights protected at law to Caines; he focused instead on picking away at the defense's interpretation of a broadly conceived common law.

When Van Ness, Harison, and Hamilton outlined the defense's arguments in favor of a new trial, they built their case on a conception of the common law as more than just the judicial output of the central courts at Westminster. As Hamilton noted in 1787, the common law was the sum total of all the courts in the English realm, and in *Croswell*, Harison looked to "the whole of English law" for guidance on questions of criminal libel.[95] This extensive notion of common law encompassed the entire English constitution, and it meant that the substantive law, rules, and processes of equity, ecclesiastical, and admiralty courts—to name only a few of many English jurisdictions—combined with those narrowly defined, and more commonly known, common law courts (held at Westminster, in county quarter sessions, and on assize) to form a broadly conceived common law shared by Englishmen. Sometimes process and doctrine from these other types of courts conflicted with the output of the King's Bench or Common Pleas, but this circumstance only made it necessary for the New York bench to sift through the sources of common law to declare the particular law in force under New York's constitution.

Parliament, the highest court of the realm, figured prominently in the defense's extensive conception of the common law because its output regularly constituted the truly common, shared law of England. Parliamentary output blurred any formal distinction between legislation and judicial determinations: historically and theoretically, its statutes were decisions of a court, either decreed retrospectively for particular petitioners or aimed prospectively for all subjects of the realm. In their broad conception of common law, the defense treated Parliament's statutes as authoritative, declaratory evidence of the common law and thus relevant for New York's bench to consider.[96]

Particularly relevant was Fox's Libel Act of 1792, the parliamentary statute declaring that in cases of criminal libel, the jury could decide on the general issue, and it should not be confined only to determining the fact of publication.[97] The defense championed Fox's Libel Act as a judicial determination handed down by the highest court of the realm to declare and clarify the actual substance of common law. Hamilton argued that the act did not alter the existing law espoused by Lord Mansfield; instead, it restored the true, time-out-of-mind law of criminal libel. Late seventeenth- and eighteenth-century King's Bench doctrine had muddied the law, and with Fox's Act, Parliament declared that the common law as embodied in ancient statutes reflected the real substance of criminal libel law. The act was not a modification to the law but a declaration of the law—the true legal doctrine of criminal libel—as it had always been. Crucially, given that the New York constitution only adopted common law dating from before April 19, 1775, the defense argued that Fox's Libel Act simply provided evidence of the true criminal libel doctrine already in place in 1775, but that had been confused by the King's Bench version of the law.[98]

During this portion of his arguments, Hamilton also raised a technical question of law for the court to consider: what constituted a valid precedent? He suggested a rubric for determining a true legal precedent: first, nothing but a uniform course of judicial conduct on a legal matter formed a precedent, and if this uniform course was not in place, then the substance of the now questionable precedent must be considered in relation to "principles of general law." If the questionable precedent did not conform to these principles, then the court was free to disregard the judicial conduct that was heretofore erroneously considered to be binding precedent, and to assume instead that the law had never been settled.[99]

According to Hamilton, this was the exact circumstance of Harry Croswell's case: ancient statutes pointed to truth as a defense, and the general principles of criminal common law allowed juries to determine not only the general issue but intent as well.[100] Criminal intent, as Hamilton elaborated earlier in his speech, was an inseparable mixture of law and fact—the one legitimate and indisputable exception to the English judge's duty to decide only on law, and the jury's duty to decide only on fact.[101] The King's Bench judges had developed a criminal libel doctrine that denied truth as a defense and limited the law to a narrow question of the fact of publication, thus denying the jury its power to determine the general issue and the publisher's intent. This meant that the law of England and the law of New York consisted of only "a mere floating of litigated questions" on criminal libel.[102]

Yet England had already taken care of this problem. With Fox's Libel Act, the "highest branch of the judicature of that country" confirmed—and for Hamilton's argument settled—the common law of criminal libel in England. Hamilton continued, "It is in evidence that what we [the defense] contend for was and had been the law, and never was otherwise settled" until Fox's Act.[103] Now Hamilton and his colleagues looked to the supreme court sitting at Albany to resolve New York's problem of unsettled law.

Hamilton argued last, but Attorney General Spencer anticipated these claims and preemptively attempted to mitigate their effects on the prosecution's case. Spencer underscored that English judges and their American counterparts shared a solemn judicial duty to separate the question of law from fact because under the English constitution, the jury "ought not to decide the question of law."[104] The defense's motions for retrial thus stood in contrast to both English and American judges' judicial duty. Furthermore, Spencer resisted the defense's claims that any law originating outside of the courts at Westminster—and especially not the ancient laws cited by Van Ness—constituted the common law of England.[105] He also warned the *Croswell* court that it should deny what amounted to the defense's prodding to change the Zengerian version of criminal libel law because it fell only to the New York legislature, and not to the courts, to make new law or to modify this existing law. Spencer lectured the court, "Let us not, in a Court of justice, attempt, by altering the law, to usurp the power of the legislature."[106] Again, he argued that the English judge served as an example for the American judge: American courts inherited the maxim *jus dicere non jus dare*, which, when further bound by uniquely American notions of separated departmental powers, did not give the court any authority to usurp legislative power and change the law of libel. The legislature altered the law, but it did not declare the law.

In addition, the attorney general denied the defense's contention that Parliament provided contrary evidence to the King's Bench version of criminal libel law. He argued that Parliament's libel act was not evidence of New York's common law because Fox's Act innovated on Mansfield's version of criminal libel law, rather than declaring the law as it existed in 1775.[107]

The defense's argument ultimately revolved around the idea that because various elements of the English constitution, including centuries-old statutes, "principles of general law," Parliament, and King's Bench determinations together formed the broadly defined common law of England, all of it gave evidence as to the common law adopted under New York's constitution. Yet the defense did not stop there in its application of an extensive notion of common law to New York state. The defense also suggested that American institutions—namely Congress and the New York legislature—operated similarly to Parliament and shared a Parliament-like authority to give evidence as to what constituted common law. In republican legislatures, as in Parliament, a fine line separated the power to make the law and the capacity to declare the law.

Defense counsel never argued that American judges could make new law. But the defense looked to Congress to give evidence of the law (the New York legislature had not yet "declared" the law on criminal libel, but they would do so after the *Croswell* court divided and failed to grant the new trial). Referring to Congress's Sedition Act of 1798—which declared truth to be a valid defense against federal sedition (criminal libel) prosecutions—William Van Ness declared:

> The supreme legislature of the union has declared, that by law, truth is a justification. . . . By a recurrence to the statute [the Sedition Act], it will be found, that *that* part of it which permits the truth to be given in evidence is *declaratory*, and the other parts remedial. Ought this Court to doubt after this solemn declaration of the nation on this point? And

is it not bound to regard it as conclusive on this subject? . . . This is an authority pure and unadulterated; above all, it is American.[108]

Hamilton agreed. He affirmed, "I say, the highest legislative body in this country, ha[s] declared that the common law is, that the truth shall be given in evidence, and this I urge as a proof of what that common law is."[109] Congress, it was implied, imitated Parliament's capacity to declare the common law.

Through these arguments, the defense advanced an important claim about the nature of governmental power in the early republic. By implicitly analogizing a congressional power to declare the law to that of Parliament, the defense suggested that while state legislatures were generally fashioned as separate and independent departments from the courts of law, the legislatures' powers often included the capacity to make certain quasi-judicial determinations, like confirming what exactly comprised the law of the land. Keep in mind, however, that Hamilton and Van Ness intended these remarks to persuade judges who also sat on the highest court in New York state, the Court for the Correction of Errors. Analogies between Congress and Parliament would have resonated particularly well with judges who were accustomed to participating in and being overseen by New York's version of the House of Lords.[110]

In 1804, just as in 1788, Hamilton remained a staunch advocate for an independent federal judiciary, and he would not (and did not) make arguments analogizing Congress to Parliament in order to describe the nature of legislative and judicial power at the federal level. But in the context of New York, where the Court of Errors held a primary place in the state's legal and constitutional apparatus, Hamilton thought that New York's bench would be willing to accept congressional law as "proof" of the common law and to adopt his broad conception of the British common law tradition as part of New York's jurisprudence.

The defense did not imply that either Congress or the New York assembly (the lower house) was actually a high judicial court of their respective federal and state realms; yet their extensive common law argument does suggest how American institutions and constitutional law continued to be intimately tied to English constitutionalism. State and federal institutions imitated and relied on British institutions as models, and American jurists and statesmen looked to English law for guidance and precedent.[111] Indeed, the defense's extensive conception of the common law was premised on the notion that American courts could answer novel questions about republican law by scouring the corpus of English law.

Before advocating for Harry Croswell, Hamilton defended Congress's Sedition Act as an innovation on historical common law practice (under the statute, juries could decide the general issue and truth was allowed as a viable defense). At the same time, he argued that common law influenced and infused the US Constitution.[112] Hamilton endorsed the Sedition Act at the federal level for these reasons, though when arguing *Croswell*, he embraced a more enhanced conception of free press liberty as well as an admiration for juries. He further elaborated on these topics when unsuccessfully arguing against the Jeffersonians' repeal of the 1801 Judiciary Act under the pen name Lucius Crassus.[113] With the Federalists out of national power, Hamilton could only appeal to the public to try to convince them that the Republicans' actions jeopardized an independent federal judiciary. Still, the arguments about liberty and common law, made by all of the attorneys in *People v. Croswell* but especially by Alexander Hamilton, demonstrate how the influence of the English constitution and its broadly conceived, truly *common* law continued to be alive and well, and in operation in America's partisan, republican jurisprudence.

Hamilton's Rights Strategy and the Development of American Law

In 1832, Chancellor Kent remembered *People v. Croswell* as Hamilton's finest performance before the New York bench. "I have always considered General Hamilton's argument in that cause the greatest forensic effort that he ever made. He had bestowed unusual attention to the case, and he came prepared to discuss the points of law with a perfect mastery of the subject," Kent recounted. "He believed that the rights and liberties of the people were essentially concerned in the vindication and establishment of those rights of the jury and of the press for which he contended. . . . His whole soul was enlisted in the cause, and in contending for the rights of the jury and a free press he considered that he was establishing the finest refuge against oppression."[114] Kent recognized in *Croswell*, as well as in the entirety of Hamilton's career, what historians and biographers seem to have forgotten: that Alexander Hamilton was rights conscious. Hamilton devoted himself to becoming, in Kent's words, an "inflexible friend of justice and of national civil liberty."[115]

Kent also recognized Hamilton's profound impact on the substance of New York law. Hamilton's extensive common law strategy helped to reverse and amend the state's statutory treatment of unpopular Loyalists—for example, when the people of New York county elected Hamilton in 1787 to be a delegate in the tenth state assembly.[116] Moderate Whigs increasingly challenged and often defeated Anti-Loyalist legislation, and during the period from 1786 to 1788, the legislature restored Loyalists to almost complete citizenship.[117] In this increasingly tolerant atmosphere, Hamilton continued to champion the protections of due process in the law.

During his tenure in the state assembly, Hamilton campaigned for, and succeeded in passing, a modified Trespass Act that repealed "that part which was in violation of the public treaty" and put the courts of justice in "a delicate dilemma, obliged either to explain away a positive law of the state or openly violate the national faith by counteracting the very words and spirit of the treaties now in existence."[118] The amended Trespass Act reinstated the defendant's plea to a military order justification (defendants could now plea military command without relying on a law of nations plea) and granted the right of removal and review to superior courts.[119]

On January 26, 1787, New York's tenth legislature enacted its first statute, "An Act concerning the Rights of the Citizens of this State," into law.[120] This statutory bill of rights originated in the ninth assembly as an attempt by lawmakers to collect and summarize the English law still in effect in New York.[121] Neither Hamilton nor any ninth or tenth session delegate attributed the statutory bill of rights directly to Phocion's influence, yet the specific clauses enumerated in the act, as well as the moderate sentiments pervading the political climate, suggest that Phocion's ideas resonated with the people of New York and their representatives.

The statutory bill of rights addressed many of Hamilton's courtroom and public complaints about the limitations of legal process aimed at Loyalist citizens and British subjects residing in the state. The act affirmed that no citizen of the state may be "disseised of his or her freehold or liberties, or free customs, or out-lawed, or exiled, or condemned, or otherwise destroyed, but by lawful judgment of his or her peers, or by due process of law."[122] Also, no person could be put out of his franchise or freehold without the "due course of law, and if any thing be done contrary to the same, it shall be void in law and holden for none." Furthermore, "that writs and process shall be granted freely and without delay, to *all persons* requiring the same."[123] New Yorkers had regained their common law liberties.

Attorneys for remaining Loyalists must have been relieved as well to read the fourth clause in the bill: "That no person shall be put to answer, without presentment before justices, or matter of record, or due process of law, according to the law of the land, and if any thing be done to the contrary it shall be void in law and holden for error."[124] This clause summarized all that was unfair and unlawful about prosecutions under the Trespass, Citation, and Confiscation acts. Under these statutes, the necessities of presentment, review of errors, and traditional process accorded by constitutional and customary laws of the land had been rendered unnecessary to prosecutions of British subjects and Loyalists in the years during and after the war. Yet with the statutory bill of rights in place, the New York legislature and the Council of Revision—which passed the law without disagreement or comment—affirmed to themselves, to defense attorneys, to the courts, and mainly to the people of New York that the due process of law was not to be denied to any person residing in the state under any circumstances whatsoever.[125]

Hamilton's impact on American seditious libel law extended even further. At the end of its term, in May 1804, the *Croswell* court handed down a divided decision, 2–2, thus defeating the motion for Harry Croswell's retrial. However, since the beginning of February 1804, the New York assembly and senate been considering various bills to "declare" the law of criminal libel once and for all. Their legislative efforts became law on April 15, 1805, and provided that in libel actions, the jury had the right to consider both law and fact, and the jury did not have to find the defendant guilty solely on the basis of the fact of publication. The law also allowed the defendant to offer truth as a justification for his libelous publication.[126] The New York legislature codified the defense's arguments and changed the law of seditious libel in the state. By the time of the Civil War, most states in the Union had adopted the key provisions of New York's modified libel law, thus extending Hamilton's influence across the United States.[127]

Hamilton's rights strategy also affected the nature of judicial power in the American republic, first by transforming the meaning of "common law" into a vast synonym for the entire English legal tradition. This extensive interpretation treated common law as nothing less than the entire legal framework that constituted the realm—the English constitution itself—and fit England's various jurisdictions, substantive law, procedures, and institutions into this common law framework.[128] By treating the common law as the expansive, constitutive law of the land, Hamilton turned English law into a grab bag of potential arguments and examples to use to define relevant, legally valid common law principles to apply in American courts. This extensive strategy in turn positioned New York judges to be in charge of declaring the substantive, nonstatutory law of the land. The judiciary therefore became the guardians of those guaranteed rights and liberties that constituted the celebrated Anglo-American birthright.

In addition, Hamilton viewed English common law as a methodological opportunity to recombine familiar legal materials to fit new, distinctly American conclusions. His extensive conception of common law also managed an important legal sleight of hand: Hamilton's arguments allowed the New York courts to declare new legal outcomes while denying that the judges were actually innovating on existing law or improperly legislating. Because the Hamiltonian strategy treated common law doctrine as part of an expansive legal tradition rather than as only those rules handed down from the Westminster courts, Hamilton's arguments suggested that American judges had a substantial array of valid jurisprudential options available to them to determine the law of the land. The judge remained squarely within his proper judicial duty to "find" the law through other sources, like ancient or declaratory statutes, even if he declared that the law in force differed from Westminster precedent.

Alexander Hamilton thus mapped an alternative route to instrumentality in American law, one where the common law supplied a corpus of legal arguments rather than rigid rules. Hamilton deeply respected common law legal traditions, particularly those concerning common law rights; he simultaneously demonstrated how the common law could be flexible and vast, as well as capable of adapting to American policy ends when used strategically in court.[129] His strategy allowed for judges to adjudicate new legal doctrines within their traditional authority. It also offered a way for the court to resist sudden departures from established legal doctrine, and to enable lawyers and judges to excavate the past in order to meet the legal needs of the present.

Hamilton considered the entire English common law tradition to be intimately and integrally tied to American jurisprudence as a source of precedent, process, and substance for republican law. Hamilton's career, which culminated only a few months after his arguments in *Croswell*, demonstrates that defending a client's rights claim offered the best opportunity for him to invoke the extensive common law, and thus to mine English constitutional history for precedent relevant to American legal questions. Hamilton was openly and consistently concerned with the problem of securing individuals' rights under republican government, and to him, common law, in its most expansive sense, provided the last line of defense separating an individual from an overreaching government, from majoritarian despotism, or from the harmful effects of partisan politics. English law offered an effective counter to the unfavorable consequences of republican government. Because Alexander Hamilton recognized this, he relied on common law to protect his clients' access to their inherited English liberties.

The Federalist

Alexander Hamilton's influence permeates American constitutionalism, beginning with the first part of his lasting, legal legacy: his dedicated use of inherited and selectively applied English legal tools to create a strong executive and an authoritative federal judiciary fit for a constitutional republic. To Hamilton, the most important tool in that toolbox was concurrent constitutionalism, as adapted for the American federal system.

Concurrence had multiple dimensions. Hamilton created and encouraged one form, a functional concurrence between executive and judicial functions, whereby executive officers properly exercised some judgelike discretion and judges operated as administrators. This federal magistracy of cooperating judges and executive officials blurred the boundaries of any strict separation of governmental powers in the early republic. In doing this, Hamilton's magisterial model borrowed directly from the centuries-old British constitution.

More profoundly, concurrence had a lasting impact on the jurisprudence of federal–state relations under the US Constitution. This federal form of concurrence, as articulated by Hamilton in *Federalist* Nos. 32 and 82, provided guidelines for dividing and delegating sovereignty between the national and state levels of government. While early national jurists were quick to adopt Hamilton's guidelines, Hamilton also put this form of concurrent constitutionalism into practice in federal admiralty court, through marine insurance litigation, through arguments in favor of strong federal taxing and borrowing powers, and through equitable trusts and mortgage law. Finally, despite the enhanced authority vested in the newly minted national government, Hamilton demonstrated that the federal system, and especially the still-vibrant state courts, would help to preserve Americans' liberty and common law rights.

It is fitting, then, that the author of *The Federalist* essays on concurrence, federal court jurisdiction, and executive functions helped to augment the power and relevance of the federal magistracy while maintaining the states' authority in practice. While Hamilton's constitutional arguments echo loudly through decisions of the US Supreme Court, he did the most to enhance the scope of federal judicial power within the district and circuit courts, particularly by fostering a close working relationship between his energetic Treasury Department and district judges. Working alongside Hamilton and his team of customs collectors, these federal magistrates sorted out the day-to-day business of governing by resolving the practical details of everyday administration and by executing the letter and spirit of congressional statutes.

Even though scholars have emphasized the treasury secretary's various reports on economic policy as his decisive contribution to the economic successes of the 1790s, in practice, Hamilton's true policy genius was to build a close working relationship with the network of administrators and judges who managed and adjudicated the commercial republic. These executive and judicial officials ensured the success of the nation's economic interests by overseeing the collection of revenue taxes, the remission of penalties, and the prosecution of those who violated customs and neutrality statutes. For Secretary Hamilton, abstract policy recommendations and statutory law could only go so far toward building his vision of a thriving commercial republic. It fell to those who executed that policy—the combined personnel of the federal magistracy—to ensure a delicate balance among the conflicting goals of fostering trade, collecting taxes, and enforcing revenue statutes. In this way, the development and growth of both federal judicial and executive powers were inextricably linked in the early national period.

Throughout the early republic, the combined efforts of many individuals who usually go unrecognized in American history—state and federal judges, teams of administrators, and lawyers from across the states—greatly expanded federal judicial power. This development in law occurred from the concerted efforts of key actors, like Hamilton, as well as from the jurists'

wide-ranging, uncoordinated efforts to reconcile inherited English precedents and newly minted American law with pressing political circumstances.
As described above, federal court authority developed from within—from
the accommodating magisterial relationship forged among the network of
district court judges and administrators who exercised mixtures of executive and judicial powers. Congress also aided the growth of federal judicial
authority by granting the US Supreme Court its writ of error review of state
supreme court decisions (through section 25 of the 1789 Judiciary Act).[1]
Hamilton was the first legal strategist to use this review process strategically; he used it to simultaneously defend his customs collectors and protect
the Treasury's (Hamilton's) interpretation of federal revenue laws.

External political circumstances also hastened the expansion of federal
court jurisdiction. Although Article III of the US Constitution bestowed a
historically limited admiralty jurisdiction on the federal courts, it took the
unanticipated combination of a staunch US neutrality policy plus a carrying-
trade boom to empower the US Circuit Court for the District of Massachusetts to greatly widen the scope of federal admiralty jurisdiction to include
maritime contracts and tort claims. When delivering this decision in *De
Lovio v. Boit*, Justice Joseph Story did not act unilaterally in making this
power grab; instead, he stood on the shoulders of countless litigators and
judges at both the federal and state levels, who, after years of adjudicating
neutrality and marine insurance litigation, made it seem natural and even
obvious to extend the federal admiralty courts' jurisdiction over most maritime disputes.[2]

Of course, federal judicial power increased because the justices on the
federal court of last resort, the US Supreme Court, routinely handed down
nationally oriented decisions that tended not to limit or reduce their authority. But the Marshall and Taney courts frequently supported their opinions
with Hamiltonian arguments. During the early national period, the US Supreme Court, as well as the teams of Federalist, Jeffersonian, and Jacksonian lawyers pleading their causes before the supreme bench, relied heavily
on legal arguments first pronounced by Alexander Hamilton to explain and
to defend his own policy initiatives. From the proper scope of executive
power to the sanctity of the federal fiscal powers, Hamilton articulated legal
arguments to accomplish his particular statecraft goals during his lifetime;
yet after his death, lawyers and judges still cited and repurposed Hamilton's
claims and legal reasoning, thus incorporating them into a lasting American
corpus of constitutional jurisprudence. As a member of the cadre of litigators, administrators, and magistrates who worked in and out of the federal

courts, and as a policy maker, constitutional theorist, and legal strategist who made nation building his life's work, Alexander Hamilton developed American law by instrumentally expanding the authority and jurisdictional reach of all levels of the federal magistracy.

Perhaps it is no surprise that Alexander Hamilton, the leader of the Federalist Party, worked to enhance the power of national institutions like the federal courts and the executive branch, or that he, a trained common lawyer, would seek inspiration and instruction from the British constitution, which Americans had feted as the best, most liberty-loving legal system in the world until the 1760s. Yet these accomplishments comprise only certain aspects of Hamilton's influence on American law. Indeed, the most important part of Hamilton's legal legacy is the one that requires the most rethinking of our typical, uncomplicated, and now centuries-old ideas of Alexander Hamilton's policy goals. Our conceptions of Hamilton must be revised because after examining the ways in which he used law to accomplish his statecraft, Hamilton cannot be properly understood simply as a staunch nationalist. Hamilton's influence on the development of American law demonstrates that he was instead a committed, small-f federalist.

In the preceding chapters, I recast Hamilton as a constitutional strategist fully committed to maintaining and solving the unique legal problems arising from the American federal system. Of course, Hamilton desired that the national government be vested with all the vigorous powers necessary to prevent the absurdities, embarrassments, and impotence that plagued the Confederation Congress. Yet Hamiltonian jurisprudence was not a jurisprudence of nationalism; it was instead a jurisprudence of federalism. Alexander Hamilton's concurrent constitutionalism, his constant focus on identifying and properly defining the contours of national and state power, became his grandest, career-defining statecraft project. As Hamilton used law to accomplish his policy goals, he articulated key principles that outlined the jurisprudence of concurrent constitutionalism. In doing so, his most important influence on the development of American law was to concurrently define, defend, exercise, and maintain both Congress's delegated powers as well as the states' retained authority.

Hamilton's primary intellectual contribution to the jurisprudence of federalism was legislative and judicial concurrence, which again he borrowed from the British constitution, and applied, throughout his legal practice, to republican constitutionalism. He first sketched out a model for concurrence in *Federalist* Nos. 32 and 82, where he described how the national and state governments could simultaneously exercise their overlapping powers yet still coexist with minimal interference. Although in practice Hamiltonian concurrence often resulted in robust exercises of federal power, his objective was not to enhance the national government's authority beyond its constitutional boundaries (as perceived by Hamilton), nor at the expense of the states' retained powers. Instead, he aimed primarily to ensure that the federal government could act without interference from the states.

Hamiltonian concurrence thus justified the nation's sovereign sphere of authority in the face of the states' powerful and occasionally jealous governments, when the central government was still young and untried. In contrast to the new national government, the states retained and exercised formidable powers; they also commanded fierce loyalty from their inhabitants. In the aftermath of the late 1770s, when most states drafted and ratified new constitutions, Americans looked to their home state as the locus of law and order, civil and political rights, welfare regulation, and good republican government.

Hamilton did not use law to diminish these sovereign state powers. Instead, he viewed the problem of federalism in the early republic as how to establish and maintain national authority when the states posed a potentially formidable threat to the exercise of that federal power. Hamiltonian concurrence thus cast a protective bubble over the exercise of both state and national powers. We have seen how this power dynamic played out, for example, over taxes: Hamilton correctly anticipated that state governments would balk at federal revenue taxes, and in response, he articulated fiscal-legal arguments within the framework of concurrence. He argued to both New Yorkers and Virginians that federal taxes were not only constitutionally justified but also did not dilute the states' powers to tax.

The states benefited too. Because of concurrence, as Hamilton pointed out, New York could not lose its taxing or police powers just because the national government levied particular taxes or regulated the collection of its revenues. Concurrence also ensured that state courts remained vibrant and powerful throughout the nineteenth century, and New York's courts in particular handed down cutting-edge legal doctrine arising from its commercial docket. As Morton Horwitz demonstrates, state courts generated most of the transformations in contract, tort, eminent domain, and property law that propelled the expansion of the American marketplace throughout the antebellum era.[3]

By actively litigating important legal questions in state courts, Hamilton also practiced what he preached: he acknowledged the states' concurrent role in defining the character and jurisprudence of the new republic. Where else but in the state courts could Hamilton resolve the finer points of maritime contract law? Or argue that all of New York inhabitants enjoyed the protections of the common law, particularly the due process of law? Also, in the aftermath of Congress's Sedition Act, the state courts became key battlegrounds for contemplating the meaning of the freedom of the press in a republic—an opportunity to shape the law that Hamilton eagerly seized.[4] New York helped to redefine the meaning of freedom of the press across the nation.

In Hamilton's day, the state of New York also proved itself to be a more effective forum for attracting foreign capital than the federal government. Like other foreign and domestic investors in the early national and antebellum years of the republic, Hamilton recognized that state legislatures and courts would be key jurisdictions for attracting, developing, and financing beneficial activities like commerce, manufacturing, and agriculture in the new nation. As a true federalist, Hamilton viewed his national statecraft as working in tandem with—that is, concurrently with—state efforts to achieve the same sorts of policy goals. That he took the opportunity to promote his national goals in state courtrooms is a testament to his commitment to concurrent constitutionalism.

For these reasons, Alexander Hamilton is best understood as a committed federalist—a legacy recognized by those early national judges and lawyers who incorporated Hamiltonian arguments about concurrence, executive discretion, and judicial power into Jacksonian constitutionalism. Dual federalism, the product of Andrew Jackson and Roger Taney's combined constitutional theories, posited that the state and national governments coexisted in separate, sovereign spheres of authority (borrowing from Hamiltonian concurrence) and that the US Supreme Court presided over them, resolving national versus state conflicts like a constitutional umpire. Hamiltonian principles sit at the core of this brand of constitutionalism, as dual federalism embraces Hamilton's robust conception of federal judicial power and his notion of coexistence through concurrence. Even Hamilton's defensive federalism anticipates the notion that law and courts would be responsible for strictly policing the boundaries separating the sovereign state and national spheres.

Hamilton's legal influence thus reaches far into the development of the jurisprudence of American federalism, and it therefore becomes part of the formative core of American constitutionalism itself. Acknowledging this legacy is significant in part because it recasts Hamilton as a dedicated federalist who worked to resolve the unique problems of American federalism rather than as a one-dimensional, die-hard nationalist. Hamilton's formative influence over the jurisprudence of federalism is also important because negotiating the precise boundaries of the federal system became the dominant constitutional problem of the nineteenth century. During the antebellum era, the exact dimensions of federal authority and state sovereignty spilled over into the interwoven questions of states' rights, slavery, comity, and territorial governance, and eventually erupted into a constitutional crisis and civil war. Yet even after war restored the Union, the problem of state and national sovereignty persisted, though in altered forms and through different legal questions. After the war, the US Supreme Court still maintained the doctrine of dual federalism, but the Court applied it to novel questions arising from African Americans' claims to civil and political rights, from the working classes' pleas for workplace reform, and from Congress's still "dormant" commerce powers, which the Court leveraged to establish itself as "the umpire of the nation's free-trade network."[5]

Hamilton's preferred legal toolbox, the corpus of the English common law, offered few solutions to resolve these persistent, shape-shifting problems of federalism and rights in American jurisprudence. During the mid-nineteenth century, American courts slowly abandoned the common law writ system; after Reconstruction, formalist lawyers and judges reduced the remnants of the common law tradition to a rigid set of rules.[6] Deprived of its flexibility and distinct process, the inherited common law no longer provided lawyers with the viable litigation strategy that Hamilton embraced. Positivism, with its emphasis on the will of the sovereign people expressed through statutory law, reigned as well, further reducing and relegating the common law to the interstices or periphery of American law.

Still, even though references to the King's Bench or to the British constitution largely disappeared from American law by the end of the nineteenth century, the common law strategies used by Hamilton, and later discarded by subsequent lawyers, have implications for modern constitutional law. With the rise of legal positivism—and then formalism, followed by realism, and finally originalism—the options and flexibility provided by the founding generation's common law traditions seem to be far removed from modern judging. Yet the eighteenth- and early nineteenth-century embrace of English legal traditions remains relevant even today because it complicates twentieth- and twenty-first-century modes of constitutional interpretation.

If, for example, modern originalist judges seek to uncover and then adhere to lawmakers' original intentions, what does it mean for modern constitutional law that constitutional framers like Hamilton viewed written constitutions through the prism of the (sometimes unwritten) English common law? Are so-called activist judges wrong to rely on "penumbras," substantive due process, or any other extratextual jurisprudential foundations, when Hamilton and his lawyerly brethren looked to the expansive common law tradition to give meaning to both state and federal law? Does judging outside the text of the US Constitution repudiate positivism, or can it coexist by reclaiming an older, revered legal tradition practiced by the Founding Fathers themselves? While these questions await consideration by other legal scholars, they may also persuade historians of Hamilton's contemporaries, like Thomas Jefferson, James Madison, and other lawyer-statesmen of the founding generation, to further uncover how these men used the common law tradition to accomplish their own lawmaking or administrative objectives.[7]

But of that generation, Alexander Hamilton remains the preeminent federalist, lawyer, and lawmaker. One posthumous admirer may even be correct to say, "The nation has not yet produced [one] greater." Recovering Hamilton's legal legacy, therefore, is crucial for understanding the development of American law, as well as for recognizing, to an even greater extent, Hamilton's formative influence on the early republic. We do well, then, to think of Alexander Hamilton as a lawyer, first and foremost, and to reflect on this most fitting of epitaphs:

> Alexander Hamilton sleeps in Trinity churchyard, in the heart of the great metropolis. Scores of lawyers may look from their windows upon his grave; thousands more pass it by heedlessly each day. . . . Pause a moment, heedless thousands! He who sleeps in this churchyard was a lawyer. . . . And how laboriously did he strive, how deep did he delve into the hidden treasures of the right! Great was his victory, and greatly did he deserve it. Pause, hasting thousands! Alexander Hamilton, the lawyer, sleeps here.[8]

And so we pause.

Notes

Introduction: Alexander Hamilton, Lawyer and Lawmaker

1. Hamilton, *Law Practice*, 1:47.

2. See Hamilton, "List of Books" (1773), in Hamilton, *Papers*, 1:42; Hamilton to Richard Varick, "Enclosure: Deficient Books of Mr. Hamilton's Law Library" (June 16, 1795), in Hamilton, *Papers*, 18:378; Elkins and McKitrick, *Age of Federalism*, 97. For a complete list of Hamilton's legal citations, see Hamilton, *Law Practice*, 1:853–867.

3. Staloff, *Hamilton, Jefferson, Adams*; Gould, *Among the Powers of the Earth*; Onuf and Onuf, *Federal Union, Modern World*.

4. Hamilton, "Notes" (June 18, 1787), in *Papers*, 4:184.

5. Burke, "Alexander Hamilton as a Lawyer," 181. Burke, a graduate of Hamilton College's class of 1893, identified three cases which "present Alexander Hamilton, the lawyer, as the defender of truth, the champion of justice, and the expositor of liberty," and include *People v. Levi Weeks* (Court of Oyer and Terminer and General Gaol Delivery for the City and County of New York, 1800), the extended litigation involving merchant Louis Le Guen, and *People v. Harry Croswell*, 3 Johns. Cas. 337 (N.Y. Sup. Ct., 1804).

6. See *Elizabeth Rutgers v. Joshua Waddington* (N.Y. Mayors Ct., 1784); *Hylton v. US*, 3 U.S. (3 Dall.) 171 (1796); and *People v. Croswell*, 3 Johns. Cas. 337 (N.Y. Sup. Ct., 1804).

7. Kent, "Alexander Hamilton: Address," 13; McDonald, *Alexander Hamilton*, 63.

8. Political scientists and the occasional legal scholar have also examined Hamiltonian constitutionalism, a topic that routinely includes the political science of

Publius (Hamilton's shared pseudonym with James Madison and John Jay in the *Federalist* essays), the Hamilton–Jefferson divide over broad constitutional construction, the origins and development of judicial review, and sometimes Hamilton's tax-clause advocacy in *Hylton v. US* as well as his freedom of the press arguments in *People v. Croswell*. See Konefsky, *John Marshall and Alexander Hamilton*; Finkelman, "Alexander Hamilton, Esq."; Meyerson, *Liberty's Blueprint*; Flaumenhaft, *Effective Republic*; Staloff, *Hamilton, Jefferson, Adams*; Federici, *Political Philosophy of Alexander Hamilton*; Staab, *Political Thought of Justice Antonin Scalia*.

9. See, e.g., Hurst, "Alexander Hamilton, Law Maker"; McCraw, *Founders and Finance*; Edling and Kaplanoff, "Alexander Hamilton's Fiscal Reform"; Edling, "So Immense a Power"; Elkins and McKitrick, *Age of Federalism*, 107–131; Nelson, *Liberty and Property*; McCoy, *Elusive Republic*, 136–165; McDonald, *Alexander Hamilton*.

10. For scholarship on Hamilton's political legacy, partisan disagreements, and foreign policy, see Wood, *Empire of Liberty*; Ellis, *Founding Brothers*, 48–80; Freeman, *Affairs of Honor*; Stourzh, *Alexander Hamilton and the Idea of Republican Government*; Harper, *American Machiavelli*.

11. For the details of Hamilton's post-Cabinet career, refer to the scores of Hamilton biographies. Many biographies date from the nineteenth century, but select modern biographies include Miller, *Alexander Hamilton: Portrait in Paradox*; McDonald, *Alexander Hamilton*; Cooke, *Alexander Hamilton*; Kennedy, *Burr, Hamilton, and Jefferson*; Chernow, *Alexander Hamilton*; and Ferling, *Jefferson and Hamilton*. Also, for a survey of Hamilton's popular reception, see Knott, *Alexander Hamilton*.

12. See, e.g., *Youngstown Sheet & Tube Co. v. Sawyer*, 343 US 579 (1952).

13. Edmund Randolph, "Notes on the Common Law" (c. September 1799), written for Madison, *Papers*, 17:261–269.

14. See Dalzell, "Prudence and the Golden Egg" and "Taxation with Representation"; Rao, *National Duties*.

15. For the classic works on common law reception, see Goebel, *Antecedents and Beginnings*, 116–118; Stoebuck, "Reception of English Common Law"; Reinsch, "English Common Law"; Goebel, "King's Law and Local Custom" and "Common Law and the Constitution"; Brown, *British Statutes in American Law*. For modern legal debates about the nature and scope of English law in the early republic, see Hulsebosch, *Constituting Empire*; Hamburger, *Law and Judicial Duty*; Bilder, *Transatlantic Constitution*; Stoner, *Common Law and Liberal Theory*; Parker, *Common Law, History, and Democracy*; Pearson, *Remaking Custom*.

16. A vast literature contemplates the radical change—or lack thereof—that followed the Declaration of Independence. Some of the most important, as well as the most recent, work weighing in on this question includes Beard, *Economic Interpretation*; Bailyn, *Ideological Origins*; Wood, *Creation of the American Republic* and *Radicalism of the American Revolution*; Reid, *Constitutional History*; Breen, *Marketplace of Revolution*.

17. See the "Case of the Duchy of Lancaster, at Serjeant's Inn," in Plowden, *Com-

mentaries, 213–214, pt. 1; Blackstone, *Commentaries*, "Of the King's Prerogative," bk. 1, ch. 7, 1:249; Kantorowicz, *King's Two Bodies*.

18. Black, "Constitution of Empire."

19. Hobson, *Great Chief Justice*; Goebel, *Antecedents and Beginnings*; Haskins and Johnson, *Foundations of Power*; White, *Marshall Court and Cultural Change*; Ellis, *Aggressive Nationalism*; Casto, *Supreme Court*.

20. Gilmore, *Ages of American Law*, 41.

21. For influential titles emphasizing history "from the bottom up," see Nash, *Red, White, and Black*; Kerber, *Women of the Republic*; Johansen, *Forgotten Founders*; Holton, *Forced Founders*; McDonnell, *Politics of War*; Wilf, *Law's Imagined Republic*. Also, Robin L. Einhorn warned against putting too much emphasis on the elites of the founding generation in *American Taxation*.

22. Mashaw, *Creating the Administrative Constitution*; White, *Federalists*; White, *Jeffersonians*; White, *Jacksonians*; Rao, *National Duties*.

Chapter 1. Creating the Federal Magistracy: Discretionary Power and the Energetic Executive

1. Hamilton introduced these "ingredients" in *Federalist* No. 70 and expounded on them in Nos. 71–77.

2. Historical, legal, and political science scholarly commentary on Hamilton and executive power includes Flaumenhaft, *Effective Republic*; Rossiter, *Alexander Hamilton and the Constitution*; Federici, *Political Philosophy of Alexander Hamilton*; Calabresi and Yoo, *Unitary Executive*; Corwin, *President*; Chernow, *Alexander Hamilton*. Hamilton's arguments about executive discretionary authority also have an intellectual lineage that includes not only Marshall and Taney court decisions but also twentieth-century Court decisions on executive power such as *Youngstown Sheet & Tube Co. v. Sawyer*, 343 US 579 (1952), and *US v. Nixon*, 418 US 683 (1974).

3. Otho H. Williams to Hamilton (July 27, 1792), in Hamilton, *Papers*, 12:119–122. Caldwell identified the law as an important, stabilizing force that undergirded Hamilton's administrative theories and practices in *Administrative Theories*, 18–22.

4. For a recent analysis of Hamilton's strident defense of the royal prerogative, as well as the presidential prerogative, throughout the imperial crisis, Confederation era, and the constitutional debates of 1787–1788, see Nelson, *Royalist Revolution*, 53–56, 102–103, 168–170, 190–195, 210–213, 217–226. See also Prakash, *Imperial from the Beginning*.

5. Leonard D. White referred to Hamilton as "the greatest administrative genius of his generation in America, and one of the great administrators of all time." White, *Federalists*, 125–126. See also Mashaw, *Creating the Administrative Constitution*, 29–33, 56.

6. Wood, *Creation of the American Republic*, 132–150.

7. James Madison, for example, warned that "if [the executive power is] large, we shall have the Evils of Elective Monarchies." Qtd. from Rufus King's notes on the 1787 Convention in King, *Life and Correspondence*, 1:588. President George

Washington also expressed concerns that the public suspected his administration of establishing monarchical practices, among other misdeeds. See, e.g., Washington to Hamilton (July 29, 1792), in Washington, *Papers*, 10:588–592; Bartoloni-Tuazon, *For Fear*; Ketcham, *Presidents Above Party*, 3.

8. On early American views of the prerogative power, see Nelson, *Royalist Revolution* and "Patriot Royalism"; Wood, "Problem of Sovereignty"; Maier, "Whigs against Whigs against Whigs"; Hulsebosch, "Plural Prerogative."

9. White, *Federalists*, 450–455.

10. Hamilton was not alone in describing judges and executive officials as "magistrates"; other members of the founding generation, including James Madison, Thomas Jefferson, and George Washington, did so as well. Jefferson spoke of "the most determined zeal of our chief magistrate," and Madison referred to the "present chief magistrate" when discussing the president's removal powers. Washington did the same. At the outset of his second inaugural address, the unanimously reelected president gratefully acknowledged that "I am again called upon, by the voice of my country, to execute the functions of its Chief Magistrate." Jefferson to Harry Innes (March 7, 1791), in Jefferson, *Papers*, 19:521; Madison's "Removal Power of the President" speech in Congress (June 16, 1789), in Madison, *Papers*, 19:225–226; Washington's "Second Inaugural Address" (March 4, 1793), in Washington, *Papers*, 12:264.

11. Scholarship on English and colonial magistrates includes Landau, *Justices of the Peace*; Henretta, "Magistrates, Common Law Lawyers, Legislators"; Langbein, Lerner, and Smith, *History of the Common Law*, 229–238, 880.

12. If the Treasury was going to successfully collect revenue, the collectors at port needed to process incoming vessels efficiently. Therefore, initiating lawsuits to clarify each detail of statutory construction would be time-consuming and not conducive to active trade. In response, Hamilton advised his customs collectors to turn to him, rather than to the courts, to clarify points of law. Hamilton instructed the collectors: "It is true that a remedy, in a large proportion of the cases, might be obtained from the Courts of Justice; but the vexatious course of tedious law suits to decide whether the practice of one Officer, or of another, was the most legal, would be a mode of redress very unsatisfactory to suffering parties—and very ill suited, as an ordinary expedient, to the exigencies and conveniences of Trade." See "Treasury Department Circular to the Collectors of the Customs" (July 20, 1792), in Hamilton, *Papers*, 12:59.

13. G. Edward White's seminal volume on the Marshall Court, *Marshall Court and Cultural Change*, is an extended study on how Chief Justice John Marshall and his associates put the Hamiltonian concept of coextensivity into practice.

14. Hamilton, "Explanation" (November 11, 1795), in Hamilton, *Papers*, 19:423.

15. See *Federalist* Nos. 66 and 67.

16. This formulation of the judge's "judicial duty" was inherited from English common law judges and is described in Hamburger, *Law and Judicial Duty*.

17. Landau, *Justices of the Peace*, 6; Baker, *Introduction to English Legal History*, 149. See also Gillis, "Conduits of Justice."

18. Michael Dalton's *Countrey Justice*, a thick handbook published in 1619 for local English magistrates that was also widely read in America, indicated just how extensive local magisterial responsibilities could be. These obligations included administering the poor laws, imposing quarantines during plague outbreaks, organizing and implementing efforts to repair local infrastructure (particularly bridges, roads, and sewers), setting and overseeing weights and measures used in trade, and keeping the peace throughout the county. Dalton, *Countrey Justice*, 34–36, 58–64, 79–90, 118–122, 128–135.

19. Landau, *Justices of the Peace*, 21.

20. Baker, *Introduction to English Legal History*, 143, 149. The writ of certiorari could not be used to call into question or overturn the magistrates' purely administrative (discretionary) decisions, however, a distinction that the US Supreme Court would later maintain for mandamus actions. Baker described the central courts' use of certiorari: "As with error, the superior court was limited to an examination of the record to ensure that no order or conviction was *ultra vires*. It could not conduct a new trial or act as a court of appeal" (149).

21. Dalton, *Countrey Justice*, 18.

22. Surrency, "Courts in the American Colonies," 267–268; Olwell, "Practical Justice."

23. Henretta, "Magistrates, Common Law Lawyers, Legislators," quote at 569, but see in general 555–582.

24. See, e.g., the Remitting Act ("An Act to provide for mitigating or remitting the forfeitures and penalties accruing under the revenue laws, in certain cases therein mentioned"), ch. 12, 1 Stat. 122 (1790), and the 1792 Invalid Pensions Act ("An Act to provide for the settlement of the Claims of Widows and Orphans barred by the limitations heretofore established, and to regulate the Claims to Invalid Pensions"), ch. 11, 1 Stat. 243 (1792). For federal process acts, see sections 13 and 14 of the 1789 Judiciary Act ("An Act to establish the Judicial Courts of the United States"), ch. 20, 1 Stat. 73, 81 (1789), and the Process Act ("An Act to regulate Processes in the Courts of the United States"), ch. 21, 1 Stat. 93 (1789). See also Mashaw, *Creating the Administrative Constitution*, 40–64.

25. *Federalist*, 438–439 (No. 78).

26. Ibid., 441, 437 (emphasis added).

27. Ibid., 441.

28. 5 U.S. (1 Cranch) 137 (1803).

29. Hamburger, *Law and Judicial Duty*, 380–383.

30. See the 1790 Funding Act ("An Act making provision for the Debt of the United States"), ch. 34, 1 Stat. 138 (1790). *US v. Hopkins* (1794) went unreported but can be found in the minutes of the Supreme Court during February 13–15, 1794. See also Marcus, *Documentary History*, 6:356–363.

31. *Federalist*, 402 (No. 70), emphasis added.

32. Blackstone, *Commentaries*, "Of the King's Prerogative," bk. 1, ch. 7, 1:240.

33. Ibid., 1:239.

34. Ibid., 1:250.

35. Ibid., 1:270.

36. *Federalist*, 418 (No. 73).

37. See *Federalist* Nos. 73, 74, 76, and 77 for Hamilton's discussions of these powers.

38. *Federalist*, 410 (No. 71).

39. *Federalist*, 422 (No. 74).

40. See "Philip Vigol Stay of Execution" (June 16, 1795), in Washington, *Papers*, 18:242–243, as well as Washington's stay of execution for John Mitchell in US National Archives and Records Administration, Washington, DC, RG59, "Copies of Presidential Pardons and Remissions, 1794–1893." Washington's pardons for Mitchell and Vigol can be found at the US National Archives as well.

41. See Washington to Hamilton (September 17, 1792), in Hamilton, *Papers*, 12:391–392. Washington published the final draft of his proclamation on August 7, 1794; see "Proclamation," in Washington, *Papers*, 16:531–537.

42. *Federalist*, 423 (No. 74).

43. See George Washington to Edmund Randolph (March 1, 1791), in Washington, *Papers*, 7:493–495, note 1, as well as the 1790 Collection Act ("An Act to provide more effectually for the collection of the duties imposed by law on goods, wares, and merchandise imported into the United States, and on the tonnage of ships or vessels"), ch. 35, 1 Stat. 145 (1790). The 1790 act went into effect on October 1, 1790 (per section 74).

44. See Washington to Edmund Randolph (March 1, 1791), in Washington, *Papers*, 7:493–495, including note 1, which reproduces parts of Dodge's petition. For the entire petition, see Samuel Dodge's petition, dated February 24, 1791, in US National Archives and Records Administration, Washington, DC, RG59, "Miscellaneous Letters, 1790–1799."

45. 1 Stat. 122 (1790).

46. See Hamilton to Harison (March 18 and April 26, 1791), in Hamilton, *Papers*, 8:202, 312–314, and Harison to Hamilton (May 24, 1791), in ibid., 8:352.

47. Hamilton to Harison (April 26, 1791), in Hamilton, *Papers*, 8:312–314, and Washington to Randolph (March 1, 1791), in Washington, *Papers*, 7:493.

48. Hamilton and Harison both thought that common law principles governed this question. Hamilton noted, "There is a general rule that a power to pardon cannot be exercised so as to divest Individuals of a right of action for their sole benefit, or of a *vested* right which they have in conjunction with the sovereign; as where there is a penalty part to the use of the Public and part to the use of an informer." Harison agreed: "The principles of the Common Law of England upon this Subject appear to be founded in good sense and I think must govern where-ever they apply." Hamilton to Harison (April 26, 1791), in Hamilton, *Papers*, 8:312, and Harison to Hamilton (May 24, 1791), in ibid., 8:352.

49. Harison to Hamilton (May 24, 1791), in ibid., 8:352–354.

50. See Nicholas Romayne to Hamilton (April 9, 1792), in ibid, 11:257n2.

51. Pacificus No. 1 (June 29, 1793), in Hamilton, *Papers*, 15:38.

52. Ibid., 40; emphasis added in second quote.

53. Ibid., 43; emphasis added.

54. Casto, *Foreign Affairs*, 82.

55. I borrow Jerry L. Mashaw's apt characterization of Hamilton's administrative style. See Mashaw, *Creating the Administrative Constitution*, 56.

56. Mashaw observed that in the early republic, "The most impressive contribution to [administrative] lawfulness came . . . from the system of internal control established by the Treasury." Ibid., 100, 104. Hamilton began this system —particularly the circular communications—and Oliver Wolcott Jr. and Albert Gallatin continued it to great effect.

57. James Madison considered the comptroller's claims adjudication function to be partaking of both executive and judicial duties. See *Annals of Congress*, House of Representatives, 1st Congress, 1st Session, 635–636 (June 29, 1789).

58. The first Congress received hundreds of petitions, which ranged from citizens' unsolicited advisory opinions to Congress regarding policy to protests against slavery. For a summary of the various types of petitions submitted to the First Federal Congress, see diGiacommantonio, "Petitioners and Their Grievances," 29–56. For a brief history of the right to petition in America, see Higginson, "Short History."

59. The Gilder Lehrman Institute of American History, New York, holds documents relating to Knox's claims adjudication process. Included are a 1790 statement of facts relating to *US v. George Tyler*, a libel brought by a John Lee, a collector at Penobscot, as well as a letter between Tyler and Knox; Gilder Lehrman Collection, GLC02437.04749 and GLC02437.04748. Also, Gilder Lehrman holds a 1793 list of Revolutionary War officers' claims under consideration by Knox (GLC02437.05837).

60. "Report on the Petition of Jacob Rash" (August 5, 1790), in Hamilton, *Papers*, 6:543–544.

61. *Journal of the House*, 1st Congress, 2nd Session, 253 (June 29, 1790).

62. Hamilton's proposed solution created a procedure that, if legalized by statute, would help to identify these creditors who lost their certificates through a verifiable accident. First, the renewed certificates could only be reissued to those who held them at the time the certificates were destroyed; second, the holders must adhere to the common law practice of presentment, or advertising in newspapers, the time, place, and means for the destructions of their certificates; third, a copy of the advertisements had to be on file with the state office of the commissioner of loans; fourth, the holders would enter into a bond with other freeholders to indemnify the United States against the possibility of the certificates suddenly reappearing as possessions of other holders; and finally, no certificates would be renewed until three months after the newspaper advertisements had been published. He concluded the petition with a warning that proving ownership of certificates that had been lost or captured would be so difficult that no remedy could be available. Otherwise, these claims would "subject the United States to so much hazard of imposition and injury." See "Report on the Petition of Jacob Rash" (August 5, 1790), in Hamilton, *Papers*, 6:543–544.

63. "Report on Sundry Petitions" (April 18, 1792), in ibid., 11:299–315.

64. "Report on Sundry Petitions" (April 18, 1792), No. 7, in ibid., 11:305.

65. "Report on Sundry Petitions" (April 18, 1792), No. 11, in ibid., 11:307–308.

66. "Report on Sundry Petitions" (April 16, 1792), in ibid., 11:282–288.

67. "Report on the Petition of Joseph Bennett" (February 27, 1794), in ibid., 16:62–63.

68. Hamilton avoided the unworkable precedent of compensating for depreciation in his "Report on the Memorial of James Warren" (April 12, 1790), in ibid., 6:362–364. Hamilton stated, "That every precedent of an admission of a claim upon that ground [depreciation], beyond the limits now observed at the Treasury, must be more or less dangerous" (363–364).

69. See, in general, Mashaw, *Creating the Administrative Constitution*; Hamburger, *Is Administrative Law Unlawful?*

70. "Treasury Department Circular to the Collectors of the Customs" (July 20, 1792), in Hamilton, *Papers*, 12:57–62. Regarding the duty on spikes and nails, see "An Act for laying a Duty on Goods, Wares, and Merchandises imported into the United States," ch. 2, 1 Stat. 24 (1789), and "An Act making further provision for the payment of the debts of the United States," ch. 39, 1 Stat. 180 (1790). Regarding the fees under the Coasting Act, see "An Act for Registering and Clearing Vessels, Regulating the Coasting Trade, and for other purposes," ch. 11, 1 Stat. 55 (1789).

71. "Treasury Department Circular to the Collectors of the Customs" (July 20, 1792), in Hamilton, *Papers*, 12:58.

72. Ibid. Hamilton's quote referred to section 2 of "An Act to establish the Treasury Department," ch. 12, 1 Stat. 65 (1789).

73. "Treasury Department Circular to the Collectors of the Customs" (July 20, 1792), in Hamilton, *Papers*, 12:59–60.

74. Ibid., 12:58.

75. "An Act for Registering and Clearing Vessels, Regulating the Coasting Trade, and for other purposes," ch. 11, 1 Stat. 55, 63 (1789).

76. "Treasury Department Circular to the Collectors of the Customs" (August 5, 1791), in Hamilton, *Papers*, 9:17.

77. "Treasury Department Circular to the Collectors of the Customs" (November 30, 1789), in ibid., 5:575.

78. See Hamilton to Harison, with Enclosure (November 9, 1789), in ibid., 5:504–506; Harison and Jones to Hamilton (November 18, 1789), in ibid., 5:521–522; Heth to Hamilton (November 20, 1791), in ibid., 9:511–513; Randolph to Hamilton (June 21, 1792), in ibid., 11:536–541.

79. "Treasury Department Circular to the Collectors of the Customs" (November 30, 1789), in ibid., 5:578.

80. "An Act repealing, after the last day of June next, the duties heretofore laid upon Distilled Spirits imported from abroad, and laying others in their stead; and also upon Spirits distilled within the United States, and for appropriating the same," ch. 15, 1 Stat. 199 (1791).

81. "Treasury Department Circular to the Collectors of the Customs," and "[Enclosure:] Explanations and Instructions Concerning the Act" (May 26, 1791), in Hamilton, *Papers*, 8:365–387.

82. "Report on the Difficulties in the Execution of the Act Laying Duties on Distilled Spirits" (March 5, 1792), in Hamilton, *Papers*, 11:79.

83. Ibid., 11:80–81.

84. Hamilton proposed a tax on spirits in his first "Report Relative to a Provision for the Support of Public Credit," submitted to Congress on January 14, 1790.

85. Hamilton responded to the criticism of "A Calm Observer," written to the editor of Philadelphia's *Aurora General Advertiser* on October 23, 1795. See Hamilton's "Explanation" (November 11, 1795), in Hamilton, *Papers*, 19:426, note 1.

86. "Explanation" (November 11, 1795), in Hamilton, *Papers*, 19:410–411, and "An Act for allowing a Compensation to the President and Vice President of the United States," ch. 19, 1 Stat. 72 (1789).

87. "Explanation" (November 11, 1795), in Hamilton, *Papers*, 19:408–409.

88. Ibid., 19:423.

89. Judiciary Act of 1801, "An Act to provide for the more convenient organization of the Courts of the United States," ch. 4, 2 Stat. 89 (1801), and "An Act for altering the times and places of holding certain Courts therein mentioned, and for other purposes," ch. 32, 2 Stat. 123 (1801), were repealed in spring 1802.

90. *Marbury v. Madison*, 5 U.S. (1 Cranch) 137 (1803), and *Little v. Barreme*, 6 U.S. (2 Cranch) 170 (1804).

91. *Gilchrist et al. v. Collector of Charleston*, 10 F. Cas. 355 (C.C.D. S.C., 1808), and *Kendall v. US ex. rel. Stokes et al.*, 37 U.S. (12 Pet.) 524 (1838).

92. Marshall reasoned that section 13 of the 1789 Judiciary Act, which gave the Court authority to issue the writ, violated the US Constitution. Article III granted the US Supreme Court original jurisdiction in only certain, enumerated cases; however, section 13 of the Judicial Act violated Article III by granting the Court original jurisdiction to hear mandamus actions.

93. Thomas W. Merrill argues that *Marbury* should be considered today as nineteenth-century jurists conceived of the decision: as a guide for limiting or allowing executive actions, as opposed to a check on congressional legislation. See Merrill, "*Marbury v. Madison.*"

94. 5 U.S. (1 Cranch) 137, 166 (1803).

95. Ibid.

96. Ibid., 170, 171.

97. Ibid., 158.

98. What I call the "ministerial distinction" comports with what Thomas W. Merrill identified as Marshall's "two tier standard of review" for executive actions that originated in *Marbury* and lives on in modern constitutional decisions like *Chevron USA, Inc. v. Natural Resources Defense Council, Inc.*, 467 U.S. 837 (1984). See Merrill, "*Marbury v. Madison,*" 498–499.

99. Ibid., 146–152.

100. Ibid. 152.

101. Ibid., 149. There is no indication that Hamilton found the Supreme Court's jurisdiction lacking or complicated when he brought *Hopkins* before the 1794 bench.

102. "An Act further to suspend the Commercial Intercourse between the United States and France, and the dependencies thereof," ch. 2, 1 Stat. 613 (1799).

103. The fifth section of the 1799 act authorized the president to instruct the armed merchant marine "to stop and examine any ship or vessel of the United States on the high sea which there may be reason to suspect to be engaged in any traffic or commerce contrary to the true tenor" of the law (1 Stat. 615). If the suspicious vessel was headed to the French Republic, then it could be seized and libeled at port. President Adams subsequently issued instructions to the merchant marine that outright ignored the statute's precise permission for making seizures. Adams instructed his merchant marine that the act "will require the exercise of a sound and impartial judgment," and that they were to "do all that in you lies to prevent all intercourse . . . between the ports of the United States and those of France and her dependencies." (Note how Adams ignored the statute's specific rule that seized vessels be traveling *to* French ports.) His instructions continued, "In cases where the vessels or cargoes are apparently, as well as really, American . . . but you are to be vigilant that vessels or cargoes really [are] American, but covered by Danish or other foreign papers, and bound *to or from* French ports do not escape you." *Little v. Barreme*, 6 U.S. (2 Cranch) 170, 171 (1804).

104. *Little v. Barreme*, 6 U.S. (2 Cranch) 170, 179 (1804).

105. See "An Act laying an Embargo on all ships and vessels in the ports and harbors of the United States," ch. 5, 2 Stat. 451 (1807); Rao, *National Duties*, 147–151.

106. *Gilchrist et al. v. Collector of Charleston*, 10 F. Cas. 355, 356 (C.C.D. S.C., 1808).

107. Rodney noted that if the US Supreme Court denied itself jurisdiction for an original jurisdiction mandamus suit, then the Circuit Court for the District of South Carolina should as well. Ibid., 357.

108. Ibid., 358.

109. Ibid.

110. Jefferson articulated the idea that the president held a coequal power with the federal courts to engage in constitutional review in a September 11, 1804, letter to Abigail Adams and in a September 28, 1820, letter to William Charles Jarvis. See Jefferson, *Writings*, vols. 8 and 10, 8:311n1 and 10:160–161. See also Calabresi and Yoo, *Unitary Executive*, 69–70.

111. According to Johnson, Rodney misunderstood the jurisdictional component of *Marbury*. The case did not preclude the federal courts from issuing mandamus writs as outside the scope of Article III powers. To the contrary, Johnson said, *Marbury* restricted mandamus writs to exercises of its appellate jurisdiction only. Furthermore, he thought that the 1789 Process Act implicitly conferred on the federal courts the authority to issue the writ of mandamus. *Gilchrist et al. v. Collector of Charleston*, 10 F. Cas. 355, 362–363 (C.C.D. S.C., 1808).

112. *Kendall v. US ex. rel. Stokes et al.*, 37 U.S. (12 Pet.) 524 (1838).

113. Ibid., 540, 544, 600.

114. Ibid., 571, 572.

115. Ibid., 611.

116. Ibid., 613.

117. Ibid., 610.

118. Ibid., 626; emphasis added.

119. McCloskey, *American Supreme Court*, 26–27.

120. After its decision in *Kendall v. US ex. rel. Stokes*, however, the Taney Court would be more deferential to executive power than the Marshall Court. Taney's Supreme Court issued a series of decisions that narrowed its ruling in *Kendall v. US* and created uncertainty as to just how far coordinate judicial review could extend. See, e.g., *Kendall v. Stokes*, 44 U.S. (3 How.) 87 (1845), the supplementary decision to *Kendall v. US ex. rel. Stokes*, *Rankin v. Hoyt*, 45 U.S. (4 How.) 327 (1846), and *Bartlett v. Kane*, 57 U.S. (16 How.) 263 (1853).

121. For scholarly debates over modern administrative law, see Jerry L. Mashaw's synthesis of the history and development of administrative law, *Creating the Administrative Constitution*, as well as Hamburger, *Is Administrative Law Unlawful?* Adrian Vermeule and Gary Lawson offered critical responses to Hamburger in Vermeule, "'No': Review of Philip Hamburger, *Is Administrative Law Unlawful?*," and Lawson, "Return of the King."

122. See Konefsky, *John Marshall and Alexander Hamilton*.

Chapter 2. Administrative Accommodation in the Federal Magistracy

1. See, e.g., coordinate judicial review in *Marbury v. Madison*, 5 U.S. (1 Cranch) 137 (1803), and *Kendall v. US ex. rel. Stokes et al.*, 37 U.S. (12 Pet.) 524 (1838); the early national Supreme Court also positioned itself as the final arbiter of constitutional questions in the federal system in *Martin v. Hunter's Lessee*, 14 U.S. (1 Wheat.) 304 (1816), *McCulloch v. Maryland* 17 U.S. (4 Wheat.) 316 (1819), and *Cohens v. Virginia* 19 U.S. (6 Wheat.) 264 (1821).

2. See Hobson, *Great Chief Justice*; Haskins and Johnson, *Foundations of Power*; White, *Marshall Court and Cultural Change*; Ellis, *Aggressive Nationalism*.

3. "An Act to provide for the settlement of the Claims of Widows and Orphans barred by the limitations heretofore established, and to regulate the Claims to Invalid Pensions," ch. 11, 1 Stat. 243 (1792).

4. 2 U.S. (2 Dall.) 409 (1792). The Court also disavowed its administrative role in *Hayburn*'s companion cases *Ex parte Chandler* (1794) and *US v. Yale Todd* (1794).

5. Hamburger, *Is Administrative Law Unlawful?*, 211–215. Mashaw has uncovered the one exception to this rule—but an exception that did not involve an administrator reviewing and potentially overturning the courts' decisions. Under the 1790 Naturalization Act, Congress authorized any federal or state common law court of record to bestow persons of "good character" with US citizenship. See "An Act to establish an uniform Rule of Naturalization," ch. 3, 1 Stat. 103 (1790); Mashaw, *Creating the Administrative Constitution*, 74.

6. "An Act for the government and regulation of Seamen in the merchants ser-

vice," ch. 29, 1 Stat. 131 (1790). See Mashaw, *Creating the Administrative Constitution*, 73–74.

7. "An Act to provide for mitigating or remitting the forfeitures and penalties accruing under the revenue laws, in certain cases therein mentioned," ch. 12, 1 Stat. 122 (1790).

8. "An Act in addition to the act for the punishment of certain crimes against the United States," ch. 50, 1 Stat. 381 (1794).

9. See, e.g., the case of the *Young Ralph*, discussed in Chapter 3: *US v. The Ship Young Ralph*, D.C.D. N.Y., 1802; C.C.D. N.Y., 1802–1805.

10. For the December 1807 embargo act, see "An Act laying an Embargo on all ships and vessels in the ports and harbors of the United States," ch. 5, 2 Stat. 451 (1807); and for the 1798 Sedition Act, see "An Act in addition to the act, entitled 'An act for the punishment of certain crimes against the United States,'" ch. 74, 1 Stat. 596 (1798).

11. *Olney v. Arnold*, 3 U.S. (3 Dall.) 308 (1796). *US v. Hopkins* (1794) was unreported.

12. Ann Woolhandler described a fluctuating degree of deference given by the nineteenth-century federal courts to executive administrators in "Judicial Deference to Administrative Action." Also, Thomas W. Merrill argued that *Marbury v. Madison* originated the "rise of the deference doctrine" in modern administrative law. Merrill, "*Marbury v. Madison*," 512.

13. "Report on the Petition of Christopher Saddler" (January 19, 1790), in Hamilton, *Papers*, 6:191–192, 192n2.

14. Saddler most likely violated "An Act for laying a Duty on Goods, Wares, and Merchandises imported into the United States," ch. 2, 1 Stat. 24 (1789).

15. During the 1790s, Congress enacted, repealed, and modified tonnage, duty, and excise acts numerous times. See the *US Statutes at Large* for statutes enacted on July 20, 1789 (ch. 3, 1 Stat. 27), July 4, 1789 (ch. 2, 1 Stat. 24), September 16, 1789 (ch. 15, 1 Stat. 69), July 20, 1790 (ch. 30, 1 Stat. 135), August 4, 1790 (ch. 35, 1 Stat. 145), March 3, 1791 (ch. 15, 1 Stat. 199; ch. 26, 1 Stat. 219), May 2, 1792 (ch. 27, 1 Stat. 259), June 5, 1794 (ch. 49, 1 Stat. 378), and January 29, 1795 (ch. 17, 1 Stat. 411).

16. "Report on the Petition of Christopher Saddler" (January 19, 1790), in Hamilton, *Papers*, 6:191,192.

17. 1 Stat. 122 (1790).

18. Congress first extended, then renewed, the Remitting Act on May 8, 1792 (ch. 35, 1 Stat. 275), and March 3, 1797 (ch. 13, 1 Stat. 506).

19. Hamilton teased his sister-in-law, Angelica Church, about stepping down from his treasury post: "You would lose the pleasure of speaking of your brother[-in-law as] 'The Chancellor of the Exchequer' if I am to give up the trade." From "Alexander Hamilton to Angelica Church," April 4, 1794, as quoted in Chernow, *Alexander Hamilton*, 457.

20. 1 Stat. 122, 123 (1790).

21. Jeremiah Olney to Hamilton (August 25, 1792), in Hamilton, *Papers*, 12:273.

See also section 70 of "An Act to provide more effectually for the collection of the duties imposed by law on goods, wares, and merchandise imported into the United States, and on the tonnage of ships or vessels," ch. 35, 1 Stat. 145, 177 (1790). Discrepancies existed between foreign regulations of tonnage and the American method of measuring tonnage, which resulted, in the case of the *Rising Sun*, in a vessel that was too light to meet the American tonnage requirement for importation. See Hamilton, *Papers*, 12:300n4.

22. Henry Marchant to Hamilton (August 31, 1792), in ibid., 12:299–300.

23. Hamilton to Jeremiah Olney (September 13, 1792), in ibid., 12:376.

24. Hamilton to David Sewall (November 13, 1790), in ibid., 7:150–152.

25. Ibid., 151–152.

26. See Mashaw, "Recovering American Administrative Law," 1333.

27. "Treasury Department Circular to the District Judges" (October 17, 1791), in Hamilton, *Papers*, 9:402.

28. 3 U.S. (3 Dall.) 171 (1796).

29. *US v. Hopkins* went unreported by Alexander Dallas, but references to the case can be found in the minutes of the Supreme Court for February 13–15, 1794, and on the docket of the Supreme Court, February 1794 term.

30. See Marcus, *Documentary History*, 6:356–357, and the 1790 Funding Act ("An Act making provision for the Debt of the United States"), ch. 34, 1 Stat. 138 (1790).

31. Marcus, *Documentary History*, 6:357.

32. Hamilton to William Skinner (August 12 and September 8, 1791), in Hamilton, *Papers*, 9:32–33, 191–192; Hamilton to Benjamin Hawkins (December 9, 1791), in ibid., 10:353–355; Hamilton to Theodore Foster (September 1, 1791), in ibid., 9:153–157.

33. Marcus, *Documentary History*, 6:357.

34. Ibid. For Randolph's supporting opinion, see Edmund Randolph to Hamilton (November 9, 1791), in Hamilton, *Papers*, 9:486.

35. Marcus, *Documentary History*, 6:357.

36. Ibid., 6:358.

37. Hamilton to Henry Lee (March 22, 1793), in Hamilton, *Papers*, 14:232–234.

38. Ibid.

39. Ibid.

40. *US v. Hopkins* did not reach the Supreme Court until the February 1794 term, and by this time, Randolph had become the secretary of state, succeeded by William Bradford as attorney general (Marcus, *Documentary History*, 6:360).

41. Ibid.

42. Ibid., 361.

43. North Carolina had previously requested an explanation of the Treasury's subscription policy before the *Hopkins* action began. See ibid., 361n35.

44. Ibid. The final settlement of accounts concluded on June 29, 1793, months before the ruling in *Hopkins*.

45. Ibid., 361.

46. See *Olney v. Arnold*, 3 U.S. (3 Dall.) 308 (1796), and "An Act to provide more effectually for the collection of the duties imposed by law on goods, wares, and merchandise imported into the United States, and on the tonnage of ships or vessels," ch. 35, 1 Stat. 145, 168, 169 (1790). For a detailed account of the complicated proceedings, see Marcus, *Documentary History*, 7:565–577. Marcus noted that this system benefited both the merchants and the US Treasury, as merchants had a window of time to sell their goods in order to pay their duties, while the Treasury secured future payment on the duties owed.

47. Hamilton to Olney (October 12, 1792), in Hamilton, *Papers*, 12:579; see also Hamilton to Olney (September 19, 1792), in ibid., 12:404.

48. *US v. Arnold* (1792) went unreported; see Marcus, *Documentary History*, 7:567n12.

49. Hamilton to Jeremiah Olney (November 27, 1792), in Hamilton, *Papers*, 13:239–240.

50. "An Act to establish the Judicial Courts of the United States," ch. 20, 1 Stat. 73, 85 (1789).

51. Marcus, *Documentary History*, 7:570.

52. When under section 25 review in the US Supreme Court, lawyers for Arnold argued that the Rhode Island General Assembly, and not the Supreme Court of Judicature, constituted the highest court in the state. The US Supreme Court rejected this argument. Ibid., 7:575–576.

53. Hamilton to Olney (April 24, 1794), in Hamilton, *Papers*, 16:333–334; see also Olney to Hamilton (April 14 and 24, 1794), in ibid., 16:258, 331–332; Olney to Hamilton (May 5, 1794), in ibid., 16:378–379.

54. Chief Justice Oliver Ellsworth's opinion for the court is incomplete. See "Judgments of the Supreme Court" (August 11, 1796), in Marcus, *Documentary History*, 7:617. See also ibid., 7:572–577, for the procedural issues involved.

55. See section 62 of "An Act to regulate the collection of duties on imports and tonnage," ch. 22, 1 Stat. 627, 675 (1799), and Marcus, *Documentary History*, 7:577.

56. *Federalist*, 460 (No. 82).

57. For scholarship focused on the more contentious side to the executive–judicial relationship in the early republic, see Ellis, *Jeffersonian Crisis, Union at Risk*, and *Aggressive Nationalism*; Ackerman, *Failure of the Founding Fathers*; Haskins and Johnson, *Foundations of Power*.

58. *Marbury v. Madison*, 5 U.S. (1 Cranch) 137, 166 (1803), *Stuart v. Laird*, 5 U.S. (1 Cranch) 299 (1803), *Gilchrist et al. v. Collector of Charleston*, 10 F. Cas. 355 (C.C.D. S.C., 1808), *Kendall v. US ex. rel. Stokes et al.*, 37 U.S. (12 Pet.) 524 (1838), and *US v. Burr*, 25 F. Cas. 55 (C.C.D. Va., 1807).

59. The original Remitting Act passed on May 26, 1790 (ch. 12, 1 Stat. 122), and was extended, renewed, or revised on May 8, 1792 (ch. 35, 1 Stat. 275), March 3, 1797 (ch. 13, 1 Stat. 506), and January 2, 1813 (ch. 7, 2 Stat. 789). On February 11, 1800, Congress passed an amendment to the 1797 Remitting Act that removed the sunset provision on the treasury secretary's remitting powers (ch. 6, 2 Stat. 7).

Congress also inserted remitting clauses in subsequent revenue acts that authorized or slightly altered the remitting process under those particular statutes. See section 3 of "An Act further to regulate the entry of merchandise imported into the United States from any adjacent territory," ch. 14, 3 Stat. 616, 617 (1821). Also, in an 1823 tonnage act amendment, Congress gave the treasury secretary a remitting-like power to admit entry of foreign goods or persons if he did not suspect fraud. In this provision, district judges are not involved in the secretary's adjudication process. See section 10 of "An Act supplementary to, and to amend an act, entitled 'An act to regulate the collection of duties on imports and tonnage,' passed second March, one thousand seven hundred and ninety-nine, and for other purposes," ch. 21, 3 Stat. 729, 734 (1823).

60. US v. the Hawke, 26 F. Cas. 233 (D.C.D. S. C., 1794). See the 1793 Enrollment and Licensing Act ("An Act for enrolling and licensing ships or vessels to be employed in the coasting trade and fisheries, and for regulating the same"), ch. 8, 1 Stat. 305 (1793).

61. On March 26, 1794, Congress passed a joint resolution declaring "that an embargo be laid on all ships and vessels in the ports of the United States"; res. 2, 1 Stat. 400 (1794).

62. See sections 8 and 32, at 1 Stat. 305, 308, 316 (1793).

63. US v. The Hawke, 26 F. Cas. 233, 235 (D.C.D. S. C., 1794).

64. The Cotton Planter, 6 F. Cas. 620 (C.C.D. N.Y., 1810) and the 1807 embargo, "An Act laying an Embargo on all ships and vessels in the ports and harbors of the United States," ch. 5, 2 Stat. 451 (1807).

65. The Cotton Planter, 6 F. Cas. 620, 621 (C.C.D. N.Y., 1810).

66. Ibid., 622.

67. Section 22 of an 1818 amended duty act described cargo-to-invoice search requirements for customs collectors to follow, and then section 25 incorporated the 1797 Remitting Act's process if the invoice and cargo did not match. See "An Act supplementary to an act, entitled 'An act to regulate the collection of duties on imports and tonnage,' passed the second day of March, one thousand seven hundred and ninety-nine," ch. 79, 3 Stat. 433, 438 (1818), and "An Act to provide for mitigating or remitting the Forfeitures, Penalties and Disabilities accruing in certain cases therein mentioned," ch. 13, 1 Stat. 506 (1797).

68. US v. One Case of Hair Pencils, 27 F. Cas. 244, 247 (C.C.D. N.D. N.Y., 1825).

69. Gallego et al. v. US, 9 F. Cas. 1105, 1107 (C.C.D. Va., 1820); "An Act directing the Secretary of the Treasury to remit fines, forfeitures and penalties in certain cases," ch. 7, 2 Stat. 789 (1813).

70. Gallego et al. v. US, 9 F. Cas. 1105, 1108 (C.C.D. Va., 1820).

71. US v. Lancaster, 26 F. Cas. 859 (C.C.D. E.D. Pa., 1821).

72. US v. Morris, Marshal of the Southern District of New York, 23 U.S. (10 Wheat.) 246, 291 (1825). The Court closely read and interpreted the 1797 Remitting Act, found at ch. 13, 1 Stat. 506, 507 (1797).

73. US v. The William, 28 F. Cas. 614 (D.C.D. Mass., 1808). At issue were "An

Act laying an Embargo on all ships and vessels in the ports and harbors of the United States," ch. 5, 2 Stat. 451 (1807), and the March 12, 1808, supplementary statute, "An Act in addition to the act, intitled 'An act supplementary to the act, intitled An act laying an embargo on all ships and vessels in the ports and harbors of the United States,'" ch. 33, 2 Stat. 473 (1808).

74. Mashaw, *Creating the Administrative Constitution*, 96.

75. *US v. The William*, 28 F. Cas. 614, 618 (D.C.D. Mass., 1808).

76. *US v. Vowell and M'Clean*, 9 U.S. (5 Cranch) 368, 372 (1810).

77. *Crowell and others v. M'Fadon*, 12 U.S. (8 Cranch) 94 (1814). See section 6 and 11 of "An Act in addition to the act intitled 'An act laying an embargo on all ships and vessels in the ports and harbors of the United States,' and the several act supplementary thereto, and for other purposes," ch. 66, 2 Stat. 499, 500, 501 (1808).

78. *Crowell and others v. M'Fadon*, 12 U.S. (8 Cranch) 94, 98 (1814).

79. *Otis v. Watkins*, 13 U.S. (9 Cranch) 339, 356–357 (1815).

80. See section 11 of "An Act in addition to the act intitled 'An act laying an embargo on all ships and vessels in the ports and harbors of the United States,' and the several act supplementary thereto, and for other purposes," ch. 66, 2 Stat. 499, 501 (1808).

81. Administrators in the public land offices also adjudicated land claims, and federal courts tended to treat their patent decisions as binding unless jurisdictional errors arose. See Mashaw, *Creating the Administrative Constitution*, 137; Woolhandler, "Judicial Deference to Administrative Action," 216–219.

82. For example, Andrew Jackson's 1832 Nullification Proclamation, and Taney Court decisions like *Kendall v. US ex. rel. Stokes et al.*, 37 U.S. (12 Pet.) 524 (1838), and *The Propeller Genesee Chief v. Fitzhugh*, 53 U.S. (12 How.) 443 (1851). See Jackson, "Proclamation."

83. *Martin v. Hunter's Lessee*, 14 U.S. (1 Wheat.) 304, 348 (1816).

84. Jackson, "Proclamation," December 10, 1832.

85. *Decatur v. Paulding*, 39 U.S. (14 Pet.) 497 (1840). The Taney Court accommodated administrative action in a number of cases, which narrowed the scope of the Court's decision in *Kendall v. US ex. rel. Stokes*. More so than the Marshall Court, Taney's Supreme Court was conflicted about just how much coordinate oversight it could exercise. See *Kendall v. Stokes* 44 U.S. (3 How.) 87 (1845), the supplementary decision to *Kendall v. US ex. rel. Stokes*; *Rankin v. Hoyt*, 45 U.S. (4 How.) 327 (1846), and *Bartlett v. Kane*, 57 U.S. (16 How.) 263 (1853). Jaffe, *Judicial Control*, 178–179; Mashaw, *Creating the Administrative Constitution*, 210–218.

Chapter 3. Creating the "Commercial Republic": Neutrality
and Law in the American Courts

1. Elkins and McKitrick, *Age of Federalism*, 396, 399. On the relationship between neutrality and economic growth, see North, *Economic Growth of the United States*, 24–58; Adams, "American Neutrality," 713, 714, 720, 726, quote at 727; Kingston, "Marine Insurance in Philadelphia."

2. Despite Article III's seemingly broad grant of federal jurisdiction "to all Cases of admiralty and maritime Jurisdiction," the first federal Congress allowed suitors to bring claims that could have been heard in admiralty to the state common law courts, if the common law was "competent" to provide a remedy—thus "saving to suitors" a remedy at common law. If the claim met certain statutory jurisdictional requirements, the suitor could also initiate an action in the common law, rather than the admiralty, side of the federal courts. See section 9 of "An Act to establish the Judicial Courts of the United States," ch. 20, 1 Stat. 73, 76–77 (1789).

3. *Federalist*, 106 (No. 6). See McCoy, *Elusive Republic*, 77, 166–184.

4. *Federalist*, 133 (No. 11).

5. Elkins and McKitrick, *Age of Federalism*, 107–131. For historiographical treatments of Hamilton's policies and their effect on American commerce, see Edling and Kaplanoff, "Alexander Hamilton's Fiscal Reform"; Edling, "So Immense a Power"; Ferguson, *Power of the Purse*; McCraw, *Founders and Finance*; McCoy, *Elusive Republic*, 136–165; Nettels, "The Federalist Program," in *Emergence of a National Economy*, 109–129; Hurst, "Alexander Hamilton, Law Maker."

6. Nettels, *Emergence of a National Economy*, 112–126; North, *Economic Growth of the United States*, 46; and Sylla, "Transition to a Monetary Union," 73, 73–79.

7. *Marbury v. Madison*, 5 U.S. (1 Cranch) 137 (1803); *Martin v. Hunter's Lessee*, 14 U.S. (1 Wheat.) 304 (1816); *McCulloch v. Maryland*, 17 U.S. (4 Wheat.) 316 (1819); and *Gibbons v. Ogden*, 22 U.S. (9 Wheat.) 1 (1824).

8. Charles Hobson and Gordon Wood suggested that the Marshall Court decided cases in ways intended only to limit state power rather than to deliberately augment federal power. See generally Hobson, *Great Chief Justice*, and Wood, *Empire of Liberty*. G. Edward White, Charles Sellers, and Richard E. Ellis, however, argued that the Marshall Court acted aggressively to increase the federal courts' power whenever it could. In his chapter on admiralty, White used Story's opinion in *De Lovio v. Boit*, 7 F. Cas. 418 (C.C.D. Mass., 1815), to make just this point. See generally Sellers, *Market Revolution*; Ellis, *Aggressive Nationalism*; White, *Marshall Court and Cultural Change*, 427–484.

9. The US Supreme Court first considered the meaning of Article I, section 8's commerce clause in *Gibbons v. Ogden*, 22 U.S. (9 Wheat.) 1 (1824).

10. Nettels, *Emergence of a National Economy*, 227, 232–238; North, *Economic Growth of the United States*, 25–26.

11. As James Kent put it, Hamilton's *Federalist* No. 82 "laid down as a rule that the state courts retained all pre-existing authorities, or the jurisdiction they had before the adoption of the constitution, except where it was taken away" by Hamilton's three exceptions. Kent, *Commentaries*, 1:370.

12. *Federalist*, 458–459 (No. 82).

13. Ibid., 460.

14. 7 F. Cas. 418 (C.C.D. Mass., 1815). See also Newmyer, *Supreme Court Justice Joseph Story*, 125.

15. Section 9 of the 1789 Judiciary Act extended the federal courts' admiralty

jurisdiction over revenue-related lawsuits ("seizures under laws of imposts, naviga-tion or trade of the United States"), whereas in England, the common law side of the Court of the Exchequer adjudicated revenue-related cases. However, courts of vice admiralty presided over revenue and navigation laws for the British North American colonies. See "An Act to establish the Judicial Courts of the United States," ch. 20, 1 Stat. 73, 76–77 (1789). Note, however, that while section 9 seemed to make clear that revenue-related seizures would be adjudicated in the federal district courts, it was not always clear whether the suit should be heard in admiralty or at common law.

16. Bourguignon, *First Federal Court*, 13–14.

17. Ibid., 22–26. Parliament passed the 1696 Navigation Act "for Preventing Frauds, and Regulating Abuses in the Plantation Trade," 7 and 8 Will. III, ch. 22. Before the act, the colonial admiralty system was incoherent; provincial courts as-sumed for themselves the authority to hear admiralty cases. The act gave structure and coherence to the colonial admiralty system, and by 1700, the eleven fully func-tioning vice admiralty courts in the British colonies corresponded to the following areas: Virginia, North Carolina/Bahamas, Maryland, Massachusetts, New Hamp-shire, Rhode Island, New York, East New Jersey/Connecticut, Pennsylvania, West New Jersey, and South Carolina. The colonies interpreted the 1696 act as allow-ing concurrent jurisdiction between the vice admiralty courts and the common law courts, and the British Board of Trade did not contradict this interpretation.

18. Ibid., 28–33. In 1666–1667, Parliament reorganized the colonial vice admi-ralty's appellate process. It created a layer of four vice admiralty courts that had concurrent and appellate jurisdiction over the eleven lower vice admiralty courts within their districts. The four districts included the following: Boston (presiding over New Hampshire, Massachusetts, Rhode Island, and Connecticut), Philadelphia (over New York, New Jersey, Pennsylvania, Delaware, Maryland, and Virginia), Charleston (over North Carolina, South Carolina, Georgia, and the Floridas), and Halifax (over Quebec, Newfoundland, and Nova Scotia). Also, in 1764, the Sugar Act granted the district-level vice admiralty courts with concurrent jurisdiction (with common law courts) over revenue cases, and allowed the petitioner to bring the case to the Halifax vice admiralty court if he chose. In addition, the Stamp Act granted the Halifax court with the appellate authority to oversee all cases brought in the various acts of trade and revenue.

19. Ibid., 192–193. Americans introduced other common law elements to ad-miralty procedure, like the motion to set aside a verdict and the motion to grant a new trial if improper evidence had been admitted. Also, because admiralty sat at the intersection of multiple types of law—Continental Europe's civil law traditions, En-glish admiralty and vice admiralty practices, the law of nations, natural law, the law merchant—during the early republic and through most of the nineteenth century, judges were willing to examine any or all of these legal traditions in order to answer a question of law arising in federal admiralty court. See Gilmore and Black, *Law of Admiralty*, 40–42; Owen and Tolley, *Courts of Admiralty*, 223–229.

20. Bourguignon, *First Federal Court*, 121, 319–323.

21. Ibid., 328–329. Bourguignon determined that "twenty-one of the fifty-five

members of the Philadelphia convention of 1787 had some direct acquaintance with the work of the Committee on Appeals or the Court of Appeals" as lawyers or judges.

22. *John Lamb Qui Tam v. Two Trunks of Merchandize*, John Baptist Riolz, Claimant (N.Y. Adm., 1785; N.Y. Ct. Err., 1785–1786), Hamilton, *Law Practice*, 2:831–841.

23. 1784 Impost Law, *Laws of the State of New York*, 8 Sess. 1784, ch. 7; amended, 8 Sess. 1785, ch. 34. See Hamilton, *Law Practice*, 2:829–832.

24. "Answer and Claim of J. Riolz" (July 23, 1785), Hamilton, *Law Practice*, 2:833.

25. Hamilton, "Riolz & Lamb" (undated), Hamilton, *Law Practice*, 2:832.

26. See Hamilton, *Law Practice*, 2:861–874, 881–890.

27. Ibid., 2:892–903.

28. Emphasis added. As James Kent noted, the phrase "waters which are navigable from the sea" was ambiguous as to whether seizures made "on tide waters in ports, harbours, arms, and creeks of the sea" were cognizable exclusively in admiralty, or if they could be heard on the common law side of the district courts. Over time, the Supreme Court determined that cases arising from these appendages of the sea would be heard in admiralty. Kent, *Commentaries*, 1:347. Other qualifications to this exclusive, original district court cognizance included, "Where the seizures are made, on waters which are navigable from the sea by vessels of ten or more tons burthen . . . saving to suitors, in all cases, the right of a common law remedy, where the common law is competent to give it; and shall also have exclusive original cognizance of all seizures on land, or other waters than as aforesaid, made, and of all suits for penalties and forfeitures incurred, under the laws of the United States." "An Act to establish the Judicial Courts of the United States," ch. 20, 1 Stat. 73, 76–77 (1789).

29. Gilmore and Black, *Law of Admiralty*, 33–36. On the changing meaning of the *in rem/in personam* distinction, see *The Moses Taylor*, 71 U.S. (4 Wall.) 411 (1866); *The Hine v. Trevor*, 71 U.S. (4 Wall.) 555 (1866); Casto, "Origins of Federal Admiralty Jurisdiction," 117, 140–149; McCurdy, "Prelude to Civil War," 3.

30. The majority of all admiralty suits filed from 1789 to 1797 were seizures made to enforce revenue laws. See Henderson, *Courts for a New Nation*, 55.

31. See Hamilton to Jeremiah Olney (April 2, 1793) and Hamilton to John Brown (April 5, 1793), in Hamilton, *Papers*, 14:276, 283–284.

32. Frederick Dalzell and Gautham Rao have noted how careful Hamilton and his Treasury Department were to maintain good relationships with the local merchants paying their duties, and thus increasing the federal coffers. Hamilton and his customs collectors attempted to accommodate local merchants to achieve a smoothly running and effective revenue collection operations. See Dalzell, "Prudence and the Golden Egg"; Rao, *National Duties*, 1–14, 40–42, 75–99.

33. See, e.g., William Ellery to Hamilton (March 15, 1791) and Hamilton to William Ellery (April 11, 1791), in ibid., 8:183, 271–272.

34. Hamilton to Jeremiah Olney (July 31, 1792), in ibid., 12:140.

35. William Ellery to Hamilton (August 27, 1792), in ibid., 12:278–279.

36. See, e.g., the case of Jeremiah Olney and Welcome Arnold, discussed in Chapter 2.

37. William Ellery to Hamilton (September 3, 1792), in Hamilton, *Papers*, 12:315.

38. Ibid., 315–316. Ellery referred to section 69 of the 1790 Collection Act, or "An Act to provide more effectually for the collection of the duties imposed by law on goods, wares, and merchandise imported into the United States, and on the tonnage of ships or vessels," ch. 35, 1 Stat. 145, 177 (1790).

39. William Ellery to Hamilton (September 4, 1792), in Hamilton, *Papers*, 12:318–319.

40. William Ellery to Hamilton (October 1, 1792), in ibid., 12:512–513.

41. "Treasury Department Circular to the Collectors of the Customs" (August 4, 1793), in ibid., 15:179.

42. See "Treasury Department Circular to the Collectors of the Customs" (April 18, 1794) and Meletiah Jordan to Hamilton (May 7, 1794), in ibid., 16:239–240, 387–388; Congress's joint resolution, "That an embargo be laid on all ships and vessels in the ports of the United States," res. 2, 1 Stat. 400 (1794).

43. The Napoleonic wars complicated the treasury secretaries' abilities to tolerate discretion and accommodation at the local level. For a direct comparison of Hamilton's adjudicatory style with another treasury secretary, see *US v. The Ship Huron, Francis Hill and Ephraim Hart, Claimants* (D.C.D. N.Y., 1800–1803), where Treasury Secretary Albert Gallatin considered a remission petition for a claimant whose ship was libeled in federal admiralty court by Hamilton (acting again as a prosecutor, alongside Richard Harison and Edward Livingston). See Hamilton, *Law Practice*, 2:823–825.

44. Counted on November 26, 2013, from the LexisNexis Academic database of reported federal cases.

45. 3 U.S. (3 Dall.) 6 (1794).

46. Sloss, "Judicial Foreign Policy," 145, 147.

47. See the Registry Act ("An Act concerning the registering and recording of ships or vessels"), ch. 1, 1 Stat. 287 (1792), and the Enrollment and Licensing Act ("An Act for enrolling and licensing ships or vessels to be employed in the coasting trade and fisheries, and for regulating the same"), ch. 8, 1 Stat. 305 (1793). See also Hamilton, *Law Practice*, 2:791.

48. See, e.g., "Agreement" by Peter du Ponceau (representing the claimant) and Hamilton (representing the libellant) in *Don Diego Pintado v. The Ship San Joseph, Jean Antoine Berard, Claimant* (D.C.D. N.Y., 1795; C.C.D. N.Y., 1795–1796; US, 1796), which Harison also borrowed and signed for use in his companion case, *US v. La Vengeance*, 3 U.S. (3 Dall.) 297 (1796). Also, Hamilton and Harison tag-teamed in court for *US v. The Ship Lydia, Henry Treadwell, Claimant* (D.C.D. N.Y., 1801). See Hamilton, *Law Practice*, 2:804–805, 825–826.

49. *US v. The Ship Young Ralph* (D.C.D. N.Y., 1802; C.C.D. N.Y., 1802–1805).

50. See section 1 of "An Act to prohibit the carrying on the Slave Trade from the

United States to any foreign place or country," ch. 11, 1 Stat. 347, 347–349 (1794); Hamilton, *Law Practice*, 2:847.

51. Harison admitted as much in his "Draft Opinion" (April 6, 1802), in Hamilton, *Law Practice*, 2:854.

52. Hamilton, "Opinion" (March 29, 1802), in ibid., 2:850–854, quote at 852.

53. Richard Harison, "Draft Opinion" (April 6, 1802), in ibid., 2:854–857. Harison cited section 9 of "An Act to establish the Judicial Courts of the United States," ch. 20, 1 Stat. 73, 76–77 (1789).

54. Even James Kent, when publishing his *Commentaries* in the 1820s, would cast doubt on the legitimacy and good sense of the expansion of federal admiralty jurisdiction beyond the high seas. He suggested that because Congress and the US Supreme Court had defied English admiralty precedent and had extended the scope of federal admiralty jurisdiction to include revenue-related seizures and to waters not confined to the high seas, their actions were insufficiently considered and possibly illegitimate. The US Supreme Court consistently upheld its earliest expansion of the federal admiralty jurisdiction in *US v. La Vengeance*, 3 U.S. (3 Dall.) 297 (1796). However, before *The Propeller Genesee Chief v. Fitzhugh*, 53 U.S. (12 How.) 443 (1851), the Court confined its admiralty jurisdiction to only the high seas and to coastal waters where the tide ebbed and flowed. See, in general, Kent, *Commentaries*, 1:331–361; see also Farrar, "Extension of the Admiralty Jurisdiction," 459, 472–474, 482–486.

Also, in the early republic period, even authorities on law sent mixed messages as to where exactly admiralty jurisdiction extended. Blackstone said "on the seas," but while writing on *La Vengeance* in his *Commentaries*, Kent suggested that the admiralty jurisdiction extended to bays and harbors (corresponding to the ebb and flow of the tide rule that the Supreme Court would adopt for the first half of the nineteenth century). Richard Harison distinguished between the "high seas" and waters "within a County," but the Court in *La Vengeance* did not specify where on the water the admiralty jurisdiction extended; it bluntly stated that the unlawful act in question (exportation, in violation of US law) was an act that took place wholly on the water (not in a county vicinity) and was part of their civil admiralty jurisdiction. Thus, in the 1790s, the exact boundaries of admiralty's extension over local waters remained muddled.

55. *The Propeller Genesee Chief v. Fitzhugh*, 53 U.S. (12 How.) 443 (1851).

56. *US v. La Vengeance*, 3 U.S. (3 Dall.) 297 (1796). James Kent thought that the Supreme Court wrongly decided the case, and he complained that the whole body of federal admiralty decisions was premised on this one questionable decision. Kent, *Commentaries*, 1:347–348.

57. *Pintado v. The Ship San Joseph* went unreported; its journey through the federal court system can be traced through the minutes and dockets of the US District Court for New York (1795), the US Circuit Court for New York (1795–96), and the US Supreme Court (1796).

58. "An Act in addition to the act for the punishment of certain crimes against the United States," ch. 50, 1 Stat. 381 (1794).

59. "An Act prohibiting for a limited time the Exportation of Arms and Ammunition, and encouraging the Importation of the same," ch. 33, 1 Stat. 369 (1794).

60. Hamilton, *Law Practice*, 2:794.

61. *La Vengeance* and *Pintado* had a complex journey through the federal courts. For a complete narrative of the relevant events, legal maneuvers, and holdings, see Marcus, *Documentary History*, 7:524–537, and Hamilton, *Law Practice*, 2:792–797.

62. Marcus, *Documentary History*, 7:535–537.

63. *US v. The Schooner Sally of Norfolk*, 6 U.S. (2 Cranch) 406 (1805).

64. *US v. The Schooner Betsey and Charlotte and her Cargo*, 8 U.S. (4 Cranch) 443 (1808).

65. *The Emulous*, 8 F. Cas. 697, 701 (C.C.D. Mass., 1813), emphasis added.

66. Despite James Kent's critique of the Court's decision in *La Vengeance*, the Court's holding that seizures made under US revenue laws did not require a civil jury trial was firmly upheld in subsequent cases. In addition to *US v. The Schooner Sally of Norfolk* and *US v. The Schooner Betsey and Charlotte and her Cargo*, the case of *Waring v. Clarke*, 46 U.S. (5 How.) 441 (1847), upheld *La Vengeance*'s decision. See Farrar, "Extension of the Admiralty Jurisdiction," 472–474.

67. The federal courts were hesitant to claim an expanded territorial jurisdiction over criminal cases, however. The courts confined their criminal jurisdiction to the high seas only, unless Congress specifically granted jurisdiction via statute. See Kent, *Commentaries*, 1:337–342.

68. Julius Goebel Jr., "The Business of Marine Insurance in New York," in Hamilton, *Law Practice*, 2:391–413; and Kingston, "Marine Insurance in Britain and America."

69. North, *Economic Growth of the United States*, 50. In 1792, the Insurance Corporation of North America, the first incorporated American marine insurance company, opened for business.

70. Kingston, "Marine Insurance in Philadelphia," 174–176.

71. According to Douglass C. North, US shipping carried only 59 percent of foreign trade in 1790. Yet by 1795, US shippers carried 90 percent of foreign trade, and by 1807, their market share increased to 92 percent. Yet revisionist Donald R. Adams Jr. had a more sober view of the period. Although he calculated that US shipping, in total and foreign tonnage, increased from 1793 to 1807, he observed that the increase in US tonnage shipped began in the period 1789–1792. Whereas North considered neutrality to be an overall positive force on the US economy in the early republic, Adams saw neutrality as having limited effects. Nevertheless, both economic historians demonstrated that during the years of American neutrality, the carrying trade grew. See North, *Economic Growth of the United States*, 41, and Adams, "American Neutrality," 723–724.

72. President Thomas Jefferson's December 1807 embargo put an end to American economic growth in the early republic period. Shipping activity somewhat rebounded when Congress repealed the embargo and replaced it with the Non-Intercourse Act of March 1809, which permitted commercial intercourse with all coun-

tries except England and France. When the War of 1812 broke out, however, the British "effectively ended [US] external trade and concluded an era of growth based on American neutrality in a world at war." See North, *Economic Growth of the United States*, 38, 42, 46.

73. Wright and Kingston, "Corporate Insurers," 449.

74. Horwitz, *Transformation of American Law, 1780–1860*, 226–237. Alexander Hamilton helped introduce actuarial science to marine insurance law in *Barnewall v. Church*, 1 Cai. 217 (N.Y. Sup. Ct., 1803).

75. See, e.g., *Warren Manufacturing Company v. Etna Insurance Company*, 29 F. Cas. 294 (C.C.D. Conn., 1837). Section 11 of "An Act to establish the Judicial Courts of the United States," ch. 20, 1 Stat. 73, 78–79 (1789), gave this jurisdiction to the circuit courts.

76. "An Act concerning the District of Columbia," ch. 15, 2 Stat. 103, 106 (1801).

77. Bottomry bonds were agreements whereby the owner/master of a vessel borrowed money for the use or repair of the vessel upon pledging the "bottom" of the ship as security. Bottomry was a means for the shipmaster to raise money for unexpected repairs or to continue the voyage while at a foreign port. The borrower and lender entered into the agreement knowing that bottomry bonds were made with the condition that if the vessel reached the destination safely, the money advanced plus interest would be paid back to the lender. If, however, the vessel were lost at sea, then the borrower would not be obligated to pay anything back to the lender. (If something of the cargo or vessel could be salvaged, then the lender would receive some recompense from the salvaged items.) Shippers relied on two main types of bottomry bonds, respondentia and hypothecation. A respondentia bond applied to a loan of money on merchandise laden on board a ship, where the repayment depended on the safe arrival of the goods at the destined port. Hypothecation bonds referred to the pawn of the ship itself or its cargo for relief funds when the ship found itself in distress at sea. Hypothecation bonds specifically required the loan to fund repairs needed on the voyage. See Hamilton, *Law Practice*, 2:238–239, 861.

78. Kent, *Commentaries*, 300, 303. Kent analogized the two because the bottomry bond was a contract that had similar terms as marine insurance policies and was decided, at law, on similar principles. The lender took the risk that he would be made whole (with interest) if the ship or cargo completed the voyage successfully; likewise, the underwriter would collect the premium and would not have to pay out if the insured ship or cargo completed the voyage successfully and without peril.

79. I refer to Hurst's lecture on "The Release of Energy" in his *Law and the Conditions of Freedom*, 3–32, and to Horwitz's *Transformation of American Law, 1780–1860*, 83.

80. See Kent, *Commentaries*, 2:527–528.

81. These lawyer-colleagues included two of Hamilton's closest friends and trusted advisors, Richard Harison and Robert Troup, as well as Josiah Ogden Hoffman, Nathaniel Pendleton, George Caines, and, before he assumed his position on the state Supreme Court, Henry Brockholst Livingston.

82. English treatise writer James Allan Park issued multiple editions of his *A system of the law of marine insurances: With three chapters on bottomry; on insurances on lives; and on insurances against fire* in the late eighteenth century. American Wendell Phillips also wrote *A Treatise on the Law of Insurance* in 1823, before James Kent summarized the principles of American marine insurance law in his *Commentaries*.

83. American jurists considered cases like *Hughes v. Cornelius*, 89 Eng. Rep. 907 (K.B., 1683), *Beak v. Thyrwhit*, 87 Eng. Rep. 124 (K.B., 1688), and *Phillips v. Hunter*, 126 Eng. Rep 618 (Ex., 1795), as indicative that England had adopted the principle that foreign sentences were conclusive and would have the same force as domestic decrees.

84. *Ludlow & Ludlow v. Dale*, 1 Johns. Cas. 16 (N.Y. Sup. Ct., 1799); *Goix v. Knox*, 1 Johns. Cas. 337 (N.Y. Sup. Ct., 1800); *Goix v. Low*, 1 Johns. Cas. 341 (N.Y. Sup. Ct., 1800) and 2 Johns. Cas. 480 (N.Y. Ct. Err., 1802); *Vandenheuvel v. United Insurance Company*, 2 Johns Cas. 127 (N.Y. Sup. Ct., 1801) and 2 Johns Cas. 451 (N.Y. Ct. Err., 1802).

85. *Goix v. Knox*, 1 Johns. Cas., 337, 340 (N.Y. Sup. Ct., 1800) and *Goix v. Low*, 1 Johns. Cas. 341, 343 (N.Y. Sup. Ct., 1800).

86. 2 Johns. Cas. 451 (N.Y. Ct. Err., 1802). Alexander Hamilton's thoughts on the conclusiveness of foreign decrees remain unclear. Hamilton successfully defended Dale and participated in the defense of Low and Knox by arguing in favor of the conclusiveness of foreign decrees. Yet there is evidence to suggest that Hamilton did not personally agree with this principle and only made it when defending his underwriter clients. See Hamilton, *Law Practice*, 2:617–620 (for Hamilton's memorandum in *Goix*) and 622.

87. 2 U.S. (2 Dall.) 270 (Pa. Sup. Ct., 1797).

88. As quoted from the policy at issue in *Calhoun for the use of Fitzsimmons and another v. The Insurance Company of Pennsylvania*, 1 Binn. 293, 302 (Pa. Sup. Ct., 1808), emphasis added. According to notes in *Calhoun*, the Pennsylvania case establishing the conclusiveness of foreign decrees was *Dempsey v. The Insurance Co. of Pennsylvania* (unreported, but cited on 1 Binn. 299 and in Kent, *Commentaries*, 2:103, note c). Kent referred to *Dempsey* as evidence that the Pennsylvanian courts also adopted the rule of conclusiveness for a foreign decree before their legislature intervened.

89. Kent, *Commentaries*, 2:103, note c.

90. *Croudson and Others v. Leonard*, 8 U.S. (4 Cranch) 434 (1808) and *Fitzsimmons v. The Newport Insurance Company*, 8 U.S. (4 Cranch) 185 (1808).

91. 7 U.S. (3 Cranch) 458 (1806). *Maley* arose as a libel in federal district court and came to the Supreme court on appeal from the Pennsylvania Circuit Court in 1805; see *Shattuck v. Maley*, 21 F. Cas. 1181 (C.C.D. Pa., 1805).

92. *Croudson and Others v. Leonard*, 8 U.S. (4 Cranch) 434, 442 (1808).

93. 8 U.S. (4 Cranch) 185, 196 (1808).

94. *John Baxter et al. v. The New England Marine Insurance Company*, 6 Mass. 277, 296 (Mass. Sup. Ct., 1810).

95. Day 142 (Conn. Sup. Ct. Err., 1803).

96. *Baxter v. New England Insurance Co.*, 6 Mass. 277, 298 (Mass. Sup. Ct., 1810).

97. Ibid. Kent, *Commentaries*, 2:103, note c.

98. *Baxter v. New England Insurance Co.*, 6 Mass. 277, 299 (Mass. Sup. Ct., 1810).

99. Ibid., emphasis added.

100. Kent, *Commentaries*, 3:236.

101. The exception was carrying contraband. Hamilton participated in at least two cases that helped establish this rule in the New York courts. See *Seton, Maitland & Co. v. Low*, 1 Johns. Cas. 1 (N.Y. Sup. Ct., 1799), and *Juhel v. Rhinelander*, 2 Johns. Cas. 120 (N.Y. Sup. Ct., 1800). Massachusetts followed New York's lead, and by 1823, Wendell Phillips considered it a rule that carrying contraband did not violate the neutrality warranty. See Phillips's *Treatise on the Law of Insurance*, 102; for the cases that generated this rule, including Hamilton's abovementioned litigation, see *Skidmore & Skidmore v. Desdoity*, 2 Johns. Cas. 77 (N.Y. Sup. Ct., 1800), *Richardson and another v. The Maine Fire & Marine Insurance Company*, 6 Mass. 102 (Mass. Sup. Ct., 1809), and *Stocker v. The Merrimack Marine & Fire Insurance Company*, 6 Mass. 220 (Mass. Sup. Ct., 1810).

102. 1 Cai. R. 549 (N.Y. Sup. Ct., 1804). In *Bowne v. Shaw*, 1 Cai. R. 489, 491 (N.Y. Sup. Ct., 1803), Hamilton claimed that the illicit trade clause was "framed by myself." He explained, "It is contrary to the principles of a warranty, that it should extend to all things. It can relate only to the subject matter insured. When we warrant of a certain thing, we warrant of that thing alone. . . . [Therefore] the intent of the clause cannot be doubted. It was framed by myself to avoid the construction contended for on the other side, and to confine the operation of it simply to the article insured." As included in a cargo policy written by the United Insurance Co. in October 1799, the clause read: "It is also agreed, That the property be warranted by the assured free from any charge, damage or loss, which may arise in consequence of a seizure or detention, for or on account of any illicit or prohibited trade, or any trade in articles contraband of war." Hamilton, *Law Practice*, 2:654–655.

103. According to the case report, this was done in order to take advantage of a Spanish royal order that restricted North American trade with Spanish colonies ("the royal order of His Most Catholic Majesty of the 17th November, 1797"), whereby American goods shipped in American bottoms would be introduced to the Cartagena market. To do this, it was necessary that the cargo appear to be Spanish property, and so the cargo was consigned to Thorres as his property, shipped for him by Blagge as Thorres's agent based in New York. Thorres would receive a cut of the net proceeds in return for facilitating the transaction. See *Blagge v. The New York Insurance Company*, 1 Cai. R. 549 (N.Y. Sup. Ct., 1804) and Hamilton, *Law Practice*, 2:658–660.

104. *Blagge v. The New York Insurance Company*, 1 Cai. R. 549, 563 (N.Y. Sup. Ct., 1804).

105. Ibid., 561.

106. 4 F. Cas. 1030 (C.C. D. Pa., 1805). The plaintiff and defendant's names were also commonly found as "Calbraith" and "Gracie."

107. See, e.g., *Pollock v. Babcock*, 6 Mass. 234 (Ma. Sup. Ct., 1810), and *Calhoun for the use of Fitzsimmons and another v. The Insurance Company of Pennsylvania*, 1 Binn. 293 (Pa. Sup. Ct., 1808).

108. *The Phoenix Insurance Company v. Pratt and Clarkson*, 2 Binn. 308 (Pa. Sup. Ct., 1810).

109. *Carrere v. The Union Insurance Company of Maryland*, 3 H. & J. 324, 329 (Md. Ct. App., 1813). Counsel cited *Blagge v. New York Insurance Co.* and *Vandenheuvel v. United Insurance Co.* in their arguments before the court.

110. Kent, *Commentaries*, 3:203, 237.

111. White, *Marshall Court and Cultural Change*, 443.

112. See Horwitz, *Transformation of American Law, 1780–1860*, 226–237.

113. *Martin v. Hunter's Lessee*, 14 U.S. (1 Wheat.) 304 (1816).

114. Kent, *Commentaries*, 1:352.

115. Ibid., 1:370–379.

116. Federal judges cited Hamilton's *Federalist* No. 82 in *US v. New Bedford Bridge*, 27 F. Cas. 91, 102 (C.C.D. Mass., 1847) when drawing a boundary around federal admiralty jurisdiction. Also, Rhode Island's Supreme Court referred to Hamilton to justify its concurrent jurisdiction over Narragansett Bay. See *Philip B. Chase, Administrator v. The American Steamboat Company*, 9 R.I. 419, 430–431 (R.I. Sup. Ct., 1870).

Chapter 4. Developing the Jurisprudence of Federalism: Hamilton's Defense of Federal Fiscal Powers

1. William Lowder to Hamilton (July 14, 1791), in Hamilton, *Papers*, 8:549–550. Lowder published the letter in the August 30, 1791, edition of the *Federal Gazette and Philadelphia Daily Advertiser*. See also Tobias Lear to George Washington (October 9, 1791), in Washington, *Papers*, 9:62–63.

2. Only months before, in February 1791, President Washington called on the treasury secretary to defend the constitutionality of the proposed central bank. After much political wrangling, Hamilton's assumption plan passed through Congress in July 1790.

3. *Plowden Weston and others v. The City Council of Charleston*, 27 U.S. (2 Pet.) 449 (1829).

4. Ibid., 450, emphasis added.

5. In Hamilton's "Report on a Plan for the Further Support of Public Credit" (written January 16, 1795, and communicated to the House and Senate within the following week), the outgoing treasury secretary listed the fourteen revenue-raising acts that Congress had passed since June 1789. See Hamilton, *Papers*, 18:59–65.

6. 3 U.S. (3 Dall.) 171 (1796).

7. Edling, "So Immense a Power"; Edling and Kaplanoff, "Alexander Hamilton's Fiscal Reform"; see generally Edling, *Revolution in Favor of Government*; North, *Economic Growth of the United States*, 46; Nettels, *Emergence of a National Econ-*

omy, 121–126; Bruchey, *Roots of American Economic Growth*, 108–113; Sylla, "Shaping the US Financial System," 254–262.

8. Nelson, *Liberty and Property*, 22–36; Wood, *Empire of Liberty*, 95–97; Miller, *Alexander Hamilton: Portrait in Paradox*, 238–254; McDonald, *Alexander Hamilton*, 163–188; Ellis, *Founding Brothers*, 48–80; Freeman, *Affairs of Honor*, 22–23, 36.

9. Brown, *Redeeming the Republic*. In *American Taxation*, however, Robin L. Einhorn briefly considered the effects of the US Supreme Court's decision in *Hylton v. US*.

10. See McCraw, *Founders and Finance*, 354–356.

11. 17 U.S. (4 Wheat.) 316 (1819). Richard E. Ellis has most recently argued that Marshall seized on *McCulloch* as an opportunity to instill a particularly "aggressive nationalism" in the Supreme Court's jurisprudence. Ellis noted the close connection between Hamilton and Marshall's constitutional interpretations, and Samuel J. Konefsky went farther, calling Marshall a "conscious disciple of the Hamiltonian brand of nationalism," as evidenced by the *McCulloch* decision. Clinton Rossiter discussed broad construction of the US Constitution as Hamilton's particular brand of constitutional theory—"the fortress of logic" from which Marshall determined *McCulloch*. See Ellis, *Aggressive Nationalism*, 34–36, 95; Konefsky, *John Marshall and Alexander Hamilton*, 165; Rossiter, *Alexander Hamilton and the Constitution*, 185–208, quote at 200.

12. There are two mostly nonoverlapping threads of *Hylton* historiography: one discusses the case within the context of the origins or development of judicial review in America, and the other is concerned with the consequences of the Supreme Court's interpretation of the direct tax clauses. Examples of this judicial review line of scholarship include Goebel, *Antecedents and Beginnings*, 778–784; Casto, "James Iredell"; Casto, *Supreme Court*, 221; Frankel, "Before *Marbury*"; Kramer, *The People Themselves*, 102–103. On the meaning of "direct tax," see Ackerman, "Taxation and the Constitution"; Jensen, "Taxation and the Constitution"; Campbell, "Dispelling the Fog"; Alicea and Drakeman, "Limits of New Originalism."

13. Hamilton to Robert Morris (May 18, July 22, and August 13, 1782), with enclosure, in Hamilton, *Papers*, 3:89–90, 114–117, 132–144, and Hamilton to the County Treasurers of the State of New York (September 7, 1782), in ibid., 3:160. See also Miller, *Alexander Hamilton: Portrait in Paradox*, 83–84.

14. Elkins and McKitrick, *Age of Federalism*, 117; Edling, "So Immense a Power," 291.

15. The states retained a concurrent authority to levy the following types of taxes, which they relied on before ratification: land, poll, slave, marriage and tavern licenses, court fees, professional fees, penalties (e.g., for refusing militia service), and "duties on billiard tables, playing cards, dice, on carriages, sales at auction, and alcohol." Edling and Kaplanoff, "Alexander Hamilton's Fiscal Reform," 720–721.

16. New York's convention proposed an amendment to the Constitution that required a two-thirds majority of both the House and Senate before Congress could exercise their power to borrow. Edling, *Revolution in Favor of Government*, 175.

17. Ibid., 163.

18. The American Colonies Act of 1766, which is better known as the Declaratory Act (6 Geo. III, c. 12).

19. Hamilton's New York Ratifying Remarks (Francis Childs's version, made on June 27, 1788), in Hamilton, *Papers*, 5:99, 102.

20. Hamilton's New York Ratifying Remarks, Third Speech (Francis Childs's version, made on June 28, 1788), in ibid., 5:116.

21. *Federalist*, 220 (No. 32). This would come to be seen like an out-of-character admission coming from Hamilton, but nineteenth-century states' rights proponents quoted from the Arch-Federalist himself to support their claims to their "concurrent sovereignty theory." White discussed this theory in *Marshall Court and Cultural Change*, 538–541, 571–585.

22. *Federalist*, 220 (No. 32).

23. Ibid., 221.

24. See, in general, Hamilton's "Report Relative to a Provision for the Support of Public Credit" (January 9, 1790), in Hamilton, *Papers*, 6:65–110. For Hamilton's tax proposals, see the report's enclosed Schedule K, along with a discussion in the body of the report. Hamilton, *Papers*, 6:102–107, 137. A few months later, Hamilton critiqued certain revenue statutes enacted by Congress in his "Report on the Defects in the Existing Laws of Revenue" (April 22, 1790), in ibid., 6:373–397.

25. Edling and Kaplanoff, "Alexander Hamilton's Fiscal Reform," 715–716, 717–718, 732–733, 736, and Brown, *Redeeming the Republic*, 236.

26. Edling, "So Immense a Power," 290–291, 322–324.

27. Fisher Ames to Hamilton (January 26, 1797), in Hamilton, *Papers*, 20:485.

28. Richard Wooddesson stated that civil laws "may be repealed, either expressly, or by implication, founded on disuse." Wooddesson, "Positive or Instituted Law," in *Lectures on the Law of England*, 1:xxxii.

29. Ibid., 1:xxxiii, note 2.

30. Wilson, "Lectures on Law," in *Works*, 2:39.

31. Reid, *Constitutional History*, 5, 26–48.

32. See Schedule K of Hamilton's "Report Relative to a Provision for the Support of Public Credit" (January 9, 1790), in Hamilton, *Papers*, 6:137, for his proposed duties. The treasury secretary made suggestions to improve the revenue laws in his "Report on the Defects in the Existing Laws of Revenue" (April 22, 1790) and "Report on the Improvement and Better Management of the Revenue of the United States" (January 31, 1795).

33. See "Report on a Plan for the Further Support of Public Credit" (January 16, 1795), in ibid., 18:59–65. Congress passed the first, apportioned direct tax with "An Act to provide for the valuation of Lands and Dwelling-Houses, and the enumeration of Slaves within the United States," ch. 70, 1 Stat. 580 (1798).

34. William Lowder to Hamilton (July 14, 1791), in Hamilton, *Papers*, 8:549–550.

35. Hamilton to the Board of Assessors of the Town of Boston (July 27, 1791), in ibid., 8:580–581.

36. Fisher Ames to Hamilton (September 8 and July 31, 1791), in ibid., 9:188, 591.

37. Tobias Lear to George Washington (October 9, 1791), in Washington, *Papers*, 9:62.

38. "An Act laying duties on property sold at Auction," ch. 65, 1 Stat. 397 (1794).

39. Josiah Ogden Hoffman to Hamilton (September 11, 1799), in Hamilton, *Papers*, 23:408.

40. Josiah Ogden Hoffman to John Jay (August 15, 1799), in ibid., 23:410n. 2.

41. "Final Version of an Opinion on the Constitutionality of an Act to Establish a Bank" (February 23, 1791), in ibid., 8:98.

42. Julius Goebel suggested that Hoffman's opinion prevailed because New York state passed a law in 1801 that regulated public auctions and recognized auctioneers acting under the authority of the United States. See Hamilton, *Law Practice*, 4:505–507, and "An Act to regulate sales by public auction, and to prevent stock jobbing," *Laws of the State of New York*, 24 Sess. 1801, c. 116.

43. See Thomas Jefferson to George Washington, "Opinion on the Constitutionality of the Bill for Establishing a National Bank" (February 15, 1791), in Jefferson, *Papers*, 19:275–282, and Edmund Randolph to George Washington, and its enclosures, "Opinion on the Constitutionality of the Bank" and "Additional Considerations on the Bank Bill" (February 12, 1791), in Washington, *Papers*, 7:330–340.

44. "Final Version of an Opinion on the Constitutionality of an Act to Establish a Bank" (February 23, 1791), in Hamilton, *Papers*, 8:107.

45. Ibid., 8:102–103.

46. Ibid., 8:104–105.

47. Ibid., 8:105.

48. Hamilton observed that a central bank would facilitate the federal government's exercise of its taxing powers in his "Final Version of the Second Report on the Further Provision Necessary for Establishing Public Credit (Report on a National Bank)" (December 13, 1790), in ibid., 7:309–310.

49. "Final Version of an Opinion on the Constitutionality of an Act to Establish a Bank" (February 23, 1791), in ibid., 8:113, 121.

50. Ibid., 122, emphasis added.

51. Ibid., 124.

52. Ibid., 125.

53. 3 U.S. (3 Dall.) 171 (1796). See also Marcus, *Documentary History*, 7:358.

54. The rates for the other types of carriage were as follows: $6 for every phaeton and coachee, $2 for every other four- and two-wheel top carriage, and $1 for every other two-wheel carriage; ch. 45, 1 Stat. 373, 374 (1794).

55. Hamilton suggested a federal tax on carriages in his "Report on the Redemption of the Public Debt" (November 30, 1792), in Hamilton, *Papers*, 13:270. The US Constitution uses the term "direct tax" but not "indirect tax"; Article I, section 8, stipulated duties, imposts, and excises be levied uniformly across the states, thereby implicitly categorizing those taxes as indirect.

56. Article I, sections 2 and 9.

57. Samuel Dexter, a Federalist from Massachusetts, quoting John Nicholas of Virginia in the *Annals of Congress*, House of Representatives, 3rd Congress, 1st Session, 645–646 (May 6, 1794). See also Hamilton, *Law Practice*, 4:306.

58. James Madison to Thomas Jefferson (May 11, 1794), in Jefferson, *Papers*, 28:72.

59. Hamilton to Tench Coxe (undated, but written during August 1–15, 1794), in Hamilton, *Papers*, 17:2.

60. Hamilton, *Law Practice*, 4:310. The state suit was dropped or deferred at some point.

61. Hylton had previously been involved in another federal case, *Ware v. Hylton*, 3 U.S. (3 Dall.) 199 (1796). Daniel Hylton, citing a Virginia statute, refused to pay a bond he owed to a British creditor, and the creditor's agent sued in federal court to recover the bond. In *Ware*, the US Supreme Court held that Virginia's statute authorizing the confiscation of debts owed to foreign creditors was in violation of the 1783 Treaty of Paris and was therefore unconstitutional.

62. Interestingly, Hamilton and Bradford miscalculated, making the *Hylton* suit worth exactly $2,000 (back taxes plus penalties) when the Judiciary Act stipulated that only suits valued in excess of $2,000 could be heard in the US Supreme Court on a writ of error from the circuit courts. This technicality did not affect the litigation, however. See section 22 of "An Act to establish the Judicial Courts of the United States," ch. 20, 1 Stat. 73, 84 (1789), and Hamilton, *Law Practice*, 4:313.

63. Hamilton, *Law Practice*, 4:315.

64. Marcus, *Documentary History*, 7:358–369, Hamilton, *Law Practice*, 4:297–340.

65. On August 20, 1787, Rufus King directly asked the members of the Philadelphia Convention, "What was the precise meaning of *direct* taxation?" According to James Madison's notes, "No one answd." See Farrand, *Records of the Federal Convention*, 2:350.

66. Einhorn, *American Taxation*, 161. Einhorn demonstrated that the total population for tax purposes (including three-fifths of enslaved persons) was 3,650,668 in 1796.

67. Einhorn, *American Taxation, American Slavery*, 160, and table on page 161.

68. In their seriatim opinions, both Justices William Paterson and James Iredell called the idea of an apportioned carriage tax "absurd." See *Hylton v. US*, 3 U.S. (3 Dall.) 171, 179, 182 (1796).

69. By internal taxes, I mean those that were not levied on goods leaving or entering the country. There were other problems with levying direct taxes that had to do with how they would be administered. Did the federal government assign the calculated tax burden to each state as a requisition, in which case the states would administer taxes as part of their own tax system, and just pay the federal government out of the state treasury? Or would federal direct taxes be levied as a separate federal tax, administered and collected by federal personnel (without any state involvement)? Furthermore, as Einhorn quipped, the apportionment of direct

taxes "was and remains an almost laughably unfair way to distribute the tax burden." She calculated a modern federal income tax that would result in a greater tax rate for poorer states and a lesser tax rate for the wealthiest states. The inequality of apportioning direct taxes worsened if applied to the 1794 carriage tax. Einhorn, *American Taxation*, 158–160).

70. Einhorn calculated that US citizens owned 18,384 carriages in 1796. On the basis of her data, the six Southern states (Delaware, Maryland, South Carolina, North Carolina, Virginia, and Georgia) housed less than half of the total number of extant carriages. When the federal government eventually levied a tax on slaves in 1798, it did so as a direct tax. Einhorn, *American Taxation*, 158, 161, and "An Act to provide for the valuation of Lands and Dwelling-Houses, and the enumeration of Slaves within the United States," ch. 70, 1 Stat. 580 (1798).

71. John Taylor, "Argument on the Carriage Tax, &c." (May [27], 1795), in Marcus, *Documentary History*, 7:392–393.

72. Ibid., 7:404.

73. Ibid., 7:387.

74. Ibid., 7:399, 400.

75. Taylor took shots at Hamilton's fiscal program through his extensive, meandering arguments before the court. He criticized in particular the tax immunity enjoyed by the Bank of the United States and by federal securities. Taylor was critiquing Hamilton's recently submitted "Report on a Plan for the Further Support of Public Credit" and the treasury secretary's comments on the nontaxable nature of federal debt. Ibid., 405–406.

76. Alexander Hamilton's "Brief" (composed before February 17, 1796), in Marcus, *Documentary History*, 7:463.

77. Alexander Hamilton's "Opinion" (composed before February 17, 1796), in ibid., 7:465.

78. Ibid.

79. "Final Version of an Opinion on the Constitutionality of an Act to Establish a Bank" (February 23, 1791), in Hamilton, *Papers*, 8:97, 107.

80. 3 U.S. (3 Dall.) 171, 173 (1796).

81. Ibid., 179.

82. Ibid., 182.

83. Hamilton, "Report Relative to a Provision for the Support of Public Credit" (January 9, 1790), in Hamilton, *Papers*, 6:73. Forrest McDonald also argued that two "philosophical premises" run through the entire corpus of Hamilton's arguments in favor of restoring the public credit. These premises are, first, that "the sanctity of contracts is the foundation of all private morality and the indispensable condition of every sane social order," and second, that "good government"—that is, "active, affirmative" governing—"is essential to the happiness and freedom of society." McDonald, *Alexander Hamilton*, 165.

84. *Annals of Congress*, House of Representatives, 3rd Congress, 2nd Session, 535 (March 27, 1794).

85. When discussing these resolutions as a Committee of the Whole, some con-

gressmen objected to the proposals and declared that the sanctity of contracts should lead Congress to oppose the measures. Referring to the sequestration resolutions, William Loughton Smith, of South Carolina, observed that "the sacredness with which the modern usages of nations has shielded debts is a great bar to our proceeding in the present case. Contracts between individuals are now considered as out of the reach of Governments." Connecticut representative Uriah Tracy also noted that "a breach of bargain was a breach of honesty" with regard to taxing the transference of federal securities. None of these resolutions became law, but Hamilton was alarmed enough to address the debates, and to expound on the legality of taxing federal securities and violating the sanctity of contracts. See the *Annals of Congress*, House of Representatives, 3rd Congress, 2nd Session, 540, 617, 619 (March 27 and May 1, 1794).

86. "Report on a Plan for the Further Support of Public Credit" (January 16, 1795), in Hamilton, *Papers*, 18:116, 121.

87. Hamilton addressed each of these specific situations separately. Foreign creditors should enjoy the same contractual sanctity bestowed on American debt holders because "when a Government enters into a contract with the Citizen of a foreign country it considers him *as an individual in a state of Nature, and Contracts with him as such*. It does not contract with him as *the member of another society*." Hamilton objected to the transfer tax proposed on federal bonds, because "the Stock in its *creation* is *made transferrable*. This quality constitutes a material part of its value, and the existence of it is a part of the contract with the Government. . . . It is as completely a breach of contract to derogate from this quality in diminution of the value of Stock, by incumbering the transfer with a charge or tax, as it is to take back in the same shape a portion of the principal or interest" (emphases in original). "Report on a Plan for the Further Support of Public Credit" (January 16, 1795), in Hamilton, *Papers*, 18:120, 123.

88. After all, Hamilton noted, "The true definition of public debt is *a property subsisting in the faith of the Government. Its essence is promise.* Its definite value depends upon the reliance that the promise will be definitely fulfilled." Ibid., 18:118.

89. Ibid., 18:119, 121; emphasis in original.

90. Note, however, that Hamilton never claimed that Congress would have violated its constitutional authority if it taxed federal securities. The Constitution granted the national government extensive power to tax and to borrow, but it never alludes to a collision between the two exercises of sovereign power. Moreover, Article I, section 10, bars the states, but not the federal government, from impairing the obligations of contracts. He therefore had to rely on principle, policy, and a balancing of opposing federal powers in order to craft his argument that securities were inviolable contracts. Hamilton was involved in developing contracts clause jurisprudence, however. In 1796, Hamilton drafted a legal "Case and Answer" for a client involved in Georgia's land speculation scandals. In that document, Hamilton argued that Georgia's legislature acted in violation of Article I, section 10's contracts clause by granting, then subsequently rescinding, titles to contested land. Hamilton's argument that the legislature's first grant of land constituted a contract

would ultimately influence John Marshall's opinion on the nature of contracts and the contracts clause in *Fletcher v. Peck*, 10 U.S. (6 Cranch) 87 (1810). See Hamilton, *Law Practice*, 4:420–422, 428–431, and Konefsky, *John Marshall and Alexander Hamilton*, 123.

91. *Federalist*, 220 (No. 32).

92. Story, "Rules of Interpretation of the Constitution," in *Commentaries on the Constitution of the United States*, 3:§436. He then cited Hamilton as the authority consulted in the following Supreme Court cases: *Sturges v. Crowninshield*, 17 U.S. (4 Wheat.) 122 (1819), *Houston v. Moore*, 18 U.S. (5 Wheat.) 1 (1820), *Gibbons v. Ogden*, 22 U.S. (9 Wheat.) 1 (1824), and *Ogden v. Saunders*, 25 U.S. (12 Wheat.) 213 (1827).

93. *Robert R. Livingston and Robert Fulton v. James Van Ingen et al.*, 9 Johns. Cas. 507, 567–568 (N.Y. Ct. Err., 1812) (Yates, J.). Hamilton would have agreed. In *Federalist* No. 32, he indicated that if the states acted in direct contradiction or repugnancy to constitutional authority, then their prerogative to legislate would be abridged. Hamilton did not suggest outright that the supremacy clause would trump exercises of the states' concurrent powers, but admitting such a thing to the people of New York state before their ratifying convention would have been ill-advised.

94. 9 Johns. Cas. 507, 568 (N.Y. Ct. Err., 1812).

95. Ibid., 576.

96. Ibid. 507, 539.

97. Ibid. 507, 547, 548.

98. *Houston v. Moore*, 18 U.S. (5 Wheat.) 1 (1820), and *Gibbons v. Ogden*, 22 U.S. (9 Wheat.) 1 (1824).

99. See, e.g., *Sturges v. Crowninshield*, 17 U.S. (4 Wheat.) 122 (1819). In *Gibbons*, however, the idea that congressional inaction permitted state action remained confused and muddled, and legal historian G. Edward White critiqued Marshall for failing to clarify this doctrine when the opportunity arose. Marshall missed such an opportunity to clarify his confused preclusion doctrine in *Brown v. Maryland*, 25 U.S. (12 Wheat.) 419 (1827), a combined tax and commerce clause case where Maryland required that importers be licensed by the state. The Court found that this violated both the commerce clause and the Constitution's prohibition on states to lay any imposts or duties on imports or exports. See White, *Marshall Court and Cultural Change*, 535, 580–583.

100. Section 5 of "An Act to provide more effectually for the Settlement of Accounts between the United States, and Receivers of public Money" reads: "And be it further enacted, That where any revenue officer, or other person hereafter becoming indebted to the United States, by bond or otherwise, shall become insolvent . . . the debt due to the United States shall be first satisfied." See ch. 20, 1 Stat. 512, 515 (1797).

101. *United States v. Fisher et al. Assignees of Blight, a Bankrupt*, 6 U.S. (2 Cranch) 358 (1805).

102. Ibid., 396.

103. Ibid., 396, 397.

104. In his lecture entitled "Of the Concurrent Jurisdiction of the State Governments," James Kent used Hamilton's *Federalist* No. 32 as the basis of his discussion of concurrent federal and state powers. When considering *US v. Fisher*, Kent recalled Hamilton's first-come, first-served approach in convention, but he noted that in *Fisher*, along with later concurrent sovereignty cases, the doctrine of federal supremacy trumped most state claims when federal and state powers directly collided. Kent, *Commentaries*, 1:369–370.

105. Maryland levied a tax of $15,000 per year on the Baltimore branch of the second Bank of the United States in February 1817. Over the next two years, five other states taxed bank stock or local branches. In contrast to Maryland, Kentucky and Ohio levied enormous sums intended not to raise revenue but to attack the unpopular national bank. Ellis, *Aggressive Nationalism*, 65.

106. *McCulloch v. Maryland*, 17 U.S. (4 Wheat.) 316, 344 (1819).

107. Ibid., 345.

108. Ibid., 372.

109. Ibid., 434, emphasis added.

110. Ibid., 435.

111. Quote at 436–437. See also Marshall on federal supremacy at 425.

112. "Let the end be legitimate, let it be within the scope of the constitution, and all means which are appropriate, which are plainly adapted to that end, which are not prohibited, but consist with the letter and spirit of the constitution, are constitutional." Ibid., 421.

113. *J. Bulow and J. Potter v. The City Council of Charleston*, 10 S. C. L. (1 Nott & McC.) 527, 529 (S.C. Ct. App., 1819). In *McCulloch*, Marshall declared that the national bank's tax immunity did not extend to the shares of bank stock held by private citizen shareholders. *McCulloch v. Maryland* (17 U.S. [4 Wheat] 316, 436 (1819)).

114. *J. Bulow and J. Potter v. The City Council of Charleston*, 10 S. C. L. (1 Nott & McC.) 527, 530–531 (S.C. Ct. App., 1819).

115. Ibid., 532–533.

116. *Weston and Others v. The City Council of Charleston*, 27 U.S. (2 Pet.) 449 (1829).

117. 27 U.S. (2 Pet.) 449, 454, 465, 466, 468, 469 (1829).

118. Ibid., 479, emphasis added.

119. Ibid., 477, 478.

120. 78 U.S. (11 Wall.) 113, 125 (1870).

121. 158 US 601, 630 (1895). See also Zimmerman, *Private Use of Tax-Exempt Bonds*, 41–43.

122. Rossiter, *Alexander Hamilton and the Constitution*, 199.

123. Richard E. Ellis deemed Marshall's nationalistic jurisprudence in *McCulloch* an "aggressive nationalism." My interpretation comports instead with Charles F. Hobson's argument that the Marshall Court "endors[ed] a limited, essentially defensive form of constitutional nationalism that left ample room for the exercise of state sovereignty." See, generally, Ellis, *Aggressive Nationalism*, and Hobson, *Great Chief Justice*, xiii, 122.

Chapter 5. "A Most Valuable Auxiliary": Securing Foreign
Capital with the Law of the Land

1. "Final Version of the Report on the Subject of Manufactures" (December 5, 1791), in Hamilton, *Papers*, 10:275.

2. Ibid., 10:276.

3. For historical studies of land speculation and land management during the early republic, see "Transatlantic Land Speculation," in Furstenberg, *When the United States Spoke French*, 227–285; Taylor, *William Cooper's Town*; Blaakman, "Speculation Nation"; Rohrbough, *Land Office Business*; Livermore, *Early American Land Companies*; Hulbert, "Methods and Operations"; Jones, *King of the Alley*.

4. Hamilton, *Law Practice*, 4:129.

5. Wilkins, *History of Foreign Investment*; see 32 for foreign and domestic loans, as well as 28–48. For foreign investment in the first half of the nineteenth century, see 49–89. See also Van Winter, *American Finance and Dutch Investment*; Hidy, *House of Baring*; Furstenberg, *When the United States Spoke French*, 280.

6. For one such critique of Hamilton, see Bradburn, *Citizenship Revolution*, 68–69. Yet even favorable biographers tend to emphasize his nationalistic leanings without recognizing that Hamilton also accepted and even relied on state authority to accomplish his objectives.

7. In practice, once the federal system was established, Hamilton resisted state encroachments of what he viewed as proper national power, but he also considered the states to be powerful venues to accomplish his statecraft. See "James Madison's Version of Hamilton's Remarks" (June 18, 1787), in Hamilton, *Papers*, 4:191, and "Constitutional Convention. Remarks on the Abolition of the States" (June 19, 1787), in Hamilton, *Papers*, 4:211n1

8. Story, *Commentaries on Equity Jurisprudence* 2:295 (§964).

9. Sullivan, "Alien Land Laws," 16–17.

10. Article II, section 2, of the US Constitution gave the federal courts exclusive jurisdiction only when a state was a party to the litigation (except in disputes between the state and its own citizens). The 1789 Judiciary Act qualified and elaborated the federal courts' concurrent jurisdiction with the states. See sections 11 and 13 of "An Act to establish the Judicial Courts of the United States," ch. 20, 1 Stat. 73, 78, 80 (1789).

11. *Fowler v. Lindsley et al.; Fowler et al. v. Miller*, 3 U.S. (3 Dall.) 411 (1799), and its companion case, *New York v. Connecticut*, are discussed in detail in Marcus, *Documentary History*, 8:178–191.

12. Wilkins, *History of Foreign Investment*, 35.

13. For in-depth scholarship on the formation, composition, and operations of the Holland Land Company, see Evans, *Holland Land Company*; Wyckoff, *Developer's Frontier*; Chazanof, *Joseph Ellicott*.

14. In 1803, foreign investors held $48.7 million of the federal debt. Wilkins, *History of Foreign Investment*, 36, 48.

15. Table 2.3, "Corporate Stock Held by Foreigners, 1803," in ibid., 37.

16. Van Winter, *American Finance and Dutch Investment*, 2:568, 577–580, 624–630.

17. "Report on Vacant Lands" (July 20, 1790), in Hamilton, *Papers*, 6:503, 505n1.

18. This is the primary insight and argument of Onuf, *Origins of the Federal Republic*.

19. The Committee of Style issued a September 10, 1787, report that limited the federal judiciary's authority "to controversies between two or more States (except such as shall regard Territory and Jurisdiction)." Hamilton, James Madison, Rufus King, Gouverneur Morris, and William Samuel Johnson submitted another version on September 12 that excluded the parenthetical limitation, thus allowing territorial dispute jurisdiction to the federal courts. Farrand, *Records of the Federal Convention*, 2:576, 600.

20. See Mashaw, *Creating the Administrative Constitution*, 127, and "An Act providing for the Sale of the Lands of the United States, in the territory northwest of the river Ohio, and above the mouth of Kentucky river," ch. 29, 1 Stat. 464 (1796).

21. Mashaw, *Creating the Administrative Constitution*, 127.

22. Haskins and Johnson, *Foundations of Power*, 590.

23. Section 11 of "An Act to Amend the act intitled 'An act providing for the sale of the lands of the United States, in the territory northwest of the Ohio, and above the mouth of Kentucky River,'" ch. 55, 2 Stat. 73, 77 (1800).

24. Mashaw, *Creating the Administrative Constitution*, 126.

25. Section 4 of "An Act making provision for the disposal of the public lands in the Indiana Territory, and for other purposes," ch. 35, 2 Stat. 277, 278 (1804).

26. Mashaw, *Creating the Administrative Constitution*, 129.

27. Ibid., 136–137.

28. The federal courts reviewed land office decisions only for jurisdictional errors. See Woolhandler, "Judicial Deference to Administrative Action," 216–219.

29. *Fletcher v. Peck*, 10 U.S. (6 Cranch) 87 (1810), and *Martin v. Hunter's Lessee*, 14 U.S. (1 Wheat.) 304 (1816).

30. 7 U.S. (3 Cranch) 1 (1805). For a full description of the case, see Haskins and Johnson, *Foundations of Power*, 317–322, 590–603.

31. Warren, *Supreme Court in United States History*, 1:370.

32. Marcus, *Documentary History*, 8:178.

33. The company initiated litigation in 1796 in the Connecticut Circuit Court before New York filed in either the Circuit Court for the District of New York or the US Supreme Court. The company brought two ejectment actions, *Fowler v. Lindsley* and *Fowler v. Miller*, on diversity grounds, claiming that Massachusetts citizen and company proprietor Samuel Fowler wished to try the titles of the *Connecticut citizens* Lindsley, Miller, and their codefendants living in the Gore. With these legal maneuvers, the company achieved a strategically advantageous position over New York: not only did the company maintain that Gore's inhabitants were Connecticut citizens (thus denying New York's title claims from the outset) but it also brought suit in a federal court that would assemble a Connecticut jury to hear the case. See Marcus, *Documentary History*, 8:178–191.

34. See ibid., 8:183, as well as "Notes of Arguments in the Circuit Court" (April

[13–16], 1798), in ibid., 8:218–223, and "Notes on Opinions of the Circuit Court" (April [16], 1798), in ibid., 8:223–224.

35. Another lawyer acting on behalf of New York, William Lewis, moved that the US Supreme Court issue an order to the plaintiffs to "shew cause . . . why a Venire should not be awarded to summon a Jury from some District of the United States other than the Districts of Connecticut or of New York." In February 1799, the justices heard arguments about whether and how the Court should adjudicate the *Fowler* cases. After disagreeing that New York was in fact a party to the litigation, the Court also dismissed the defendants' argument that the writ of certiorari could be used to move a case from a lower to a higher court on jurisdictional grounds. Marcus, *Documentary History*, 8:184, 186.

36. Section 16 of "An Act to establish the Judicial Courts of the United States," ch. 20, 1 Stat. 73, 82 (1789).

37. Marcus, *Documentary History*, 8:189.

38. Ibid. See also "An Act to authorize the President of the United States to accept, for the United States, a cession of jurisdiction of the territory west of Pennsylvania, commonly called the Western Reserve of Connecticut," ch. 38, 2 Stat. 56 (1800).

39. McCurdy, *Anti-Rent Era*, 1, 28.

40. The writ of right was an old English action to settle the question of proprietorship between the demandant-plaintiff and the defendant tenant to land. The plaintiff used the right in order to make claims about his ancestor's seisin in the property used by the tenant. See Hamilton, *Law Practice*, 3:340–343. For Hamilton's representation of New York patroons, see the section titled "Real Property: The Colonial Patents" in Hamilton, *Law Practice*, vol. 3.

41. See, in general, McCurdy, *Anti-Rent Era*.

42. Baker, *Introduction to English Legal History*, 291–292. For the origins of equity jurisprudence in English law, see Story, *Commentaries on Equity Jurisprudence*, 1:38–66 (ch. 2).

43. Story, *Commentaries on Equity Jurisprudence*, 2:347–349 (§1013).

44. Section 35 of the 1777 state constitution incorporated English common law into New York state law.

45. Hamilton, *Law Practice*, 3:614–615.

46. Ibid., 3:623.

47. "An Act for the relief of Wilhem Willinck, Nicholaas Van Staphorst, Christian Van Eeghen, Hendrick Vollenhoven, Rutger Jan Schimmelpenninck and Pieter Stadnitski being aliens," *Laws of the State of New York*, 19 Sess. 1796, c. 58 (April 11, 1796), and Hamilton, *Law Practice*, 3:625.

48. Hamilton, *Law Practice*, 3:612, 619–620.

49. "An Act to enable aliens to purchase and hold real estates within this State under certain restrictions therein mentioned," *Laws of the State of New York*, 21 Sess. 1798, c. 72 (Apr. 2, 1798). Restrictions on the Alien Act of 1798 included that alien landholders could not lease their lands, that they had to record their land transactions properly and within twelve months of purchase, and that the act would be in effect for only three years. See Hamilton, *Law Practice*, 3:628.

50. Hamilton, *Law Practice*, 3:632–633.

51. Hamilton, Richard Harison, and David A. Ogden, "Opinion Letter" (May 28, 1798), Hamilton, *Law Practice*, 3:717.

52. The trust was abolished on December 31, 1798. See Hamilton, *Law Practice*, 3:633.

53. Baker, *Introduction to English Legal History*, 311.

54. Kent, *Commentaries*, 4:132.

55. Baker, *Introduction to English Legal History*, 313.

56. Ibid., 313–314.

57. *Rex v. The Inhabitants of St. Michaels in Bath*, 2 Doug. 630 (K.B., 1781); Hamilton, *Law Practice*, 3:637.

58. "An Act for establishing an easier and cheaper mode of recovering Money secured by Mortgage on Real Estates, and barring the Equity of Redemption; and for abolishing the fictitious proceedings in the action of Ejectment." *Acts of the General Assembly of the State of South Carolina*, 1:63 (February 19, 1791), as cited in Hamilton, *Law Practice*, 3:637.

59. 1 Cai. Cas. (Cas. Err.) 47 (N.Y. Ct. Err., 1804).

60. Ibid., 47–49. Sarah had conveyed her interest in the property to her brother, Thomas Waters, before initiating the bill in chancery, which explains why he appears as complainant.

61. "An Act for making lands and tenements, liable to be sold by execution for debt, and for the more easy discovery of judgments, and the better security and relief of purchase and creditors," *Laws of the State of New York*, 10 Sess. 1787, c. 56 (March 19, 1787), and reenacted in "An Act concerning judgments and executions," *Laws of the State of New York*, 24 Sess. 1801, c. 105 (March 31, 1801). See Hamilton, *Law Practice*, 3:639.

62. Hamilton, *Law Practice*, 3:639.

63. 1 Cai. Cas. (Cas. Err.) 47, 57 (1804).

64. One caveat to the Court's decision, however, was that their rule only applied when the mortgagor was in possession when the equity of redemption was sold. Kent stated, "But when the mortgagee's rights are not in question, a mortgagor in possession, and before foreclosure, is a totally distinct character. He is regarded as the owner of the land, and the mortgage is treated as a mere incumbrance." Ibid., 68.

65. Ibid., 66 (Spencer).

66. Kent noted, "In equity, the mortgagor has been uniformly regarded as the legal owner; and the courts of law have latterly, in many respects, adopted the more rational ideas of chancery on this subject. If the mortgagor is to be deemed the owner of the land, as respects his own acts, and as respects the world, subject only to the *lien* of the mortgagee, it is neither unreasonable nor improper that courts of law, at the instance of other creditors, should treat the land as his, under the same limitation." Ibid., 69.

67. Ibid., 71. For New York mortgagors, the *Waters* decision meant that an equity of redemption qualified as "real estate" to be liquidated at law to pay debts—so

the Waters family was out of luck. However, New York courts would now acknowledge the mortgagor as the title holder to the property and the mortgagee as possessing only a lien.

68. See *Jackson ex dem. Benton v. Laughhead*, 2 Johns. 75 (1806); Hamilton, *Law Practice*, 3:643.

69. 11 Johns. 534 (N.Y., 1814). See also Hamilton, *Law Practice*, 3:643.

70. Kent, *Commentaries*, 4:148–158.

71. The quote is from Kent's opinion in *Waters v. Stewart*, 1 Cai. Cas. (Cas. Err.) 47, 73 (1805). Kent commented on the inconvenience that would arise (and probably had already occurred) if the Court determined that equities of redemption could only be forfeited by a decree in equity. Because *Waters* determined that this was not the case, the Court's decision excused mortgagees from the double expense and the resort to both law and equity. See also Hamilton, *Law Practice*, 3:643.

72. Hamilton, *Law Practice*, 3:644.

73. The Holland Land Company purchased, in total, 3.3 million acres of New York lands from Robert Morris in the early 1790s. While Morris conveyed deeds for the land to the company for most of the acreage, he would not do so for a western parcel of 1.5 million acres. Because Morris refused to convey deeds for that tract, the company could not confirm its title to those lands. Morris withheld the deeds because he and his attorneys suspected that the original agreement made between Morris and the company (a 1793 conveyance) remained a mortgage and never formally became an absolute sale. Morris and his attorneys believed that the absolute sale remained merely a mortgage because, through an inconvenient clerical oversight, none of the Holland Land Company's American agents or attorneys saw to it that the agreement was properly recorded. In the meantime, before the Holland Land Company could fix the clerical error and properly record their 1793 agreement with Morris, creditors had won legal judgments attached to the land in order to satisfy debts Morris owed to them. The judgments entitled two separate groups of creditors to different portions of Morris's interests in the property, including any equities of redemption. Morris also conveyed some acreage to a trust created to benefit another set of creditors. The result of all this was that in 1799, the Holland Land Company not only held a questionable title to 1.5 million acres in western New York, but Morris's creditors now had competing, if not superior claims, to the land. This morass of claims, judgments, trusts, and counterclaims could have been sorted out by New York's chancellor—and indeed Hamilton and other counsel considered this option. But instead, the company's attorneys opted for another, two-part strategy. First, the company bought out some of Morris's judgment creditors, thus acquiring the titles and property interests that judges had previously assigned to the creditors to execute Morris's debts. Then Hamilton and co-counsel David A. Ogden sorted out the remaining creditor interests by arbitrating the dispute, which meant, in essence, that the attorneys acted as if presiding in chancery.

The lawyers arbitrated a tangle of interests that arose from an agreement made between Gouverneur Morris, one of Morris's friends turned creditors, and Adam Hoops, an agent for the separate trust of creditors. Gouverneur Morris and Hoops agreed that Robert Morris's holdings in Ontario County would be sold to Hoops, and through this transaction, both Gouverneur Morris and the creditors in trust would receive payments toward settling Morris's outstanding debts. The deal did not go through as planned, however, and the Holland Land Company ended up buying the creditor judgment from Gouverneur Morris. This move now gave the company a stake in the Ontario parcel of land. At this time, David A. Ogden proposed that the Holland Land Company, Gouverner Morris, and the trust reach a tripartite agreement whereby the company acquired title to the land (by buying it outright at an 1800 sale, or vendue), and Morris and the trust receive cash from the company to compensate them for their interests in the land. The creditors would thus finally have repayment for Morris's debts. The agreement hinged on fixing and then monetizing each party's respective interest in the lands, and Hamilton suggested that a group of arbitrators make this determination. Hamilton, Ogden, and another lawyer and master in the Court of Chancery, Thomas Cooper, served as the arbitrators. See Hamilton, *Law Practice*, 3:651–682, and the accompanying documents.

74. See *Fitzsimmons and Others v. Ogden and Others*, 11 U.S. (7 Cranch) 2 (1812), and Hamilton, *Law Practice*, 3:678–679. Another interested creditor, Hamilton's brother-in-law, John B. Church, also questioned the arbitrators' award but brought suit in New York's chancery. No record exists of the Chancellor's final disposition of the case. Hamilton, *Law Practice*, 3:679–680.

75. Goebel and Smith devote an entire section to Hamilton's work on "Creditors' Rights" in Hamilton, *Law Practice* 2:232–374.

76. For other rules governing the doctrine of tacking, see Kent, *Commentaries*, 4:169.

77. Hamilton, *Law Practice*, 2:296–300.

78. 1 Cai. Cas. (Cas. Err.) 112, 119 (N.Y. Ct. Err., 1804).

79. Ibid., 120.

80. Kent, *Commentaries*, 4:171nc.

81. Hamilton to Gouverneur Morris (February 29, 1802), in Hamilton, *Papers*, 25:544.

Chapter 6. Litigation, Liberty, and the Law: Hamilton's Common Law Rights Strategy

1. Twentieth-century scholars including Richard Hofstadter, Louis Hartz, and Adrienne Koch have incorrectly characterized Hamilton as villainous, power hungry, or harmful to the American republic. Hartz even referred to Hamilton's absolute "hatred of the people." Hartz, *Liberal Tradition*, 111. For examples of other unflattering assessments of Hamilton, see Hofstadter, *United States*, 130, 147–148, 153–154, and Koch, "Hamilton, Adams," 46–47. In contrast, Knott, *Alexander Hamilton*, offered a historiographical survey of the waxing and waning of Hamilton's legacy over time. More recent historians have offered more nuanced perspectives on Hamilton. On Hamilton's suspicions of the people's ability to govern themselves, see Robert W. T. Martin's insightful reconciliation of Hamilton's distrust of democracy with his conception of republican citizenship and a free press,

"Reforming Republicanism." On Hamilton's skepticism of juries, particularly civil juries, see Hamilton's *Federalist* No. 83, and Amar, *Bill of Rights*, 89–92.

2. For the infamous murder case of Levi Weeks, see *People v. Weeks* (Court of Oyer and Terminer and General Gaol Delivery for the City and County of New York, 1800); "The Manhattan Well Mystery: *People v. Weeks*" section in Hamilton, *Law Practice*, 1:693–774; and Collins, *Duel with the Devil*.

3. Hamilton's concern for the protection of common law rights has been hinted at biographer John C. Miller, but otherwise, his rights consciousness goes largely unacknowledged by scholars. Miller, *Alexander Hamilton: Portrait in Paradox*, 101–105.

4. For the scholarship on common law reception, see Stoebuck, "Reception of English Common Law"; Reinsch, "English Common Law"; Goebel, "King's Law and Local Custom" and "Common Law and the Constitution"; Brown, *British Statutes in American Law.*

5. See section 35 of New York state's 1777 constitution.

6. "Remarks on an Act for settling Intestate Estates, Proving Wills, and Granting Administrations," made in the New York Assembly (February 14, 1787), in Hamilton, *Papers*, 4:69–70.

7. Hamilton, *Papers*, 4:69.

8. James Kent to Elizabeth Hamilton, or "Chancellor Kent's Memories of Alexander Hamilton" (December 10, 1832), in Kent, *Memoirs and Letters*, 290.

9. Hamilton to Gouverneur Morris (February 21, 1784), in Hamilton, *Papers* 3:512.

10. See Jasanoff, *Liberty's Exiles*; Ranlet, *New York Loyalists*; Spaulding, *New York in the Critical Period, 1783–1789*; Van Tyne, *Loyalists in the American Revolution.*

11. See "The War Cases," in Hamilton, *Law Practice*, 1:197–544, and Bloomfield, "Peter Van Schaack," 16. For selections from the enormous scholarship on judicial review, see Gordon S. Wood's two chapters "Law and an Independent Judiciary" and "Chief Justice John Marshall and the Origins of Judicil Review" in *Empire of Liberty*. See also Harrington, "Judicial Review before John Marshall," 53; Hulsebosch, "Discrete and Cosmopolitan Minority"; Treanor, "Judicial Review before *Marbury*," 483; Hulsebosch, *Constituting Empire*, 189–202; Kramer, *The People Themselves*, 65–67; Snowiss, *Judicial Review*, 16–22; Corwin, "Establishment of Judicial Review," 115–116.

12. Hamilton's conception of judicial power conformed to the eighteenth-century idea of judicial duty. Philip Hamburger defined "judicial duty" as the duty of English and American judges to decide in accordance with the law of the land. See Hamburger, *Law and Judicial Duty*, 17.

13. A British pamphlet published in 1786 and titled "Laws of the Legislature of the State of New York, in force against the Loyalists, and affecting the trade of Great Britain, and British Merchants, and others having property in that state" listed thirty-two laws against British sympathizers in New York state.

14. *Laws of the State of New York*, 6 Sess. 1783, c. 31 (March 17, 1783).

15. *Laws of the State of New York*, 3 Sess. 1779, c. 25 (October 22, 1779).

16. Hamilton, *Law Practice*, 1:197.

17. Ibid., 1:198–199.

18. *Laws of the State of New York*, 6 Sess. 1782, c. 1 (July 12, 1782).

19. Julius Goebel Jr. estimated that Hamilton was involved in forty-five cases involving the Trespass Act and nine cases involving the Citation Act (Hamilton, *Law Practice*, 1:419, 265). Because of the scarcity of extant records dealing with Confiscation Act litigation, Goebel cited Hamilton's involvement in only one Confiscation Act case, *People v. Nicholas Hoffman*. However, Hamilton also provided a number of opinions on the effects of the Confiscation Act for Loyalist clients, and he submitted petitions to the New York legislature on their behalf as well.

20. See Hamilton's *Rutgers* Brief No. 6 (undated), Hamilton, *Law Practice*, 1:368–369.

21. Hamilton inferred general amnesty to those identifying themselves as British subjects from Article VI of the Treaty of Peace. Hamilton, *Law Practice*, 1:299, 373.

22. Ibid., 1:289–292.

23. *Elizabeth Rutgers v. Joshua Waddington* (N.Y. Mayors Court, 1784).

24. See notes from Hamilton's *Rutgers* Brief No. 6 (undated), Hamilton, *Law Practice*, 1:377, 380, 383, 388.

25. See, in general, Hamburger, *Law and Judicial Duty*; Hamilton, *Rutgers* Brief No. 6, Hamilton, *Law Practice*, 1:381; "Remarks on an Act Repealing Law Inconsistent with the Treaty of Peace" (April 17, 1787), in Hamilton, *Papers*, 4:150–153.

26. "Opinion of the Mayor's Court" (August 27, 1784), Hamilton, *Law Practice*, 1:402.

27. Hamilton, *Law Practice*, 1:415, 417.

28. Ibid., 1:411, 419. Some contemporary New Yorkers interpreted Duane's equitable construction as a power play by the Mayor's Court to exercise legislative power, but equitable interpretation was a traditional way for courts to deal with two conflicting laws without pronouncing one void. See Hamburger, *Law and Judicial Duty*, 344–357.

29. "Opinion of the Mayor's Court" (August 27, 1784), in Hamilton, *Law Practice* 1:412; also 1:308–309.

30. *Thomas Tucker v. Henry Thompson* (N.Y. Mayor's Ct., 1784–1785), Plea (May 29, 1784), Hamilton, *Law Practice*, 1:432–447; *Moses Gomez v. Thomas Maule* (N.Y. Sup. Ct., unknown date), Plea (April 7), Hamilton, *Law Practice*, 1:449–453; see also Hamilton, *Law Practice*, 1:419–420.

31. *Walter Quackenbos v. Thomas Underhill* (N.Y. Mayor's Ct., 1784–1785), Plea (undated), Hamilton, *Law Practice*, 1:465–467; Jacob Morton and Mary S. Morton, Administrator and Administratrix of *John Morton v. William Seton* (N.Y. Sup. Ct., 1785–1786), Plea by John Lawrence, attorney for the plaintiff (undated), Hamilton, *Law Practice*, 1:468–474.

32. "Remarks on Trespass act Litigation in Connection with the Ratification of the Jay Treaty," extract from a letter from Hamilton to George Washington, July 9–10, 1795, Hamilton, *Law Practice*, 1:540–541.

33. *Daniel Shaw v. John Stevenson* (N.Y. Mayor's Ct., 1784), Plea, drafted by Hamilton for use by George Bond, attorney for defendant (April 6, 1784), Hamilton, *Law Practice*, 1:459–464. Quotation from Hamilton, *Law Practice*, 1:535.

34. *John Lloyd Jr. Executor of Joseph Lloyd v. John Williams* (N.Y. Sup. Ct., 1784–1785), Hamilton, *Law Practice*, 1:475–478; *John Lloyd Jr. Executor of Joseph Lloyd v. Charles Hewlett* (N.Y. Sup. Ct., 1784–1790), Hamilton, *Law Practice*, 1:478–488; *Isaac Hendrickson v. Whitehead Cornwell* (Queens County Common Pleas, 1786; N.Y. Sup. Ct., 1787–1788), Hamilton, *Law Practice*, 1:499–504; *John Lloyd Jr. Executor of Joseph Lloyd v. Barrack Sneathen* (N.Y. Sup. Ct., 1784–1788), Hamilton, *Law Practice*, 1:488–494.

35. Hamilton to Cornelius Glen, "Opinion on the Application of Abraham Cuyler" (February 13, 1784), Hamilton, *Law Practice*, 1:250.

36. Hamilton's "Remarks on Trespass act Litigation in Connection with the Ratification of the Jay Treaty," extract from a letter from Hamilton to George Washington (July 9–10, 1795), ibid., 1:541.

37. Although I have focused on the Trespass Act here, Hamilton also used a removal strategy in Citation Act litigation. See *Abel Belknap v. Elizabeth Van Cortlandt, et al.* (N.Y. Mayor's Ct., 1784; N.Y. Sup. Ct., 1786), Hamilton, *Law Practice*, 1:274.

38. Hamilton stated to Washington that he was "afraid myself of the event in the Supreme Court"—that the pleas of the law of nations and of the treaty would be ruled contrary to the Trespass Act and thus inadmissible. Hamilton's "Remarks on Trespass act Litigation in Connection with the Ratification of the Jay Treaty," extract from a letter from Hamilton to George Washington (July 9–10, 1795), in Hamilton, *Law Practice*, 1:541.

39. Hamilton, *Law Practice*, 1:201–202.

40. Ibid., 1:310–311.

41. For the quote, see the New York Assembly Proceedings, as reported in the *Pennsylvania Packet and Daily Advertiser*, November 20, 1784, issue 1807, p. 3; Melacton Smith, Peter Riker, Thomas Tucker, Daniel Shaw, Jonathan Lawrence, Anthony Rutgers, Peter T. Curtenius, Adam Gilchrist Jr., and John Wiley, "To the People of the State of New York," *New York Packet and the American Advertiser*, November 4, 1784, issue 434, p. 2.

42. *Benjamin Birdsall v. Obadiah Valentine* (Queen's County Justice's Court, 1785; N.Y. Sup. Ct., 1786), Hamilton, *Law Practice*, 1:495–499.

43. "Petition of the Executors of John Aspinwall to the New York Legislature" (undated), in ibid., 1:269–270.

44. "Petition of Phoebe Ward to the Governor and the General Assembly of New York" (August 11, 1789), in ibid., 1:262.

45. Ibid., 1:226.

46. *People v. Nicolas Hoffman* (N.Y. Sup. Ct., 1783–1784); "Plea of Autrefois Attaint" (undated), in ibid., 1:249.

47. Ibid., 1:227–230, 232, 235–237.

48. Ibid., 1:228.

49. *Jackson ex dem. James Leonard v. Anthony Post, John Stiles* (N.Y. Sup. Ct., 1784–1786); Hamilton, *Law Practice*, 1:228–230.

50. Brutus, "To All Adherents to the British Government and Followers of the British Army, Commonly Called Tories, Who are at Present within the City and County of New-York," *New-York Gazetteer or Northern Intelligencer*, October 27, 1783, vol. 2, issue 74, p. 2.

51. James H. Kettner argued that in the period after the Revolution, Americans began to consider citizenship as a status voluntarily chosen. In the aftermath of the war, some British sympathizers in America chose to remain British subjects; others chose to switch their allegiance to the new American nation. I refer to these former British sympathizers who chose to remain in the states and remake themselves as Americans as Loyalists throughout, and Hamilton argued that they had become bona fide citizens and members of New York state. See Kettner, *Development of American Citizenship*, 213–247.

52. "A Letter from Phocion to the Considerate Citizens of New York" (January 1784), in Hamilton, *Papers*, 3:484, 485.

53. Ibid., 3:484.

54. Hamilton's emphasis. Hamilton cited "Coke upon Magna Charta, Chap. 29, Page 50" in a footnote to this passage. See ibid., 3:485. He similarly defined due process when remarking on an "Act for Regulating Elections" in the New York Assembly on February 6, 1787. During that debate, Hamilton added, "The words *'due process'* have a precise technical import, and are only applicable to the process and proceedings of the courts of justice; they can never be referred to an act of legislature." See ibid., 4:35.

55. "No citizen can be deprived of any right which the citizens in general are entitled to, unless forfeited by some offence. . . . Can we then do by act of legislature, what the treaty disables us from doing by due course of law?" "A Letter from Phocion to the Considerate Citizens of New York" (January 1784), in ibid., 3:488.

56. Mechanic, "An Address from a Mechanic to Phocion," *New-York Journal and State Gazette*, March 25, 1784, issue 1951, p. 3, and "Conclusion of the Mechanic's Address to Phocion," *New York Journal and State Gazette*, April 1, 1784, issue 1952, p. 2.

57. Ledyard, "Mentor's Reply to Phocion's Letter," 7–9.

58. For details on how Hamilton dismissed Mentor's interpretation of the treaty, see "Second Letter from Phocion" (April 1784), in Hamilton, *Papers*, 3:535–540.

59. "First, That no man can forfeit or be justly deprived, without his consent, of any right, to which as a member of the community he is entitled, but for some crime incurring the forfeiture. Secondly, That no man ought to be condemned unheard, or punished for supposed offences, without having an opportunity of making his defence. Thirdly, That a crime is *an act* committed or omitted, in violation of a public law, either forbidding or commanding it. Fourthly, That a prosecution is in its most precise signification, an *inquiry* or *mode of ascertaining*, whether a particular person has committed, or omitted such act. Fifthly, That *duties* and *rights* as applied to sub-

jects are reciprocal; or in other words, that a man cannot be a *citizen* for the purpose of punishment, and not a *citizen* for the purpose of privilege." Ibid., 3:532–533.

60. Ibid., 3:533–535, 541–547.

61. Ibid., 3:534.

62. Ibid., 3:535.

63. Ibid., 3:548.

64. See "Note on the Development of the Right of a New Trial in English Law," Hamilton, *Law Practice*, 3:117–132; Robert R. Livingston's "Notes on Hamilton's Argument of Facts and Relevant Law in support of defendant's motion for new trial" (undated), ibid., 3:237–244; Hamilton's "Brief on Facts and Relevant Law for Argument of Motion for New Trial" (undated), ibid., 3:220–224; all relating to *Jackson ex dem. Livingston v. Hoffman* (N.Y. Sup. Ct., 1783–1785).

65. 3 Johns. Cas. 337 (N.Y. Sup. Ct., 1804). Harry Croswell published two libelous remarks about President Thomas Jefferson: that he was hostile to the US Constitution, and that he paid scandalmonger James Callender to attack former presidents John Adams (calling him a "hoary headed incendiary") and to posthumously libel George Washington (as a "traitor, a robber, and a perjurer"). For these assertions, the Republican powers in New York brought Croswell to court on criminal libel charges, and he was indicted on January 10, 1803. For a complete narrative of the case, see Hamilton, *Law Practice*, 1:775–790. Hamilton was only involved in the arguments for retrial.

66. Only a few historians consider the constitutional question in *Croswell*. Julius Goebel Jr. and Daniel J. Hulsebosch both described *Croswell*'s significance as a common law "reception" problem. Goebel, *Antecedents and Beginnings*, 116–118; Hulsebosch, *Constituting Empire*, 398n60. Also, most scholars have missed the constitutional question at the heart of *Croswell* because they have relied primarily on Johnson's case reports and its condensed summary of arguments. George Caines, representing the state in *Croswell*, published a more complete account of the attorneys' speeches in 1804. These published speeches reveal the constitutional uncertainty undergirding the attorneys' arguments. When referring to Van Ness's, Caines's, Spencer's, and Harison's arguments, I cite this publication instead of the Johnson reports. See Caines, *Speeches at Full Length*. When I refer to Hamilton's arguments, I cite a reprinted excerpt of *Speeches at Full Length* that can be found in Hamilton, *Law Practice*, 1:808–833.

67. Leonard W. Levy cited *Croswell* in his chapter "The Emergence of an American Libertarian Theory," in *Emergence of a Free Press*, 338–340. See also Berns, "Freedom of the Press," 111; Curtis, *Free Speech*, 112–115; Martin, *Free and Open Press*, 155, 160.

68. In November 1799, Hamilton urged New York attorney general Josiah Ogden Hoffman to charge Republican publisher David Frothingham with criminal libel for accusations Frothingham had made against Hamilton in the press. Hoffman prosecuted Frothingham, and a jury found him guilty. See Bird, *Press and Speech under Assault*, 280–281.

69. James Morton Smith has been critical of Hamilton in particular, but also of the general suppression of the press in this period. See, in general, Smith, *Freedom's Fetters*. Smith portrayed Hamilton as a leading suppressor of the press in "Alexander Hamilton, the Alien Law, and Seditious Libels," particularly for Hamilton's failure to come out strongly against the Sedition Act and for his complicity in the 1799 trial of David Frothingham.

70. There could be a fine line between "declaring" the law and "changing" the law. Yet in *Croswell*, the court's duty to declare the law resulted from the opposing premises adopted by each side. The defense assumed that the law of criminal libel was never settled in New York state, so no matter what outcome the judges selected, the court would not be "legislating," or actively changing what they acknowledged to be existing law. Instead, the court would be determining criminal libel law's official, doctrinal starting point on the New York record. In this way, a new legal outcome could be generated within the boundaries of a proper judicial adjudication. The prosecution adopted the opposite premise: that the law had been already in force in New York, and to deviate from King's Bench and colonial precedent (Peter Zenger's case) would be to inappropriately alter the law by judicial judgment. Thus, neither side asked the *Croswell* court to change the existing law.

71. See below, as well as Lobban, "From Seditious Libel to Unlawful Assembly."

72. Attorney General Ambrose Spencer, for example, referred to the common law's distinction between law and fact in *Speeches at Full Length*, 49.

73. Hamilton, *Law Practice*, 1:789–790.

74. Both the prosecution and the defense retained different combinations of legal counsel at each stage of the *Croswell* proceedings. Only Ambrose Spencer and William Van Ness appeared consistently. For details, see ibid., 1:793.

75. *Rex v. John Peter Zenger* (N.Y., 1738) and "Tryal of John Peter Zenger."

76. *Rex v. Shipley*, 21 State Trials 847 (K.B., 1784); *Queen v. Tutchin*, 14 State Trials 1095 (Q.B., 1704); *Rex v. Franklin*, 21 *State Trials* 1039 (K.B., 1731); *Rex v. Owen*, 18 State Trials 1203 (K.B., 1752). See also Oldham, *English Common Law*, 228–229. Note that each *Croswell* attorney also addressed one or more of these King's Bench cases throughout their speeches.

77. Oldham, *English Common Law*, 229. Mansfield suggested that jurymen, who were subject to bias and prejudice, would disrupt the staid course of the law if they could rule on law—in this case, on the intent of publication.

78. Caines, *Speeches at Full Length*, 28.

79. 12 State Trials 183 (K.B., 1688). While this has been generally true for criminal libel actions, the larger story of English prosecutions against seditious publications suggests a more complex story behind English libel law. According to Philip Hamburger, the doctrine of criminal libel described by Mansfield only developed around 1700, and before the mid-1690s, criminal libel actions were not regularly used as a means to restrain the press. The English Crown used other legal actions and statutes to prosecute libel, some of which—like *Scandalum Magnatum*—allowed truth as a defense to the publication of libelous news. Hamburger's findings lend historical support to the *Croswell* defense's argument that King's Bench libel

doctrine could be considered as a relatively new legal position and not evidence of the true common law. However, while the *Seven Bishops Case* allowed truth as a defense, as a result of the political nature of the decision, Hamburger considered the case to be an exception from the developing doctrine of criminal libel law that did not allow truth as a defense. Hamburger, "Development of the Law of Seditious Libel," 663, 668–669, 699.

80. Lobban, "From Seditious Libel to Unlawful Assembly," 307–322.

81. This outline of late eighteenth-century developments in English seditious libel law comes directly from ibid., 307–322, 349–352. Fox's Libel Act, or the Libel Act, 32 Geo. III, c. 60 (1792), declared that juries should determine the general issue of guilt or innocence for criminal libel actions, but it did not mention truth as a defense. Yet even if Parliament did not declare truth to be a viable defense to criminal libel prosecutions, under the Libel Act, the jury had more discretion to consider truth and intent of publication as part of its general verdict. As Lord Mansfield's experience made clear, English juries resisted the narrow question of the fact of publication and would welcome the opportunity to decide under the general issue. Oldham, *English Common Law*, 218–219.

82. Van Ness in Caines, *Speeches at Full Length*, 9; Hamilton, *Law Practice*, 1:820.

83. Caines, *Speeches at Full Length*, 33.

84. Ibid., 35, 48.

85. Ibid., 41.

86. Ibid., 22. Some scholars seem to doubt Caines's assertion that the law developed to protect against breaches of the peace. See Hamburger, "Development of the Law of Seditious Libel," 664–665, 692, 697–714.

87. Caines, *Speeches at Full Length*, 42.

88. Caines, referring to the *Dean of St. Asaph's Case*, in ibid., 43.

89. As counsel for the defense in *Rex v. Shipley* (or the *Dean of St. Asaph's Case*), Thomas Erskine would have turned Caines's argument back around on the *Croswell* prosecution. To Erskine, precisely because seditious publications could incite discord, determining the seditious nature of the words necessarily relied on the context of the publication and thus was a fact (and not a question of law) for the jury to decide. (Context was difficult to capture on the written record, yet according to common law rules, the judge could only base his decision on the law from the information and evidence captured on the record.) Thus, when placed in the changing context of the late eighteenth-century law of seditious libel, Caines's point about protecting against breaches of the peace would serve to aid Croswell's argument that under New York law, the jury should decide the general issue. See Lobban, "From Seditious Libel to Unlawful Assembly," 316–317.

90. Caines, *Speeches at Full Length*, 20, 38, 44. Considering the "right of reputation" as a form of property right to be enforced by a libel prosecution was common in England. Lobban, "From Seditious Libel to Unlawful Assembly," 311. It also made sense in the context of prevailing Anglo-American cultural norms—namely, the honor culture of the late eighteenth century. See generally Freeman, *Affairs of Honor*.

91. Caines, *Speeches at Full Length*, 40.

92. Van Ness in ibid., 10.

93. Caines did not specify how unpunished libels would affect a person's property, real or chattel, unless he was referring to the public man's reputation as property. Ibid., 44.

94. Spencer in ibid., 53.

95. Harison in ibid., 55.

96. Matthew Hale described Parliament as "the high and supreme court of this kingdom." Hale elaborated on the dual nature of Parliament's adjudicatory and law making powers: "Touching the power of parliament, either it respects things done or things to be done. In respect of things already done. This is the judicative power of parliament, which is the supreme judicature. . . . In respect of things to be done, wherein it acts under a double notion, *viz.* either by way of council or by way of law. . . . As touching the legislative power . . . this power of law making is exercised: (1) in imposing charges as subsidies &c. (2) in enacting new laws, (3) in declaring laws." Hale, *Prerogatives of the King*, 135, 140–141.

97. *The Libel Act*, 32 Geo. III, c. 60 (1792).

98. Hamilton, *Law Practice*, 1:826.

99. Ibid.

100. Van Ness cited four statutes, passed between 1275 and 1554, which suggested that the law of England only punished false or malicious publications. Van Ness in Caines, *Speeches at Full Length*, 7.

101. Hamilton, *Law Practice*, 1:814–815, and Van Ness in Caines, *Speeches at Full Length*, 10, 11.

102. Hamilton, *Law Practice*, 1:826.

103. Ibid., 1:827. Hamilton looked to Fox's Libel Act as a declaration, or confirmation, of the law of seditious libel, but a declaration that had the imprimatur of the highest court in the realm.

104. Spencer, quoting Lord Chief Justice Mansfield, in Caines, *Speeches at Full Length*, 50.

105. Ibid., 48; Caines had previously made a similar point (35).

106. Ibid., 47. Fox's Libel Act did not declare "truth" to be a defense to criminal libel actions, so even if the prosecution granted that the 1792 Libel Act was declaratory of common law, argued Spencer, the court could not apply the act to Croswell's second ground for retrial.

107. Ibid., 49.

108. Van Ness in Caines, *Speeches at Full Length*, 9. See also the 1798 Sedition Act, or "An Act in addition to the act, entitled 'An act for the punishment of certain crimes against the United States,'" ch. 74, 1 Stat. 596 (1798).

109. Hamilton, *Law Practice*, 1:830.

110. See Julius Goebel Jr., in ibid., 1:17–18, 78. In addition, see "Collision between the Supreme Court and the Court of Errors." In *Constituting Empire*, Hulsebosch discussed how the Court for the Trial of Impeachments and the Correction of Errors fit into New York's late eighteenth-century constitutional fabric, 180–182.

Philip Hamburger described how Parliament, as the highest court in the realm, presided as the dernier resort of the English legal system. See "No Appeal from Parliament," in Hamburger, *Law and Judicial Duty*, 237–254.

111. Take, for example, Congress relying on parliamentary precedent as a model to run the trial of Robert Randall and Charles Whitney; see the *Annals of Congress* from Monday, December 28, 1795, to Friday, January 8, 1796. Also, eighteenth-century American statesmen often consulted George Petyt's *Lex Parliamentaria* (1748).

112. A concern for citizen security was what made Congress's Sedition Act such a "valuable" statute to Hamilton, as the sedition law allowed the jury to consider the truth of the publication as a defense. According to Hamilton, Congress premised the 1798 Sedition Act on "common law principles," and in doing so, it followed the wise example set by the Framers of the US Constitution. Because the US Constitution relied on the common law, it created a strong but limited government that could not infringe on individuals' rights. "The Constitution of the US," Hamilton warned, "would have been melted away or borne down by Faction, if the Com[mo]n law was not applicable." Hamilton elaborated on the wisdom of reading common law principles into the US Constitution: "The Habeas Corpus is mentioned, and as to treason, it adopts the very words of the common law. Not even the Legislature of the union can change it. Congress itself can not make constructive, or new treasons. Such is the general tenor of the constitution of the United States, that it evidently looks to antecedent law. What is, on this point, the great body of common law? Natural law and natural reason applied to the purposes of Society." Hamilton, *Law Practice*, 1:829–830.

113. During winter 1801–1802, Hamilton published eighteen essays, titled "The Examination," in the *New York Evening Post*, under the pseudonym Lucius Crassus. He intended these articles to be his public response to President Jefferson's first annual message to Congress (December 8, 1801), as well as an opportunity to address Hamilton's larger concerns about the state of the nation. To Hamilton, the most pressing of these concerns involved the state of the federal judiciary, which, according to the former treasury secretary, had been compromised and rendered dependent by the repeal of the 1801 Judiciary Act. With the successful repeal of the act, Congress abolished sixteen federal circuit court judgeships, even though judges had already been selected to fill those positions. Hamilton found this to be an unconstitutional violation of Article III's guarantee that federal judges hold their offices as long as they maintained "good behavior." He argued that to divest the judges of these offices, once created, was to violate the judge's vested right in the office, in addition to violating Article III's good behavior clause. Furthermore, the repeal of the circuit court judgeships meant that the independence of the federal judiciary had been successfully nullified by the national legislature, and that the wisdom and benefits of separating governmental institutions had been abrogated.

114. James Kent to Elizabeth Hamilton, or "Chancellor Kent's Memories of Alexander Hamilton" (December 10, 1832), in Kent, *Memoirs and Letters*, 323–324, 326.

115. Ibid., 300. In the full quote, Kent wrote to Hamilton's widow, Elizabeth Schuyler Hamilton, and lauded Hamilton's entire career for its devotion to liberty: "All his actions and all his writings as a public man show that he was the uniform, ardent, and inflexible friend of justice and of national civil liberty."

116. During the 1780s, Hamilton was not only concerned with protecting Loyalists' rights. He argued against the New York assembly's proposed requirement that naturally born Roman Catholics take an oath of abjuration that effectively would have barred them from holding office. See "Remarks on an Act of Regulating Elections" (January 24, 1787), made in the New York assembly, in Hamilton, *Papers*, 4:22, as well as Miller, *Alexander Hamilton: Portrait in Paradox*, 104.

117. Spaulding, *New York in the Critical Period, 1783–1789*, 130–131.

118. Alexander Hamilton's remarks in the New York assembly, as reported in the *Daily Advertiser: Political, Historical, and Commercial*, March 23, 1787, vol. 3, issue 648, p. 2.

119. *Laws of the State of New York*, 10 Sess. 1787 c. 71 (April 4, 1787).

120. *Laws of the State of New York*, 10 Sess. 1787 c. 1 (January 26, 1787).

121. Emery, "New York's Statutory Bill of Rights," 369. Lawyers Samuel Jones and Richard Varick assumed control over the project and drew up "An Act concerning the Rights of Citizens" along with nine other sundry bills.

122. *Laws of the State of New York*, 10 Sess. 1787 c. 1, clause 2 (January 26, 1787).

123. Ibid., clauses 5 and 6.

124. Ibid., clause 4.

125. In the New York assembly, the statutory bill of rights "was unanimously agreed to after a very few alterations." Assembly proceedings, as reported in the *New-York Journal and Weekly Register*, January 18, 1787, vol. 41, issue 3, p. 3. The Senate and Council also passed the bill without opposition. Emery, "New York's Statutory Bill of Rights," 369.

126. "An Act concerning Libels," *Laws of the State of New York*, 28 Sess. 1805, c. 90. James Kent referred to the law as a "declaratory statute," thus underscoring his assumption that the legislature had exercised its Parliament-like capacity to declare the common law in force in New York state. See Forkosch, "Freedom of the Press," 447, and Roper, "James Kent and the Emergence of New York's Libel Law," 223–231.

127. Levy, *Emergence of a Free Press*, 339–340.

128. The idea that common law constituted the English polity and regulated the English people, along with all of the institutions, jurisdictions, and authorities of the government, derived from sixteenth- and seventeenth-century English common lawyers and their notions of the ancient constitution of England. See Burgess's *Politics of the Ancient Constitution*, chaps. 1–3, and Reid, *Constitutional History*, 3–25.

129. Bernadette Meyler, in "Towards a Common Law Originalism," argued that Americans of the revolutionary generation considered the common law to be flexible and adaptive, but she focused mainly on interpreting references to the common law in the federal Constitution. Michael Lobban also argued that common law was

inherently flexible, though his reasoning differed from the Hamiltonian "extensive" common law described here. Lobban, *Common Law and English Jurisprudence*, 1–16.

Conclusion: The Federalist

1. "An Act to establish the Judicial Courts of the United States," ch. 20, 1 Stat. 73, 85 (1789).

2. 7 F. Cas. 418 (C.C.D. Mass., 1815).

3. See, in general, Horwitz, *Transformation of American Law, 1780–1860*.

4. "An Act in addition to the act entitled, 'An act for the punishment of certain crimes against the United States,'" ch. 74, 1 Stat. 596 (1798).

5. McCurdy, "American Law," 648.

6. See Horwitz, *Transformation of American Law, 1870–1960*. Also, Michael Lobban argues that the rigors of pleading and writs gave the common law its adaptive flexibility to provide a variety of remedies to claimants. Lobban, *Common Law and English Jurisprudence*, 1–16.

7. Historians who have already begun this inquiry include Bilder, "James Madison, Law Student," and Johnson, "John Jay."

8. All quotes in this paragraph are from Burke, "Alexander Hamilton as a Lawyer," 184.

Bibliography

Archival Materials

Annals of Congress
Gilder Lehrman Collection, New York, NY
Journal of the House
National Archives and Records Administration, Washington, DC
US Statutes at Large

Federal Cases

Bartlett v. Kane, 57 US (16 How.) 263 (1853).
Brown v. Maryland, 25 US (12 Wheat.) 419 (1827).
Calbreath v. Gracy, 4 F. Cas. 1030 (C.C.D. Pa., 1805).
Chevron USA., Inc. v. Natural Resources Defense Council, Inc., 467 US 837 (1984).
Cohens v. Virginia 19 US (6 Wheat.) 264 (1821).
Collector v. Day, 78 US (11 Wall.) 113 (1870).
The Cotton Planter, 6 F. Cas. 620 (C.C.D. N.Y., 1810).
Croudson and Others v. Leonard, 8 US (4 Cranch) 434 (1808).
Crowell and others v. M'Fadon, 12 US (8 Cranch) 94 (1814).
Decatur v. Paulding, 39 US (14 Pet.) 497 (1840).
De Lovio v. Boit, 7 F. Cas. 418 (C.C.D. Mass., 1815).
Don Diego Pintado v. The Ship San Joseph, Jean Antoine Berard, Claimant (D.C.D.
    N.Y., 1795; C.C.D. N.Y., 1795–1796; US, 1796).
The Emulous, 8 F. Cas. 697 (C.C.D. Mass., 1813).
Fitzsimmons and Others v. Ogden and Others, 11 US (7 Cranch) 2 (1812).

Fitzsimmons v. The Newport Insurance Company, 8 US (4 Cranch) 185 (1808).

Fletcher v. Peck, 10 US (6 Cranch) 87 (1810).

Fowler et al. v. Lindsey et al.; Fowler et al., v. Miller, 3 US (3 Dall.) 411 (1799).

Gallego et al. v. US, 9 F. Cas. 1105 (C.C.D. Va., 1820).

Gibbons v. Ogden, 22 US (9 Wheat.) 1 (1824).

Gilchrist et. al. v. Collector of Charleston, 10 F. Cas. 355 (C.C.D. S.C., 1808).

Glass v. The Sloop Betsey, 3 US (3 Dall.) 6 (1794).

Hayburn's Case, 2 US (2 Dall.) 409 (1792).

The Hine v. Trevor, 71 US (4 Wall.) 555 (1866).

Houston v. Moore, 18 US (5 Wheat.) 1 (1820).

Huidekooper's Lessee v. Douglas, 7 US (3 Cranch) 1 (1805).

Hylton v. US, 3 US (3 Dall.) 171 (1796).

Kendall v. Stokes, 44 US (3 How.) 87 (1845).

Kendall v. US ex. rel. Stokes et. al., 37 US (12 Pet.) 524 (1838).

Little v. Barreme, 6 US (2 Cranch) 170 (1804).

Maley v. Shattuck, 7 US (3 Cranch) 458 (1806).

Marbury v. Madison, 5 US (1 Cranch) 137 (1803).

Martin v. Hunter's Lessee, 14 US (1 Wheat.) 304 (1816).

McCulloch v. Maryland 17 US (4 Wheat.) 316 (1819).

The Moses Taylor, 71 US (4 Wall.) 411 (1866).

Ogden v. Saunders, 25 US (12 Wheat.) 213 (1827).

Olney v. Arnold, 3 US (3 Dall.) 308 (1796).

Otis v. Watkins, 13 US (9 Cranch) 339 (1815).

Plowden Weston and others v. The City Council of Charleston, 27 US (2 Pet.) 449 (1829).

Pollock v. Farmers Loan & Trust Co., 158 US 601 (1895).

The Propeller Genesee Chief v. Fitzhugh, 53 US (12 How.) 443 (1851).

Rankin v. Hoyt, 45 US (4 How.) 327 (1846).

Shattuck v. Maley, 21 F. Cas. 1181 (C.C.D. Pa., 1805).

Stuart v. Laird, 5 US (1 Cranch) 299 (1803).

Sturgis v. Crowninshield, 17 US (4 Wheat.) 122 (1819).

US v. Burr, 25 F. Cas. 55 (C.C.D. Va., 1807).

US v. Fisher et al Assignees of Blight, 6 US (2 Cranch) 358 (1805).

US v. The Hawke, 26 F. Cas. 233 (D.C.D. S. C., 1794).

US v. Lancaster, 26 F. Cas. 859 (C.C.D. E.D. Pa., 1821).

US v. La Vengeance, 3 US (3 Dall.) 297 (1796).

US v. Morris, Marshal of the Southern District of New York, 23 US (10 Wheat.) 246 (1825).

US v. New Bedford Bridge, 27 F. Cas. 91 (C.C.D. Mass., 1847).

US v. Nixon, 418 US 683 (1974).

US v. One Case of Hair Pencils, 27 F. Cas. 244 (C.C.D. N.D. N.Y., 1825).

US v. The Schooner Betsey and Charlotte and her Cargo, 8 US (4 Cranch) 443 (1808).

US v. The Schooner Sally of Norfolk, 6 US (2 Cranch) 406 (1805).

US v. The Ship Huron, Francis Hill, and Ephraim Hart, Claimants (D.C.D. N.Y., 1800–1803).

US v. The Ship Lydia, Henry Treadwell, Claimant (D.C.D. N.Y., 1801).

US v. The Ship Young Ralph (D.C.D. N.Y., 1802; C.C.D. N.Y., 1802–1805).

US v. Vowell and M'Clean, 9 US (5 Cranch) 368 (1809).

US v. The William, 28 F. Cas. 614 (D.C.D. Mass., 1808).

Ware v. Hylton, 3 US (3 Dall.) 199 (1796).

Waring v. Clarke, 46 US (5 How.) 441 (1847).

Warren Manufacturing Company v. Etna Insurance Company, 29 F. Cas. 294 (C.C.D. Conn., 1837).

Youngstown Sheet & Tube Co. v. Sawyer, 343 US 579 (1952).

New York State Cases

Abel Belknap v. Elizabeth Van Cortlandt, et al., (N.Y. Mayor's Ct., 1784; N.Y. Sup. Ct., 1786).

Barnewall v. Church, 1 Cai. 217 (N.Y. Sup. Ct., 1803).

Benjamin Birdsall v. Obadiah Valentine (Queen's County Justice's Court, 1785; N.Y. Sup. Ct., 1786).

Blagge v. The New York Insurance Company, 1 Cai. R. 549 (N.Y. Sup. Ct., 1804).

Bowne v. Shaw, 1 Cai. R. 489 (N.Y. Sup. Ct., 1803).

Daniel Shaw v. John Stevenson (N.Y. Mayor's Ct., 1784).

Goix v. Knox, 1 Johns. Cas. 337 (N.Y. Sup. Ct., 1800).

Goix v. Low, 1 Johns. Cas. 341 (N.Y. Sup. Ct., 1800).

Goix v. Low, 2 Johns. Cas. 480 (N.Y. Ct. Err., 1802).

Isaac Hendrickson v. Whitehead Cornwell (Queens County Common Pleas, 1786; N.Y. Sup. Ct., 1787–1788).

Jackson ex dem. Benton v. Laughhead, 2 Johns. 75 (N.Y. Sup. Ct., 1806).

Jackson ex dem. Leonard v. Post, Stiles (N.Y. Sup. Ct., 1784–1786).

Jackson ex dem. Livingston v. Hoffman, (N.Y. Sup. Ct., 1783–1785).

Jacob Morton and Mary S. Morton, Administrator and Administratrix of John Morton v. William Seton (N.Y. Sup. Ct., 1785–1786).

James Grant et al. v. The Bank of the United States, 1 Cai. Cas. (Cas. Err.) 112 (N.Y. Ct. Err., 1804).

John Lamb Qui Tam v. Two Trunks of Merchandize, John Baptist Riolz, Claimant (N.Y. Adm., 1785; N.Y. Ct. Err., 1785–1786).

John Lloyd Jr. Executor of Joseph Lloyd v. Barrack Sneathen (N.Y. Sup. Ct., 1784–1788).

John Lloyd Jr. Executor of Joseph Lloyd v. Charles Hewlett (N.Y. Sup. Ct., 1784–1790).

John Lloyd Jr. Executor of Joseph Lloyd v. John Williams (N.Y. Sup. Ct., 1784–1785).

Juhel v. Rhinelander, 2 Johns. Cas. 120 (N.Y. Sup. Ct., 1800).

Ludlow & Ludlow v. Dale, 1 Johns. Cas. 16 (N.Y. Sup. Ct., 1799).

Moses Gomez v. Thomas Maule (N.Y. Sup. Ct).

People v. Croswell, 3 Johns. Cas. 337 (N.Y. Sup. Ct., 1804).

People v. Levi Weeks (Court of Oyer and Terminer and General Gaol Delivery for the City and County of New York, 1800).

People v. Nicolas Hoffman (N.Y. Sup. Ct., 1783–1784).

Robert R. Livingston and Robert Fulton v. James Van Ingen, et al., 9 Johns. Cas. 507 (N.Y. Ct. Err., 1812).

Runyan v. Mersereau, 11 Johns. 534 (N.Y. Sup. Ct., 1814).

Rutgers v. Waddington (N.Y. Mayors Ct., 1784).

Seton, Maitland & Co. v. Low, 1 Johns. Cas. 1 (N.Y. Sup. Ct., 1799).

Skidmore & Skidmore v. Desdoity, 2 Johns. Cas. 77 (N.Y. Sup. Ct., 1800).

Thomas Tucker v. Henry Thompson (N.Y. Mayor's Ct., 1784–1785).

Vandenheuvel v. United Insurance Company, 2 Johns. Cas. 127 (N.Y. Sup. Ct., 1801).

Vandenheuvel v. United Insurance Company, 2 Johns Cas. 451 (N.Y. Ct. Err., 1802).

Walter Quackenbos v. Thomas Underhill (N.Y. Mayor's Ct., 1784–1785).

Waters v. Stewart, 1 Cai. Cas. (Cas. Err.) 47 (N.Y. Ct. Err., 1804).

Other State Cases

Calhoun for the use of Fitzsimmons and another v. The Insurance Company of Pennsylvania, 1 Binn. 293 (Pa. Sup. Ct., 1808).

Carrere v. The Union Insurance Company of Maryland, 3 H. & J. 324 (Md. Ct. App., 1813).

Dempsey v. The Insurance Co. of Pennsylvania (Pa. Sup. Ct.).

J. Bulow and J. Potter v. The City Council of Charleston, 1 S. C. L. (1 Nott & McC.) 527 (S.C. Ct. App., 1819).

John Baxter et al v. The New England Marine Insurance Company, 6 Mass. 277 (Mass. Sup. Ct., 1810).

Philip B. Chase, Administrator v. The American Steamboat Company, 9 R.I. 419 (R.I. Sup. Ct., 1870).

Phoenix Insurance Company v. Pratt and Clarkson, 2 Binn. 308 (Pa. Sup. Ct., 1810).

Pollock v. Babcock, 6 Mass. 234 (Ma. Sup. Ct., 1810).

Richardson v. Maine Fire & Marine Insurance Company, 6 Mass. 102 (Mass. Sup. Ct., 1809).

Stewart v. Warner, 1 Day 142 (Conn. Sup. Ct. Err., 1803).

Stocker v. Merrimack Marine & Fire Insurance Company, 6 Mass. 220 (Mass. Sup. Ct., 1810).

Vasse v. Ball, 2 US (2 Dall.) 270 (Pa. Sup. Ct., 1797).

English Cases

Beak v. Thyrwhit, 87 Eng. Rep. 124 (K.B., 1688).

Hughes v. Cornelius, 89 Eng. Rep. 907 (K.B., 1683).

Phillips v. Hunter, 126 Eng. Rep 618 (Ex., 1795).

Queen v. Tutchin, 14 State Trials 1095 (Q.B., 1704).
Rex v. Franklin, 21 State Trials 1039 (K.B., 1731).
Rex v. The Inhabitants of St. Michaels in Bath, 99 Eng. Rep. (K.B., 1781).
Rex v. Owen, 18 State Trials 1203 (K.B., 1752).
Rex v. Shipley, 21 State Trials 847 (K.B., 1784).
Seven Bishop's Case, 12 State Trials 183 (K.B., 1688).

Unreported Cases

Ex parte Chandler (U.S., 1794).
New York v. Connecticut (U.S., 1799)
Rex v. John Peter Zenger (N.Y., 1735).
US v. Arnold (D.C.D. R.I., 1792).
US v. George Tyler (D.C.D. Me, 1790).
US v. Hopkins (U.S., 1794).
US v. Yale Todd (U.S., 1794).

Congressional Statutes

"An Act concerning the District of Columbia," ch. 15, 2 Stat. 103 (1801).
"An Act concerning the registering and recording of ships or vessels," ch 1, 1 Stat. 287 (1792).
"An Act directing the Secretary of the Treasury to remit fines, forfeitures and penalties in certain cases," ch. 7, 2 Stat. 789 (1813).
"An Act for allowing a Compensation to the President and Vice President of the United States," ch. 19, 1 Stat. 72 (1789).
"An Act for altering the times and places of holding certain Courts therein mentioned, and for other purposes," ch. 32, 2 Stat. 123 (1801).
"An Act for enrolling and licensing ships or vessels to be employed in the coasting trade and fisheries, and for regulating the same," ch. 8, 1 Stat. 305 (1793).
"An Act for laying a Duty on Goods, Wares, and Merchandises imported into the United States," ch. 2, 1 Stat. 24 (1789).
"An Act for raising a further sum of money for the protection of the frontiers, and for other purposes herein mentioned," ch. 27, 1 Stat. 259 (1792).
"An Act for Registering and Clearing Vessels, Regulating the Coasting Trade, and for other purposes," ch. 11, 1 Stat. 55 (1789).
"An Act for the government and regulation of Seamen in the merchants service," ch. 29, 1 Stat. 131 (1790).
"An Act further to regulate the entry of merchandise imported into the United States from any adjacent territory," ch. 14, 3 Stat. 616 (1821).
"An Act further to suspend the Commercial Intercourse between the United States and France, and the dependencies thereof," ch. 2, 1 Stat. 613 (1799).
"An Act imposing duties on the tonnage of ships or vessels," ch. 30, 1 Stat. 135 (1790).
"An Act imposing Duties on Tonnage," ch. 3, 1 Stat. 27 (1789).

"An Act in addition to the act, entitled 'An act for the punishment of certain crimes against the United States,'" ch. 74, 1 Stat. 596 (1798).

"An Act in addition to the act for the punishment of certain crimes against the United States," ch. 50, 1 Stat. 381 (1794).

"An Act in addition to the act, intitled 'An act supplementary to the act, intitled An act laying an embargo on all ships and vessels in the ports and harbors of the United States,'" ch. 33, 2 Stat. 473 (1808).

"An Act in addition to the act intitled 'An act laying an embargo on all ships and vessels in the ports and harbors of the United States,' and the several act supplementary thereto, and for other purposes," ch. 66, 2 Stat. 499 (1808).

"An Act laying an Embargo on all ships and vessels in the ports and harbors of the United States," ch. 5, 2 Stat. 451 (1807).

"An Act laying duties on property sold at Auction," ch. 65, 1 Stat. 397 (1794).

"An Act laying duties upon Carriages for the Conveyance of Persons," ch. 45, 1 Stat. 373 (1794).

"An Act making further provision for the collection of the duties by law imposed on Teas, and to prolong the term for the payment of the Duties on Wines," ch. 26, 1 Stat. 219 (1791).

"An Act making further provision for securing and collecting the Duties on foreign and domestic distilled Spirits, Stills, Wines, and Teas," ch. 49, 1 Stat. 378 (1794).

"An Act making further provision for the payment of the debts of the United States," ch. 39, 1 Stat. 180 (1790).

"An Act making provision for the Debt of the United States," ch. 34, 1 Stat. 138 (1790).

"An Act making provision for the disposal of the public lands in the Indiana Territory, and for other purposes," ch. 35, 2 Stat. 277 (1804).

"An Act prohibiting for a limited time the Exportation of Arms and Ammunition, and encouraging the Importation of the same," ch. 33, 1 Stat. 369 (1794).

"An Act providing for the Sale of the Lands of the United States, in the territory northwest of the river Ohio, and above the mouth of Kentucky river," ch. 29, 1 Stat. 464 (1796).

"An Act repealing, after the last day of June next, the duties heretofore laid upon Distilled Spirits imported from abroad, and laying others in their stead; and also upon Spirits distilled within the United States, and for appropriating the same," ch. 15, 1 Stat. 199 (1791).

"An Act supplementary to an act, entitled 'An act to regulate the collection of duties on imports and tonnage,' passed the second day of March, one thousand seven hundred and ninety-nine," ch. 79, 3 Stat. 433 (1818).

"An Act supplementary to, and to amend an act, entitled 'An act to regulate the collection of duties on imports and tonnage,' passed second March, one thousand seven hundred and ninety-nine, and for other purposes," ch. 21, 3 Stat. 729 (1823).

"An Act supplementary to the several acts imposing duties on goods, wares and merchandise imported into the United States," ch. 17, 1 Stat. 411 (1795).

"An Act to Amend the act intitled 'An act providing for the sale of the lands of the

United States, in the territory northwest of the Ohio, and above the mouth of Kentucky River,'" ch. 55, 2 Stat. 73 (1800).

"An Act to authorize the President of the United States to accept, for the United States, a cession of jurisdiction of the territory west of Pennsylvania, commonly called the Western Reserve of Connecticut," ch. 38, 2 Stat. 56 (1800).

"An Act to continue in force the act intitled, 'An Act to provide for mitigating or remitting the Penalties and Forfeitures accruing under the Revenue Laws in certain Cases,' and to make further Provision for the payment of Pensions to Invalids," ch. 35, 1 Stat. 275 (1792).

"An Act to establish an uniform Rule of Naturalization," ch. 3, 1 Stat. 103 (1790).

"An Act to establish the Judicial Courts of the United States," ch. 20, 1 Stat. 73 (1789).

"An Act to establish the Treasury Department," ch. 12 1 Stat. 65 (1789).

"An Act to prohibit the carrying on the Slave Trade from the United States to any foreign place or country," ch. 11, 1 Stat. 347 (1794).

"An Act to provide for mitigating or remitting the forfeitures and penalties accruing under the revenue laws, in certain cases therein mentioned," ch. 12, 1 Stat. 122 (1790).

"An Act to provide for mitigating or remitting the Forfeitures, Penalties and Disabilities accruing in certain cases therein mentioned," ch. 13, 1 Stat. 506 (1797).

"An Act to provide for the more convenient organization of the Courts of the United States," ch. 4, 2 Stat. 89 (1801).

"An Act to provide for the settlement of the Claims of Widows and Orphans barred by the limitations heretofore established, and to regulate the Claims to Invalid Pensions," ch. 11, 1 Stat. 243 (1792).

"An Act to provide for the valuation of Lands and Dwelling-Houses, and the enumeration of Slaves within the United States," ch. 70, 1 Stat. 580 (1798).

"An Act to provide more effectually for the collection of the duties imposed by law on goods, wares, and merchandise imported into the United States, and on the tonnage of ships or vessels," ch. 35, 1 Stat. 145 (1790).

"An Act to provide more effectually for the Settlement of Accounts between the United States, and Receivers of public Money," ch. 20, 1 Stat. 512 (1797).

"An Act to regulate Processes in the Courts of the United States," ch. 21, 1 Stat. 93 (1789).

"An Act to regulate the collection of duties on imports and tonnage," ch. 22, 1 Stat. 627 (1799).

"An Act to repeal part of an act, intitled 'An Act to provide for mitigating or remitting the forfeitures, penalties and disabilities, accruing in certain cases therein mentioned, and to continue in force the residue of the same,'" ch. 6, 2 Stat. 7 (1800).

"An Act to suspend part of an Act, intitled 'An Act to regulate the collection of the Duties imposed by Law on the Tonnage of Ships and Vessels, and on Goods, Wares, and Merchandises, imported into the United States,' and for other purposes," ch. 15, 1 Stat. 69 (1789).

British Statutes

7 & 8 Will. III, ch. 22 (1696).
6 Geo. III, c. 12 (1766).
32 Geo. III, c. 60 (1792).

New York State Statutes

Laws of the State of New York, 3 Sess. 1779, c. 25.
Laws of the State of New York, 6 Sess. 1782, c. 1.
Laws of the State of New York, 6 Sess. 1783, c. 31.
Laws of the State of New York, 8 Sess. 1784, c. 7.
Laws of the State of New York, 8 Sess. 1785, c. 34.
Laws of the State of New York, 10 Sess. 1787, c. 1.
Laws of the State of New York, 10 Sess. 1787, c. 56.
Laws of the State of New York, 10 Sess. 1787, c. 71.
Laws of the State of New York, 19 Sess. 1796, c. 58.
Laws of the State of New York, 21 Sess. 1798, c. 72.
Laws of the State of New York, 24 Sess. 1801, c. 105.
Laws of the State of New York, 24 Sess. 1801, c. 116.
Laws of the State of New York, 28 Sess. 1805, c. 90.

Newspapers

Daily Advertiser: Political, Historical, and Commercial.
New-York Gazetteer or Northern Intelligencer.
New-York Journal and State Gazette.
New-York Journal, and Weekly Register.
New York Packet and the American Advertiser.
Pennsylvania Packet and Daily Advertiser.

Published Sources

Ackerman, Bruce. The Failure of the Founding Fathers: Jefferson, Marshall, and the Rise of Presidential Democracy. Cambridge, MA: Belknap Press of Harvard University Press, 2005.
———. "Taxation and the Constitution." Columbia Law Review 99 (1999): 1–58.
Acts of the General Assembly of the State of South Carolina, from February 1791 to December, 1794, Both Inclusive, 1:63 (1791).
Adams, Donald R. "American Neutrality and Prosperity, 1793–1808: A Reconsideration." Journal of Economic History 40 (1980): 713–737.
Alicea, Joel and Donald L. Drakeman. "The Limits of New Originalism." University of Pennsylvania Journal of Constitutional Law 15 (2013): 1161–1219.
Amar, Akhil Reed. The Bill of Rights: Creation and Reconstruction. New Haven, CT: Yale University Press, 1998.
Bailyn, Bernard. The Ideological Origins of the American Revolution. Cambridge, MA: Belknap Press, 1967.

Baker, J. H. *An Introduction to English Legal History*. 4th ed. New York: Oxford University Press, 2007.

Bartoloni-Tuazon, Kathleen. *For Fear of an Elective King: George Washington and the Presidential Title Controversy of 1789*. Ithaca, NY: Cornell University Press, 2014.

Beard, Charles A. *An Economic Interpretation of the Constitution of the United States*. New York: Free Press, 1913, 1986.

Berns, Walter. "Freedom of the Press and the Alien and Sedition Laws: A Reappraisal." *Supreme Court Review* 1970 (1970): 109–159.

Bilder, Mary Sarah. "James Madison, Law Student and Demi-Lawyer." *Law and History Review* 28 (2010): 389–449.

———. *The Transatlantic Constitution: Colonial Legal Culture and the Empire*. Cambridge, MA: Harvard University Press, 2004.

Bird, Wendell. *Press and Speech under Assault: The Early Supreme Court Justices, the Sedition Act of 1798, and the Campaign against Dissent*. New York: Oxford University Press, 2016.

Blaakman, Michael A. "Speculation Nation: Land Speculators and Land Mania in the Early Republic, 1776–1803." PhD diss., Yale University, 2016.

Black, Barbara A. "The Constitution of Empire: The Case for the Colonists." *University of Pennsylvania Law Review* 124 (1976): 1157–1211.

Blackstone, William. *Commentaries on the Laws of England*. 2 vols. Philadelphia: J. B. Lippincott, 1893.

Bloomfield, Maxwell. *American Lawyers in a Changing Society, 1776–1876*. Cambridge, MA: Harvard University Press, 1976.

Bourguignon, Henry J. *The First Federal Court: The Federal Appellate Prize Court of the American Revolution, 1775–1787*. Philadelphia: American Philosophical Society, 1977.

Bradburn, Douglas. *The Citizenship Revolution: Politics and the Creation of the American Union, 1774–1804*. Charlottesville: University Press of Virginia, 2009.

Breen, T. H. *The Marketplace of Revolution: How Consumer Politics Shaped American Independence*. New York: Oxford University Press, 2004.

Brown, Elizabeth Gaspar. *British Statutes in American Law, 1776–1836*. Ann Arbor: University of Michigan Law School, 1964.

Brown, Roger H. *Redeeming the Republic: Federalists, Taxation, and the Origins of the Constitution*. Baltimore, MD: Johns Hopkins University Press, 1993.

Bruchey, Stuart. *The Roots of American Economic Growth, 1607–1861*. New York: Harper & Row, 1965.

Burgess, Glenn. *The Politics of the Ancient Constitution: An Introduction to English Political Thought, 1603–1642*. University Park: Pennsylvania State University Press, 1992.

Burke, Daniel W. E. "Alexander Hamilton as a Lawyer." In *Alexander Hamilton: Thirty-one orations delivered at Hamilton College from 1864 to 1895 upon the prize foundation established by Franklin Harvey Head, A.M.* Edited by Melvin Gilbert Dodge, 180–184. New York: G. P. Putnam's Sons, 1896.

Caines, George, ed. *The Speeches at Full Length of Mr. Van Ness, Mr. Caines, The Attorney-General, Mr. Harrison, and General Hamilton, in the Great Cause of the People, against Harry Croswell, on an Indictment for a Libel on Thomas Jefferson, President of the United States.* New York: G. &. R. Waite, 1804.

Calabresi, Steven G., and Christopher S. Yoo. *The Unitary Executive: Presidential Power from Washington to Bush.* New Haven, CT: Yale University Press, 2008.

Caldwell, Lynton K. *The Administrative Theories of Hamilton and Jefferson: Their Contribution to Thought on Public Administration.* Chicago: University of Chicago Press, 1944.

Campbell, James R. "Dispelling the Fog about Direct Taxation." *British Journal of American Legal Studies* 1 (2012): 109–172.

Casto, William R. *Foreign Affairs and the Constitution in the Age of Fighting Sail.* Columbia: University of South Carolina Press, 2006.

———. "James Iredell and the American Origins of Judicial Review." *Connecticut Law Review* 27 (1995): 329–363.

———. "The Origins of Federal Admiralty Jurisdiction in an Age of Privateers, Smugglers, and Pirates." *American Journal of Legal History* 37 (1993): 117–157.

———. *The Supreme Court in the Early Republic: The Chief Justiceships of John Jay and Oliver Ellsworth.* Columbia: University of South Carolina Press, 1995.

Chazanof, William. *Joseph Ellicott and the Holland Land Company.* Syracuse, NY: Syracuse University Press, 1970.

Chernow, Ron. *Alexander Hamilton.* New York: Penguin, 2004.

Collins, Paul. *Duel with the Devil: The True Story of How Alexander Hamilton and Aaron Burr Teamed Up to Take on America's First Sensational Murder Mystery.* New York: Crown, 2013.

"Collision between the Supreme Court and the Court of Errors of the State of New York." *American Law Magazine* 3 (1844): 317–333.

Cooke, Jacob E. *Alexander Hamilton.* New York: Scribner's, 1982.

Corwin, Edward S. *The President—Office and Powers, 1787–1948: History and Analysis of Practice and Opinion.* New York: New York University Press, 1948.

Corwin, Edwin S. "Establishment of Judicial Review." *Michigan Law Review* 9 (1910): 102–125.

Curtis, Michael Kent. *Free Speech, "The People's Darling Privilege": Struggles for Freedom of Expression in American History.* Durham, NC: Duke University Press, 2000.

Dalton, Michael. *Countrey Justice.* Classical English Law Texts. London: Professional Books, 1973.

Dalzell, Frederick. "Prudence and the Golden Egg: Establishing the Federal Government in Providence, Rhode Island." *New England Quarterly* 65 (1992): 355–388.

———. "Taxation with Representation: Federal Revenue in the Early Republic." PhD diss., Harvard University, 1993.

diGiacommantonio, William C. "Petitioners and Their Grievances: A View from the First Federal Congress." In *The House and Senate in the 1790s: Petitioning, Lob-*

bying, and Institutional Development, edited by Kenneth R. Bowling and Donald R. Kennon, 29–56. Athens: Ohio University Press, 2002.

Edling, Max M. *A Revolution in Favor of Government: Origins of the US Constitution and the Making of the American State.* New York: Oxford University Press, 2003.

———. "'So Immense a Power in the Affairs of War': Alexander Hamilton and the Restoration of Public Credit." *William and Mary Quarterly* 64 (2007): 287–326.

Edling, Max M., and Mark D. Kaplanoff. "Alexander Hamilton's Fiscal Reform: Transforming the Structure of Taxation in the Early Republic." *William and Mary Quarterly* 61 (2004): 713–744.

Einhorn, Robin L. *American Taxation, American Slavery.* Chicago: University of Chicago Press, 2006.

Elkins, Stanley, and Eric McKitrick. *The Age of Federalism.* New York: Oxford University Press, 1993.

Ellis, Joseph J. *Founding Brothers: The Revolutionary Generation.* New York: Vintage Books, 2002.

Ellis, Richard E. *Aggressive Nationalism: McCulloch v. Maryland and the Foundation of Federal Authority in the Young Republic.* New York: Oxford University Press, 2007.

———. *The Jeffersonian Crisis: Courts and Politics in the Young Republic.* New York: Oxford University Press, 1971.

———. *The Union at Risk: Jacksonian Democracy, States' Rights and the Nullification Crisis.* New York: Oxford University Press, 1987.

Emery, Robert. "New York's Statutory Bill of Rights: A Constitutional Coelacanth." *Touro Law Review* 19 (2003): 363–392.

Evans, Paul Demund. *The Holland Land Company.* Buffalo, NY: Buffalo Historical Society, 1924.

Farrand, Max, ed. *The Records of the Federal Convention of 1787.* Rev. ed., 4 vols. New Haven, CT: Yale University Press, 1966.

Farrar, Edgar H. "The Extension of the Admiralty Jurisdiction by Judicial Interpretation." *Annual Report to the American Bar Association* 33 (1908): 459–488.

Federici, Michael P. *The Political Philosophy of Alexander Hamilton.* Baltimore, MD: Johns Hopkins University Press, 2012.

Ferguson, E. James. *The Power of the Purse: A History of American Public Finance, 1776–1790.* Chapel Hill: University of North Carolina Press, 1961.

Ferling, John. *Jefferson and Hamilton: The Rivalry that Forged a Nation.* New York: Bloomsbury Press, 2013.

Finkelman, Paul. "Alexander Hamilton, Esq.: Founding Father as Lawyer." *American Bar Foundation Research Journal* 9 (1984): 229–252.

Flaumenhaft, Harvey. *The Effective Republic: Administration and Constitution in the Thought of Alexander Hamilton.* Durham, NC: Duke University Press, 1992.

Forkosch, Morris D. "Freedom of the Press: *Croswell's Case.*" *Fordham Law Review* 33 (1965): 415–448.

Frankel Jr., Robert P. "Before *Marbury: Hylton v. United States* and the Origins of Judicial Review." *Journal of Supreme Court History* 28 (2003): 1–13.

Freeman, Joanne B. *Affairs of Honor: National Politics in the New Republic.* New Haven, CT: Yale Nota Bene, 2002.

Furstenberg, François. *When the United States Spoke French: Five Refugees Who Shaped a Nation.* New York: Penguin, 2014.

Gillis, Brendan. "Conduits of Justice: Magistrates and the British Imperial State, 1732–1834." PhD diss., Indiana University, 2015.

Gilmore, Grant. *The Ages of American Law.* New Haven, CT: Yale University Press, 1977.

Gilmore, Grant, and Charles L. Black Jr. *The Law of Admiralty.* Brooklyn, NY: Foundation Press, 1957.

Goebel Jr., Julius. "The Common Law and the Constitution." In *Chief Justice John Marshall: A Reappraisal,* edited by W. Melville Jones, 101–123. Ithaca, NY: Cornell University Press, 1956.

———. "King's Law and Local Custom in Seventeenth Century New England." *Columbia Law Review* 31 (1931): 416–448.

———. *The Oliver Wendell Holmes Devise: History of the Supreme Court of the United States.* Vol. 1, *Antecedents and Beginnings to 1801.* New York: Macmillan, 1971.

Gould, Eliga H. *Among the Powers of the Earth: The American Revolution and the Making of a New World Empire.* Cambridge, MA: Harvard University Press, 2012.

Hale, Matthew. *The Prerogatives of the King.* Edited by D. E. C. Yale. London: Selden Society, 1976.

Hamburger, Philip. "The Development of the Law of Seditious Libel and the Control of the Press." *Stanford Law Review* 37 (1985): 661–765.

———. *Is Administrative Law Unlawful?* Chicago: University of Chicago Press, 2014.

———. *Law and Judicial Duty.* Cambridge, MA: Harvard University Press, 2008.

Hamilton, Alexander. *The Law Practice of Alexander Hamilton: Documents and Commentary.* Edited by Julius Goebel Jr. et al. 5 vols. New York: Columbia University Press, 1964–1981.

———. *The Papers of Alexander Hamilton.* Edited by Harold C. Syrett et al. 27 vols. New York: Columbia University Press, 1961–1987.

Harper, John Lamberton. *American Machiavelli: Alexander Hamilton and the Origins of US Foreign Policy.* New York: Cambridge University Press, 2004.

Harrington, Matthew P. "Judicial Review before John Marshall." *George Washington Law Review* 72 (2003): 51–94.

Hartz, Louis. *The Liberal Tradition in America: An Interpretation of American Political Thought since the Revolution.* New York: Harcourt, Brace, & World, 1955.

Haskins, George Lee, and Herbert A. Johnson. *The Oliver Wendell Holmes Devise:*

History of the Supreme Court of the United States. Vol. 2, *Foundations of Power: John Marshall, 1801–15.* New York: Macmillan, 1981.

Henderson, Dwight F. *Courts for a New Nation.* Washington, DC: Public Affairs Press, 1971.

Henretta, James A. "Magistrates, Common Law Lawyers, Legislators: The Three Legal Systems of British America." In *The Cambridge History of Law in America,* Vol. 1, *Early America (1580–1815),* edited by Michael Grossberg and Christopher Tomlins, 555–592. New York: Cambridge University Press, 2008.

Hidy, Ralph W. *The House of Baring in American Trade and Finance: English Merchant Bankers at Work, 1763–1861.* Cambridge, MA: Harvard University Press, 1949.

Higginson, Stephen A. "A Short History of the Right to Petition Government for the Redress of Grievances." *Yale Law Journal* 96 (1986): 142–166.

Hobson, Charles F. *The Great Chief Justice: John Marshall and the Rule of Law.* Lawrence: University Press of Kansas, 1996.

Hofstadter, Richard. *The United States: The History of a Republic.* Englewood Cliffs, NJ: Prentice-Hall, 1957.

Holton, Woody. *Forced Founders: Indians, Debtors, Slaves, and the Making of the American Revolution in Virginia.* Chapel Hill: University of North Carolina Press, 1999.

Horwitz, Morton J. *The Transformation of American Law, 1780–1860.* Cambridge, MA: Harvard University Press, 1977.

———. *The Transformation of American Law, 1870–1960: The Crisis of Legal Orthodoxy.* New York: Oxford University Press, 1992.

Hulbert, Archer Butler. "The Methods and Operations of the Scioto Group of Speculators." *Mississippi Valley Historical Review* 1 (1915): 502–515.

Hulsebosch, Daniel J. *Constituting Empire: New York and the Transformation of Constitutionalism in the Atlantic World, 1664–1830.* Chapel Hill: University of North Carolina Press, 2005.

———. "A Discrete and Cosmopolitan Minority: The Loyalists, the Atlantic World, and the Origins of Judicial Review." *Chicago-Kent Law Review* 81 (2006): 825–866.

———. "The Plural Prerogative." *William and Mary Quarterly* 68 (2011): 583–587.

Hurst, James Willard. "Alexander Hamilton, Law Maker." *Columbia Law Review* 78 (1978): 483–547.

———. *Law and the Conditions of Freedom in the Nineteenth-Century United States.* Madison: University of Wisconsin Press, 1956.

Jackson, Andrew. "Proclamation by Andrew Jackson, President of the United States." In *A Compilation of the Messages and Papers of the Presidents,* edited by James D. Richardson, 3:1203–1219. New York: Bureau of National Literature, 1897.

Jaffe, Louis L. *Judicial Control of Administrative Action.* Boston: Little, Brown, 1965.

Jasanoff, Maya. *Liberty's Exiles: American Loyalists in the Revolutionary World.* New York: Knopf, 2011.

Jefferson, Thomas. *The Papers of Thomas Jefferson.* Edited by Julian P. Boyd. 42 vols. Princeton, NJ: Princeton University Press, 1950–.

———. *The Writings of Thomas Jefferson.* Edited by Paul Leicester Ford. 10 vols. New York: G. P. Putnam's Sons, 1892–1899.

Jensen, Erik M. "Taxation and the Constitution: How to Read the Direct Tax Clause." *Journal of Law and Politics* 15 (1999): 687–716.

Johansen, Bruce E. *Forgotten Founders: Benjamin Franklin, the Iroquois, and the Rationale for the American Revolution.* Ipswich, MA: Gambit, 1982.

Johnson, Herbert Alan. "John Jay: Lawyer in a Time of Transition, 1764–1775." *University of Pennsylvania Law Review* 124 (1976): 1260–1292.

Jones, Robert F. *The King of the Alley: William Duer, Politician, Entrepreneur, and Speculator, 1768–1799.* Philadelphia: American Philosophical Society, 1992.

Kantorowicz, Ernst Hartwig. *The King's Two Bodies: A Study in Mediaeval Political Theology.* Princeton, NJ: Princeton University Press, 1957.

Kennedy, Roger G. *Burr, Hamilton, and Jefferson: A Study in Character.* New York: Oxford University Press, 1999.

Kent, James. "Alexander Hamilton: Address Delivered before the Law Association of New York, October 21, 1836" [pamphlet]. Brooklyn, NY: George Tremlitt, 1889.

———. *Commentaries on American Law.* 4 vols. New York: O. Halsted, 1826–1830.

Kent, William. *Memoirs and Letters of James Kent, LL.D.* Boston: Little, Brown, 1898.

Kerber, Linda. *Women of the Republic: Intellect and Ideology in Revolutionary America.* Chapel Hill: University of North Carolina Press, 1980.

Ketcham, Ralph. *Presidents Above Party: The First American Presidency, 1789–1829.* Chapel Hill: University of North Carolina Press, 1984.

Kettner, James H. *The Development of American Citizenship, 1608–1870.* Chapel Hill: University of North Carolina Press, 1978.

King, Rufus. *The Life and Correspondence of Rufus King.* Edited by Charles R. King. 6 vols. New York: G. P. Putnam's Sons, 1894–1900.

Kingston, Christopher. "Marine Insurance in Britain and America, 1720–1844: A Comparative Institutional Analysis." *Journal of Economic History* 67 (2007): 379–409.

———. "Marine Insurance in Philadelphia during the Quasi-War with France, 1795–1801." *Journal of Economic History* 71 (2011): 162–184.

Knott, Stephen F. *Alexander Hamilton and the Persistence of Myth.* Lawrence: University Press of Kansas, 2002.

Koch, Adrienne. "Hamilton, Adams, and the Pursuit of Power." *Review of Politics* 16 (1954): 37–66.

Konefsky, Samuel J. *John Marshall and Alexander Hamilton: Architects of the American Constitution.* New York: Macmillan, 1964.

Kramer, Larry D. *The People Themselves: Popular Constitutionalism and Judicial Review*. New York: Oxford University Press, 2004.

Landau, Norma. *The Justices of the Peace, 1679–1760*. Berkeley: University of California Press, 1984.

Langbein, John H., Renée Lettow Lerner, and Bruce P. Smith. *History of the Common Law: The Development of Anglo-American Legal Institutions*. New York: Aspen/Wolters Kluwer Law & Business, 2009.

"Laws of the Legislature of the State of New York, in force against the Loyalists, and affecting the trade of Great Britain, and British Merchants, and others having property in that state" [pamphlet]. London: H. Reynell, 1786.

Lawson, Gary. "The Return of the King: The Unsavory Origins of Administrative Law." *Texas Law Review* 93 (2015): 1521–1545.

Ledyard, Isaac. "Mentor's Reply to Phocion's Letter" [pamphlet]. New York: Shepard Kollock, 1784.

Levy, Leonard W. *Emergence of a Free Press*. New York: Oxford University Press, 1985.

Livermore, Shaw. *Early American Land Companies: Their Influence on Corporate Development*. New York: Octagon Books, 1968.

Lobban, Michael. *The Common Law and English Jurisprudence, 1760–1850*. New York: Oxford University Press, 1991.

———. "From Seditious Libel to Unlawful Assembly: Peterloo and the Changing Face of Political Crime, c. 1770–1820." *Oxford Journal of Legal Studies* 10 (1990): 307–352.

Madison, James. *The Papers of James Madison*. Edited by William T. Hutchinson et al., vols. 11–17. 1st ser. Charlottesville: University Press of Virginia, 1977–1991.

Madison, James, Alexander Hamilton, and John Jay. *The Federalist Papers*. Edited by Isaac Kramnick. New York: Penguin Books, 1987.

Maier, Pauline. "Whigs against Whigs against Whigs: The Imperial Debates of 1765–76 Reconsidered." *William and Mary Quarterly* 68 (2011): 578–582.

Marcus, Maeva, et al., eds. *The Documentary History of the Supreme Court of the United States: 1789–1800*. 8 vols. New York: Columbia University Press, 1985–2007.

Martin, Robert W. T. *The Free and Open Press: The Founding of American Democratic Press Liberty, 1640–1800*. New York: New York University Press, 2001.

———. "Reforming Republicanism: Alexander Hamilton's Theory of Republican Citizenship and Press Freedom." *Journal of the Early Republic* 25 (2005): 21–46.

Mashaw, Jerry L. *Creating the Administrative Constitution: The Lost One Hundred Years of American Administrative Law*. New Haven, CT: Yale University Press, 2012.

———. "Recovering American Administrative Law: Federalist Foundations, 1787–1801." *Yale Law Journal* 115 (2006): 1256–1344.

McCloskey, Robert G. *The American Supreme Court*. 2nd ed. Revised by Sanford Levinson. Chicago: University of Chicago Press, 1994.

McCoy, Drew R. *The Elusive Republic: Political Economy in Jeffersonian America*. New York: Norton, 1982.

McCraw, Thomas K. *The Founders and Finance: How Hamilton, Gallatin, and Other Immigrants Forged a New Economy.* Cambridge, MA: Belknap Press, 2012.

McCurdy, Charles W. "American Law and the Marketing Structure of the Large Corporation, 1875–1890." *Journal of Economic History* 38 (1978): 631–649.

———. *The Anti-Rent Era in New York Law and Politics, 1839–1865.* Chapel Hill: University of North Carolina Press, 2001.

———. "Prelude to Civil War: A Snapshot of the California Supreme Court at Work in 1858." *California Supreme Court Historical Society Yearbook* 1 (1994): 3–32.

McDonald, Forrest. *Alexander Hamilton: A Biography.* New York: Norton, 1982.

McDonnell, Michael A. *The Politics of War: Race, Class, and Conflict in Revolutionary Virginia.* Chapel Hill: University of North Carolina Press, 2007.

Merrill, Thomas W. "*Marbury v. Madison* as the First Great Administrative Decision." *John Marshall Law Review* 37 (2004): 481–522.

Meyerson, Michael I. *Liberty's Blueprint: How Madison and Hamilton Wrote the Federalist Papers, Defined the Constitution, and Made the Democracy Safe for the World.* New York: Basic Books, 2008.

Meyler, Bernadette. "Towards a Common Law Originalism." *Stanford Law Review* 59 (2006): 551–600.

Miller, John C. *Alexander Hamilton: Portrait in Paradox.* New York: Barnes and Noble Books, 1959.

Nash, Gary B. *Red, White, and Black: The Peoples of Early America.* Englewood Cliffs, NJ: Prentice-Hall, 1974.

Nelson, Eric. "Patriot Royalism: The Stuart Monarchy in American Political Thought, 1769–75." *William and Mary Quarterly* 68 (2011): 533–572.

———. *The Royalist Revolution: Monarchy and the American Founding.* Cambridge, MA: Belknap Press, 2014.

Nelson Jr., John R. *Liberty and Property: Political Economy and Policymaking in the New Nation, 1789–1812.* Baltimore, MD: Johns Hopkins University Press, 1987.

Nettels, Curtis P. *The Emergence of a National Economy, 1775–1815.* New York: Harper & Row, 1962.

Newmyer, R. Kent. *Supreme Court Justice Joseph Story: Statesman of the Old Republic.* Chapel Hill: University of North Carolina Press, 1985.

North, Douglass C. *The Economic Growth of the United States, 1790–1860.* New York: Norton, 1966.

Oldham, James. *English Common Law in the Age of Mansfield.* Chapel Hill: University of North Carolina Press, 2004.

Olwell, Robert. "'Practical Justice': The Justice of the Peace, the Slave Court, and Local Authority in Mid-Eighteenth-Century South Carolina." In *Money, Trade, and Power: The Evolution of Colonial South Carolina's Plantation Society,* edited by Jack P. Greene, Rosemary Brana-Shute, and Randy J. Sparks, 256–277. Columbia: University of South Carolina Press, 2001.

Onuf, Peter S. *The Origins of the Federal Republic: Jurisdictional Controversies in the United States, 1775–1787.* Philadelphia: University of Pennsylvania Press, 1983.

Onuf, Peter S., and Nicholas Greenwood Onuf. *Federal Union, Modern World: The Law of Nations in an Age of Revolutions, 1776–1814.* Madison, WI: Madison House, 1993.

Owen, David R., and Michael C. Tolley. *Courts of Admiralty in Colonial America: The Maryland Experience, 1634–1776.* Durham, NC: Carolina Academic Press, 1995.

Park, James Allan. *A system of the law of marine insurances: With three chapters on bottomry; on insurances on lives; and on insurances against fire.* Philadelphia: Reprinted by Joseph Crukshank, 1789.

Parker, Kunal M. *Common Law, History, and Democracy in America, 1790–1900: Legal Thought before Modernism.* New York: Cambridge University Press, 2011.

Pearson, Ellen Holmes. *Remaking Custom: Law and Identity in the Early Republic.* Charlottesville: University Press of Virginia, 2011.

Petyt, George. *Lex Parliamentaria: or, A Treatise on the Law and Custom of Parliaments.* 3rd ed. London: Henry Lintot, 1748.

Phillips, Wendell. *A Treatise on the Law of Insurance.* Boston: Wells & Lilly, 1823.

Plowden, Edmund. *The Commentaries, or Reports, of Edmund Plowden, of the Middle Temple, Esq. An Apprentice of the Common Law: Containing Divers Cases Upon Matters of Law, Argued and Adjudged in the Several Reigns of King Edward VI, Queen Mary, King and Queen Philip and Mary, and Queen Elizabeth.* London: S. Brooke, Paternoster-Row, 1816.

Prakash, Saikrishna Bangalore. *Imperial from the Beginning: The Constitution of the Original Executive.* New Haven, CT: Yale University Press, 2015.

Ranlet, Philip. *The New York Loyalists.* Knoxville: University of Tennessee Press, 1986.

Rao, Gautham. *National Duties: Custom Houses and the Making of the American State.* Chicago: University of Chicago Press, 2016.

Reid, John Phillip. *Constitutional History of the American Revolution.* Abridged ed. Madison: University of Wisconsin Press, 1995.

Reinsch, Paul Samuel. "The English Common Law in the Early American Colonies." In *Select Essays in Anglo-American Legal History,* 1:367–415. Boston: Little, Brown, 1907–1909.

Rohrbough, Malcolm J. *The Land Office Business: The Settlement and Administration of American Public Lands, 1789–1837.* New York: Oxford University Press, 1968.

Roper, Donald. "James Kent and the Emergence of New York's Libel Law." *American Journal of Legal History* 17 (1973): 223–231.

Rossiter, Clinton. *Alexander Hamilton and the Constitution.* New York: Harcourt, Brace, & World, 1964.

Sellers, Charles. *The Market Revolution: Jacksonian America, 1815–1846.* New York: Oxford University Press, 1991.

Sloss, David. "Judicial Foreign Policy: Lessons from the 1790s." *St. Louis University Law Journal* 53 (2008): 145–196.

Smith, James Morton. "Alexander Hamilton, the Alien Law, and Seditious Libels." *Review of Politics* 16 (1954): 305–333.

———. *Freedom's Fetters: The Alien and Sedition Laws and American Civil Liberties.* Ithaca, NY: Cornell University Press, 1956.

Snowiss, Sylvia. *Judicial Review and the Law of the Constitution.* New Haven, CT: Yale University Press, 1990.

Spaulding, E. Wilder. *New York in the Critical Period, 1783–1789.* New York: Columbia University Press, 1932.

Staab, James B. *The Political Thought of Justice Antonin Scalia: A Hamiltonian on the Supreme Court.* Lanham, MD: Rowman & Littlefield, 2006.

Staloff, Darren. *Hamilton, Adams, Jefferson: The Politics of Enlightenment and the American Founding.* New York: Hill & Wang, 2005.

Stoebuck, William B. "Reception of English Common Law in the American Colonies." *William and Mary Law Review* 10 (1968): 393–426.

Stoner Jr., James. *Common Law and Liberal Theory: Coke, Hobbes, and the Origins of American Constitutionalism.* Lawrence: University Press of Kansas, 1992.

Story, Joseph. *Commentaries on the Constitution of the United States; with a Preliminary Review of the Constitutional History of the Colonies and States, before the Adoption of the Constitution.* 3 vols. Boston: Hilliard, Gray, 1833.

———. *Commentaries on Equity Jurisprudence: As administered in England and America.* 2 vols. Boston: C. C. Little & J. Brown, 1849.

Stourzh, Gerald. *Alexander Hamilton and the Idea of Republican Government.* Stanford, CA: Stanford University Press, 1970

Sullivan, Charles H. "Alien Land Laws: A Re-Evaluation." *Temple Law Quarterly* 36 (1962): 15–53.

Surrency, Erwin C. "The Courts in the American Colonies." *American Journal of Legal History* 11 (1967): 253–276.

Sylla, Richard. "Shaping the US Financial System, 1690–1913: The Dominant Role of Public Finance." In *The State, the Financial System and Economic Modernization,* edited by Richard Sylla, Richard Tilly, and Gabriel Tortella, 249–270. New York: Cambridge University Press, 1999.

———. "The Transition to a Monetary Union in the United States, 1787–1795." *Financial History Review* 13 (2006): 73–95.

Taylor, Alan. *William Cooper's Town: Power and Persuasion on the Frontier of the Early American Republic.* New York: Vintage Books, 1996.

Treanor, William Michael. "Judicial Review before *Marbury.*" *Stanford Law Review* 58 (2005): 455–562.

"The Tryal of John Peter Zenger, of New York, Printer, Who was lately Try'd and Acquitted for Printing and Publishing a Libel against the Government." London: Printed for J. Wilford, St. Paul's Church-Yard, 1738.

Van Tyne, Claude Halstead. *The Loyalists in the American Revolution.* New York: Macmillan, 1929.

Van Winter, Pieter J. *American Finance and Dutch Investment, 1780–1805: With an Epilogue to 1840.* English adaptation by James C. Riley. 2 vols. New York: Arno Press, 1977.

Vermeule, Adrian "'No': Review of Philip Hamburger, *Is Administrative Law Unlawful?" Texas Law Review* 93 (2015): 1547–1566.

Warren, Charles. *The Supreme Court in United States History.* 3 vols. Boston: Little, Brown, 1923.

Washington, George. *The Papers of George Washington.* Edited by W. W. Abbot et al. 18 vols. Charlottesville: University Press of Virginia, 1987–.

White, G. Edward. *The Marshall Court and Cultural Change, 1815–1835.* Abridged ed. New York: Oxford University Press, 1991.

White, Leonard D. *The Federalists: A Study in Administrative History.* New York: Macmillan, 1948.

———. *The Jacksonians: A Study in Administrative History, 1829–1861.* New York: Macmillan, 1954.

———. *The Jeffersonians: A Study in Administrative History, 1801–1829.* New York: Macmillan, 1951.

Wilf, Steven. *Law's Imagined Republic: Popular Politics and Criminal Justice in Revolutionary America.* New York: Cambridge University Press, 2010.

Wilkins, Mira. *The History of Foreign Investment in the United States to 1914.* Cambridge, MA: Harvard University Press, 1989.

Wilson, James. *The Works of the Honourable James Wilson.* Edited by Bird Wilson. 3 vols. Philadelphia: Lorenzo Press (printed for Bronson and Chauncey), 1804.

Wood, Gordon S. *The Creation of the American Republic, 1776–1787.* Chapel Hill: University of North Carolina Press, 1998.

———. *Empire of Liberty: A History of the Early Republic, 1789–1815.* New York: Oxford University Press, 2009.

———. "The Problem of Sovereignty." *William and Mary Quarterly* 68 (2011): 573–577.

———. *The Radicalism of the American Revolution.* New York: Vintage Books, 1993.

Wooddesson, Richard. *Lectures on the Law of England.* Edited by William Rosser Williams. 3 vols. Philadelphia: John S. Littell, 1842.

Woolhandler, Ann. "Judicial Deference to Administrative Action—A Revisionist History." *Administrative Law Review* 43 (1991): 197–245.

Wright, Robert E., and Christopher Kingston. "Corporate Insurers in Antebellum America." *Business History Review* 86 (2012): 447–476.

Wyckoff, William. *The Developer's Frontier: The Making of the Western New York Landscape.* New Haven, CT: Yale University Press, 1988.

Zimmerman, Dennis. *The Private Use of Tax-Exempt Bonds: Controlling Public Subsidy of Private Activity.* Washington, DC: Urban Institute Press, 1991.

Index

common law, 11, 16, 20, 39, 212
  admiralty and, 90–93, 97, 100, 103,
    110–111
  allodial versus nonallodial lands, 154,
    161
  American reception of, 9–10, 162,
    175–177, 181–182, 188–189,
    192–193, 195, 197–198, 200, 204
  attainder, 180, 184, 187
  certiorari, 24, 186, 219n20
  citizenship and, 188–192
  debt action, 68, 129, 180, 186
  decline of, 212
  description of, 2–3, 8
  desuetude and, 28, 115, 118, 122–123
  due process, 6, 16, 175, 177–181,
    188–192, 203–204, 211, 258–
    259n59
  duress defense, 184
  equity versus, 153–154, 160, 162,
    167–168, 171
  extensive versus strict conception of,
    175–177, 181, 192–193, 195–202,
    204–205
  federal courts and marine insurance,
    100–101, 110–111, 207
  fee simple, 161, 163, 165
  feudal rule relating to aliens, 162, 164
  freedom of the press and, 191–202,
    204–205
  general issue, 184, 194–195, 198, 202
  habeas corpus, 25
  Hamilton's use of, 2, 6, 9, 13, 16, 39,
    68, 97–98, 122–123, 174–202,
    204–206, 212–213
  King's Bench, 24, 166, 176, 194–198,
    212, 260–261n79
  magistrates (justices of the peace) and,
    24–25
  military justification (trespass defense),
    180–182, 184, 203
  mortgages develop in England, 165
  motion for new trials, 192–194, 197,
    199
  no prior restraint doctrine, 192
  originalism and, 212–213
  pardon power and, 30–31, 39, 79,
    220n48
  plea of *autrefois attaint*, 187
  plea of the law of nations, 181–185,
    191, 203
  plea of the Treaty of Peace, 181–183,
    187
  prerogative power and, 27–28, 30–31
  reception clauses, 162, 175–177, 181–
    182, 189, 192–193, 195, 198, 200
  removal to superior court safeguard,
    180, 184–186, 203
  seditious libel (criminal libel), 192–
    202, 204–205
  special assumpsit, 101
  state courts and marine insurance,
    100, 103–111
  tort liability for civil officers, 21,
    36–37, 47–49, 54
  treason, 180, 188–191
  trespass by force and arms action,
    180–181, 183–184
  trespass-on-the-case action, 71
  truth as a defense, 194–202, 204
  writ of error, 185, 191, 203–204
  writ of right, 161, 251n40
  See also British king; Chancery;
    constitutionalism; equity; executive
    power; judicial review; jury trials;
    magistracy; mandamus
concurrence (Hamiltonian)
  federal concurrence, 7, 10–12, 15, 73,
    82–83, 88–89, 102, 110–112, 114–
    118, 120–121, 136–149, 152–155,
    171–173, 206–212
  fiscal powers and, 115–121, 123, 126,
    129–133, 141–144, 148–149, 207
  functional concurrence, 10–12, 14, 60,
    74–81, 83, 206
  judicial concurrence, 10, 73, 83, 88,
    110, 112, 153, 206–207, 209
  legislative concurrence, 10, 115, 117–
    123, 136–139, 141–144, 146, 153,
    206–207, 209
  neutrality and, 88–90, 100–102, 107,
    109–112, 208

repugnancy caveat (Hamilton), 121, 137–141, 146

supremacy principle and, 114, 121–122, 136–137, 139–147, 149, 173

See also federalism; *The Federalist*: No. 32 and No. 82

Confederation Congress, 2, 118, 209

Confiscation Act, 177–181, 184, 187, 191, 203–204

Congress (US)

Article I, section 8 powers, 82, 87, 114, 119, 126–127, 132, 137, 143, 173, 209, 212

assuming state debt, 112

auction tax and, 125–126

carriage tax and, 129, 133

claims made to, 33–35, 158

Commissioners of Appeals in Cases of Capture and, 92

common law and, 176, 200–201

Connecticut Gore controversy and, 160–161

Court of Appeals in Cases of Capture and, 92

creating Circuit Court for the District of Columbia, 101

creating executive offices, 52

executive discretion and, 19–20, 23, 43, 46, 61–62, 156–158

federal court jurisdiction and, 25, 58–59

fiscal (taxing and borrowing) powers and, 6, 15, 114–116, 119, 123, 125, 132, 134–135, 152

forbidding trade with St. Domingo, 99

limitations on power, 119

neutrality and, 46, 59, 75

Parliament and, 200–201

payment of foreign debts, 122, 155

power to charter corporations (banks), 115, 126–128, 141, 143

preferred creditor status and, 139–140, 144

ratifies Treaty of Paris (Treaty of Peace), 181

Remitting Act (1790) and, 30, 59, 61–62, 65–66

remitting acts (post-1790), 77, 229n59

"Report on Manufactures" and, 151

resolutions on British creditors, 134–135, 146

Sedition Act of 1798 and, 200, 202, 211, 263n112

Senate's advice and consent, 31

tariffs and, 122

western lands and, 156–158, 160–161

Connecticut, 159–161

Connecticut Gore

Land Company, 159–160

strip of land, 159–161

Constitution (US). *See* US Constitution

constitutional conventions

at Annapolis, 2

at Philadelphia, 2, 3, 16, 19, 152, 157

Constitutional Court of Appeals (South Carolina), *Bulow and Potter v. The City Council of Charleston* and, 144

constitutionalism

American, 3, 9–10, 12, 25–29, 41, 73, 141, 147–149, 171–173, 175–177, 201, 204–205, 211–212

British (English), 3, 10–12, 21, 24–28, 123, 176–177, 193–201, 204, 206, 209, 212

broad construction of US Constitution, 115, 117, 126–128, 132–133, 140, 142, 144, 149

common law decline, 212

common law reception, 9–10, 162, 175–177, 181–182, 188–189, 192–193, 195, 197–198, 200, 204

magisterial constitutionalism, 20–22, 81–84

See also administrative accommodation; British constitution; concurrence (Hamiltonian); executive power; federalism; federal magistracy; judicial power; *The Federalist*; US Constitution

Frothingham, David, 192, 259n68
Fuller Court. *See* US Supreme Court
Fulton, Robert, 138
Funding Act of 1790. *See under* funding
  plan (Hamilton)
funding plan (Hamilton), 33, 87, 113,
  115–116, 122, 131–132
  Funding Act of 1790, 67–71

Gallatin, Albert, 8, 42, 47–48, 55, 95
  discretionary authority and, 157
  remitting acts (post-1790) and, 76–77
Gibbons v. Ogden, 87, 139
Gilchrist, Robert, 47, 49
Gilchrist v. The Collector of Charleston
  (the *Case of the Resource*), 42,
  47–50, 74
Gilmore, Grant, 13
Glass v. The Sloop Betsey, 96
Glorious Revolution, 27
Goebel, Julius, Jr., 4, 168–169, 185
Goix v. Knox, 104
Goix v. Low, 104–105
Gomez v. Maule, 183
Goshen (New York), 166
Grant, James, 170
Grant v. The Bank of the United States,
  170–171
Great Britain, 75, 103
  American diplomacy and, 86
Great Falls (Passaic River, New Jersey),
  150
Great Lakes (US), 98

Hamilton, Alexander
  administrative accommodation and,
    40, 57, 60, 64, 66, 70–71, 73–84,
    207–208
  administrative discretion and, 18,
    33–45, 47–56, 61, 66, 71, 78,
    156–158, 207
  admiralty litigation and, 92–98
  alien land law and, 162–164, 169, 171
  assumption plan, 33, 67–68, 70, 86–
    87, 113, 115–116, 122, 131–132
  attorney for Kingston, New York, 161

biographical sketch, 2, 175
Blagge v. New York Insurance Co.
  and, 108–109, 239n103
on borrowing power, 114–118, 122,
  124, 128, 134–135, 145, 149, 207
broad construction of Congress's
  powers and, 115, 117, 126–128,
  132–133, 140, 142, 144, 149
carriage tax and, 115, 128–133
citizenship rights and, 189–192
claims adjudication and, 23, 33–35,
  64, 158, 221n62
coequal creditor status and, 121, 139–
  140, 144
commentary on legal career, 4, 213
commercial republic and, 15, 85–90,
  107, 110, 150, 172, 207
common law, use of, 2, 6, 9–10, 13,
  16, 39, 68, 97–98, 122–123, 174–
  202, 204–206, 212–213
concurrence and, 10–12, 14–15, 88–
  89, 114–121, 136–137, 171–173,
  206–212
on constitutionality of the Bank of the
  United States, 116, 126–128, 132,
  149
as continental tax receiver, 118
defensive federalism and, 117, 136,
  143–144, 147–149, 211
delegate to constitutional conventions,
  2, 157
desuetude and, 115, 122–123, 136
direct versus indirect tax distinction
  and, 132
*Don Diego Pintado v. The Ship San
  Joseph* and, 98–99
due process and, 6, 16, 175, 177–179,
  188–192, 203–204, 211, 258–
  259n59
duress defense, 184
Enlightenment influences, 3
equity, use of, 154–155, 159–160, 207
equity of redemption and, 165–168, 171
on executive discretion (prerogative),
  14, 18–25, 27–45, 47–56, 61, 66,
  71, 78, 81, 156–158, 207

Hamilton, Alexander, *continued*
  on executive energy, 18, 23, 41–42,
    82, 95
  on executive power (general), 6, 8, 12,
    18, 20
  extensive versus strict conception of
    common law, 175–177, 181, 192–
    193, 195–202, 204–205
  Federalist essays, 3, 7, 10, 13, 18, 20,
    23, 25–28, 31, 45, 51, 55, 73, 80,
    83, 85, 110, 112, 120, 136–139,
    141–144, 146, 206–207, 209
  Federalist ideology versus Jeffersonian
    Republicans and, 5–8, 86, 115–
    116, 173–174, 192, 202, 263n113
  on fiscal powers, 6, 114–118, 120–
    121, 126–135, 148–149, 207
  Fitzsimmons v. Odgen and, 169
  foreign investment capital and, 15,
    150–155, 161–165, 168–169,
    171–173, 211
  Fowler v. Lindley, Fowler v. Miller,
    and *New York v. Connecticut* and,
    159–160
  freedom of the press and, 6, 16, 175,
    177, 191–202, 204–205, 259n68,
    263n112
  funding plan, 33, 67–71, 87, 113,
    115–116, 122, 131–132
  general issue, 184, 194–195, 198, 202
  Goix v. Knox and, 104
  Goix v. Low and, 104–105
  Gomez v. Maule and, 183
  *Grant v. The Bank of the United
    States,* 170–171
  Hendrickson v. Cornwell and, 184
  Holland Land Company and, 152,
    154–155, 158, 161–165, 168–169,
    253–254n73
  Hylton v. US and, 67, 70, 115–117,
    128–133, 143, 148–149
  illicit trade clause and, 108, 239n102
  installment sales contract versus
    mortgage, 168–169
  intellectual influences, 3
  judicial coextensivity, 26, 54

  on judicial power, 6, 9, 12, 15, 22,
    25–27, 40–42, 45, 48, 54, 59, 73,
    87–100, 178–179, 188, 191, 204–
    208
  judicial review and, 26, 38, 42, 55,
    128–129, 133, 178–179, 182, 208
  jury trials and, 6, 16, 39, 160, 188–
    189, 194–196, 198–199, 202–204
  land speculation and, 151
  legal influences, 3
  legal legacy, 5–6, 8–9, 12, 16, 32, 81–
    84, 115–117, 147–149, 171–173,
    202–213
  Leonard v. Post, 187
  Letters from Phocion and, 179, 188–
    191, 203
  Lloyd v. Hewlett and, 184
  Lloyd v. Sneathen and, 184
  Lloyd v. Williams and, 184
  Loyalists and, 16, 175, 177–191,
    202–204
  as Lucius Crassus (penname), 202,
    263n113
  Ludlow & Ludlow v. Dale and, 104–
    105
  Marbury v. Madison and, 26, 31,
    42–45, 47, 55, 60, 78
  marine insurance litigation and, 103–
    105, 108–110, 207
  McCulloch v. Maryland and, 116,
    141–144, 146, 149
  military justification (trespass defense),
    180–182, 184, 203
  Morton v. Seton, 183
  motion for new trials and, 192–194,
    197, 199
  necessary and proper clause, 127–128
  neutrality and, 31–32, 38, 59, 75,
    85–90, 95, 98–99, 104–105, 107,
    110–112
  in New York assembly, 176, 203–204
  New York bar and, 2, 96, 103
  Olney v. Arnold and, 71–74, 82
  "Opinion on the Constitutionality of
    an Act to Establish a Bank," 143
  Pacificus essays, 20, 31–32, 50–51

pardon power and, 29–31, 44, 53, 79,
220n48
on Parliament, 3, 175, 198–199, 201
People v. Croswell and, 16, 192–202,
204–205
People v. Hoffman and, 187
petitions to New York assembly, 163,
186
plea of *autrefois attaint*, 187
plea of the law of nations, 181–185,
191, 203
plea of the Treaty of Peace, 181–183,
187
on precedent, 198–199
private acts and, 186
procedural technicalities and, 186–187
public credit and, 33–34, 113–114,
116–117, 119, 122–125, 128,
134–135, 147–149, 155–156
Quackenbos v. Underhill and, 183
Remitting Act of 1790 and, 59, 61–66,
76, 78, 82
removal strategy, 184–186
"Report on a Plan for the Further
Support of Public Credit," 134, 145
"Report on Manufactures," 150–151,
156
"Report on the Difficulties in the
Execution of the Act Laying Duties
on Distilled Spirits," 38–39
"Report on the Petition of Christopher
Saddler," 61
"Report on the Petition of Jacob
Rash," 34
report on western lands, 156
repugnancy caveat, 121, 137–141, 146
rights consciousness and, 15, 174–193,
197–205, 207, 211
Rutgers v. Waddington and, 16, 178,
182–183, 185–186
Schuyler family and, 161
on securities (US) as contracts, 115,
124, 133–135, 145, 146, 246nn87–
88, 246–247n90
settlement strategies, 184–186
Shaw v. Stevenson and, 183

Society for Establishing Useful
Manufactures and, 150
staged cases and, 66–71, 82, 130
on Star Chamber court, 195–196
state sovereignty and, 12, 88, 109–
112, 117–118, 120, 125–126,
130–131, 141–144, 147, 152–155,
206–207, 209–212
statutory construction and, 67–74,
79–80, 207–208
superintending power and, 36–37, 43,
47–48, 51–52, 54
tacking doctrine (creditors' rights) and,
170–171
taxes and, 39, 67, 86, 113, 115, 127
on taxing power, 114–122, 126–135,
149, 207, 210
"Treasury Department Circular to the
District Judges," 65
Treasury Department defense and, 39
as treasury secretary, 5, 21, 28, 30,
32–39, 45, 58, 61–71, 74–75, 86,
93–96, 113, 115, 118, 122, 123–
129, 134–135, 155–156, 207–208,
218n12
treaty-making power and, 29
on truth as a defense, 199–202, 204
Tucker v. Thompson and, 183
US v. Hopkins and, 26, 45, 60, 67–71,
82
US v. La Vengeance and, 98–99
US v. The Ship Young Ralph and,
97–99
*Vandenheuvel v. United Insurance
Company* and, 104–105
Waters v. Stewart and, 166–169
writ of right and, 161, 251n40
See also *Federalist, The*
Hammond, George, 86
Harison, Richard, 30–31, 38
admiralty litigation and Hamilton,
96–99, 108–109
on Hamilton's ratifying convention
remarks, 121
Holland Land Company and, 163–164
People v. Croswell and, 194, 197

Gilchrist et al. v. The Collector at Charleston (the *Case of the Resource*) and, 47–50, 74
growth of, through administrative accommodation, 13, 62, 66–84, 207–208
Hamilton and, 6, 9, 12, 15, 22, 25–27, 40–42, 45, 48, 54, 59, 73, 87–100, 178–179, 188, 191, 204–208
interstate boundary disputes and, 157, 159–161
judicial duty, 197, 199–200, 204–205, 260n70
Kendall v. US ex. rel. Stokes and, 52–53, 74, 83
Marbury v. Madison and, 44–45, 47, 53, 55, 60, 74, 78
neutrality and, 88–90, 95–102, 107, 109–112, 208
Olney v. Arnold and, 71–74, 82
responsibility to uphold individual rights, 21, 26, 31, 44–45, 53–54, 178–179, 189–191, 197, 204–205
state-level development, 178
as umpire of the federal system, 13, 60, 66–84, 158, 173, 207, 211–212
See also judicial review; mandamus; US Supreme Court; writ of error review
judicial review, 26, 38, 208
coextensivity, 21
historical narrative and, 13
Hylton v. US and, 128–130, 133
judicial duty, 197, 199–200, 204–205, 260n70
Loyalists and, 178–179, 182–183, 185–186
Marbury v. Madison and, 42–45
McCulloch v. Maryland and, 141–144
over executive action, 15, 21, 26, 41–55, 67–71, 73, 82–84
Rutgers v. Waddington and, 178, 182–183, 185–186
US v. Hopkins and, 67–71
See also mandamus; writ of error review

Judiciary Act
of 1789, 72–73, 83, 90, 93, 97, 99–100, 130, 160, 208, 231–232n15
of 1801, 6, 41, 173, 202, 263n113
See also "saving to suitors" clause; waters "navigable from the sea" clause; writ of error review
jury trials, 6, 16, 39
as due process of law, 188–189, 203–204, 258–259n59
lack of, in admiralty, 91, 99
lack of, in equity, 160
lack of, in Star Chamber, 196
People v. Croswell and, 194–196, 198–199, 202, 204
justice of the peace. *See* magistracy

Kaplanoff, Mark D., 122
Kendall, Amos, 50
Kendall v. US ex. rel. Stokes, 43, 50–53, 74, 83
Kent, James
on admiralty jurisdiction, 99, 111–112
on bottomry bonds, 102, 237n78
Commentaries on American Law, 112, 168
Hamilton's influence on, 8
on Hamilton's legal reputation, 4, 202
on Hamilton's ratifying convention remarks, 121
on legal uncertainty in New York, 177
Livingston v. Van Ingen and, 138
on marine insurance law, 103, 107–109, 111–112
on New York bar, 177
People v. Croswell and, 194, 202, 204
repugnancy caveat and, 138–141
on tacking doctrine (creditors' rights), 170–171
US v. Fisher and, 140–141, 144
Waters v. Stewart and, 168
Key, Francis Scott, 50–51
King's Bench
certiorari review, 24
common law and, 176
equity of redemption and, 166

Pennsylvania Supreme Court
  *Dempsey v. The Insurance Company
    of Pennsylvania* and, 105, 107
  Huidekooper's Lessee v. Douglas and,
    158
  Phoenix v. Platt and, 109
  Vasse v. Ball and, 105
Penobscot (Maine), 65
"people's writ of error," 185
People v. Croswell, 4, 16, 192–202,
  204–205
People v. Hoffman, 187
Philadelphia (Pennsylvania), 113
Phillips, Wendell, 103
Phoenix v. Platt, 109
Pickering, John, 41
Pinkney, William, 141
Pintado, Don Diego, 98
Pintado v. The Ship San Joseph, 98–99
Pollock v. Farmers Loan & Trust Co.,
  147–148
Pope, Edward, 94
popular sovereignty. *See* sovereignty
positivism, 212–213
prerogative. *See* executive power
Privy Council (Great Britain), 11, 91
Propeller Genesee Chief v. Fitzhugh, 98
Providence (Rhode Island), 64, 66, 94
public credit
  foreign investment capital and, 155–156
  Hamilton and, 33–34, 113–114, 116–
    117, 119, 122–125, 128, 134–135,
    147–149, 155–156
  "Report on a Plan for the Further
    Support of Public Credit," 134, 145

Quackenbos v. Underhill, 183
Quasi-War with France, 96, 100
Queen's County Justice's Court (New
  York), 186
Queen v. Tutchin, 194

Randolph, Edmund, 8, 30, 38
  on constitutionality of the first Bank of
    the United States, 126–127
  US v. Hopkins and, 68–70

Rash, Jacob, 34
realism (legal realism), 212–213
redemption (debt), 67–70. *See also*
  subscription
Registry Act of 1792, 96
Remitting Act
  of 1790, 30, 59, 61–66, 75–76
  of 1797, 77, 228–229n59
  of 1813, 78
  of 1818, 77
"Report on a Plan for the Further Support
  of Public Credit," 134, 145
"Report on Manufactures," 150–151,
  156
"Report on the Difficulties in the
  Execution of the Act Laying Duties
  on Distilled Spirits" (Hamilton),
  38–39
"Report on the Petition of Christopher
  Saddler" (Hamilton), 61
"Report on the Petition of Jacob Rash,"
  34
Republicans. *See* Jeffersonian
  Republicans
repugnancy caveat (Hamilton), 121,
  137–141, 146
Resource (vessel), 47–49
Revolutionary War, 19, 87, 100
  British occupation of New York City,
    180–181, 183, 188
  claims, 23, 33–35, 64, 158
  debt, 67–70, 113, 115, 122, 152, 155
  Hamilton and, 2
  Loyalists and, 175, 177–191
  taxes and, 117–118, 122–123
  Whiggism and, 175, 189, 191
"Revolution of 1800," 22, 41
Rex v. Franklin, 194
Rex v. Owen, 194
Richardson, Laurana, 35
Riggs, Caleb, 170
Riolz, John, 92
Rising Sun (schooner), 64
Roane, Spencer, 8, 129
Rodney, Caesar A., 47–49, 51
Runyan v. Mersereau, 168

Rutgers, Elizabeth, 182–183, 185
Rutgers v. Waddington, 4, 16, 178, 182–183, 185–186

Saddler, Christopher, 61
Sandy Hook (New Jersey), 99
"saving to suitors" clause (section 9 of the 1789 Judiciary Act), 93, 97, 99–100, 231n2
Schuyler family, 161
Scotland, 123
securities (US), 113–115
    as contracts, 115, 124, 133–135, 145–146
Sedgwick, Theodore, 106–107
Sedition Act of 1798, 59, 75, 192, 200, 202, 211, 263n112
seditious libel (criminal libel), 192–202, 204–205
    truth as a defense, 194–202, 204
    See also common law; Fox's Libel Act of 1792; freedom of the press; *People v. Croswell*; Sedition Act of 1798
Seven Bishop's Case, 195
Seven Years' War, 3, 91
Sewall, David, 65, 78
Shaw v. Stevenson, 183
slaves
    criminal trials for, 25
    taxation and, 118, 120, 131
Slave Trade Act of 1794, 97, 99
Sloop Polly of Sandwich (vessel), 94–95
Smith, Joseph H, 4, 168–169
Smyth, Richard, 69–70
Society for Establishing Useful Manufactures, 150
South Carolina courts, 166. *See also* Constitutional Court of Appeals (South Carolina)
sovereignty
    coequal/preferred creditors, 121, 139–140, 144
    federal sovereignty, 7, 10–12, 16, 114, 117–121, 125–126, 130–131, 140–

144, 147–149, 152–155, 172–173, 206–210, 212
    popular sovereignty, 10, 212
    state sovereignty, 10–12, 16, 88, 114, 117–121, 125–126, 130–131, 140–144, 147–149, 152–155, 172–173, 206–207, 209–212
    See also concurrence (Hamiltonian); federalism; writ of error review
Spain, 155
Spencer, Ambrose, 168, 170, 194, 197, 199
Stamp Act of 1765, 93, 123
Star Chamber, 195–196
state common law courts. *See* common law; marine insurance; New York Supreme Court
state sovereignty. *See* sovereignty
St. Domingo (Hispaniola), 99
Stewart, John, 166–167
Stewart v. Warner, 106
Story, Joseph, 13, 81
    Commentaries on Equity Jurisprudence, 154
    De Lovio v. Boit and, 89, 99, 107, 110–111, 208
    on *Federalist* No. 32, 137
    growth of judicial power and, 8, 208
    Martin v. Hunter's Lessee and, 83, 111–112
    nationalistic mindset, 87
St. Thomas (Caribbean island), 46
Stuart v. Laird, 74
subscription (debt), 26, 67–70. *See also* redemption
superintending power, 36–37, 43, 47–49, 51–52, 54. *See also* executive power
Superior Court of Judicature (Rhode Island), 72
Supreme Court (New York state). *See* New York Supreme Court
Supreme Court of the United States. *See* US Supreme Court

tacking doctrine (creditors' rights), 170–171
Taney, Roger, 8, 211
Taney Court. *See* US Supreme Court
taxes, 24, 25, 32
  apportionment of taxes, 129–131, 133, 147–148
  auctions and, 125–126
  Boston's tax on US securities, 113–114, 123–125, 144, 146
  carriage tax, 115, 118, 129–133
  Charleston's taxes on bank stock and US securities, 114, 141, 144–146
  direct tax clauses (Article I, sections 2 and 9), 67, 117, 129–133, 147–148
  direct tax on houses, 115
  direct versus indirect tax, 129–132
  on distilled spirits, 39, 115
  on dwelling houses, 118, 123
  Hamilton's funding plan and, 33, 67–71, 86–87, 113, 115–116, 122, 131–132
  income tax (federal), 147–148
  Maryland's tax on the second Bank of the United States, 141–143
  nonapportioned income taxes, 147–148
  prohibition on states to tax imports and exports (Article I, section 10), 119
  prohibition on taxing state exports (Article I, section 9), 119
  on rum, 127
  on slaves, 118, 120, 131
  Stamp Act taxes, 93, 123
  tariffs, 122
  taxable real and personal property, 118, 120
  types of direct taxes, 129–130
  uniform duties, imposts, and excises (Article I, section 9), 119
  Weston v. Charleston and, 114, 117, 145–147
tax immunity, 115, 124, 133–135
taxing powers (federal). *See* fiscal powers (US)
Taylor, John (of Caroline), 129, 131–132

Theus, Simon, 47–48
Thompson, Smith, 51–52, 77–78
  Livingston v. Van Ingen and, 137–138
  People v. Croswell and, 194
  Weston v. Charleston and, 146–147
Thorres, Thomas, 108
Tilghman, Edward, 69–70
Treasury Department, 13, 14, 20–22, 26, 32–33
  administrative accommodation and, 40, 74–84, 207–208
  administrative discretion and, 23, 25, 33–42, 46–50, 61–62, 66, 70, 78–79, 81, 156–158, 207–208, 218n12
  admiralty litigation and, 93–96
  claims adjudication, 33–35, 64, 158
  Crowell et al. v. M'Fadon and, 80
  Hamilton defends, 39
  Olney v. Arnold and, 71–74, 82
  Remitting Act (1790) and, 61–66, 75–76
  remitting acts (post-1790) and, 77–79
  US securities and, 113, 115, 124, 133–135
  US v. Hopkins and, 67–71, 82
  US v. One Case of Hair Pencils and, 77–78
  western lands and, 155–158
"Treasury Department Circular to the District Judges" (Hamilton), 65–66
Treaty of Amity and Commerce (Franco-American Treaty of 1778), 31
Treaty of Ghent (1814), 111
Treaty of Paris (Treaty of Peace) (1783), 181–184, 187–190
Trespass Act, 177–187, 191, 203–204
trusts (equitable instrument), 15, 154, 162–164, 171, 207
  "cestuy"/"cestuy que use"/"cestuy que trust" (beneficiary), 162–163
  mortgages (form of trust), 154, 162, 165–171, 207
Tucker, St. George, 8
Tucker v. Thompson, 183
Tyler, George, 65

ministerial versus political
(discretionary) distinction, 42–45,
49–54, 81, 83
New York v. Connecticut (Connecticut
Gore controversy) and, 159–160
Olney v. Arnold and, 71–74, 82
Otis v. Watkins and, 80–81
Pollock v. Farmers Loan & Trust Co.
and, 147–148
Propeller Genesee Chief v. Fitzhugh
and, 98
Taney Court, 41, 43, 50–51, 54, 58,
82–83, 98, 208
as umpire of the federal system, 60,
66–84, 207–208, 211–212
US v. Fisher and, 139–141, 143, 149
US v. Hopkins and, 26, 45, 60, 67–71,
82
US v. La Vengeance and, 98–99
US v. One Case of Hair Pencils and,
77–78
US v. The Schooner Betsey and, 99
Weston v. Charleston and, 114, 117,
144–147, 149
See also admiralty jurisdiction; judicial
power; judicial review; mandamus;
writ of error review
US v. Arnold, 71
US v. Lancaster, 79
US v. The Hawke, 75–76
US v. The Ship Young Ralph, 97–98
US v. The William, 79–80

*Vandenheuvel v. United Insurance
Company*, 104–106
Van Ness, William, 194–195, 199–201
Van Rensselaer family, 161
Van Vechten, Abraham, 138
Vasse v. Ball, 105–106
veto, 28
vice admiralty courts (colonial). *See*
admiralty jurisdiction
Vigol, Philip, 29
Virginia
canal building, 151

Hylton v. US and, 115, 128–133
US v. Hopkins and, 67–71
Waddington, Joshua, 181–183, 185
Ward, Phoebe, 186
War of 1812, 6, 109
Washington, Bushrod, 79
Washington, George, 5
accused of corruption, 39
Bank of the United States (first) and,
127–128
Cabinet, 1, 2, 3, 31, 74, 116, 123
carriage tax and, 129
economic vision of, 150
executive power and, 19, 23, 29, 32,
39
fiscal policy and, 115, 123–124, 128
as justice of the peace, 25
land speculation and, 151
Loyalists' litigation strategy and, 183
neutrality and, 31, 59, 75, 85, 95, 99
pardon power and, 29–31, 39
relationship to Hamilton, 2, 175
seditious libel and, 259n65
Waters, Sarah, 166–167
Waters, Thomas, 166
waters "navigable from the sea" clause
(from section 9 of the 1789
Judiciary Act), 93, 98–99,
233n28
Waters v. Stewart, 166–169
Webster, Daniel, 141
Weeks, Levi, 175
Wells, John, 138
western lands (US), 155–158, 160–161
Western Reserve (Ohio territory), 160–
161
Weston, Plowdon, 145
Weston v. Charleston, 114, 117, 136,
144–147, 149
Whiskey Insurrection, 29, 38–39, 115
Williams, Otho H., 18
Wilson, James, 123, 175
Wirt, William, 141
Wolcott, Oliver, Jr., 39, 95, 115, 158
Wooddesson, Richard, 123

writ of error review (common law), 185,
191, 203–204
writ of error review (from section 25 of
the 1789 Judiciary Act), 83, 208
Crowell et al. v. M'Fadon, 90
Hylton v. US, 128–130, 133
Kendall v. US ex. rel. Stokes, 50

Olney v. Arnold and, 71–74, 82
Otis v. Watkins, 80–81
See also judicial review

Yorktown (Virginia), 2

Zenger's case, 194, 199